The Making of Capitalism in France

Historical Materialism Book Series

The Historical Materialism Book Series is a major publishing initiative of the radical left. The capitalist crisis of the twenty-first century has been met by a resurgence of interest in critical Marxist theory. At the same time, the publishing institutions committed to Marxism have contracted markedly since the high point of the 1970s. The Historical Materialism Book Series is dedicated to addressing this situation by making available important works of Marxist theory. The aim of the series is to publish important theoretical contributions as the basis for vigorous intellectual debate and exchange on the left.

The peer-reviewed series publishes original monographs, translated texts, and reprints of classics across the bounds of academic disciplinary agendas and across the divisions of the left. The series is particularly concerned to encourage the internationalization of Marxist debate and aims to translate significant studies from beyond the English-speaking world.

For a full list of titles in the Historical Materialism Book Series available in paperback from Haymarket Books, visit:
https://www.haymarketbooks.org/series_collections/1-historical-materialism

The Making of Capitalism in France

Class Structures, Economic Development, the State and the Formation of the French Working Class, 1750–1914

Xavier Lafrance

Haymarket Books
Chicago, IL

First published in 2018 by Brill Academic Publishers, The Netherlands
© 2018 Koninklijke Brill NV, Leiden, The Netherlands

Published in paperback in 2020 by
Haymarket Books
P.O. Box 180165
Chicago, IL 60618
773-583-7884
www.haymarketbooks.org

ISBN: 978-1-64259-188-0

Distributed to the trade in the US through Consortium Book Sales and
Distribution (www.cbsd.com) and internationally through Ingram
Publisher Services International (www.ingramcontent.com).

This book was published with the generous support of Lannan
Foundation and Wallace Action Fund.

Special discounts are available for bulk purchases by organizations and
institutions. Please call 773-583-7884 or email info@haymarketbooks.org
for more information.

Cover design by Jamie Kerry and Ragina Johnson.

Printed in the United States.

10 9 8 7 6 5 4 3 2 1

Library of Congress Cataloging-in-Publication data is available.

Pour Bénédicte et Félix

Contents

Acknowledgements

My work on this book first began during my Ph.D. studies at York University, in Toronto, where I had the pleasure and privilege of developing my knowledge of issues related to the origins of capitalism with the late Ellen Meiksins Wood, as well as David McNally and George Comninel. Ellen's work has been the single most important source of inspiration for this book. Our conversations have made an inestimable contribution to the clarification of my thought on some of the topics discussed here. I feel incredibly fortunate to have had the chance to know her and to appreciate her impressively sharp intellect and disarmingly generous personality in the last decade of her life. I am also greatly indebted to David, whose comments on my work and comradely support have been of immeasurable value.

Though the basic argument remains essentially the same, this book is much more mature and developed than the original dissertation from which it originates. Years of subsequent work have made this possible. During these years, I had the opportunity to test some of my ideas on panels and via email exchanges with Chris Isett, Steve Miller, Benno Teschke and Mike Zmolek. Their support and comments have been of great assistance to me in the process of revising the book for publication. I also want to thank François Jarrige for his very helpful comments and suggestions, as well as another, anonymous reviewer. The editing work on the manuscript by Alexandre Lemay-Roche and Danny Hayward has been fantastic, and I am also grateful for it.

While intellectual work is always collective and irrigated by the thoughts of a multitude of individuals, the process of writing a book is often a lonely one. I have been incredibly fortunate, through the years, to count on the friendship and support of Élène Beaudoin, Crystelle Bédard, Marc-André Cyr, Thierry Drapeau, Thomas Chiasson-Lebel, Frantz Gheller, Claudia Hébert, Benoit Marsan, Jonathan Martineau, Sébastien Rioux, Gary Romanuk, Jean-Pierre Roy, Alan Sears (whose support has been invaluable) and Jonathan Veillette. Our intellectual exchanges have been stimulating; our laughs have kept me going.

Special thanks go to David Mandel, a dear friend, for his support ever since the very first week of my undergraduate studies, and to Charlie Post, who has been the number one fan of this book project, for his comradely friendship and invaluable comments on my work.

Finally, I want to thank my family: Bénédicte, Félix, Gaëtan, Marie-Hélène, Charles, Justin, Laetitia, Rachel, Raphaël, Renaud, and Clémence. I love you and thank you for support.

Introduction

This book is an attempt to think the transition to capitalism and its impact on the making of the working class in France. One might expect and maybe welcome an effort to *re*-think, to *reconsider*, the rise of French capitalism, yet I would argue that we have to begin with a long overdue attempt to approach this issue *historically*. There is certainly something provocative, and apparently ironic, in such a statement. There is after all a very large and very rich literature on the history of French capitalism, from the early modern to the contemporary period. Indeed, it can be argued that the issue of the birth and development of capitalism has been central in the field of economic history in France and elsewhere, from Marx to Fernand Braudel, for whom this was a central problematic.[1] Yet, while many highly valuable works of French economic and social history will be mobilised to develop the argument presented in this book, I contend that most of these contributions take for granted the existence of capitalism without really considering its historical origins. When the issue is considered, a strong, in fact almost universal, tendency is to assume the very things that need to be explained. Explanations are circular, and capitalism is presented as emerging out of pre-existing, embryonic capitalist dynamics that were already gestating in the womb of feudalism or absolutism.

Capitalism is thus generally presented as a quantitative expansion of trade in ways that resonate with the 'commercial model', tied to the historical narrative put forward by Enlightenment thinkers and classical political economists. The most famous version of this model was presented by Adam Smith, for whom capitalism evolved out of a natural propensity to 'truck, barter, and exchange'.[2] Smith suggested that, given the opportunity, economic actors would unproblematically respond to growing market demand by developing the division of labour – specialising and maximising returns by reducing production costs via productivity-improving investments. This Smithian perspective continues to inform most contemporary historical works interested in the origins of capitalism and economic development.

The *Annales* school, in which Braudel emerged as a major figure, devoted considerable energy to the historical analysis of capitalism, acquiring major influence in the field of history and across the social sciences in France and

---

1   Verley and Mayaud 2001, p. 6.
2   Wood 2002a, pp. 11–12, 28.

indeed worldwide. Braudel insists that the genesis of capitalism is 'strictly' related to trade,[3] but also distinguishes the market economy from the capitalist system.[4] While the former has to do with transparent, equal exchange, taking place mostly on a local plane, the latter is generally tied to long-distance trade and allows a limited number of large capitalist merchants to corner markets using state-granted trade monopolies. This conception of capitalism, as noted by Benno Teschke, leads Braudel to offer a reified conception of capitalism that is retroprojected across the history of human civilisations. In his own words:

> I have long argued that capitalism had been potentially visible since the dawn of history, and that it has developed and perpetuated itself down the ages. Far in advance, there were signs announcing the coming of capitalism: the rise of the towns and of trade, the emergence of a labour market, the increasing density of society, the spread of the use of money, the rise in output, the expansion of long-distance trade or to put it another way the international market.[5]

Capitalism thus appears as an outgrowth of commercial activities that have always been present in one form or another. Consequently, no explanation of its historical origins appears to be really necessary.

Likewise, in a major multi-volume contribution to the economic history of modern France, co-edited by Braudel and Ernest Labrousse, we again find that capitalism is not really problematised as a distinct form of historical society.[6] Once again, capitalism is equated with commercial exchange and is said to result from its expansion, which resumed in France during the mid-fifteenth century. 'Capitalist structures' then rapidly matured due to the 'call of the market', from the mid-sixteenth and across the seventeenth centuries, laying the ground for a 'final explosion' that led to a 'bourgeois era' and hastened economic development.

This narrative, summarised by Labrousse in the final section of Volume 2 of the *Histoire Économique et sociale de la France*, is clearly reminiscent of the ostensibly Marxist 'social interpretation' of the 1789 French Revolution. Inspired by Marx's discussion of the 'bourgeois revolution' in the *Commun-*

---

3 Braudel 1979, p. 535.
4 Braudel 2008.
5 Quote in Teschke 2003 p. 133. For an excellent critique of Braudel's thought, on which many of the points put forth here are based, see Teschke 2003, pp. 129–33.
6 Braudel and Labrousse 1993.

ist Manifesto, this interpretation is based on 'strong'[7] Smithian assumptions, insofar as it maintains that proto-capitalist dynamics directed history toward a revolutionary clash that destroyed the feudal shackles holding back the full development of capitalism. After the invalidation of this thesis by 'revisionist' historians of the French revolution,[8] Marxists put forward a 'consequentialist' interpretation, according to which the Revolution eventually led to the development of a capitalist society even if it was not itself led by capitalists. Here we find 'weak' Smithian assumptions, whereby the removal of obstacles – most importantly the elimination of guilds and of state regulations of industry by the National Assembly in 1791 – would create a context in which economic actors were able to seize market opportunities and behave as capitalists.[9] While empirically incorrect (as will be argued in detail in Chapter 3), and saturated with liberal teleology, this narrative of the Revolution is still accepted as a given by many historians and social scientists.[10]

Since the origins of capitalism *as a historically distinct system* are often left unaddressed, or are approached, as a rule, by assuming what needs to be explained, it is probably not really surprising that much of the economic history of modern France has been focused on debating the *pace* of French economic development. Until the late 1970s the analysis of growth rates formed the core of the economic historiography of nineteenth-century France.[11] Since then, while the analysis of growth rhythms has remained a research topic,[12] the issue of the development of capitalism has been largely abandoned.[13]

---

7   I owe this distinction between 'strong' and 'weak' Smithian assumptions to an exchange with Charlie Post.

8   These historiographical debates will be summarised and discussed in Chapter 3.

9   See Lemarchand (2008) for an example of a recent, and otherwise rich and informative, iteration of this thesis. Unable to shake off teleological assumptions, Lemarchand explains how 'structural brakes' continued to impede the capitalist tendencies that he sees as stemming from 'mutations of economic structures' brought about by the Revolution.

10   Miller (2012, p. 156) explains that in the sub-field of French rural economic history 'the current consensus ... is that a transition to capitalism requires no explanation whatsoever', since it is generally believed that '[a]griculture became productive when stimulated by the economic demands of the towns'. This statement also applies more broadly to the field of French economic history, in which it also tends to be true that '[m]arket dynamism and bourgeois revolution permit liberal historians to present the essential relations of capitalism without any explanation, as the inherent response to prospects for gain'.

11   Fureix and Jarrige 2015, pp. 70–1.

12   For a wide-ranging review of the historiography of French economic growth in the nineteenth century, see Crouzet 2003. This historiography will be discussed in Chapter 2 and, with greater emphasis, in Chapter 3.

13   Barjot 2012, p. 7; Verley and Mayaud 2001, pp. 6–7.

Most research programmes in French economic history in recent decades have focused on market dynamics,[14] on the one hand, and on business history, especially innovating entrepreneurs and the organisation of firms, on the other.[15] This book, unfashionably, reconnects with the issue of *capitalism* and stresses that explaining the transition to this specific type of historical society is actually key to our understanding of both modern French economic growth and the related propensity (or lack thereof) of business owners to innovate and invest in a sustained way. I contend that, in order to provide this explanation, we need to adopt a distinctive understanding of what capitalism is.

1   Problematising Capitalism

An exception in the historical literature on the modern French economy is the outstanding work of Stephen Miller, which, focusing on the agrarian sector, refuses to equate the expansion of trade with the origins of capitalism.[16] While sharing Miller's theoretical perspective and building on his important contributions, my work focuses on the rise of industrial capitalism, which in France preceded agrarian capitalism.

The theoretical framework used in this book has generally been called 'Political Marxism', though it might be more appropriate to speak of a '*Capital*-centric Marxism'. It is rooted in Marx's mature critique of political economy, which has been theoretically systematised as a tool of historical analysis by Robert Brenner and Ellen Meiksins Wood.[17] Marx's early work, and especially the *German Ideology* and the *Communist Manifesto*, accepted the narrative of historical development promoted by liberal historians and political economists. With the *Grundrisse* and *Capital*, however, Marx broke with the liberal paradigm, offering a radical critique of classical political economy's notion of

---

14   Verley (1996; 1997a; 1997b) has offered outstanding contributions on this topic. He develops a comparative analysis of the original Western countries' industrialisation by relating it to the evolution of domestic and international demand. His perspective, however, remains anchored in a Smithian paradigm: sustained industrial development is explained by the emergence of new market outlets that stimulate productivity gains, and contributes in turn to reduce consumer good prices, leading to renewed growth in demand and, consequently, production growth. The difference between industrialisation processes in Britain and France are thus explained by the absence of a large middle class that limited the size of the consumer market in the latter country.

15   Barjot 2012, pp. 5–6, 22.

16   Miller 2008; 2009; 2012; Isett and Miller 2017.

17   Brenner 1986 and 2007; Wood 1995 and 2002a.

'primitive accumulation' as the gateway to capitalism.[18] In these mature works, Marx insisted that the accumulation of capital stock and expansion of trade cannot on their own explain the origins of capitalism. As he explains, 'capital is not a thing, but a social relation', and for monetary wealth or machinery to be turned into capital, a radical transformation of class relationships of exploitation needs to take place. Focusing his attention on the English countryside, Marx explained that the secret behind the 'so-called primitive accumulation' is 'the historical process of divorcing the producer from the means of production' – the mass expropriation of the English peasantry and the transformation of means of production (land and tools) into *capital* whose reproduction must take place through market competition.[19]

In the late 1970s, building on Marx's theoretical and historical insights, Robert Brenner developed a devastating critique of the 'commercialisation' and the 'demographic' models of the transition to capitalism, which were preeminent at the time.[20] Both of these models accepted that the early modern agrarian economy responded in a basically automatic manner to changes in the supply and demand of land and labour. Because they asserted that specifically capitalist dynamics existed transhistorically, they were unable to account for the divergent paths of development across Europe in the wake of the fourteenth-century crisis of feudalism. As Brenner pointed out, the spread of towns and trade that had begun from the eleventh century, on the one hand, and the demographic collapse tied to the feudal crisis, on the other, were cross-European phenomena, yet led to divergent regional outcomes. These were shaped by diverging 'vertical' balances of power between lords and peasants, which varied according to the 'horizontal' relationship of conflict or solidarity within these classes.

In Eastern Europe, a formerly free peasantry lacking strong communal village organisations was reduced to a 'second serfdom'. In Western continental Europe, including France, stronger village communities allowed peasants to free themselves from serfdom. This, however, did not lead to capitalism. Peasants remained in possession of their plots through stable customary rents and taxes and engaged in 'safety first' agriculture, marketing surpluses only after the needs of the household and villagers were satisfied. Moreover, the rise of absolutist monarchies, whose main source of revenue was taxing the peasantry, limited the ability of landlords to consolidate leaseholds and to raise rents in response to increased agricultural prices. Only in England, Brenner showed, did

---

18   Brenner 1989; Comninel 1987.
19   Marx 1990, pp. 873–940.
20   Brenner 1985a; 1985b. For a discussion of the 'Brenner Debate' and its evolution, see Lafrance and Post 2018.

capitalist social property relations emerge, as the unintended consequence of the landlords' attempts to reproduce their class position. In this case, lords took advantage of their ability to raise customary feudal rents and thus undermine peasant possession of the land; these rents then become commercial leases set by market competition among richer peasants who themselves became tenant farmers. Backed by a relatively more centralised state, commercial landlords and capitalist tenants joined forces to expropriate peasants.[21] The upshot was the emergence of capitalist social property relations, in which tenant farmers were compelled by competitive market imperatives to specialise, innovate and accumulate by exploiting a growing mass of agrarian wage-labourers. English capitalist social property relations led to epoch-making, sustained economic development.

This book applies Brenner's Marxist framework to explore the origins of capitalism in France. It should be clear from the preceding discussion that capitalism won't be approached here merely as an economic system. Capitalism is never simply economic; it is a *social* system that has its own developmental logic – with regard to both economic development and patterns of class conflict. Marx's mature critique of classical political economy, stressing the distinctiveness of capitalism, implies that each historical mode of production functions according to its own distinctive internal logic. This logic, as Marx explains, arises out of the specific way in which 'unpaid surplus-labor is pumped out of direct producers' by an exploiting class.[22] Modes of production are thus always simultaneously *modes of exploitation* – in other words: sets of social property relations. Our analysis must begin with the multi-layered and complex configuration of social power that shapes how classes reproduce themselves while allowing one class to appropriate a surplus at the expense of another (or several others). Put another way, we begin with an assessment of social property relations – which always involve *horizontal* relationships of competition and collaboration *within* classes as well as vertical conflicts *between* classes – that impose 'rules of reproduction' on social agents and consequently orient macro-level social and economic phenomena.

In pre-capitalist modes of production, class exploitation took an extra-economic form – the ruling class relied on a superior socio-legal status granting privileged access to state coercive powers used to directly appropriate surplus-labour. This mode of class exploitation tended to stifle economic development. Under feudalism, for instance, peasants did not have an incentive to max-

---

21   On this point see also Dimmock (2015), who develops Brenner's analysis.
22   Marx 1991, p. 927.

imise surpluses, which would be siphoned off by rent or tax payments. Nor were they under any compulsion to accumulate, because they were secure in their possession of land and tools. Meanwhile, in order to maintain a pool of exploitable peasants, landlords were compelled by geopolitical competition to direct surpluses toward *political* accumulation (engaging in state-building processes) instead of economic accumulation. Even leaving aside the simple logic of local trade – 'the exchange of reciprocal requirements' – within a single community or among adjacent communities (which did not in itself generate the need to produce competitively), commerce can and did grow substantially in non-capitalist modes of production. Long-distance trade undertaken by merchants was based on commercial profit-taking – buying cheap in one market and selling dear in another. The strategy of appropriation via arbitrage between markets did not depend on the transformation of production. Competition between merchants or groups of traders backed by states or city-states could be fierce, but had 'less to do with competitive production of the capitalist kind, than with "extra-economic" factors such as superior shipping, domination of the seas and other transport-routes, monopoly privileges, or highly-developed financial institutions and instruments of arbitrage, typically supported by military force'. While '[s]ome of these extra-economic advantages, such as those in shipping or, indeed, military superiority, certainly depended on technological innovations, ... this was not a matter of a systematic need to lower the costs of production in order to prevail in price competition'.[23]

Under capitalism, by contrast, exploiters and direct producers are both market dependent – all economic actors must (directly or indirectly) rely on market exchange to gain and to maintain access to the means of life and the means of production. Both exploiters and producers can be 'formally' free – though this has historically always been the result of struggles from below, and many remain unfree – without compromising the extraction of surplus labour. In this case, the surplus acquires the form of surplus value appropriated through an 'economic' process of exploitation. Under capitalism, we find 'the market as a compulsion rather than an opportunity'.[24] While market-dependent wage-labourers are competing to sell their labour power, capitalists are compelled by market imperatives to exploit this labour-power so as to maximise their profits. This maximisation becomes a matter of survival for capitalists who are facing price competition that coerces them into systematically reinvesting surpluses so as to cut labour costs. The 'law of value' leads to relentless specialisation and innovation, as employers must turn a portion of their profits into capital to

---

23   Wood 2002a, pp. 76–7.
24   Wood 1994.

be able to remain in business. They are obligated to develop and adopt state of the art methods and technologies with a view to producing according to the standards of 'socially necessary labour time'. Put another way, capitalists must constantly extend capital so as to preserve it, and the result is historically unprecedented economic growth. Capitalism, then, 'is not simply production for the market, but competitive reproduction on the market'.[25]

So, when looking at the transition to capitalism in France – or elsewhere – what we are analysing is a radical remaking of class relations of exploitation. This implies deep *social* and *political* transformations and the emergence of a new form of *competitive* market. It implies paying specific attention to the evolution of state structures and initiatives and to socio-legal institutions supporting relations of exploitation. Likewise, studying the making of the French working class will lead us beyond a mere consideration of economic relations of production and the amalgamation of workers in new forms of workplaces. We will have to situate the (re)formation of the working class on the material terrain of specific sets of social property relations – which will once again call for close consideration of state initiatives and of the evolution of socio-legal forms. Before proceeding with these analyses, let me first briefly summarise my thesis and the content of the book.

2   Importing Capitalism to France

I contend that capitalism *did not* develop endogenously in France, and much of this book will be devoted to demonstrating this. The country in fact entered the modern period on a path that was leading it away from capitalism. Attempts to reform the French economy because of British geopolitical competition failed under the old regime, and the Revolution of 1789 did not bring capitalism to France, but actually maintained non-capitalist, customary regulations of industrial production. The French working class first emerged in a self-conscious form during the 1830s and 1840s in this non-capitalist context, and in opposition to a ruling class whose material interests were still largely and directly tied to the state.

I argue that the transition to capitalism in France was incited by dominant sectors of the French state from around the 1860s, against the will of most industrial employers and different political actors. Capitalism did not emerge spontaneously in France but was *made* at the initiative of the state, in a context

---

25   Teschke 2005, p. 11.

of intensifying geopolitical competition. As the transition to capitalism took root in France, the working class remade itself through a new cycle of struggles during the closing decades of the century.

The book begins with a chapter that assesses the political economy of the French Old Regime. A comparative analysis of the social property relations in place in England and France at the time allows us to explain how labour productivity tended to stagnate or decline in the latter country, which remained an overwhelmingly agrarian society. The chapter then discusses liberal attempts to develop the French economy, induced by geopolitical pressures coming from a British rival undergoing a transition to agrarian capitalism, and describes the failure of these attempts to break out of an essentially extensive mode of growth.

I then move, in Chapter 2, directly to an examination of economic structures and growth in post-revolutionary France up until the Second Empire. I again begin with a systematic comparison with capitalist Britain. After a presentation of historiographical debates on nineteenth-century French economic growth, I argue that France's industrialisation remained non-capitalist and therefore much less dynamic over the period. In the absence of a competitive national market, and as a consequence of strongly protectionist policies, I argue, French economic development was propelled by the emulation of British industrial technology, and by market opportunities that in part derived from the use of this technology, as opposed to market imperatives.

Chapter 3 then comes back to the Revolution and its social, judicial and economic impact. On the basis of a discussion of different historical interpretations, and building on the works of different 'political Marxists', I present 1789 as a bourgeois, but non-capitalist, revolution. I also show that the abolition of guilds in 1791 derived mostly from long-standing workers' struggles and did not bring about a capitalist transformation of industry. In addition to consolidating small traditional peasant production in the countryside and extra-economic forms of surplus appropriation, the French Revolution had a direct and decisive impact on industrial labour relations that ruled out the subsumption of labour by capital.

After demonstrating that France did not undergo a capitalist transition until the coming of the Second Empire, I face the challenge of explaining how the French working class made itself during the 1830s and 1840s – an issue tackled in Chapter 4. Sticking to a materialist approach, I contend that workers came to form a self-conscious class, and to adhere to a republican-socialist agenda, through a process of struggle against a class of 'notables' whose members reproduced themselves in a non-capitalist manner – largely by monopolising access to a state that still served as a means of surplus appropriation.

The transition to capitalism in France is addressed in Chapter 5. The capitalist restructuring of French industry was encouraged by sectors of the state
under the authoritarian regime of the Second Empire. Sectors of the French
elite were still opposed to this initiative, but a new international context
marked by the rapid maturation of British industrial capitalism made the transformation of the economy an increasingly pressing matter, and the new executive powers gained by the French emperor finally settled the issue. Through
different measures – including the liberalisation of foreign trade, the economic
integration of the country, and the eradication of customary regulations of
industrial production – the state imposed new social property relations that
revolutionised investment and industrial growth patterns, and announced the
rise of new economic strategies of surplus appropriation.

The book's sixth chapter explores how the capitalist transformation of
French society led to a re-formation of the French working class. From the
1880s, workers reacted to the rise of industrial capitalism by embarking on
what at the time was the largest strike wave in French history, expressing a
deep-seated refusal of the de-politicisation of the social relations of production
entailed by capitalism. While continuities with earlier working-class forma-
tions are noticeable, ruptures also took place, as workers began to construct an
increasingly autonomous labour movement. Significantly larger trade unions
and socialist parties began to emerge, especially at the turn of the twentieth
century.

This is, it goes without saying, a very ambitious research agenda. I did not
undertake it on the basis of original historical research. What I am offering is
an essay of historical and political sociology based on a critical engagement
with a wide range of historical works. My hope is that my argument will open
up new fields of research and answer questions about French economic and
social history that have never been answered satisfactorily, despite all of the
detailed research underpinning the existing historical literature. This body of
work is rich, but its analytic frameworks have often been flawed, and I hope that
my work can help to refocus research and to provide more satisfying answers
to old questions, while keeping in mind the historical nature of capitalism.

CHAPTER 1

The Old Regime False Start: Attempts at Liberal Reforms and the Absence of a Transition to Capitalism in Absolutist France

If industrialisation came fairly early to France, capitalism arrived relatively late. The non-capitalist mode of industrialisation of early nineteenth-century France will be analysed in the following chapter. The present chapter deals with the historical roots of this mode of industrialisation, which dig deep into the soil of Old Regime France. It will be argued that capitalist dynamics did not develop endogenously in France – the French state was compelled by British geopolitical competition to attempt capitalist reforms that ultimately proved unsuccessful.

Historians have long agreed that compared to Britain, economic development in Old Regime France was slow. According to the standard argument, the entrenchment of smallholder peasant production explained the sluggishness of French economic growth.[1] Over the post-war period, and especially since the 1960s and 1970s, this historiographical orthodoxy has been challenged by revisionist historians, who have downplayed the institutional differences between early modern France and Britain and put the economic development of these two countries on a par.[2] Important recent historical works, however, have reasserted the profound qualitative differences that existed between the economic institutions of early modern France and England, and convincingly demonstrated the much lower labour productivity and general economic dynamism of the former country when compared to the latter.[3] The argument presented in this chapter adheres to the latter perspective. Agricultural output did grow in eighteenth-century France, and commercial and (mostly proto-) industrial activities did expand. As we will see, though, the amplitude of this growth needs to be qualified. Most importantly, it is crucial to take note of the fact that French growth over the period took an extensive form – it was more of the same. Growth did not derive from any substantial, sustained and widespread

---

1 Bloch 1966; Goubert 1970; Le Roy Ladurie 1974.
2 See for instance Heywood 1981; Hoffman, 1996; Moriceau, 1994; Toutain 1961. We will deal with the way in which revisionist historians assess the economic performance of nineteenth-century France in a section of the upcoming chapter.
3 Comninel 2000; Jones 1995; Miller 2008; Parker 1996; Teschke 2003.

gains in labour productivity, either in the agrarian or in the industrial sector of the country.

Mobilising the ground-breaking comparative historical work of Robert Brenner[4] on the economic development of early modern Europe, we will first contrast the developmental paths taken by absolutist France and capitalist England. This will provide the opportunity to assess the French extra-economic mode of surplus extraction that will be reintroduced, in a modified but fundamentally similar (i.e. non-capitalist) form, during the post-revolutionary period. Our approach will also allow us to see how the rise of agrarian and subsequently industrial capitalism in England exercised growing geopolitical and economic pressures, which led parts of the French elite to wield state institutions so as to implement liberal economic reforms. This began as early as the second half of the eighteenth century. It was out of these pressures that the history of the transition to capitalism first began in France.

However, as will also be seen, these efforts to reform the political economy of Old Regime France in the wake of the capitalist transformation of England were frustrated. As will be explained, France did not transition toward capitalism before the Revolution. The main reason for this failure to adapt to mounting pressures emanating from England was that the absolutist French regime functioned according to a logic that was foreign and even antithetical to the basic mechanisms of capitalism. The ruling class needed to act in order to maintain its increasingly challenged geopolitical might, but the changes necessary for this adaptation undermined the very foundations of the mode of surplus appropriation that sustained its class reproduction. Only when British capitalist industrialisation had been consolidated and prompted capitalist transitions in different European countries (that is to say, over the second half of the nineteenth century) did the French state successfully engage in a capitalist restructuring of its economy, in the face of rapidly intensifying geopolitical competition – as we will discuss in Chapter 5. During the eighteenth century, however, reformists' efforts failed, and the upshot was not a capitalist transition but a revolution.

1   Absolutist France vs Capitalist England

The tendency to present French absolutism as a transitory regime toward capitalism goes back to Marx and Engels and has been kept alive by different Marxist

---

4   Brenner 1987a and 1987b.

authors.[5] Against this conceptualisation, it is argued here that the building of the absolutist state was not a prelude to capitalism but rather an alternative route out of the crisis of feudalism that hit fourteenth-century Europe; one that perpetuated an extra-economic structure of surplus appropriation. The non-capitalist character of the (never fully stabilised) French absolutist project for the reassertion of its class power can be best understood when compared to the political and economic evolution of early modern England.

The absolutist French state emerged out of a protracted process stretching over centuries and was motivated by the double threats of peasant rebellion from below, and geopolitical pressures from above.[6] It represented a restructuring of inter-ruling class political and jurisdictional bonds, undertaken by landlords whose aim was to reassert their class power against a defiant peasantry. In the wake of the crumbling of the Carolingian Empire, and as the French kingdom was emerging over the late medieval period, French landlords became embroiled in an intense competition for jurisdiction over land and peasants. This competition was only mitigated by the 'unstable bonds of vassalage' and proved increasingly debilitating for the ruling landlord class.[7] Struggles led by French peasants during late medieval times had allowed them to gain increasingly secure proprietorship of their lands. By the thirteenth and fourteenth centuries, capitalising on internal lordly dissensions, and relying on solidarities embedded in their village communities, peasants had secured possession of much of the land available in France.[8] They were also able to gain their freedom and the right to pay fixed monetary dues to lords for the use of the land.[9]

The gains made by peasants progressively jeopardised the capacity of French seigneurs to appropriate a surplus by means of rents. Facing fixed rents that were devalued by inflation, landlords were increasingly compelled to turn to the concentrated power of the monarchical state apparatus to secure revenues and reproduce themselves.[10] During this protracted process, members of the ruling class were integrated into a contested process of 'political accu-

---

5   Perry Anderson 1974 has offered one of the most sophisticated versions of this argument. According to Anderson, absolutism represented a 'redeployed and recharged' form of feudal domination that simultaneously facilitated a capitalist transformation of economic structures. For an incisive critic of Anderson's thesis, see Teschke 2003.
6   Brenner 1987a and 1987b; Teschke 2003.
7   Teschke 2003, pp. 107–8.
8   Miller 2009, p. 4.
9   Miller 2012, p. 142.
10 Brenner 1987b, pp. 284–9; Miller 2012, p. 142.

mulation', building a 'tax/office state'. While rent remained a major mode of surplus appropriation, the state represented an increasingly important form of pumping surplus labour out of the massive French peasantry. Competing with landlords to access these surpluses, the French state developed the coercive means necessary to both safeguard and tax small peasant property, as well as the administrative channels to redistribute the surpluses appropriated within the ruling class.[11] The monarchy struggled to assimilate and pacify an often reluctant, and at times violently rebellious, nobility into a centralised state structure. Even at the height of absolutism, 'France remained a confusing welter of competing jurisdictions, as nobility and municipal authorities clung to the remnants of their autonomous feudal powers, the residues of feudal "parcellized sovereignty"'.[12]

The incorporation of the nobility into state structures of surplus appropriation was archetypically realised through the granting or sale of venal offices (as well as honours and privileges). Offices became inheritable from 1604, and could be bought and sold as commodities on an increasingly vast market.[13] This selling of venal offices amounted to an actual privatisation of a state power that was pulverised by the very process that was meant to consolidate it.[14] Until the final fall of the Old Regime in 1789, 'politically constituted private property – seigneurial rights, venal offices, tax farms, noble titles, and bonds sold by office holders, municipal magistracies, and provincial estates – redistributed income from the peasantry to the nobility and bourgeoisie'.[15] Bourgeois, including merchants, were not capitalists. Merchants made their profits out of circulation and aspired to political careers and land proprietorship as sources of income. Competing with the nobility for access to state power, great bourgeois families also relied on politically constituted means of appropriation 'as the sole means of appropriating the surplus from the mass of resources possessed by the peasantry'.[16]

Both the rise of the tax/office state and the evolution of landlord-tenant relationships under absolutist France contributed to the perpetuation of an extra-economic mode of class exploitation that was not conducive to sustained economic development. A number of historians have asserted that the emergence of dynamic, capitalist agricultural production could be observed in

---

11   Brenner 1987b, pp. 288–9.
12   Wood 2002a, p. 104.
13   Brenner 1987b, pp. 289–90; Gerstenberger 2009.
14   Teschke 2003, pp. 173, 176.
15   Miller 2012, p. 149.
16   Miller 2012, p. 149. See also Parker, pp. 100–1, 263–5.

France during the eighteenth century.[17] According to them, important mutations took place on both large estates and modest farms and were driven
by expanding urban demand. These transformations, amounting to a passage
from 'malthusien' economic stagnation to 'smithian growth', were characterised by regional specialisation and sustained improvements. While taking place
in different regions, they were especially noticeable in the Paris Basin, where
they were steered by the capital's market demand.[18] Moriceau suggests that the
30 percent population growth experienced by the French kingdom over the
century could not have taken place had its agriculture not undergone what he
depicts as capitalist changes.[19] But as impressive as such population growth
might have been, it seems unlikely to have signalled the rise of agrarian capitalism in France – the country's demographic weight within Europe actually
decreased over this period and its population growth remained much lower
than Britain's, as will be discussed below.

France did experience substantial agricultural output growth, probably
amounting to a 25 to 40 percent net rise over the eighteenth century.[20] Much
of this growth, however, simply allowed the country to return to earlier output
levels that had already been reached before the sharp downturn of the later
part of the seventeenth century. In any case, as Moriceau himself recognises,
this increase of agricultural production was 'undeniably' only barely sufficient
to answer to the needs of the growing French population.[21]

Overall, subsistence agriculture remained overwhelmingly dominant in the
French countryside and 70 percent of agricultural production was still consumed on the farm where it had been produced.[22] It is true that the pull
of urban market demand did lead to an expanded 'commercialisation of the
rural economy' at the time.[23] Landlords and merchants seized these market
opportunities and significant numbers of peasants forsook traditional subsistence polyculture to engage in specialised agricultural production and proto-
industrial activities. Such commercialisation of the countryside could be
observed in Normandy, in littoral zones of the Garonne, around the Medi-
terranean coasts and, above all, in the Paris basin. This commercialisation,
however, should not be confused with a process of capitalist transformation.

---

17   Hoffman 1996; Moriceau 1994; Moriceau and Postel-Vinay 1992; Postel-Vinay 1974.
18   Moriceau 1994, pp. 59–60.
19   Moriceau 1994, p. 29.
20   Jones 1995, p. 84.
21   Moriceau 1994, p. 29.
22   Jones 1995, p. 87.
23   Jones 1995, p. 86.

In the Paris Basin, where the phenomenon was most prominent, one could find numerous large and relatively consolidated farms, specialised in grain production for the Parisian market and worked by wealthy tenant farmers employing landless or semi-landless wage workers.[24] Yet, even in this region, 'peasant farms, mostly smaller than 2 hectares existed in nearly every parish and covered anywhere from 5 to 45% of the farmland', and 'these small holdings grew at the expense of the large farms of the bourgeoisie and nobility in the eighteenth and nineteenth centuries, as the peasants took on debts to buy as much land as possible in the hopes of attaining self-sufficiency and security in old age'.[25] In other words, the development of commercial agriculture – which had been present for several centuries – over the second half of the eighteenth century, far from signalling the decline of small peasant production, was actually related to its expansion.

Only a minority possessed the land and livestock necessary to avoid leasing small plots of land, but 'the nobility and bourgeoisie' in possession of this rented land 'had no thought of expropriating the peasants and turning them into proletarians ... The routine practice of pinning down ever more of the peasants' labour to the soil ... generated much wealth for the landed classes. This form of appropriation did not involve the calculation of labour costs, the competitive pressure to reduce them, or the accumulation of surpluses'. In Paris and other regions, 'traditional, quasi-feudal, arrangements for the payment of seigneurial dues, and for labour services' remained the rule. Rental agreements 'contained many indications that the tenants were bound to the soil in debts they could never redeem. Leases spelled out traditional methods and crop rotations, and restricted the lands for seeding through binding rotations of grains and fallows so as to prevent soil exhaustion'.[26]

The large numbers who possessed insufficient land to support their families, and who were also often compelled to work as wage-labourers on commercial farms, were not thereby reduced to a pure and malleable commodity – to *labour-power* – by landlords and their tenants.[27] Contrary to their English counterparts, tenant farmers of the Paris Basin acted as 'seigneurial stewards', engaging wage-labourers, storing grain and collecting dues.[28] As Comninel explains, commercial grain production

---

24   Comninel 1987, p. 183.
25   Miller 2012, p. 148.
26   Miller 2012, pp. 150–1.
27   Miller 2012, p. 145, 149.
28   Isett and Miller 2017, pp. 95–103.

remained bound by the considerations and social relations of peasant community reproduction – even in production under tenant farmers on consolidated seigneurial farms ... [F]arm workers themselves remained peasants, producing their own subsistence on land for which they also had to pay landowners exploitive rents ... [T]his underlying structure of exploitation and subsistence production required maintenance of the tradition structure of peasant rights, obligations, and practices.[29]

Feudal-like extractive relations were well alive in the Paris Basin and elsewhere, and French peasants were 'kept in place and "squeezed" by rents' and royal taxation.[30] Tenants did not face competitive imperatives to preserve their access to the land, and 'French agriculture was to an astonishing extent untouched by the revolutionary techniques of improved farming which had swept England over the previous century or century and a half'.[31]

It was not capitalist dynamics but the intensification of rural labour that sustained the output growth of French agriculture during the eighteenth century.[32] More land was put under cultivation – which contributed to increasing output – but population pressure also led to land morcellation as peasants subdivided their plots on inheritance.[33] Small and shrinking peasant plots meant that landlords had access to large reserves of cheap rural labour and could make copious profits without having to make substantial labour-saving capital investments.[34] As urban demand increased, '[l]arge landowners did not respond to market opportunities by producing more efficiently but rather by taking advantage of the unequal distribution of land, of the opportunities for unequal exchange, and redistributing income and wealth from others'. The evolution of the agrarian structure, 'characterised by peasant possession of the land, led the producers to increase output in response to population pressure on the land through the intensification of labour and stagnating or declining returns to each additional hour of work'.[35] Rather than appropriating surplus value by improving labour productivity, as was done on English lands, French '[l]andowners relied on traditional leasing practices to appropriate extra work

29   Comninel 1987, pp. 189–90.
30   Comninel 1987, p. 190; Isett and Miller 2017, pp. 95–103.
31   Comninel 1987, p. 189. Miller (2012, p. 154) provides a long list of references that support this view.
32   Isett and Miller 2017, pp. 95–103.
33   Brenner 1987b, pp. 290, 302.
34   Miller 2009, p. 6.
35   Ibid.

and produce from the peasantry'.[36] The ruling class was thus squeezing surpluses out of the peasantry by forcing the production of additional outputs through traditional and unproductive means.[37]

Social property relations of Old Regime France were 'to prove disastrous to economic development'.[38] The French ruling class relied on extra-economic means of squeezing surpluses out of peasants and channelled economic resources away from potential agricultural improvements and toward conspicuous consumption and warmongering. The vast process of enclosure that took place in England had no equivalent in France, and the French peasantry retained customary rights and stuck to traditional agricultural practices.[39] As Parker concludes, in Old Regime France, we have 'stasis rather than capitalist social relations', and 'agricultural techniques and productivity did not improve at all'.[40]

Things evolved in a radically different way in early modern England, which was characterised by the development of agrarian capitalism, rather than state absolutism. This implied a fundamentally different relationship between the English ruling class and the state. In the wake of the eleventh-century Norman conquest, this ruling class had developed a mode of exploitation resting on remarkably higher levels of inter-lordly cooperation, under the auspices of the crown. The early modern English state centralised military and political power relatively rapidly. In doing so, it safeguarded the landed property of an aristocracy that was demilitarised well before similar processes took hold in continental Europe. Landed property and economic rent, rather than politically constituted property, eventually became the cornerstone of English ruling class reproduction.[41] The Stuarts' absolutist temptations were definitely put to bed during the seventeenth century, and the so-called 'Glorious Revolution' of 1688 allowed English landlords to assert their parliamentary power over the crown. In sharp contrast to French developments, landlords began to tax themselves to finance state activities instead of mobilising political power as a means of surplus appropriation.[42]

From the mid-fifteenth century, capitalising on the large landholdings they possessed, English landlords began to extract surpluses by establishing 'eco-

---

36   Miller 2012, p. 154.
37   Miller 2012, p. 149, 153.
38   Brenner 1987b, p. 290.
39   Parker 1996, pp. 50–1.
40   Parker 1996, p. 58; see also Brenner 1987b, pp. 307–8.
41   Wood 2002a, p. 99.
42   Brenner 1987b, pp. 298–9.

nomic' leases tied to rents established through market competition.[43] By doing so – and relying on the judicial and military might of the crown – landlords supressed customary land tenure that had been enforced by village and manorial institutions.[44] This erosion of custom was at the heart of a process of land enclosure that signalled the advent of new forms of property and class relations.

This emerging mode of surplus-extraction triggered a process of sustained economic development. English tenants had become market-dependent in a historically unprecedented way, and had to compete in order to secure their access to the land. Facing market imperatives, they were compelled to reduce costs, increase labour productivity, innovate, and to reinvest surpluses to reproduce themselves. Land tenure was now dependent on levels of productivity and profitability. Successful tenants consolidated their plots and joined the yeomanry. Meanwhile, and as land became increasingly enclosed and customary rights declined in parallel, many tenants ended up on the losing end of market competition and were expelled from their land. They joined the ranks of a rapidly growing class of wage-labourers working on the land, and eventually in cottages, workshops and factories in the countryside – and increasingly in towns and cities. Together with landlords and capitalist tenants, this swelling class of wage-labourers formed the triadic class structure of modern England.

The new English agrarian economy proved highly dynamic and laid the groundwork for subsequent socio-economic and political transformations that eventually led to an industrial revolution. The capitalist transformation of the English countryside brought about a secular tendency of rising labour productivity in agriculture that was exceptional in comparison to continental Europe.[45] Robert Brenner and Christopher Isett explain that, in the England of 1500 to 1750, 'agricultural labor productivity grew by between 52 and 67 percent. Its trajectory thus diverged sharply and decisively from that of virtually all the rest of Europe in this period, reaching, for example, *a level that was double that of France by 1750*'.[46] David Parker reports a doubling of labour productivity in English farming over the period from 1600 to 1800, the last fifty years of which were marked by an intense wave of parliamentary land enclosures.[47]

---

43   Brenner 1987b, pp. 291–6.
44   Comninel 2000, p. 46.
45   Miller (2009, p. 3) provides a list of recent works that amply confirm the superiority of early modern England's agricultural productivity. Spencer Dimmock 2014 offers an important defence of Robert Brenner's thesis and historical research on the emergence of agrarian capitalism.
46   Brenner and Isett 2002, p. 627. Emphasis added.
47   Parker 1996, p. 211.

This unprecedented and sustained improvement of its productivity levels allowed English agriculture to support a rapidly expanding population and a growing labour force outside of the agrarian sector. As noted by E.A. Wrigley, 'the population of England grew by approximately 280 per cent between 1550 and 1820 while the population of Western Europe minus England grew by about 80 per cent'.[48] Moreover, 'urban growth in England accelerated so dramatically that during the second half of the eighteenth century 70 per cent of all urban growth taking place in Europe as a whole occurred in England alone, even though the population of England was only about 8 per cent of that of Europe'.[49] By 1700, slightly more than half of the English population was engaged in agricultural activities, and by 1800, only around 38 percent of adult male labour was involved in this sector, whereas on the European continent the average figure ranged from 60 to 80 percent.[50] By 1840, the proportion of the English labour force active outside of agriculture had increased to about seventy-five percent, and this proportion – unique at the time – was itself made possible by a growth in agricultural labour output of about sixty percent between 1750 and 1850.[51]

While England's population nearly tripled from the mid-sixteenth to the early nineteenth century, and the country remained broadly self-sufficient in basic foodstuffs, the massive labour productivity increase activated by agrarian capitalism also allowed for a substantial rise of real wages, fuelled by falling food prices. As Parker explains, 'even the most revisionist of quantitative historians accept that in the 1780s real wages may have been as much as a third higher in England' than in France.[52] As food became cheaper, much broader sections of the English population were able to devote a growing part of their income to discretionary expenditures. This process initiated a 'consumer revolution' and the rise of a mass domestic consumer market. From the seventeenth century and in particular throughout the eighteenth, English wage labourers – whose numbers were rapidly growing as they were expelled from the land – began to consume an ever-growing number of manufactured goods for basic necessities such as cutlery, pottery, candles or printed fabrics.[53] So important was the growth of domestic consumption that, by 1700, the English 'home market was variously estimated at from 6 to 32 times the foreign market'.[54] Even though

---

48   Wrigley 1999, p. 118.
49   Wrigley 1999, p. 122.
50   Ibid.; Brenner 1987b, p. 318.
51   Brenner and Isett 2002, p. 643.
52   Parker 1996, p. 211.
53   Brenner and Isett, pp. 635, 648–9.
54   Hill quoted in Zmolek 2014, p. 158.

British exports were booming, nearly tripling from 1720 to 1790, the main stimulus behind the development of British manufacturing and the industrial revolution that began during the second half of the century remained the spectacular rise of domestic demand.[55] Indeed, around the mid-eighteenth century and on the eve of the first industrial revolution, 'British domestic trade was of perhaps four or five times the volume of foreign trade and ... four-fifths of industrial output was consumed at home'.[56]

Over the seventeenth and the eighteenth centuries, an ever more dynamic and diversified industrial economy was developed in England in response to the pull of a rapidly growing demand for consumer goods, as well as for capital goods used for agricultural and industrial production. Enterprises responding to this expanding domestic and foreign demand did so in the context of an increasingly integrated and competitive national market, which was unique to England at the time. Meanwhile, the state was actively dismembering the customary regulations of trades.[57]

In absolutist France, by contrast, important obstacles to the political and economic integration of the realm remained in place. One of the main reasons for this was that channels of exploitation 'were political and economic at the same time, in the form of state office as well as the remnants of old aristocratic and municipal jurisdiction, [and] tended to fragment both state and economy even under absolutism'.[58] Local authorities and tax farmers – but also many merchants who made their profits as brokers in fragmented markets – often opposed the rationalisation of internal tolls, tariffs and customs.[59] Many of the over 5,500 internal custom posts that were in place under Louis XV had been eliminated as a results of several waves of rationalisation pushed through by the 'enlightened monarchy', but over 2,500 still existed in the final years of the Old Regime.[60]

Back in England, a clearer differentiation of political and economic powers meant that the private economic powers of the ruling class did not represent a major obstacle to political unity. As Wood explains, 'there was both a truly centralized state and an integrated national economy'.[61] Already by the

---

55   Zmolek 2014, pp. 193, 258.
56   Parker 1996, p. 216.
57   Zmolek, 2014.
58   Wood 2002a, p. 105.
59   Parker 1996, p. 30; Wood 2002a, p. 77.
60   Jones 1995, pp. 92, 95.
61   Wood 2002a, p. 105.

seventeenth century, there was in England 'something like a unified national market, without the disjunctions that had characterized international trade ... and without the internal trade barriers that still affected domestic economies elsewhere, not just fragmented city-states but even a centralized kingdom like France'.[62] Subsequently, 'the effective annexation of Scotland in 1707 broadened this domestic market and made Great Britain the largest free-trade area in the world'.[63]

This political unity of the British national market was completed and became an ever more tangible reality through major improvements in transportation infrastructures.[64] Already in the sixteenth century, a network of roads and waterways unified the English territory to an extent that was exceptional at the time and that would be greatly developed over subsequent centuries.[65] Starting in the late seventeenth century, and accelerating from the mid-eighteenth century, road improvements were accomplished through the establishment of turnpikes by private trusts. Also from the seventeenth century, the navigability of rivers was greatly enhanced and provided a cheaper means of transporting bulky goods such as coal. So did the improvement of coastal shipping infrastructures over the first half of the eighteenth century – again through private initiatives – that resulted in a steady fall in transport costs and times, and was followed by the construction of an elaborate network of canals during the second half of the century. As a result of these successive improvements, mostly undertaken by private interests in conjunction with the rapid swelling of trade that was propelled by the capitalist transformation of the countryside, 'by the end of the eighteenth and early nineteenth centuries, Britain had developed the most advanced transport and communication infrastructure in the world'.[66]

Agrarian capitalism, then, supported rapid demographic growth and an unprecedented rise in the proportion of the labour force that was found outside of agriculture. It created and was able to sustain a massive dispossession of customary tenants from their land and provided the waged labour power and market-dependent consumers who respectively fuelled the supply and demand sides of a process of industrialisation. It did this by driving a steady rise in agricultural labour and land productivity, which was ample enough to reduce food prices in a way that allowed for the growth of discretionary

---

62   Wood 2002a, p. 136.
63   Zmolek 2014, p. 213.
64   Zmolek 2014, pp. 197–8, 262.
65   Wood 2002a, p. 99.
66   Zmolek 2014, p. 265. See also Marzagalli 2012, p. 255.

expenditures, and thus to underpin a distinctively large domestic market. But agrarian capitalism did not simply create a mass consumer market for basic commodities. This exceptionally large and integrated domestic market was also qualitatively unique. It was an integrated national market that implied an unprecedented connection between consumption and production that submitted the latter to the exigencies of the former in a new way, compelling first agricultural and eventually industrial productive units to adopt cost-effective and profit-maximising production strategies so as to retain and expand market shares. In other words, the large domestic consumer market produced by the development of agrarian capitalism was also *uniquely integrated and competitive*. British industrial enterprises did not simply seize opportunities offered by expanding consumer demand; evolving in an integrated and competitive market, they were also compelled to compete in a new way in order to respond to this demand. The upshot was an obligation to accumulate and to develop productive forces in a manner that supported unprecedented and sustained economic growth. Agrarian capitalism, emerging from the mid-fifteenth century, eventually led to a British industrial revolution that blossomed from the second half of the eighteenth century. These processes of economic growth provided a decisive geopolitical advantage to Britain.

In France, the stagnant and even declining productivity of agricultural labour discussed above imposed strict limits on demographic growth and on the share of the labouring population that could move away from the land and out of agricultural work. The French population increased by about 30 percent over the eighteenth century and continued to grow at a similar pace into the nineteenth. The modesty of this growth is brought home by the fact that 'from constituting 18 per cent of the European total, the French population dropped to just 16 per cent'.[67] What is more, while the percentage of the English population living in towns of over ten thousand people went from 13 percent in 1700 to 24 percent in 1800, in France, in 1789, 'those living in cities of over 10,000 accounted for 9 per cent of the population, more or less what the figure had been at the beginning of the century'.[68]

All the while, as we saw, British real wages increased rapidly as a consequence of cheapening food prices – in spite of the strain on the agricultural sector imposed by rapid urbanisation and impressive demographic dynamism – and stagnated in France. As a result, and as was mentioned above, on the eve of the French Revolution, real wages were about one-third higher in

---

67   Parker 1996, p. 211.
68   Brenner and Isett 2002, p. 636; Parker 1996, p. 211.

England then they were in France. In fact, across the eighteenth century, the real income of rural and urban wage-labourers is estimated to have decreased by around twenty-five percent.[69] The relative poverty of French peasants and workers, exacerbated by a heavy tax burden and punitive rents, reduced the French internal market to much smaller proportions than in Britain. Far from stimulating the development of a mass market that could sustain an expanding industrial sector, French agriculture precluded its formation.

The sluggishness of the French economy was tied to recurrent Malthusian cycles, in which – in a context characterised by stagnant or declining agrarian labour productivity – 'as non-agrarian employment expanded, demand for food rose, driving up food prices, wages and thus the price of manufactured goods. As prices rose, buying power was undermined, thus forcing the domestic economy to contract'.[70] Unprecedented levels of agricultural productivity in early modern England had lifted this Malthusian cap on industrial development.[71] This was not the case in France, where market outlets were much more limited and production remained overwhelmingly oriented towards luxury production aimed at elite consumption, as had been the case since medieval times.

Again, however, it must be stressed that the depth of the market is not the only factor that needs to be considered here. Limited agricultural productivity and demographic development bounded the growth of the domestic market and thus limited the pace of French industrial development. French industrial producers lacked the growing opportunities that their British counterparts were benefiting from. But they were also freed from the market compulsions that the latter faced, and this turned out to be a decisive factor for the evolution of the French economy.[72] Indeed, if France's internal market lacked the elasticity to support a sustained process of industrialisation, it was also much less integrated than Britain's, and was devoid of competitive compulsions to improve productive forces. The unified national market that had existed in England since the seventeenth century was in fact absent in Old Regime France, and the removal of internal barriers to trade did not take place until the First Empire. On top of these numerous regional trade barriers, we have to consider

---

69   Kasdi 2014, p. 22.

70   Zmolek 2014, p. 173.

71   Brenner 1987b, pp. 324–5.

72   As we will see in Chapter 5, however, even though it was only sustained by mild demo-
      graphic growth and relatively slow – yet not altogether insignificant – urbanisation rates,
      capitalist industrialisation did emerge in France from the last third of the nineteenth cen-
      tury, before finally accelerating, as the world market rapidly expanded at the turn of the
      twentieth century.

the very poor quality of transport infrastructures. Improvements to these infra-structures remained much too limited to eliminate the major inter-regional price disparities that existed in a French economic space that remained deeply compartmentalised and deprived of effective price competition.[73] As Parker summarises, 'there was no such thing as the French economy; only a number of regional ones and, within these, many local ones'.[74]

These fragmented eighteenth-century French markets did not impose price competition on economic actors. The characteristics of competitive markets identified by Wood, which will be discussed in more detail in the next chapter, were all but absent. Constraints on market entry were abundant, intermedi-aries between supply and demand were numerous, products were not substi-tutable, consumers rarely had access to competing providers, and price and quality information was often incomplete and not straightforwardly available. In the words of Minard, 'competition, in truth, cannot be much more imperfect' than it was in France at the time.[75]

In such a fragmented and non-competitive economic context, French mer-chants, often presiding over large networks of 'proto-industrial' workers, made their profits by arbitrating between separate regional and international mar-kets and by attempting to control the conditions of exchange rather than by controlling processes of production so as to lower prices. Major firms con-trolling large-scale factories did the same. French merchant-manufacturers did not have to adjust to external price indicators – they actively shaped prices and market structures.[76] They did not have to calculate and assess profits so as to maximise returns and did not engage in systematic efforts to gather price data in order to guide their commercial activities.[77] Their profits were heavily dependent on their ability to develop and maintain 'networks of trust-worthy representatives' and 'to exploit information and connections to capture advantage' in market exchanges.[78] French consumers were confined in local and regional economic spaces erratically connected by commercial networks, and consequently dependent upon price-setting merchants. In this context,

---

73   Minard 1998, p. 280; Minard 2008, p. 84; Margairaz 1986.

74   Parker 1996, p. 32.

75   Minard 1998, p. 281.

76   Minard 2008, p. 84.

77   Gervais, Lemarchand and Margairaz 2016, p. 7; DuPlessis 2016, p. 172. As Pollard (1965, p. 48) explains, many merchant-manufacturers also benefited from state-granted monopolies and privileges and did not face 'any necessity of comparing costs competitively with other firms'.

78   DuPlessis 2016, p. 174; Marzagalli, 2012, p. 259.

consumers complained of insufficient choices, deficient quality and overinflated prices, as merchants and middlemen made profits at their expense.[79]

French industry remained labour-intensive. This corresponded to the availability of large reserves of cheap labour in rural France.[80] But the mild capital-intensity of French factories also stemmed from the absence of competitive constraints that would have compelled economic agents to engage in cost-effective production. French enterprises did not have to deal with imperatives forcing them to adopt a more progressive attitude toward technological innovations, and to implement capitalist managerial practices, in the way that their British counterparts did from the mid-eighteenth century especially.[81]

The economy of Old Regime France – both its agrarian and industrial sectors – lagged considerably behind Britain's. During the eighteenth century, the French extra-economic mode of exploitive production that lay behind this poor record appeared increasingly inefficient, and inadequate to sustain France's geopolitical position. The French state seemed unable to compete with a British rival regime erected on the basis of an agrarian capitalist economy.

2   British Competition and French Liberal Reactions

As Wrigley aptly puts it, during the eighteenth century, 'the remarkable relative increase in English power sprang principally from what might be described as an intensification rather than an extensification of her territory'.[82] Notwithstanding its capacity to expand territories under its control (which was in fact remarkable outside of continental Europe), the British state had a vital advantage over its French rival in that it could tap into steadily increasing taxable resources provided by its capitalist mode of economic development. Not only was the taxable pool of economic resources steadily growing, but the British state was also engaged, in the wake of the Revolution of 1688, in the building of modernised and rationalised state-administrative institutions that allowed it to tax and channel economic resources with an efficiency that was well above European continental standards at the time.[83] The efficiency with which Britain was able to create and channel wealth greatly improved its capacity to bor-

---

79   Margairaz 1986, pp. 1225–32.
80   Miller 2009, p. 23.
81   Pollard 1965, p. 51.
82   Wrigley 2000, p. 118. See also Teschke 2005.
83   Brewer 1989; Teschke 2003.

row from private sponsors at advantageous rates, just as it decisively enhanced its capacity to subsidise allies in wartime.[84]

Benefiting from these developments, by the time of the Utrecht Treaty in 1713, England had acquired the status of a great power.[85] In spite of the fact that its population was over three times smaller than that of its French rival, Britain's economic and administrative advantages materialised in its capacity to impose repeated military defeat upon France over the eighteenth century.[86] The French state reacted to this series of setbacks by continuously enlarging its military expenditures, which forced it to borrow and to increase its already heavy taxation of the peasantry, in a relatively stagnant economic setting. Spiralling military expenditures and limited state revenues resulted in a series of fiscal crises, which intensified intra-ruling class conflicts over the form of the French state and its economic policies – and eventually became a critical factor leading to the Revolution.[87]

French elites had been well aware of the magnitude of the problem even before the Revolution. As David McNally has shown, the French Enlightenment was in large part a reaction to the crisis of a French state that was unable to efficiently cope with British geopolitical competition.[88] For growing numbers of French intellectuals and state officials, it became clear that British economic prosperity had to be emulated in order for France to match its rival's military might. Matching this level of state-economic resources called for a thorough reform aimed at rationalising fiscal and state accounting structures of tax farming. In Absolutist France, these structures remained attached to venal offices and, as such, were dispersed and highly inefficient. Successive enlightened state officials attempted to centralise and rationalise the state's fiscal apparatus.[89] In addition to these fiscal reforms, the need to galvanise the country's productive forces was also sharply felt. The essential impetus to transform the country's economic structures came not from an incipient capitalist class – which was absent under the Old Regime – but from within the Bourbon state itself.[90]

French individuals travelling in England, as well as official reports, showed a sharp awareness of the impressive economic wealth of their neighbours.

---

84   Zmolek 2014, p. 165.
85   Teschke 2003, pp. 258–262.
86   England lost only one of the six major wars in which it was opposed to France from 1688
      to 1815 (Zmolek 2014, p. 165).
87   Teschke 2005, p. 21.
88   McNally 1988, p. 90.
89   Jones 1995, pp. 10, 112–15.
90   Jones 1995, pp. 107–8.

French statesman shared a widespread inferiority complex toward British economic dynamism, and saw Britain not only as a military, but also as a commercial threat.[91] The need for economic reforms was strongly felt, and many
were attempted. But such attempts were often undone by counter-reforms.
The need for change was experienced in the context of an extra-economic,
strongly state-mediated, mode of exploitive production, relying on intricate
and multilayered individual and corporative privileges. This was a mode of
exploitive production that had its own internal logic and rigidities, which
often could not accommodate the institutional and legislative arrangements
of a British political and economic regime that functioned in quite different
ways.

For a while, the growing military threat was interpreted from a still dominant mercantilist perspective that lauded Britain's 'immense' and 'prodigious'
external trade activities while relating this success to the strongly protectionist policy of the British state. By the seventeenth century, mercantilist France
had become one of the most industrialised European regions, together with
England, the Low Countries and Northern Italy.[92] After a sharp crisis during
the second half of the seventeenth century, the country's industrial sector continued to grow during the eighteenth century, in a non-capitalist, spotty, and
still largely mercantilist framework. The French state supported this growth
by maintaining protectionist tariffs, and granting monopolies, fiscal advantages, and diverse subsidies to both bourgeois and aristocratic merchants and
industrialists. In collaboration with guilds, the state established and enforced
general production rules aimed at ensuring product quality so as to support
French merchants' selling efforts on international markets.[93] As French industrial trades developed across the eighteenth century, prohibitive tariffs were
multiplied in order to protect and insulate them from foreign (mostly British) competition.[94] Yet, the capacity of the French government to accelerate
economic development in a mercantilist framework that limited competition,
regulated production, and prioritised product quality, remained significantly
constrained, and the economic policies put forward proved unable to address
the underlying flaws of the country's economic structure.

As these flaws became ever more magnified by British successes, new liberal
perspectives on how to cope with the economic challenge began to emerge.
Already in the late 1720s, memoirs were being published that emphasised

91   Crouzet 1985, pp. 106–7.
92   Lemarchand 2008, p. 53.
93   Beaud 2010, pp. 59–61.
94   Ballot 1978, p. 11.

English agrarian superiority.[95] During the following decades, many different authors and pamphlets praised English agrarian innovations and improvements, until the issue was addressed in a systematic manner and identified as the decisive source of British wealth by the Physiocrats. Worried by the military and financial difficulties of the French state, the Physiocrats made finding a solution to the state revenue crisis a main priority. Their central preoccupation was to restore the military power of the Crown. To achieve this – and clearly taking their inspiration from Britain – they developed a radically new notion according to which economic prosperity, permitting the expansion of taxable national wealth, determines state power.[96]

Moving away from the mercantilist strategy of luxury production for international markets, the aim of which was to capture foreign monetary wealth, and writing just before the take-off of the English industrial revolution, the Physiocrats asserted that commerce and manufacturing were economically sterile. As the leading intellectual figure among the Physiocrats, François Quesnay maintained that France needed to emulate English agrarian capitalism, and the systematic increase in agricultural productivity that it had brought about, so as to enlarge the stock of economic resources on which the central state could draw to support its military endeavours. However, the arguments of anglophile agronomists for agricultural improvements were running head-first into existing traditional land tenure patterns and customary claims of tenants, and also into the absolutist state-mediated structures of extra-economic surplus appropriation. In consequence, they were compelled to support state intervention to restructure the French economy along the lines of agrarian capitalism.[97]

What the Physiocrats were proposing would indeed have amounted to a radical transformation of France's *political* economy. The goal was to develop in France the private property of land, freed from customary regulations, that had made Britain so wealthy by fostering steady growth in agricultural productivity. But it was also – and again with an eye on Britain – to move away from the heavy taxation of the peasantry on which French absolutism rested, by adopting a new scheme in which capitalist landlords would tax themselves through the central state, while deriving their wealth from rents paid by improving capitalist farmers (who would be exempted from taxation) employing wage-labourers.[98] As McNally explains, the Physiocrats saw the liberalisation of trade

95   Crouzet 1985, p. 112.
96   McNally 1988, pp. 109, 118, 121.
97   McNally 1988, pp. 93, 108.
98   McNally 1988, p. 106.

in grains, and the expansion of markets that would ensue, as a policy from which land enclosure and the proletarianisation of agrarian labourers would naturally follow.[99]

The monarchy became especially responsive to Physiocratic requisitions because British superiority was so evidently demonstrated during the Seven-Year War. But Quesnay and his followers were also rapidly confronted by intellectual opponents who produced an imposing and aggressive anti-physiocratic literature.[100] From the end of the 1760s, a shift in opinion led to the growing isolation and declining influence of the Physiocrats.[101] And yet the declining favour in which Quesnay's intellectual circle was held, did not amount to the political marginalisation of economic liberalism.

Already from the second half of the 1740s, a group of liberal state servants aiming to reform not only the agrarian but also the industrial economy of the kingdom, had assembled under the intellectual influence of Vincent de Gournay and began to insinuate themselves into the corridors of power, eventually extending their influence all the way up to the *Conseil Royal*.[102] They were responsible for the liberalisation of the grain trade, but also for other measures that were sporadically implemented – and often reversed – until the end of the Old Regime.

The era of liberal reforms led by this group began with the appointment of Marchaut d'Arnouville as *Contrôleur général des finances* in 1745 and gathered momentum with the nomination of Daniel-Charles Trudaine as director of commerce in 1749 (who was succeeded by his son after 1769 and until 1777) and of Gournay himself as superintendant of commerce in 1751. These administrators were joined by others, such as Henri Léonard Jean Baptiste Bertin, Étienne de Silhouette, and François de Laverdy, also liberals.[103] Though finally his achievements were fairly unimpressive, during his tenure as controller general from 1759 to 1763, and until his retirement in 1781, Bertin dedicated himself to wielding state power in support of the rationalisation and modernisation of French agriculture, promoting 'enclosures, the partition of commons and the curtailment of collective rights'.[104] The zenith of the influence of these liberal reformers, which would also lead directly to its decline – and indeed to the marginalisation of liberal reformers during the remaining years of the Old Regime –

---

99   McNally 1988, pp. 129–30.
100 Orain 2015.
101 McNally 1988, p. 101.
102 Ballot 1978, p. 10.
103 Deyon and Guignet 1980, p. 621; Jones 1995, p. 128; Minard 1998, p. 316.
104 Jones 1995, p. 6.

came with Anne Robert Jacques Turgot's tenure as controller general from 1774 to 1776.

Also influenced by English developments, liberals gathered around Gournay promoted laissez-faire politics, opposed regulation of production and exchange, and called for the elimination of guilds. Gournay envisioned a society no longer based on privileges and corporative institutions, but rather on the unrestrained exchanges of free individuals.[105] In his *Éloge de Gournay*, published in 1759, the then youthful Turgot argued that social harmony is best guaranteed by each individual's pursuit of their own personal interest, adding that 'from all points of view in which commerce can involve the State, particular interest if left to itself will always lead to general good more surely than steps taken by government, which are always incorrect and of necessity dictated by vague and uncertain theories'.[106] The influence of such liberal ideas grew apace over the last decades of the Old Regime and penetrated salons and academic milieus, as well as the state administrative apparatus. Meanwhile, the industrial superiority of Britain continued to be admired and feared. French commentators praised the innovative prowess of British entrepreneurs and their development and usage of new labour-saving technologies and machines. Many pointed out the much greater productivity of English labourers compared to their French counterparts. The stable rule of law, safeguarding property, the 'liberty of labour', and liberal commercial policies were routinely identified by French observers as factors explaining British industrial successes.[107]

Yet, as noted by Minard, the liberal ideology being promoted by Gournay, Turgot and others, taken to its logical conclusions, had revolutionary implications in an Old Regime political society that had as its basic units not atomised individuals connected through market exchanges but *corps* interwoven under the crown's authority.[108] This was a society constituted through a myriad of particularisms and privileges. The liberal project to be carried out by reformist administrators promised the emulation of English economic successes; yet it not only attacked specific privileges, but also threatened to erode the very 'substance of privilege ... and [to] gnaw at the corporatist heart of the *ancient regime*'.[109] The broader social and political order of absolutist France was at stake. Consequently, this project was faced with relentless anti-liberal res-

---

105   Kaplan 2001, pp. 24–6; Minard 1998, p. 317.
106   Quoted in Deyon and Guignet 1980, p. 624.
107   Crouzet 1985, pp. 114–15.
108   Minard 1998, p. 318.
109   Jones 1995, p. 111.

istance.[110] Liberal reforms progressed unevenly as ministers came and went. Reforms were often only feebly enforced, and many were overturned.

As controller general, Laverdy lifted controls on the grain trade in 1763–4. According to Kaplan, Laverdy's edict signalled the end of food supply as a governmental responsibility and, as such, ranked 'among the most daring and revolutionary reforms attempted in France before 1789'.[111] Precisely because of its highly transgressive character, the edict generated campaigns in support of traditional regulatory practices that were led by members of intellectual, religious, and political elites. It also sparked popular agitation propelled by poor harvests and rising grain prices. Experiments in trade liberalisation ended in a 'spectacular failure'[112] – the government retreated and grain trade control was re-established in the early 1770s. Other liberal reforms included the lifting of the prohibition of printed calico in 1759. In 1762, freedom to engage in industrial production in the countryside, which had in fact been a widespread practice for a long time, was officially granted by central authorities.

Liberal reforms were paused under Joseph-Marie Terray's administration.[113] They were then decisively resumed with the nomination of Turgot as controller general of finances. Soon after his appointment, in 1774, in spite of strong opposition voiced in the King's council, Turgot re-established free trade in grains. This measure led rapidly to important grain riots and denunciations of hoarders, fuelled by a severe dearth. As had been the case with earlier attempts, this liberalisation of the exchange in grains was retracted.[114] Likewise, Turgot made no serious headway in his attempts to eliminate remnants of feudal land tenures.[115]

Also in 1774, the controller general announced that the enforcement of state sponsored industrial rules was indefinitely suspended. In 1776, he then announced six edicts – the most controversial an order abolishing guilds.[116] This bold decision, however, led to what came to be called 'Turgot's carnival', as artisans loudly celebrated their newfound freedom from guild masters, while many seized the opportunity to leave their employers.[117] Rapidly grow-

---

110 Minard 1998, p. 314; Jones 1995, p. 7.
111 Kaplan 1976, p. xxvi.
112 Marzagalli 2012, p. 254.
113 Deyon and Guignet 1980, pp. 611–32.
114 Beaud 2010, p. 94.
115 Jones 1995, p. 8.
116 Jones 1995, p. 110; Minard 1998, p. 321.
117 Guicheteau 2014, p. 111; Kaplan 2001, 95.

ing manifestations of worker insubordination traumatised French elites, and were remembered by reformers for decades to come. This trauma, together with a concern for the preservation of product quality overseen by guilds – a practice that underpinned much of French international commerce – led large sectors of the ruling class to demand the reinstatement of trade corporations. Conservative forces active in the Church and the Parliament of Paris declared war on Turgot, who was rapidly removed from his position while his edict was withdrawn.[118] Guilds were reinstated but also rationalised (many guilds were amalgamated by the crown) and liberalised (it became easier to enter a trade and to establish an enterprise), though this liberalisation of the guild system was widely resisted and remained unapplied in many parts of the realm.[119] The outcry caused by Turgot's attempts at reform amounted to a 'politico-social earthquake' that weakened liberals and announced the end of their aggressively reformist ambitions.[120]

After Turgot's fall, Jacques Necker was appointed controller general. Necker reinstated the industrial rules that had been suspended by Turgot, while relaxing state monitoring of textile product quality.[121] While adopting a mildly liberal economic agenda, Necker was more pugnacious when it came to fiscal reforms. In 1781, in an attempt to develop a rationalised structure of public accounting, Necker tackled the issue of the byzantine system of tax farming. (Under this system, the state was made dependent for the financial resources it desperately needed on venal office holders: as French geopolitical hegemony deteriorated, the influence of these office holders increased.)[122] Once again, however, the reform measures were rapidly reversed. This was because Necker's fiscal and administrative reforms represented a fundamental threat to venal offices and privileges on which the Bourbon political society and political economy were erected. The Old Regime structures that were under attack formed an 'interlocking whole', and the reforms being brought forward 'inevitably threw into turmoil the circuit of credit on which the crown traditionally relied'.[123] As Jones suggests, fiscal and administrative reforms on the scale of

---

118   Jones 1995, pp. 110–11; McNally 1988, p. 133.

119   Kaplan 2001.

120   Minard 1998, p. 321.

121   Every merchant-manufacturer still had to get an official mark applied to their pieces at designated bureaus, but production that did not respect regulations designed to ensure standards of quality was now authorised. Products made in accordance with existing regulations would be stamped with a mark that ensured superior quality, while other products would bear a 'mark of grace' (Minard 1998, p. 323).

122   Jones 1995, pp. 112–13.

123   Jones 1995, pp. 114–15.

those brought forward by Necker and others were 'likely to jeopardise established social hierarchy' of the Old Regime.[124]

As Minard puts it, the balance sheet of liberal reforms seems rather thin in retrospect.[125] Many of the attempted reforms were not successful or did not have an enduring impact on the kingdom's political economy. Obstacles and resistances were too robust. But insofar as they wanted to emulate British capitalist economic development, the task that lay ahead for French eighteenth-century liberals was not simply to overcome and eliminate *hindrances* to embryonic capitalistic entrepreneurial energies. Such capitalist forces simply did not exist in France. As the most aware and consistent reformists would have understood, the task was rather to create an altogether new type of economic and social order that would have positively led – indeed compelled – economic actors to act as capitalists. In this, liberal reformists of the Old Regime clearly failed.

Merchant-manufacturers continued to act in accordance with a different, non-capitalist logic; one that flowed from the socio-economic and political order in which they evolved. Late eighteenth-century French merchants were not liberals – at least not in the way that Gournay and his fellow reformers were. Many merchants opposed laissez-faire and explicitly stood for the maintenance of state enforced regulations of artisanal and industrial trades. They did so because they dreaded counterfeit products and the impact that these could have on the reputation of their own goods. Indeed, many knew from experience that disrespect for production rules could be harmful for their reputation and consequently jeopardise their access to commercial outlets.

Certainly, numerous other merchants who were engaged in the production of lower-quality products called for the loosening of state regulations, hoping to reach out to new consumers who could not afford more expensive, high-quality products. Yet, Minard insists that support for or opposition to regulation (or laissez-faire) could not simply be deduced from a merchant's involvement in the production of high- or low-quality items.[126] Within intricate commercial and production networks, each actor – from direct producers to large *négociants*, including every middleman and intermediary in between – attempted to alter the balance of power between himself and others by using rules and conventions to his own advantage. This meant that he would seek freedom for himself while insisting that constraints should apply to others. Each actor

---

124   Jones 1995, p. 116.
125   Minard 1998, p. 314. For a diverging historical assessment, see Kaplan, 2001.
126   Minard 1998, pp. 291–3.

within a given trade consistently swung between his concern to maintain commercial opportunities dependent on product quality, and the temptation to individually get around the collective rules that guaranteed this very reputation.

In a capitalist economy, business owners and operators will attempt to escape the competition that they want to see applied to their competitors – a competition that represents a fundamental condition for the economic dynamism on which their profits are, as a rule, ultimately dependent. In a similar way, albeit in a fundamentally different economic system, Old Regime merchant-manufacturers individually attempted to escape regulations, the preservation of which were ultimately essential for their success. Not capitalist market competition but regulations, and, more broadly, the social and normative organisation of trust – which did not rule out but in fact inherently implied constant power contests and the wielding of networks of influence – were the guiding principle of early modern merchant activities and the foundation stone of their profits.[127] Competitive, 'self-regulated' markets were absent, and economic activities had to be integrated and organised by other means, through minutely maintained networks and within a framework of social and political regulations and conventions.[128]

French merchant-manufacturers could not but be highly aware of this. Hence, when denouncing state enforced regulations – or bypassing urban craft guilds – merchants claiming the right to trade lower-quality products did not oppose regulations as such. They simply demanded the right to determine and enforce their own rules, most often through local merchant guilds. For instance, conceding to Lyon the production of high-end silk textiles, merchants and manufacturers from Nîmes specialised in the production of lower quality silk, a strategy that represented a blatant, yet tolerated, violation of royal regulations of the trade. But while escaping the central state's regulations, local merchant-manufacturers established their own production rules.[129]

The freedom that was claimed by numerous merchants throughout the French kingdom during the eighteenth century was not the freedom imagined by liberals such as Gournay, and did not imply the dissolution of the *corps* and privileges of Old Regime society. On the contrary, it was a freedom that subscribed to the existing logic of privileges and that was actualised through it. Within the context of the Old Regime, freedom was the privilege to freely organise as a body – as a *corps intermédiaire* – with the concurrence of the

---

127 Gervais, Lemarchand and Margairaz 2016.
128 Minard 1998, p. 281.
129 Minard 1998, p. 307.

crown. This freedom granted merchants the capacity to establish rules together, as well as the right to be consulted by the crown on matters that touched upon their collective interests. Though it might seem alien to contemporary observers, as Minard reminds us,

> one can never insist too much on this: within the universe of the Old Regime, privilege was the ordinary form of freedom, because the latter only existed in the plural form, under the form of particular freedom, conceded by favour and as an exception. [T]hrough the alchemy of privilege ... liberty and protection come together: the monarch takes under his protection these particular bodies to which he has conceded the freedom to self-administer, to deliberate, to keep their house in order, and of course to address demands to him.[130]

The material context of the Old Regime – and the logic of privilege to which they subscribed – drove French merchants away from liberal ideologues. Merchants did not form a rising capitalist class ready to support reforms put forward by Gournay, Turgot, the Physiocrats and their followers.[131] The important development of proto-industrial production in the textile trade, which had begun in the later part of the seventeenth century, took place under the auspices of merchants who contracted out the manufacturing process to rural cottage workers while providing raw material as well as collecting and marketing manufactured goods.[132] Contrary to what has often been assumed, these developments did not in any way teleologically prefigure the rise of a factory system and of a capitalist process of industrialisation.[133] They were in fact propelled by an altogether different logic.

Textile merchants rapidly and successfully attempted to bypass the guild control of urban artisans by disseminating production across the countryside.

---

130   Minard 1998, p. 309. 'On ne le répétera jamais assez: dans l'univers d'Ancien Régime, le privilège est la forme ordinaire de la liberté, parce que celle-ci n'existe qu'au pluriel, sous la forme de libertés particulières, concédées par faveur et à titre d'exception. C'est par l'alchimie du privilège, précisément, que la liberté et la protection sont réunies: le monarque prend sous sa protection ces corps particuliers auxquels il a concédé la liberté de s'auto-administrer, de délibérer, de faire leur ménage interne, et bien sûr de lui faire leurs représentations.' See also Deyon and Guignet 1980, p. 626.

131   Reddy 1984, p. 46; Minard 2008, p. 82.

132   Chassagne 1991, pp. 21–2, 25.

133   For a devastating critique of teleological theories of 'proto-industrialisation' as a first stage of capitalist development, which were offered by Mendels 1972 and many others after the publication of his work, see Zmolek 2014, pp. 91–101.

As was mentioned above, in 1762 the state legalised such practices, and forbade artisan guilds to interfere with the growth of rural industrial production. The artisan guild system overseeing many textile trades took a severe blow as a result, and urban merchant guilds increasingly imposed their unilateral control over the marketing of textile products. In doing this, the goal of merchants was to control and reduce wages so as to increase their profits; their aim was not, as we saw, the imposition of a total *laissez-faire* that would in many cases have jeopardised the reputation for quality of the products that they traded. Moreover, merchants had no intention of directly interfering with labour processes so as to *systematically* increase their productivity. To ensure optimal quality and reputation of goods, they as a rule entrusted the most critical steps in the production process to highly qualified and better-paid urban weavers.[134] Merchant-manufacturers were in fact happy to remain mere merchants and to realise profits in the sphere of circulation. They were not – and demonstrated no ambition to become – capitalist entrepreneurs like their British counterparts.[135] Assessing the activities of French textile merchants, 'nowhere can one find traces of even rudimentary entrepreneurial calculation; no breakdown for material, labor, storage or unit costs were made'.[136]

The operating logic of the Old Regime economy did not in any way encourage merchants, manufacturers or artisans to act as profit-maximising capitalists. Neither did this operating logic imply anything resembling the exceptional dynamism of the *sui generis* and self-sustained economic development that characterises capitalist economies. Facing intensifying geopolitical and commercial competition from its British rival, and lacking in dynamism of its own, the French state was prompted to act in order to stimulate its economy. Besides the largely unsuccessful attempts at liberal reform discussed above, a sustained policy of industrial support was put forward through a series of targeted measures, which often remained non-liberal in nature. A key aspect of the industrial policy that was advanced by French administrators was to facilitate the introduction of foreign techniques and the development of new ones in France through the granting of monopolies and privileges.

Officials and employees of the French *Bureau de commerce* were among the observers who became increasingly obsessed with English industrial competition during this period.[137] John Harris offers a thorough analysis of how the Commerce administrators, together with various private entrepreneurs,

---

134   Reddy 1984, p. 46.
135   Chassagne 1991, pp. 208–9.
136   Reddy 1984, p. 22.
137   Minard 2007a.

developed an intricate policy of industrial espionage that entailed the hiring of English engineers as well as machine transfer into France.[138] Yet, as signalled by Lemarchand, while many technological innovations appeared in Britain and throughout Europe (including in France) during this period, they were only sparsely adopted by French merchants and industrialists.[139] We will demonstrate this in more detail below.

In their attempts to stimulate the use of English technologies and industrial systems and to breathe dynamism into the French industrial sector, state administrators perpetuated the Colbertist strategy of conceding monopolies for the use of a given technology or the production of a given product to privileged royal manufacturers, who were also often benefiting from substantial state subsidies. In parallel, they also created numerous spaces that were freed of guild controls. Yet, in spite of the growing influence of liberal ideas, Deyon and Guignet assert that 'there is no reason for believing ... that manufacturing policy was radically transformed between the first and second halves of the [eighteenth century]'.[140] In fact, 'the frequency of letters patent and orders granting the title of royal manufactury did not decrease after 1753; on the contrary, there were 158 in 35 years: the most surprising evidence to be gleaned from this statistic is that the ten-year average for granting of the title was higher in the later XVIIIth century than it was during the previous period'.[141] Even after Necker's official 1779 announcement that the granting of titles to royal manufacture would be halted, the granting of privileges actually remained uninterrupted. As Deyon and Guignet put it, 'the liberal phraseology appears to have been merely a façade around a basically unchanging practice'.[142]

Horn offers a different historical reading that stresses the shift from the 'liberty of privilege' (monopolies on production granted to specific producers) to the 'privilege of liberty' (creation of privileged enclaves where producers were exempted from guild rules, royal taxes, etc.) after 1750. However, Horn also has to concede that the 'privilege's persistent role in fragmenting French markets and inhibiting French industry must not be minimized or ignored'. He explains that '[t]he persistent clamor for "unrestrained liberty" articulated by Enlightenment officials should be regarded mainly as a rhetorical strategy intended to justify minimizing liberties of privilege in favor of privileges of liberty', but also specifies that 'despite a growing though abstract desire to apply

---

138   Harris 1998.
139   Lemarchand 2008, pp. 63–4, 110–11; see also Parker 1996, p. 214.
140   Deyon and Guignet 1980, p. 625.
141   Deyon and Guignet 1980, pp. 625–6.
142   Deyon and Guignet 1980, p. 626.

liberty to production, in practice, privilege remained the lifeblood of almost all economic policy'.[143] Though some were certainly influenced by Gournay's ideas, reforming state officials were in fact as a rule pragmatists who reckoned with the matrix of privileges that informed the behaviour of French merchants.

While Horn insists on the 'vast potential' of the French economy of the Old Regime, he admits that structural barriers such as 'market fragmentation', 'legal hindrances', or 'rent-seeking aspects of privileges' implied that this economy 'did not maximize either profits or output'.[144] This is a crucial point. Overall, the French state's attempts to stimulate the kingdom's economy over the eighteenth century had disappointing results and were insufficient to cope with British geopolitical competition. It could be argued that, in spite of important setbacks, attempts at liberalising France's economy over the second half of the eighteenth century represented the first effort to emulate the British transitions to agrarian and, increasingly, industrial capitalism. But we also need to stress that this attempt was unsuccessful. Regardless of our evaluation of the balance between demands for liberalisation and the resistance that it faced within French political and economic circles, it is clear that no radical transformations of industrial or agricultural methods of production took place in eighteenth-century France. Horn and Kaplan might be right to believe that the old guild system and royal production regulations had essentially collapsed after the late 1770s[145] – though this has been challenged by other scholars that inform the reading presented in this chapter –[146] but this is ultimately beside the point being made here, which is that, until the very end, the Bourbon state was not successful in developing, nor did it really attempt to develop, capitalist social property relations that would have created a competitive market environment conducive to sustained economic development. What we can at least be certain of, is that whatever transformations did occur over the last decades of the absolutist regime, they were never as revolutionary as those that were taking place in Britain.

3   An Extensive Mode of Economic Development

Like its agrarian sector, French industry did not undergo revolutionary changes over the eighteenth century. France's industrial sector did grow significantly

---

143   Horn 2015, p. 107, 204–5.
144   Horn 2015, p. 14, 25, 237.
145   Horn 2015; Kaplan 2001.
146   Deyon and Guignet, 1980; Minard, 1998.

over the period. Iron production developed rapidly (from a very low start-ing point), while textile output increased at an average of 3.8 percent each year from 1700 to 1789.[147] Crouzet estimates that French industrial production grew by a yearly average of 1.1 percent up until 1790; a growth rate similar to Britain's.[148] Part of the magnitude of this growth in France can actually be explained by a replenishing of the country's industrial capacities in the wake of a deep crisis in the latter part of the seventeenth century – a crisis that capit-alist Britain was largely spared. Still, this record should not be overlooked and, quantitatively, the French and British economies evolved somewhat symmet-rically over the period. *Qualitatively*, however, the two economies went separ-ate ways, and this was of crucial important for their economic development over the subsequent century.

Part of eighteenth-century France's economic growth was due to the devel-opment of foreign trade, which quadrupled from 1716 to 1788, in the wake of the recovery from the seventeenth-century crisis.[149] Most of this dynamism was related to the development of Atlantic commercial networks that were chiefly centred on the Antilles, and especially the French colony of Saint-Domingue. The expansion of Atlantic commercial exchanges, however, scarcely contrib-uted to the industrial modernisation of France. Atlantic merchants were pri-marily involved in the exchange of foodstuffs. France mostly traded wheat and wine with its Antillean colonies, in exchange for sugar and coffee, 60 to 80 percent of which was re-exported.[150] Colonial trade did propel the swift development of proto-industrial enclaves around a handful of ports (mostly Bordeaux, Marseille, Nantes and Le Havre). Yet, on the whole, France's external and domestic economies remained very poorly integrated and, as Jean Tarrade has shown, formed 'dual economies' evolving side by side but for the most part autonomously.[151] Only a very limited proportion of commercial capital engaged in colonial ventures ended up being rechannelled as investments into the met-ropolitan industrial economy.[152] Colonial (and internal) commerce thrived, but commercial profits did not modernise industry. As Jones explains,

If we take figures for the export of manufactured goods as broadly indic-ative of the extent to which trade drove the dynamo of industrialisation,

147   Asselain 1984, p. 85.
148   Crouzet 1966, p. 265.
149   Asselain 1984, pp. 26, 55; Parker 1996, p. 210.
150   Asselain 1984, p. 64.
151   Tarrade 1972, p. 778.
152   Jones 1995, pp. 99–100.

the position of France is revealing. Between 1715 and 1787 the percentage of manufactured articles (essentially fabrics) in the total volume of
French exports scarcely altered, whereas the quantity of manufactured
imports, again measured in percentage terms, rose significantly. Britain,
by contrast, mainly imported raw materials and by the 1780s her exports
consisted overwhelmingly of manufactured goods.[153]

Marzagalli comes to similar conclusions, arguing that 'colonial imports only
gave a modest stimulus to the French economy as a whole, in contrast to the
British economy, characterized by the importance of exporting manufactures.
The growth of French overseas trade, with its strong colonial component, did
not on the whole benefit the rest of the French economy, and was only a sort of
"bubble" depending on special conditions laid down for a time by the French
state'.[154]

Because of her lack of industrial productivity, France increasingly lost
ground in the international trade competition to a much more vibrant British economy and, around 1789, the value of foreign trade per capita was two-
and-a-half times lower in France.[155] French industrial producers were much
less efficient than their British counterparts and were increasingly confined to
luxury production, since they were otherwise unable to compete on international markets. It can also be noted that, towards the end of the Old Regime,
top French state officials, who had supported the 13 colonies in their war of
independence partly in the hope of providing new market outlets to French
merchant ships, were sorely disappointed. The dynamism of capitalist Britain
allowed it to sell a value of an average of 103 million *livres tournois* (l.t.) in the
newly independent United States from 1786 to 1790, while French exportation
to this country averaged a value of only 1.4 million l.t. from 1787 to 1789. Britain
was also largely dominant on other markets, including South America and the
West Indies. As Lemarchand puts it, 'on the eve of the Revolution, Britain was
already in the process of winning the global commercial and modern industrial
battle against France'.[156]

This should not be surprising. During the second half of the eighteenth century, Britain had engaged in an industrial revolution that made its manufac-

---

153   Jones 1995, p. 99.
154   Marzagalli, 2012, p. 262.
155   Asselain 1984, p. 95.
156   Lemarchand 2008, p. 119: 'À la veille de la Révolution, la Grande-Bretagne est déjà en passe
      de gagner contre la France la bataille planétaire du commerce et celle de l'industrie mod-
      erne'.

turing sector much more diversified and productive than its European rivals, while the performance of its agrarian sector was reaching new heights. No such developments could be witnessed in France. French agricultural productivity was overall 50 percent less than the British average. Francis Démier estimates – somewhat conservatively – that, compared to its British counterpart, the French industrial sector suffered from a technological backwardness of more or less fifteen years in 1789.[157] The number of patents was three times higher in Britain around that time and, much more importantly, the ability of the British industrial sector to actually implement technical advances was much greater than in France. In the cotton trade, England had 260 spindles per 1,000 inhabitants against two in France. There were 900 spinning jennies in France against 20,000 in Britain, no more than a dozen mule-jennies in the former country against 9,000 in the latter. Eight French establishments were using Arkwright's water-frame compared with 200 in England. There were ten times more steam-engines in use in Britain than there were in France, where only a few dozen could be found. The proportion of iron produced in blast furnaces using coke reached 30 to 40 percent in Britain while it stagnated at two percent in France.[158]

While significant numbers of small cotton manufactures sprouted – over 170 could be counted during the 1760s, in the wake of the lifting of the ban of calicoes printing in 1759 – proto-industrial development remained the rule. This was true for textile manufacturing, and even more so for 'heavy industries' such as iron production, which remained extremely dispersed and technologically rudimentary.[159] Economic development in general – both agricultural and industrial – was still first and foremost based on the intense use of cheap rural labour and implied little accumulation of capital, a tendency that would continue into the nineteenth century.[160]

The relative frailness of the French economy was painfully revealed by the impact of the Anglo-French commercial treaty of 1786. If, as Horn believes, French officials were confident that their country's industrial capacities could by then allow it to compete successfully against British enterprises, they were superbly mistaken.[161] It seems much more plausible, as maintained by Asselain as well as by Ballot, to interpret the signing of the treaty as an attempt on the French side to hasten the development of a modernised industrialised sector

---

157   Démier 2000, p. 40.
158   Asselain 1984, p. 98; Démier 2000, p. 40; Parker 1996, p. 214; Reddy 1984, p. 53.
159   Jones 1995, p. 90.
160   Miller 2008, pp. 177–88; 2009.
161   Horn 2010.

by exposing the French economy to British competition.[162] Gérard de Rayneval, who negotiated the treaty for France, was aware that it would shock the French economy. He considered this shock to be necessary, and his plan was precisely to establish a commercial framework that would induce it.

The blow engendered by the treaty turned out to be real, and probably much more severe than what the authorities had hoped for. According to Asselain, its immediate effects were nothing less than 'catastrophic'.[163] Cotton production collapsed in Haute-Normandy, in the face of superior British competitors, even though the region was in the vanguard of this trade in France at the time. The quantity of raw cotton consumed by French enterprises, equivalent to 70 percent of total English consumption in 1786, plummeted to 40 percent in 1790. Industries such as metal production, pottery production, paper production and others were also harshly hit.

Lemarchand reports that, as a result of the treaty, French exports to Britain went from 20 million l.t. in 1784, up to 26,276 million l.t. in 1787 (including only eight percent of manufactured products), and up again to 30 million l.t. in 1788, and 35 million l.t. in 1789.[164] British exports heading for France, however, grew much more impressively: set at 13,250 million l.t. in 1784, by 1787 they exceeded (in absolute terms) imports coming from France in 1789, reaching 35,300 million l.t. They continued to grow to 64 million in 1788 – approaching double the amount of French products entering British territory in 1789 – before decreasing slightly to 61 million l.t. in 1789. French economic difficulties during the closing years of the Old Regime were no doubt also partly related to bad climactic conditions and harvests in 1788–9, which hiked up food prices and reduced demand for manufacturing goods. But it is very telling that, in spite of contracting demand, English manufacturers were able significantly to increase their penetration of French markets. Clearly, Britain was the great winner in this economic contest.

The first attempts of the French state to emulate the capitalist mode of development of its northern rival remained largely unsuccessful. Whereas revolutionary changes took place in the British industrial sector from the 1760s on, Crouzet asserts that the expansion of the French economy over the eighteenth century 'took place in a framework that, in its organisational aspects and in terms of methods, remained very much traditional ... On the eve of the Revolution, the French economy was not fundamentally different than what it had

---

162   Asselain 1984, p. 104; Ballot 1978, p. 12.
163   Asselain 1984, p. 107.
164   Lemarchand 2008, p. 112.

been under Louis XIV: it only produced more'.[165] Even though the usage of English industrial techniques in France intensified under the First Empire and after, this non-capitalist and extensive mode of economic development persisted well into the nineteenth century. Widespread use of productivity-enhancing, cost-cutting mechanisation remained limited to a very small number of industrial sectors and, most importantly, as will be explained, was largely derived from market opportunities rather than from market compulsion.

Because of its stagnant agriculture and industry, France lacked the economic resources that would have been necessary to finance its military needs. As British geopolitical pressures intensified, the French state experienced a persistent financial crisis and in turn intensified the taxation of the peasantry; they also sold floods of new offices (which essentially amounted to disguised loans). In addition, the crown attempted administrative reforms, which were resisted by powerful sectors of the French elite. In a context of intensifying geopolitical competition, this elite resistance, together with rebellion from below, eventually led to the spectacular revolutionary upheaval of 1789.[166] The impact of this Revolution on labour relations will be dealt with in Chapter 3. For now, we will consider how the perpetuation of a non-capitalist pattern of development was a key factor explaining the persistent gap between French and British economic performances during the decades that followed the Revolution.

---

165   Crouzet 1966, pp. 271–2: 's' est déroulée au XVIIIe siècle dans un cadre qui, du point de vue de l'organisation et des méthodes, est resté très largement traditionnel ... À la veille de la Révolution, l'économie française n'était pas fondamentalement différente de ce qu'elle avait été sous Louis XIV: simplement elle produisait beaucoup plus'.
166   Miller 2014; Skocpol 1979; Teschke 2005.

CHAPTER 2

Non-capitalist Industrialisation in Post-revolutionary France

We saw in the preceding chapter how the Old Regime economy did not provide the ammunition that would have been necessary for France to compete, let alone to catch up, with Britain, whose industrialisation was only picking up further speed in the period that followed the Napoleonic wars. The Revolution and the First Empire did bring a formal integration of the French economy. Yet, as will be discussed below, the practical integration of a national market did not occur during the first half of the nineteenth century. French industry and agriculture also remained insulated from foreign competition, due to the existence of protective trade barriers. Moreover, while the revolutionary period did bring a certain liberalisation of the economy, the result of these liberal reforms was more than mitigated by the parallel perpetuation and even expansion of the normative regulations of industrial trades, which in fact deepened the social embeddedness of the French economy. This last point will be dealt with in the next chapter. For now, we will assess the industrial growth of post-revolutionary France, comparing it with the performance of the British economy, and consider aspects of the economic structures that underlay relatively modest French economic growth.

Industrialisation certainly did take place in France during the first half of the nineteenth century. But, as substantial as it was, it remained much less spectacular and sustained than developments occurring in Britain. As we will see in the first section of this chapter, revisionist economic historians studying nineteenth-century France tend to depict French economic growth over the period in a much better light. These historians also insist that France embarked upon a unique path of industrialisation that cannot properly be assessed by a comparison with the British mode of industrialisation. Against this revisionist perspective, it will be argued that it was in fact Britain that was exceptional, in that its industrialisation was capitalist in nature, whereas France's economic development was not. Comparing these two countries' economic development is indeed important, not to establish Britain as a benchmark, but to contrast two distinct modes of production. The non-capitalist, and consequently much less dynamic, character of French industrialisation until the Second Empire stands out when we compare French and British economic performances over the period. As we will see, France in fact lagged far behind Britain in economic terms.

A following section will then relate this lag to the absence of capitalist competitive markets in France. This absence was largely due to the fragmented and protected nature of the French economic space. In the absence of capitalist competitive imperatives France engaged in a non-capitalist mode of industrialisation propelled by market opportunities, as French firms attempted to emulate British industrial successes. This opportunity-driven pattern of economic development will be assessed in a section focusing on the mechanisation of the cotton production and the modernisation of French metallurgy, and also in the concluding section of the chapter.

1   Nineteenth-Century French Economic Development: the
        Revisionist Account

The revisionist historiography on the nineteenth-century French economy emerged from the 1960s and 1970s in opposition to a 'retardation-stagnation' thesis.[1] The latter was dominant during the interwar period, when Sir John Clapham published an influential book that stressed the slowness and relative backwardness of France's economic growth, depicting nineteenth-century French businessmen as lacking entrepreneurship and the will to innovate.[2] These themes were taken over and developed by different historians,[3] and most influentially by Landes, who underlined socio-cultural and psychological factors to explain the conservatism of French entrepreneurs.[4] In the following decades, and still to this day, other historians continued to emphasise the relative slowness of French economic development across the nineteenth century.[5]

The publication of quantitative studies of France's economy since 1700 by Jean Marczewski, Tibor Markovitch, and Jean Toutain, which first began to appear in 1961, launched a counter-movement. From the 1960s, numerous economic historians have provided a new and more optimistic take on the nineteenth-century French economic record.[6] Their revisionist perspective stresses that French economic growth per capita had actually been respectable, and was comparable to that of Britain and other Western European countries

---

1   On these historiographical debates, see Barjot 2012; Crouzet 2003.
2   Clapham 1921.
3   Clough 1946; Hoffmann 1963; Sawyer 1951.
4   Landes 1949.
5   Asselain 1991; Crafts 1984a; Dormois 1997; Fohlen 1973; Kemp 1971, and 2016; Salomon 1991.
6   Barjot 1995; Cole and Deane 1965; Fridenson and Straus 1987; Heywood 1992; Lévy-Leboyer 1964; Marczewski 1961–9; Markovitch 1965; O'Brien and Keyder 1979 and 2011.

across the nineteenth century. They also claim that France's process of industrialisation was specific and should not be assessed according to standards set in Britain. Explaining the specific nature of the French process, revisionists reject socio-cultural explanations and focus on factors such as the impact of the economic turmoil caused by the French revolution and Napoleonic wars, the limited amount of strategic natural resources such as coal available on the national territory, the presence of highly qualified artisan workers in France and relatively slower demographic growth in nineteenth-century France. Many revisionist historians accept the thesis that a relatively small internal consumer market and coal scarcity, among other factors, made rational the adoption of a process of industrialisation based on the production of high-quality goods – as opposed to cheap goods manufactured in large-scale, coal powered, mechanised factories – mainly for international markets and elite consumption.

One of the most influential works published in English by revisionist historians is that of Patrick O'Brien and Caglar Keyder, who insist that France and Britain embarked upon distinct paths of industrialisation from the eighteenth century. Offering a strongly revisionist take on the issue, they assert that French industrial output was 'on par with the British achievement' for most of the nineteenth century.[7] O'Brien and Keyder also go as far as affirming that 'labour productivity in French industry [was] above British levels until the 1890s'.[8] According to them, in spite of these impressive features, the French economy did not engage as strongly in industrial factory production as Britain did, because of constraints having to do with 'the relative backwardness of agriculture in France'.[9]

Jeff Horn offers a recent formulation of the revisionist perspective.[10] He explains how, from the mid-eighteenth century, French policymakers and entrepreneurs engaged in a systematic effort to emulate Britain's model of economic development, its sustained technological innovations and its entrepreneurialism.[11] According to Horn, liberal reforms caused sustained economic development and industrialisation in France. In the wake of these successful reforms, French state authorities signed the 1786 Anglo-French treaty, which significantly reduced commercial duties, hoping that France would gain the upper hand in the economic contest that opposed it to Britain.

---

7   O'Brien and Keyder 2011, p. 61.
8   O'Brien and Keyder 2011, p. 90.
9   O'Brien and Keyder 2011, pp. 138, 167.
10   Horn 2006, 2010 and 2012.
11   Horn 2010, pp. 87–9.

Horn explains that the French Revolution and a related 'threat from below', exemplified by the fifty thousand deaths caused by the Terror as well as by a wave of machine-breaking, made impossible the continuation of intensively market-oriented reforms and compelled France to adopt an alternative model of industrialisation.[12] This model mixed market mechanisms with public interventions in the economy in order to foster those sectors in which France was internationally competitive – in particular in certain agricultural sectors and in the production of a variety of luxury artisanal goods.[13] In line with the revisionist perspective, Horn asserts that this model of development, while diverging from the British pattern, eventually allowed France to reach long-term parity with its European economic competitors, and on the eve of World War I to attain a level of per capita income that was close to Britain's.[14]

Against the revisionist perspective, the remainder of the present chapter will defend the position that French economic and industrial development was actually not only different, but also clearly much less impressive than that of Britain during the classical period of the industrial revolution (1750–1850). Proceeding with this assessment, and building on the previous chapter, we will explore the socio-economic backdrop against which this development took place, by comparing aspects of British and French economic structures over the period.

French economic growth was substantial from the end of the Old Regime and over the nineteenth century. Yet, a comparative assessment of French and British performances clearly shows the major economic gap that actually existed between these two countries. Revisionists are indeed correct in claiming that building a general model of industrialisation from the British case in order to assess other national experiences is ill advised. They are also right in saying that the British and French models of development greatly differed during most of the nineteenth century. However, revisionists are wrong to insist on the 'specificity' and 'originality' of France's experience. Until the second half of the century, the French economic structure, and its economic indicators, were in fact rather close to the European average.[15] Though, of course, significant variations also existed among continental nations, it was the British case that really was 'idiosyncratic' and that stood out.[16] It is true, as maintained by

12   Horn 2005 and 2012.
13   Horn 2010, p. 91.
14   Horn 2010, pp. 88, 91, 99–102.
15   Crafts 1984a and 1984b.
16   Crafts 1984a, pp. 52, 59, 67.

O'Brien and Keyder, and other revisionists, that British and French models of industrialisation were very different and took place in contrasting legal, political, and cultural traditions and institutions. But what revisionist historians fail to recognise is that these decisive differences derived from the fact that Britain was capitalist while France was not.

The aim of this chapter is not to show how France lost the industrialisation race to Britain (though it clearly did), so much as to demonstrate how these countries played according to very different rules, and especially how this was reflected in major disparities in their respective economic evolution and achievements. The former country was not capitalist while the latter was – and this is why their developmental models and economic indicators diverged in such significant ways.

2   Contrasting French and English Nineteenth-Century Industrial
        Development

Let us first deal with a core argument put forth by revisionists. All economic historians, including revisionists, agree that nineteenth-century France's absolute GDP growth was rather mild and that it lagged behind Britain's.[17] Yet, historians of the revisionist school use evidence of strong GDP per capita growth in an attempt to show that France's economic achievements were in fact quite impressive and could be advantageously compared with Britain's during the nineteenth century. According to Crouzet, himself a self-declared 'moderate revisionist', annual average growth rates of product per capita between 1820 and 1913 were 1.1 percent in France, 1 percent in Britain, and 1.2 percent for 12 Western European countries taken together.[18] This would seem to leave France in a reasonably good position in the race for economic development. Yet, these figures also place Britain, the 'workshop of the world' for most of the nineteenth century, not only behind its southern neighbour, but also behind Western Europe as a whole. Clearly, a piece of the puzzle is missing if we simply consider economic growth per capita. This is because we are comparing a

---

17   Crouzet 2003, p. 223.
18   Crouzet 2003, p. 224. Other estimations exist, of course. Paul Bairoch (1976, p. 283), for instance, suggests that the annual average growth rates of product per capita between 1830 and 1910 were 1.18 percent in France and 1.21 in the United Kingdom. For the period from 1820 to 1913, Angus Maddison (2001, p. 92), estimates the average growth at 1.13 in France and at 0.96 in Britain. But whatever estimation we decide is the best, the argument developed here remains valid.

maturing capitalist economy with others that remained, at least in some cases, non-capitalist (or at least only partially capitalist), often for a considerable portion of the nineteenth century. Assessing economic performances in relation to demographic data might be *useful* for the purposes of comparing these different national economies, but it is not *sufficient*, and can in fact be misleading in some cases. The divergence of demographic evolutions of France and Britain over the nineteenth century needs to be taken into account.

As we saw in the previous chapter, Britain's superior economic performances, stemming from the emergence of a capitalist set of social property relations in the countryside, implied a faster rate of demographic growth, which naturally had the effect of pushing downwards its rate of growth per capita. In other words, the very fact that Britain's per capita economic growth was dampened by its relatively faster population growth was a side effect, and indeed an indicator, of its much better economic performance.[19]

Things were profoundly different in France. French absolutism tended to safeguard small peasant property. As will be discussed in the next chapter, peasant property was consolidated by the Revolution, thus ruling out the development of a French agrarian capitalism during the nineteenth century. As a corollary, no rural exodus and no booming urbanisation took place – and the internal consumer market remained greatly limited when compared to Britain's. As Roger Price explains, from 1730 all the way through the second half of the nineteenth century, 'the full potential for the development of agriculture and the growth of population within the traditional society was developed'.[20] French demographic growth was checked by the relatively low productivity of the agricultural sector, and remained sharply inferior to that of most other European countries throughout the century.[21]

Hence, France could maintain relatively high economic growth rates per capita in spite of relatively weak overall economic performances precisely because its population increase was checked by lower agricultural productivity. France's seemingly decent economic growth per capita was in fact a side-effect of its relatively poor labour productivity (while its labour productivity was also being downwardly affected by its low population growth). It follows that the focus on economic growth per capita among revisionist economic historians

---

19   As Dormois 1997 explains, growth per capita is not a useful indicator to compare French and British economic performance over the nineteenth century, because of the distortions caused by the relatively slow population growth in France over the period. Dormois, however, does not explain why demographic trends in each country were so different.

20   Price 1981, p. 183.

21   Asselain 1984, p. 134.

of nineteenth-century France is misplaced, and does not support – and would in fact tend to undermine – their claim that France's economic achievements compared advantageously with Britain's.

Industrial growth during the first half of the nineteenth century was substantial and broke new ground in France, compared with earlier historical periods. Unprecedented levels of investment, especially in cotton and in metal production, could be witnessed at the time.[22] Taking into account its industrial output in absolute terms, France, the most populous European country (after Russia), was still the first industrial power in Continental Europe up to the 1840s. However, in spite of these achievements, France's 'economic development at the base was distinctively slower than that of other countries'.[23] The economic gap with Britain increased, while Germany as well as other European states rapidly caught up with France over the remaining decades of the century. While the economic structures of France provided room for industrial development, they did not allow the country to attain parity with states that were rapidly transitioning toward industrial capitalism. Consequently, as noted by Hobsbawm, during the nineteenth century, 'in spite of her advantages and early start, France never became a major industrial power comparable to Britain, Germany and the USA'.[24]

Economic historians have often divided French economic development over the nineteenth century into four phases: 1815–40, 1840–60, 1860–95, and 1895–1914.[25] Going rapidly through these four sub-periods, we can first observe with Barjot that, from 1815 to 1840, the French gross national product per capita grew by approximately one percent per year on average, compared to a growth rate of 1.4 percent in Britain.[26] French economic growth was then characteristically labour intensive, while the mechanisation of industrial production was limited to specific branches and remained feeble when compared to Britain.

The period stretching from 1840 to 1860 was characterised by growth largely propelled by the development of a railroad network. Yet, historians do not agree on the magnitude of this economic progress. Crouzet sees these two decades as a period of strongly improving growth rates, while Markovitch proposes that growth actually decelerated from 1830, and Lévy-Leboyer maintains that it

---

22   Asselain 1984, p. 144; Reddy 1984, p. x; Woronoff 1994, p. 234.

23   Hobsbawm 1996, p. 177.

24   Hobsbawm 1996, p. 178.

25   Caron 1995. For similar periodisations see Asselain 1984; Beltran and Griset 1994; Broder 1993; Lévy-Leboyer 1968; Rioux 1989.

26   Barjot 2014a, p. 94. Again, the comparison with Britain is distorted by the fact that France's demographic growth was much slower (due to a much less dynamic agrarian sector).

slowed from 1845.[27] Caron estimates the increase of GDP at an average of two
percent per year for 1840–60, while Lévy-Leboyer suggests the more modest
figure of 1.1 percent for the same period.[28]

Most economic historians, however, tend to agree that the period from 1860
(or 1865) to 1895 was marked by a strong deceleration in French economic
growth,[29] and preceded a period of rapid economic expansion from the mid-
1890s to 1914. The so-called 'great depression' of the later part of the century
hit France particularly hard. During this era, Britain increased its overall productivity advantage over France, while Germany, Belgium, Switzerland, and
Sweden rapidly caught up with her.[30] Yet, this period of intensified international economic competition also paradoxically brought a radical, capitalist
transformation of the French industrial sector, entailing a rapid acceleration
of industrial investments and the imposition of a new industrial work discipline.

We will deal in detail with the evolution and transformation of the French
economy from the 1860s in Chapter 5. For now, we wish to focus on the period
from 1815 to 1860. During this phase, France's economy grew modestly in comparison with Britain's, which built up an 'overwhelming' lead.[31] As Crouzet puts
it, the nineteenth century was an 'English century', and Britain remained the
'sole superpower' in Europe until the ascent of Germany in the 1880s.[32] Notwithstanding tangible industrial growth, France's economy was undergoing a
relative decline when viewed from the perspective of Europe as a whole. In
opposition to the revisionist perspective on French economic history, Craft suggests that – in spite of modest demographic growth levels – at no point during
the nineteenth century was the country's per capita national income superior
to 70 percent of the value of Britain's.[33] Crafts estimates that, valued in 1970
American dollars, Britain's per capita income was at 498 against 343 in France
in 1830, whereas in 1870 it reached 904 against 567 in France.[34]

During the first two-thirds of the century, France's economy remained principally agrarian. With the industrialisation of textile and metal production, as
well as other industrial sectors, the number of workers outside of agriculture

27   Caron 1995, p. 30.
28   Barjot 2014a, p. 94.
29   Caron 1995, p. 31; Rioux 1989, p. 115.
30   Bairoch 1965; Dormois 1997; Rioux 1989, p. 105.
31   Beaud 2010, p. 132.
32   Crouzet 1985, p. 240.
33   Crafts 1984a, p. 56.
34   Crafts 1984a, p. 51.

did increase, but most industrial and artisanal workers were still employed in remarkably small workplaces, and a large majority was still attached to the land and primarily involved in agricultural labour.[35] Moreover, the number of French peasants and agrarian labourers continued to increase in parallel – Beaud notes that the agrarian labour force grew from 5.5 million in 1781–90 to 7.2 million in 1865–74.[36]

Throughout the century, a major contrast existed between France's peasant majority and the almost complete absence of peasants in Britain.[37] Already in 1811, just below two-thirds of the British labour force belonged to the industrial, commercial, and service sectors, while 35 percent remained in the agrarian sector. In France, four decades later, in 1851, 64.5 percent of labourers were still primarily engaged in agriculture, the forest sector or fishing, while no more than 35.5 percent belonged to the industrial and service sectors of the economy (again, many were still attached to the land, while being involved in some industrial activities intermittently).[38] Even as railroad construction increasingly stimulated the French economy in the period from 1840 to 1860, agriculture remained its most important sector. Thus, in 1847, 44 percent of French national income was tied to agriculture (against 29 percent for industry) while, in Britain, agriculture (which was much more dynamic and productive than in France) contributed only 20 percent of the country's GDP in 1850.[39] As late as 1870, 53.7 percent of the French labour force was primarily involved in agriculture and resource-extractive industries, while as early as 1840, only 25 percent of the British labour force was engaged in these activities.[40]

During the first half of the nineteenth century (and beyond), French industrialisation was characterised by the preponderance of consumer good (as opposed to capital good) production, and a persistent specialisation in quality luxury goods.[41] The industrial sector was relatively weakly mechanised, and massively based on artisanal and inexpensive labour. A progressively increasing number of large manufacturing enterprises were developing, but they still represented scattered patches of industrial land in an ocean of small workshop and domestic artisanal production.[42] Parallel to the relatively slow devel-

---

35   Asselain 1984, p. 143; Noiriel 1986.
36   Beaud 2010, p. 135; see also Broder 1993, pp. 46–7.
37   Asselain 1984, p. 1239.
38   Beaud 2010, pp. 134–5.
39   Barjot 2014a, p. 121; 2014b, p. 378; Stokey 2001, p. 62.
40   Brenner and Isett 2002, p. 643; Crafts 1984a, p. 55.
41   Asselain 1984, p. 145.
42   Barjot 2014a, p. 98; Asselain 1984, p. 143.

opment of these new workplaces, the consolidation of small peasant land ownership in the wake of the Revolution had revived proto-industrial production.[43] The latter entangled industrial work with agricultural labour that took place away from factories. In Britain, by contrast, the often capital-intensive factory system, with its hierarchical form of discipline and division of labour, was rapidly expanding and was integrated into an emerging sweating system, which absorbed more and more of what previously had been domestic work. As has often been noted, the expansion of factory production in England did not cause the disappearance of the small workshop or domestic labour, both of which actually continued to develop alongside it.[44] As Calhoun explains, however,

> by mid-century the leading sectors of the economy had been conquered by machines. Mechanization itself ... created new handcrafts, or swelled the ranks of old ones, only to destroy them a short time later when it overcame the last of the bottlenecks in a particular production process ... Several rural crafts, and rather more of the high-skilled urban trades, survived with some prosperity into the last part of the century. They were nevertheless vanishing one by one from the 1820s on.[45]

Capitalist industrialisation implied a profound and rapid restructuring of industrial facilities, and over 70 percent of English cotton weavers were working in factories in 1845, up from around four percent in 1820.[46]

Back in France, small workshops and domestic labour were still prevalent, even in the cotton industry. In 1850, the French industrial sector 'was only slightly more concentrated than it had been in 1800' and, as late as the mid-1860s, 'French industry had shown little movement toward consolidation'.[47] Overall, factory production remained the exception and industrial development as a whole largely took place within the framework that was already in place during the eighteenth century.[48] The census of 1851 reveals that the vast majority of enterprises comprised less than five workers. Not much had changed even in the last decade of the Second Empire. An analysis of the Industrial Survey of 1860–5 and of the census of 1866 indicate that '95 percent of all

---

43   Démier 2000, pp. 44–5.
44   Hobsbawm 1968; Thompson 1968.
45   Calhoun 2012, p. 203.
46   Beaud 2010, p. 139.
47   Berenson 1984, pp. 26, 28.
48   Beltran and Griset 1994, p. 93.

industrial firms and about 80 percent of the labor force [outside of agriculture] belonged to the artisan sector'.[49] 'Industrial' enterprises in reality remained very small, with an average of 14 workers per employer.[50]

Not only were French enterprises remarkably small, but 'as most French economic historians now agree, mechanization played only a minor role in the French economy between 1815 and 1850'.[51] Some branches were characterised by a stronger capital coefficient, while most others remained considerably less capital intensive and much less mechanised. More importantly, this duality also existed within single manufacturing branches,[52] and, in the absence of competitive compulsion to adopt state of the art technologies and techniques of production, it remained strong until the 1860s.

For most of the nineteenth century, as had been the case during the later period of the Old Regime, French industrialisation was strongly dependent on the existence of a cheap rural labour force into which merchants and industrialists could easily tap. The cost of labour was considerably lower in France than it was in Britain. Hence, around 1835, a Manchester weaver earned the equivalent of about 54 francs per week, while a French worker received an average of 24 francs, and often less, for the same task.[53] In Alsace, one of the most industrialised French regions at the time, which possessed the most mechanised and advanced cotton factories in the country, wages were on average 50 percent lower than they were in Manchester.[54] Yet not even this large wage discrepancy allowed French producers to beat, or even to cope with, British competition (apart from specific sectors where French product quality provided a decisive competitive advantage). The reason was that labour productivity was much lower in France than it was in Britain.

Most French merchant-manufacturers invested relatively sparingly in equipment and machinery and, consequently, the output by labour-unit of their firms remained significantly lower than that of their British counterparts. During the first half of the nineteenth century, outside of some textiles branches and metal-producing firms, the use of state of the art English techniques and technologies in French industry remained minimal.[55] While growth largely relied on the intensive exploitation of massive reserves of rural labour, indus-

---

49   Berenson 1984, pp. 26–7.
50   Beaud 2010, p. 142.
51   Berenson 1984, p. 29.
52   Caron 1995, p. 116.
53   Rioux 1989, p. 114.
54   Hau 1987, pp. 288–302.
55   Lévy-Leboyer 1968; Rioux 1989, p. 114.

trial investment, mechanisation and, consequently, labour productivity stayed relatively low and grew slowly until the end of the Second Empire.[56]

As we saw, O'Brien and Keyder make the rather intrepid claim that French labour productivity was superior to Britain's until the 1890s, based on findings that these two authors themselves admit to be 'certainly surprising'.[57] But their claim is not simply 'surprising'; as Crafts convincingly demonstrates, it is in fact invalid.[58] Crafts explains that methodological errors led O'Brien and Keyder greatly to underestimate the proportion of the French labour force that was actually engaged in industrial production, while also significantly overestimating the capital-labour ratio in French industry. Taking this into account, Crafts suggests that French industrial output per worker was actually only equal to 51.1 percent of the equivalent output in Britain in 1855–64.

But even this figure (the output per worker) probably does not do justice to the productivity gap that separated France and Britain. As we saw in the previous chapter, Miller explains how under the Old Regime and well into the nineteenth century, French peasants, wedged as they were into shrinking plots, supplemented their income by making themselves available as agricultural wage-labourers, or by engaging in ancillary and often domestic industrial production – the source of the massive cheap labour reserve mentioned above.[59] Large numbers of workers were thus involved in industrial activities that, for each additional hour of work, yielded stagnating or diminishing returns.[60] As a consequence, while the output per worker (the indicator used by Crafts) was increasing, the output per labour-unit was probably declining in many French industrial branches (as most were only mildly affected or unaffected by processes of mechanisation). In other words, higher labour intensity was often accompanied by decreasing labour productivity.

This was not the case, of course, in the most dynamic industrial enterprises, where mechanisation was at its strongest. There, the usage of machinery and water or steam power substantially increased labour productivity. But even in the most mechanised industries, such as cotton, the usage of machinery remained less important than it was in Britain. French cotton production progressed much more slowly than its British counterpart. The annual average consumption of raw cotton by the French industry was set at 33.5 million tons

---

56   Asselain 1984, p. 143; Caron 1995, p. 118; Verley 1989, pp. 60–2.
57   O'Brien and Keyder 2011, p. 90.
58   Crafts 1984a, pp. 64–6.
59   Miller 2009.
60   Miller 2009, p. 6.

for 1825–34 and increased to 65 million for 1845–54. For the same period, British consumption went from 104.6 million tons up to 290 million.

More to the point, British production was much more mechanised and efficient. The number of power looms in use in the French textile industries went from 5,000 in 1834 up to 31,000 in 1846.[61] As impressive as this evolution may seem, it was outshone by British figures. The combined number of power looms in England and Scotland went from 55,500 in 1829, up to 100,000 in 1833, and up again to 250,000 in 1857.[62] In France, the number of hand looms (and the attendant volume of traditional domestic production) long remained 'abnormally' high and only surpassed the number of power looms during the 1870s. In 1875, there were 85,000 power looms against 80,000 hand looms.[63] In Britain, three decades earlier, in 1845, there were already 225,000 power looms and only 60,000 hand looms remaining.[64]

The development of horsepower in French industry over the first two-thirds of the nineteenth century was also comparatively sluggish. In 1830, 3,000 steam engines could be found in France, producing a total of 15,000 horsepower, while Britain possessed 15,000 engines, having a total capacity of 220,000 horsepower.[65] In 1840, France, with a population of 35 million, possessed steam engines producing 34,000 horsepower, while Britain, with a population of 19 million, possessed steam engines producing 350,000 horsepower. In 1850, these figures had respectively increased to 67,000 horsepower against 544,000, and France had by then fallen behind Prussia.[66] While this gap was reduced during the last decades of the century, in 1870, the quantity of horsepower per industrial employee in France was equal to only 21 percent of the amount in Britain.[67]

A comparison of power sources is also useful in assessing the level of industrial development of both countries. Caron informs us that, in France, 68.1 percent of horsepower in use in 1860–5 was produced by waterwheels and windmills, whereas only 31 percent came from steam engines.[68] In Britain, by

---

61   Broder 1993, p. 67; Beltran and Griset 1994, p. 96.
62   Hills 1989, p. 117.
63   Beltran and Griset 1994, p. 96; Broder 1993, p. 67.
64   Taylor 1949, p. 117.
65   Lemarchand 2008, p. 256.
66   Beltran and Griset 1994, p. 96; Broder 1993, p. 67; Rioux 1989, p. 72.
67   Crafts 1984a, p. 65.
68   Caron 1995, p. 119. These figures exclude Paris and Lyon. Paris did possess a fair amount of steam powered machines (1,200 in 1860, while there were 6,000 in total in France by 1850) and its exclusion might have a somewhat distorting effect. The distorting effect of the exclusion of Lyon is possibly of a lesser importance. The French capital of silk production in 1880 possessed only 18,000 power looms against 105,000 hand looms. The city

contrast, already by 1830, steam power was on a par with water power (both power sources reached 47.1 percent of total, while wind power was at 5.7 per cent). By 1870, 89.6 percent of total British power came from steam whereas 10 percent was produced by water.[69] Moreover, in the cotton trade, the most rapidly mechanising branch of the French economy, the use of steam power remained marginal until the mid-century.[70]

According to Hobsbawm, the relatively weaker levels of investment and mechanisation witnessed in France represented 'one gigantic paradox'.[71] He reminds us 'that the supremacy of French science' fuelled a vibrant technological inventiveness. Moreover, the country was in possession of large capital reserves. Paris was attracting capital and bankers from all over Europe and was 'a centre of international finance lagging only a little behind London'.[72] Technological innovations were available, but had not been fully woven into the industrial fabric of the country. The large financial resources necessary to achieve this integration did indeed exist, but they were not channelled towards industrial investments to the requisite extent.

In comparison with Britain's modernised financial sector, French banking institutions looked archaic during the first half of the century.[73] Founded in 1800, the Bank of France did not play an active part in promoting industrial development during the first half of the century. It remained under the influence of the *Haute Banque*, which regrouped around 20 large and powerful family-based private financial institutions, mostly concentrated in Paris.[74] These large Parisian banks were close to, and indeed often organically related to, big merchant interests and were mostly involved in the financing of large-scale international commercial transactions as well as in lending to French and foreign states.[75] Investment banking did not develop until important modernising reforms of the French banking system were undertaken under the Second Empire.[76]

---

counted 906 industrial establishments equipped with steam engines in 1859. Yet, at 7.9, their average unit horsepower was much lower than the average of 30 horsepower per mill that could already be witnessed in Britain in 1850.

69   Hills 1989, p. 235.
70   Chassagne 1991, p. 659.
71   Hobsbawm 1996, p. 177.
72   Hobsbawm 1996, p. 117; see also Beltran and Griset 1994, p. 121; Broder 1993, p. 15.
73   Barjot 2014a, pp. 105, 112; Kemp 1971, p. 117; Rioux 1989, p. 94.
74   Barjot 2014a, pp. 118–19.
75   Barjot 2014a, p. 119; Bouvier 1968; Rioux 1989, p. 94.
76   Barjot 2014b, pp. 398–400; Hobsbawm 1996, p. 177; Kemp 1971, p. 124. A first investment bank, the *Caisse du commerce et de l'industrie*, was founded in 1827, but rapidly went bank-

French bankers hardly engaged in long-term credit in support of industry and there was in fact 'strong prejudice against the very notion of this'; a prejudice that was widely shared by political leaders and economic actors. As Zeldin explains, as leader of the government in 1840, Thiers,

> giving vent, as he so often did, to the common opinion of the ordinary middle-class man, declaimed against industry being given credit too easily or over too long a period: that would be to 'make it possible for all sorts of incapable men, men with neither ability nor money, to start up business; they would spin cotton and weave cloth blindly, without measure; they would burden the markets with a mass of products and would compete against old-established traders and these mushroom men would thus ruin men who have been in business for forty of fifty years'.[77]

Thiers was opposed to the expansion of credit out of fear of creating a competitive economic context. This was in sharp contrast to the policies put forth by the Second Empire just over a decade later, which would actively attempt to kick-start a capitalist process of industrialisation by modernising financial institutions and fostering the development of an integrated and competitive national economy (as will be discussed in Chapter 5). Conservative and protectionist manufacturers, who formed a clear majority at the time, echoed Thiers' position. The Chamber of Commerce of Amiens, for instance, claimed in 1836 that '[t]oo much capital would be an inducement to it to give its production a dangerous expansion ... Our own capital can suffice for our needs'.[78] Such claims are symptomatic of the non-capitalist context in place in France at the time.

Prior to the Second Empire, the *Haute Banque* prioritised public loans and the financing of international trade. Great families of Parisian banking were actively involved in the funding of railroad building from the 1840s, but their limited will to invest was rapidly exposed as two-thirds of capital invested in building the French network came from foreign investors, mainly from Britain.[79] Already in 1847, 60 percent of the capital invested in French railroads was British.[80] Bankers only very timidly invested in French industrial develop-

---

rupt, in large part because of the hostility manifested by the Bank of France (Barjot 2014a, p. 119).

77   Zelding 1993, pp. 81–2.
78   Zeldin 1993, p. 82.
79   Kemp 1971, p. 127; Woronoff 1994, p. 232.
80   Barjot 2014a, p. 104.

ment (judged too risky), and the *Haute Banque* was predominantly involved in a 'business of a kind which had been practised since the Middle Ages and which could grow in line with the expansion of the economy without fundamental change'.[81] This leads Kemp to assert that French bankers did not form an advanced capitalist bourgeoisie and that their political influence under Louis-Philippe's July Monarchy was in fact a symbol of French economic backwardness.[82] Indeed, the fortune of French bankers was largely dependent on the perpetuation and smooth running of a non-capitalist mode of surplus appropriation.

The supremacy of Parisian banking was accompanied by the weak development of regional banking networks. Until the 1860s, large areas of the French territory remained monetary and credit deserts.[83] As a result of an agreement between the Bank of France and the finance ministry, banking notes issued by provincial banks had no currency outside of their respective region.[84] These few provincial banks had a commercial role similar to that of the merchant bankers of Paris, only on a smaller scale, while financial transactions involving small loans to peasants were undertaken under the supervision of provincial notaries in a fashion that would already have been familiar during the sixteenth century.[85]

In general, modern deposit banking practices were largely limited and the French banking system did not possess the capacity to efficiently drain savings in a way that would have allowed for their channelling towards industrial investments. In 1850, the cumulative amount of deposits administered by French banks was still 50 times less than what it was in Britain.[86] Around the middle of the century, British banking was clearly in advance of its French counterpart. The degree of concentration and the widespread presence of limited liability banking companies with elaborated branch networks in Britain played a great role in funding the creation of a myriad of limited companies in the country's main industrial branches.[87] This evolution prefigured transformations that took place in France in the last decades of the nineteenth century and at the beginning of the twentieth.[88]

---

81   Kemp 1971, p. 120.
82   Kemp 1971, p. 123.
83   Barjot 2014a, pp. 117, 121.
84   Broder 1993, p. 32.
85   Kemp 1971, pp. 121–2.
86   Asselain 1984, p. 135; Barjot 2014a, pp. 93, 116.
87   Sée 1926, p. 156.
88   Asselain 1988, p. 1242; Plessis 2001.

The French banking system was not designed to accommodate rapid and sustained industrial investment. But while the limited access to credit that it provided was not conducive to growth, this system was less a cause of slow French industrial development than a reflection of this sluggishness.[89] French banks were part of the broader non-capitalist structure of the post-revolutionary French economy, which supported a relatively slow process of industrialisation.

3   The Non-competitive Nature of French Markets

During approximately the first two-thirds of the nineteenth century, the French economy remained 'of the old type',[90] lacking the capitalist dynamism that characterised the British economy. Economic growth in France 'remained through most of this period of "an eighteenth-century type"'.[91] Even the influential economic historian Jean Marczewski, whose quantitative work played a crucial part in the emergence of the 'revisionist' approach to French economic growth, has to concede that the 'industrialization proceeded much more slowly in France and within narrower limits than was the case in England'.[92] As we saw, up to the 1860s, the French economy was characterised by the predominance of peasant agriculture, relied heavily on large reserves of cheap, mostly rural labour, and was modernised in a slow and patchy way.

A prevalent explanation, put forward by many historians,[93] relates the slowness of French economic development over the period to the absence of a mass internal consumer market in France and the limited access of French producers to international markets that were largely dominated by their British competitors. The narrowness of market demand is presented as the key cause of limited investments and slow economic growth.

I will argue here that the limited character of the national market, while no doubt an important factor, is not in itself sufficient and satisfactory as an explanation for retarded economic growth. The lack of a large national consumer market has to do with the absence in France of capitalist social property relations of the kind that emerged in the English countryside from the

---

89   Kemp 1971, p. 121.
90   Kemp 1971, p. 133.
91   Kemp 1971, p. 112.
92   Quoted in Kemp 1971, p. 133.
93   Asselain 1988; Broder 1993; Hobsbawm 1996; Lévy-Leboyer and Bourguignon 1985; Rioux 1989; Verley 1997.

fifteen century. The absence of such property relations, and of attendant market imperatives to systematically improve and develop the productive forces, is also crucial in explaining why French industry developed more slowly. These elements are left out of the discussion if we simply relate the pace of economic development to the quantitative dimensions of the market.

Historians limiting their focus to the magnitude of the market tend to adopt what Brenner has called a 'neo-Smithian' perspective.[94] They are confined to a 'commercialisation model',[95] according to which economic development is driven by the rise of market demand (and stifled by the lack thereof). According to this model, the expansion of trade leads to an ongoing division of labour and to the adoption of improved methods of production. The propensity to respond to price indicators and market opportunities (and contractions) by systematically adapting and improving production is trans-historicised and becomes the factor triggering capitalist industrial development. This, of course, assumes what needs to be explained, and will not permit us to understand, for instance, why French producers did not answer to growing international demand (nor, for that matter, to growing domestic demand) in the same way as their British counterparts did. It cannot tell us why they failed to launch a process of sustained economic development beginning in the eighteenth century.

Hence, the issue is not simply of magnitude; it is also of market *types*. Different market types have existed historically.[96] Most markets have functioned as means of circulation and exchange, providing profit opportunities to assorted economic actors. Others have compelled market-dependent producers to maximise profits. Taking this point a step further, Wood explains that there are in fact distinct types of market dependence.[97] Peasants, merchants or artisans can be market dependent in the sense that they need to sell what they produce in order to buy the means of subsistence needed to reproduce themselves. Because they have direct access to non-market revenue sources or to goods necessary for their survival, and/or because they do not evolve in a competitive environment, these social groups can enjoy a certain room for manoeuvre and are not systematically compelled to develop the forces of production by adopting profit-maximising strategies.

This is not the case in a situation of capitalist market dependence. In such a situation, the producers' very access to the means of production – and not simply to means of subsistence – is market dependent in the sense that it

---

94   Brenner 1977.
95   Wood 2002a.
96   Wood 2002a; Polanyi 1957; Margairaz and Minard 2006.
97   Wood 2002b, pp. 62, 64.

becomes conditional to the attainment of an average rate of profit. Here, as Wood explains, the market itself becomes a social property relation, since the reproduction of capitalists as capitalists – i.e. their continuing access to the means of production and of surplus extraction – depends on their capacity to successfully compete on the market. For capitalist entrepreneurs, the optimisation of their price/cost ratio becomes a matter of survival. They are compelled 'to compete or go under', and this implies a constant effort to improve labour productivity, to boost profits, and to reinvest surpluses. Here only do we pass the threshold of capitalism, where the appropriators' means of survival become inseparable from strategies for maximising profit.[98] Herein lies not only the sources of sustained economic development, but also the foundations of the systemic antagonism between labour and capital, and of a very distinct terrain of class struggle as 'relations of producers to the means of production, and of appropriation, as well as their relation to each other, is mediated, indeed constituted, by the market'.[99]

This merging of survival (or reproduction) and profit-maximising strategies – the emergence of the market as a social property relation – takes place only in the context of competitive markets. As Wood puts it,

> [t]he conditions of capitalist competition require 'maximizing' strategies because capitalists have no guarantee of 'realization' in advance. They cannot know whether their commodities will sell, or even what conditions and production costs would ensure sale at all, let alone profit. Lacking the capacity to control prices in a competitive market, they must adopt strategies that will optimize the price/cost ratio, and their only available strategy is to reduce costs by enhancing labour productivity, to achieve the maximization of surplus value.[100]

Conditions necessary for the existence of competitive markets cannot simply be assumed to exist, as they are highly historically specific. A first and most basic requirement is 'that buyers must have ready access to alternative suppliers'.[101] The relationship between these suppliers is of a distinct kind. Supply and demand must be sufficiently connected, and the link between different producers must allow them to affect one another's costs of production. As Wood

---

98   Wood 2002b, p. 55.
99   Wood 2002b, p. 85.
100   Wood 2002b, p. 55.
101   Wood 2002b, p. 68.

stresses, 'price competition presupposes various suppliers responding to the same or similar conditions, some common standard of measure – not only some common standard of monetary exchange but, more particularly, some compelling social average of labour costs and the "socially necessary labour time" that underlies it'.[102]

We are talking here about a type of market that is integrated and integrating – a market that possesses the totalising capacity to tendentially impose on separate productive units similar standards of production. This capacity requires that 'very specific conditions, both technological and social, must be present to permit the costs and methods of production in one locale systematically to affect those in another, distant one, not to mention modern means of transport and communication – conditions very rare until quite late in history'.[103] Many factors can undercut these conditions: large distances between production and consumption, differences between social conditions and consumers' expectations at the poles of production and of consumption, numerous and multifaceted interventions by merchants and middlemen. As a rule, 'the more mediated the relation between production and consumption, the less direct will be the effect of commerce on the process of production'.[104]

Conditions for the emergence of competitive markets did not coalesce in France until the Second Empire. Two factors, discussed in what follows, importantly contributed to the lack of competitive conditions during the decades following the Revolution: the absence of an integrated national economy, and the highly protectionist policies adopted by the state in regards to foreign trade and the pressure of British competition. Proceeding with this discussion, we need to keep in mind that these factors, as important as they were, were part of a causal chain that was greater than the sum of its parts. These two factors were necessary, but not on their own sufficient, conditions. They were internally related to other dynamics that together formed a whole – one that was characterised, for instance, by the absence of agrarian capitalism discussed above, the persistence of extra-economic modes of surplus appropriation, and the persistence of normative regulations of productive activities in post-revolutionary France, as will be discussed in detail in the next chapter.

Let us begin with the issue of the limited integration of the economy. The Revolution and Napoleonic era abolished many commercial barriers, such as internal tariffs, and contributed to the formal integration of a national market.

---

102   Ibid.
103   Ibid.
104   Ibid.

Yet, in practice, the absence of adequate transport infrastructures implied that the French national economic space remained importantly fragmented.[105]

Fluvial shipping was the most widely used means of transportation during the first decades of the nineteenth century. In this domain, France was much less favoured than Britain or Germany and only a few of the country's rivers were navigable all year round.[106] Principally for political and military considerations, the state engaged in the building of a canal network and the improvement of road infrastructures under the Restoration and the July Monarchy.[107] Waterways tripled in length, but their development came relatively late and, in any case, bulky transport remained very slow and expensive in most of the country, and unreliable during parts of the year.[108]

As will be seen in Chapter 5, railroads eventually played a crucial role in the integration of the French economy, but the early phases of their development, from the 1840s, did not bring about an immediate intensification of competition between industrial producers scattered throughout different regions. The integrative effects of the development of railroads on the French economy did not come to fruition until the Second Empire, and the completion of secondary rail networks occurred under the Third Republic.[109]

The French national market did not simply derive from the inadequacies of transportation and communication infrastructures. It also had an institutional basis, related to the existence of commercial networks that mediated exchanges between the different areas of the country. Until well into the second half of the century, commercial networks and institutions composed of great merchant families had considerable power over the functioning of market exchanges and industrial activities.[110] Great *négociants* and regional

---

105   Price 1981; Szostak 1991. It should be stressed here that my argument is different from Szostaks's. Szostak's important work accounts for the industrial revolution in Britain by relating it to the superiority of this country's transportation system, while the relative sluggishness of industrial development in France is explained by the flaws of its transportation and communication networks. A first problem with Szostaks's argument is that it is monocausal. He fails, for example, to relate the British industrial revolution to the emergence of agrarian capitalism and the related development of a large consumer market. He also tends to focus on the incentives and opportunities arising from transportation improvements. By contrast, my argument insists not only on opportunities, but also on market imperatives that develop with the emergence of an integrated and competitive market economy.

106   Broder 1993, p. 41.

107   Woronoff 1994, p. 227.

108   Border 1993, pp. 42–61.

109   Caron 1995, p. 120; Rioux 1989, pp. 84, 113.

110   Bergeron 1978, pp. 39–41; Lambert-Dansette 1991, p. 154.

marchands acted as inescapable intermediaries at both ends of the production process, providing raw materials and marketing manufactured goods. Doing this, the merchant 'dictated his law to the producer'[111] and exercised much control over price-setting schemes. Merchants wielded their contact networks among regional and international elites and made bountiful profits in circulation, mediating exchanges between France and foreign countries, but also between the different regions and localities of their country. Commercial intermediaries were numerous and played a central role in the functioning of the economy – without them, there would have been no contact between producers and consumers, a fact that was often decried by the latter, who considered these intermediaries as 'parasites' who cornered markets.[112] The merchants' activities and successes were dependent on, but also constitutive of, the fragmentation of the French economic space.

France's national consumer market remained fragmented, heterogeneous, and practically fictitious. The country was composed of a mosaic of *pays* with largely diverging standards of living and important differences in customs and dress habits.[113] Because of flaws in transportation systems, many regions were practically isolated for parts of the year, if weather conditions turned out to be unfavourable.[114] Of course, this type of isolation due to bad weather conditions also existed in Britain (and elsewhere on the Continent), but to a much lesser extent, due to a transportation system that was significantly more developed and efficient. France was still 'constituted of a series of local and regional markets grouped around one or two country towns; such markets had only loose connections with each other and a national market scarcely existed'.[115] The commodities that peasants 'required in the largest amounts – cheap textiles, farm tools and domestic utensils – would generally be obtained from local sources and be produced in small units or under the putting out system'.[116]

Consequently, as Kemp explains, 'most industrial activities, outside of a few towns associated with *la grande industrie*, were concerned with the transformation of local materials and agricultural products by traditional village craftsmen and small-town artisans for a mainly local market. Even the iron industry was largely oriented towards the production of tools and implements for local use;

111   Lambert-Dansette 1991, p. 153: 'dicte sa loi à celui qui produit'.
112   Verley and Mayau 2001, pp. 8–9.
113   Broder 1993, p. 61; Kemp 1971, p. 113.
114   Broder 1993, p. 62.
115   Kemp 1971, p. 113.
116   Ibid.

the small forge using local ores and charcoal thus sufficed'.[117] Much of agricultural production was aimed at local consumption or else consumption by the producers themselves. Similarly, in the industrial sector, parcelled out, traditional, and locally rooted artisanal activities remained the rule.[118]

Evolving in a 'mainly agrarian economy of this type, made up of almost self-contained markets and with low per capita purchasing power', industrial enterprises remained 'organized in small units and on the old lines'.[119] Kemp asserts that most producers were well aware of the fact that, in this market situation, 'it would be risky and foolish for them to make large capital outlays on new techniques which could only be operated economically if their costs could be spread over a larger volume of output than the market warranted'.[120] This was certainly the case. But we need to add to this that producers were also not compelled by their economic context to invest and improve productive forces. The point is not simply that the fragmented character of the market implied smaller and dispersed demand. It is also that most producers benefited from a virtual monopoly in the local or regional markets in which they emerged. They had limited opportunities, but they were also spared the burden of having to attain an average rate of profit, and were not under threat of going bust if they were not able to do so. Facing very limited competition in self-contained economic spaces that were embedded in socio-cultural, judicial and political regulations (as will be discussed in the next chapter), most producers maintained the traditional organisation of their trade. Some of the producers who had to access larger and growing markets did invest in new English technologies. But even these investments were more about seizing opportunities than responding to market compulsion.

As was mentioned, a second important factor that explains the absence of capitalist market imperatives in post-revolutionary France was the strong economic protectionism that was adopted and renewed by the state until the Anglo-French commercial treaty of 1860. Up to this point, very high and prohibitive tariffs insulated most French industrial producers from their British competitors. Many French manufacturers had strongly opposed the 1786 commercial treaty, which, as we saw, had a catastrophic impact on their country's economy. High protective tariffs were reintroduced in 1791, and Napoleon pursued a strongly protectionist policy, even before (and then running alongside)

---

117   Kemp 1971, p. 114.
118   Perez 2012.
119   Kemp 1971, p. 113.
120   Ibid.

the continental blockade he imposed from 1806, in an attempt to stifle Britain's economy.[121]

In the meantime, the French economy remained much less dynamic than the British, and French manufacturers and merchants were incapable of capitalising on the blockade so as to make significant headway in European markets.[122] The productivity gap between Britain and France had continued to grow, and was even more important in 1815 than it had been in 1786. The end of the continental blockade following the downfall of Napoleon once again exposed the French economy to British competition, and threw many industrial branches into crisis.[123] François Caron notes that the sudden irruption of British iron products had the effect of almost definitively ruining the French metallurgic industry.[124]

French industrialists were acutely aware of the overwhelming superiority of their British competitors. Apart from luxury products, they often made little effort to seize shares of international markets, which they largely conceded to their British competitors.[125] France did export more manufactured products than it imported, but, until the 1840s, the value of these exports amounted to only 7 to 8 percent of the value of the total industrial output of the country. Around 1850, exports of cotton products counted for only a fifth of French production (against two-thirds in Britain), and the value of these exports was about fifteen times less than the value of British cotton exports.[126]

French industry, including its most rapidly mechanising branches, thus relied during the first half of the century first and foremost on internal demand. The threatening exposure to British competition rapidly led post-Restoration governments to re-establish a highly protectionist policy, as an extreme sense of economic inferiority and vulnerability became widespread in France, and as particularly strong and entrenched protectionist views became the rule among manufacturers.[127] In 1816 and 1817, the new regime adopted tariff schedules that were uniformly high and often prohibitive, and that included an outright prohibition on the importation of cotton products as well as tariffs of 50 percent on iron, hiked up to 120 percent in 1822.[128] This protectionism was of an indisputable efficacy and, on the eve of the 1860 treaty, French imports of manufactured

---

121   Kemp 1971, p. 130.
122   Crouzet 1989; Rioux 1989, p. 112.
123   Barjot 2014a, p. 92.
124   Caron 1995, p. 136.
125   Stearns 1965, pp. 50, 56–7, 61.
126   Asselain 1984, p. 137.
127   Stearns 1965, p. 57.
128   Asselain 1984, p. 136; Barjot 2014a, pp. 93, 97; Kemp 1971, p. 130.

goods amounted to a mere 0.7 percent of the national industrial product.[129] British competition was thus strongly refracted or almost completely muffled for most industrial branches, and French industrialists remained on guard to ensure that it would stay that way.[130]

Protectionist policies adopted by the French state represented an ideological continuation of the 'mercantilist' or 'colbertist' conception of international commerce that had prevailed under the Old Regime.[131] Yet, just as voices had been heard in support of liberal reforms during the second half of the eighteenth century, a liberal opposition to protectionism developed under the Restoration and persisted under the July monarchy and the Second Empire. David Todd offers a compelling and detailed account of debates that opposed protectionists and free-trade supporters after 1815 and up to 1860.[132]

From the mid-1820s, a liberal campaign was successful in propagating the pro-free-trade ideas of Jean-Baptiste Say. During the first half of the 1830s, this promotion of free trade in France was also actively backed by the British ministry of Commerce under the leadership of its agent John Bowring. Yet, the free-trade agenda was countered and defeated by an even more successful political campaign in support of protectionism, which proposed a form of industrial nationalism in defence of French enterprises and jobs. The governmental enquiry of 1834 on tariffs and prohibitions thus upheld protectionist policies.

Frédéric Bastiat reactivated the free-trade movement during the 1840s, but was checked by a counter-campaign led by the *Association pour la défense du travail national*, which secured the support of virtually all – still highly insecure – French industrialists, as well as the majority of the agrarian sector.[133] *Parlementaires* initiated enquiries, but kept backing a protectionist commercial system that remained in place until the 1860 'industrial *coup d'état*' of Napoleon III and his agent Michel Chevalier. The introduction of a strong protectionism under the Restoration, and its persistence during the following decades, entailed the survival of old-style industries and techniques, which maintained a privileged stratum of manufacturers, who were provided with access to and command over national markets without competitive imperatives to change and modernise.[134]

---

129   Asselain 1984, p. 136.
130   Stearns 1965, p. 50.
131   Todd 2008, p. 18; Kemp 1971, p. 129.
132   Todd 2008.
133   Todd 2008, p. 330.
134   Caron 1995, p. 120; Kemp 1971, pp. 129–32.

The combined effects of a fragmented national market and of protectionism, together with the perpetuation and expansion of regulatory institutions and social practices in the wake of the Revolution of 1789 (which will be discussed in the next chapter), contributed to insulating French industrial producers from capitalist rules of reproduction. Not facing capitalist competitive imperatives, French producers had a much lesser inclination to invest in the development of facilities and tools than did the English industrialist. It is noteworthy that, according to French industrialists themselves, 'the British were simply more willing to invest in industry than were the French'.[135] The archival research conducted by Stearns leads him to the conclusion that

> Many French industrialists in fact claimed that their British counterparts differed in spirit from themselves. The British loved work more than the French did. They had an 'adventurous genius' which distinguished them from all other peoples. Hence, their early start in industry. Hence, their willingness to take risks, to speculate, to be bold in the use of credit and capital. In contrast, French industrialists were slow to use new methods, timid about borrowing, less greedy in their search of markets. The French were easily discouraged, whereas British manufacturers stopped at no obstacle. For some reason ... the British had an ardour, a sense of combination in their industrial efforts which the French lacked.[136]

Economic historians endorsing the 'retardation-stagnation' thesis, tend to focus on the 'Malthusian' character of French manufacturers to explain the relatively sluggish industrialisation of nineteenth-century France. In doing so, they are echoing the self-perception of nineteenth-century French industrialists. Yet if these economic historians are right to assume that French industrialists were less disposed to rapidly invest in the development of their firms, their emphasis on the 'cultural' or 'psychological' character of French entrepreneurship is highly unsatisfactory – as is rightly stressed by 'revisionist' historians. A materialist explanation of this historical phenomenon appears much more fruitful. The so-called 'Malthusian' character of the French merchants and manufacturers in fact stemmed from the absence of capitalist social property relations and rules of reproduction in France until the later part of the nineteenth century.

---

135   Stearns 1965, p. 54.
136   Stearns 1965, p. 55.

Yet, as was mentioned above, even if comparatively slow, considerable economic growth and industrial development did take place in post-Revolutionary France, even before the emergence of capitalist social property relations, and this growth needs to be accounted for. The explanation proposed here is that it was *not* propelled by market imperatives, but rather by French producers seizing market opportunities while emulating British industrial and technological successes. This opportunities-seizing process took place in the context of an overall non-competitive French market space neighbouring a highly dynamic industrialising British capitalist economy. This perspective allows us to explain both the substantial industrial development of France and the *relative* slowness of this development in comparison to Britain during this period.

The prowess and high profits of British capitalists were plain to see, and this could not but inspire opportunistic French entrepreneurs. Patently profitable British technological innovations were adopted in France. As Stearns puts it, 'through the technical education it provided, sometimes unwillingly, Britain was in a real sense the parent of modern French industry'.[137] Over the first half of the nineteenth century, almost all the new methods diffused in French industries were from Britain.[138] The mechanisation of the cotton industry was effectuated by constant imitation of the British model, and all major technical innovations were introduced from England.[139] Commenting on this process of emulation, Charles Coquelin, author of a comparative study on the French and English linen textile industries, asserted in 1839 that '[m]ost French manufacturers behave with regard to the British as pupils to masters, and seem not to aspire to any other kind of merit than that of repeating their lessons faithfully; they believe themselves skilful only in imitating and following; they do not yet dare to act and judge by themselves'.[140]

These technological transfers were facilitated by great numbers of industrial trips to England.[141] As Stearns explains, 'an important minority of French manufacturers actually traveled to Britain in search of instruction about modern industrial methods'.[142] Alsatian cotton manufacturers paid regular visits to British factories to stay in touch with the latest innovations and regularly sent their sons north of the Channel to ensure their technical education. The leaders of every major industrial area in France possessed an acute and direct know-

---

137 Stearns 1965, p. 52.
138 Stearns 1965, p. 54.
139 Chassagne 1991, p. 657.
140 Quoted in Stearns 1965, p. 56.
141 Chassagne 1991, pp. 387–95; Woronoff 1994, p. 247.
142 Stearns 1965, p. 51.

ledge of British industry, and the information brought back from these trips was widely disseminated among French manufacturers.[143] Moreover, many English technicians and engineers were invited to France and, during the Restoration, between 15,000 and 20,000 British skilled workers were employed in the country.[144]

French industrial producers that adopted English technologies could earn high profits. They did so while being largely insulated from British competition and often while benefiting from secure and exclusive access to more or less isolated regional markets. To better understand the operating logic of what could be dubbed an 'opportunist' – as opposed to a capitalist – mode of industrialisation, it is helpful to take a closer look at two of the most dynamic industrial branches at the time.

4   The Development of Cotton Production and Metallurgy

Textiles was the largest industrial sector in nineteenth-century France, and cotton production the most mechanised branch of this sector over the period. As we saw in the previous section, the mechanisation of the cotton trade was much less intense in France than in Britain. Productivity levels reached by French cotton producers did not allow them to compete with their British counterparts – apart from Alsatian calico printers (who competed on international markets largely on the basis of the quality reputation of their products), cotton producers remained fierce supporters of highly protectionist trade policies throughout the period, and developed their activities almost exclusively in the framework of their fragmented home market.

Still, the expansion of the trade was substantial during the first decades of the century, and the number of cotton-producing enterprises almost doubled from the mid-1810s to the mid-1820s.[145] In the early 1840s, over two-thirds of French cotton production was concentrated in three departments: Seine-Inférieure, Nord, and Haut-Rhin.[146] The Alsatian department of Haut-Rhin (which was lost to Germany in the wake of the 1870–1 war) stood out as the most productive of the three, since many of its cotton entrepreneurs adopted English machinery and concentrated production in relatively large factories. By contrast, Seine-Inférieure, situated in Normandy, was the biggest cotton-producing

---

143   Stearns 1965, pp. 51–2.
144   Stearns 1965, p. 52; Woronoff 1994, p. 247.
145   Kasdi 2014, p. 241.
146   Caron 1995, p. 129.

department in France (with a turnover 30 percent above that of Haut-Rhin), and was characterised by much more widespread use of older and traditional production techniques, as well as by the persistence of semi-rural putting-out schemes.[147]

As we saw in Chapter 1, while 20,000 spinning jennies and 9,000 mule-jennies were put to use in Britain between 1773 and 1786, no more than 900 spinning jennies and almost no mules could be found in France over the same period. In other words, no spontaneous adoption of new English spinning technologies occurred in late eighteenth-century France. The socio-economic terrain was simply not conducive to the widespread propagation of these more productive machines. As stressed by Ballot, under the impulse of British competition, it was the government – via the *contrôleur general* and the *bureaux d'encouragements* it created – that acted as the true initiator of the usage of spinning jennies in France.[148] The vast majority of French jennies were built thanks to royal government sponsorship.[149]

Until the Revolution and the Empire, and in spite of growing criticism from liberal circles, the favoured strategy in stimulating the adoption of English machinery was still to grant to producers a status of royal manufacture, which bestowed exclusive rights of usage in specific regions, tax exemptions, and often subsidies as well.[150] The criterion guiding the state in granting these privileges, however, was still not so much the improvement of productivity as it was the *perfectionnement* of quality.[151] Also concerned with quality, many merchant manufacturers remained suspicious of British technology, which they perceived as gadgets, and most abstained from using it.[152]

We already saw how the commercial Treaty of 1786 with Britain exposed French producers to harsh and untenable competition. A few hundred more jennies were set to work in reaction to the coming into force of the Treaty, but the increase remained quite modest, and the intensified government efforts to stimulate their adoption between 1787 and 1789 were largely unsuccessful.[153] The reason for this was that the survival of French merchant manufacturers[154] was not threatened by the massive influx of English yarn into France. They

---

147   Caron 1995, p. 129; Kemp 1971, p. 115.
148   Ballot 1978, pp. 3, 9–10.
149   Reddy 1984, p. 52.
150   Chassagne 1991, p. 216; Reddy 1984, p. 53.
151   Kasdi 2014, p. 206.
152   Reddy 1984, p. 53.
153   Reddy 1984, pp. 53–6.
154   Who were in fact much more merchants than manufacturers, in spite of the fact that they were typically, though misleadingly, called *fabricants*.

could in fact benefit from it. French merchants, overseeing cotton spinning and weaving that were still overwhelmingly performed in a proto-industrial fashion, were not capitalists engaged in price competition: they were not making profits through the accumulation of surplus value by investing in production and increasing labour productivity. They operated according to a different logic. In the wake of the signing of the Treaty, any attempt to face British competition head on by investing in new machines and concentrating production would have proved exceedingly risky. As it happened, it turned out to be unnecessary.

As cheaper English yarn depressed prices in the aftermath of the 1786 Treaty, French merchants simply reacted by decreasing the rates paid to their factors, who collected goods from spinners and weavers. As Reddy explains, '[if] a factor refused to accept the lower price, the merchants manufacturer could simply stop dealing with him and buy English yarn. Factors were forced in turn to pass the price drop through to their spinners. It was the spinners in the end ... who competed with English machinery, and they alone who suffered'.[155] Over the summer of 1788, the earnings of the spinners decreased by 30 to 40 percent. As we saw, many of them were simultaneously peasants, and hundreds of thousand of spinners reacted by abandoning the cotton trade altogether.[156] This was the process that led to the collapse of the Norman cotton trade in 1787–8.

With the Revolution, the return to protectionist policies, and the subsequent continental blockade, capitalist competition originating from Britain receded. As Reddy puts it, the new English 'mode of production continued to make its influence felt on thinking but not on prices'.[157] The spectacular development of British industry, along with memories of the shock caused by the 1786 Treaty, contributed to the influence of liberal ideas and a belief in the importance of developing labour productivity (as opposed to exclusively reaching for quality) in many official government circles. Many merchants, by contrast, remained attached to regulations and the pursuit of quality. Still, a growing number became aware of the benefits that could be derived from the adoption of modern equipment.

The argument put forward here is that this interest was not fostered by market imperatives. Reddy explains that, during this period, the market 'was not well organized enough to provide that stable competitive pressure that one usually supposes to be the chief virtue of the market system'.[158] Markets

---

155   Reddy 1984, p. 57.
156   Reddy 1984, pp. 57, 61.
157   Reddy 1984, p. 61.
158   Reddy 1984, p. 79.

in which cotton producers emerged were not 'price-forming markets',[159] and did not compel producers to engage in 'cost-conscious management'.[160] At the same time, the much greater productivity and profits deriving from the usage of English looms were easily noticed. Even if markets produced highly fluctuating prices and were not vehicles for competitive imperatives, to quote Reddy again, 'it does not take great efficiency for prices to reflect a twenty-fold advantage in productivity'.[161] French manufacturers became aware of the new opportunities offered to them, and it was this awareness, rather than capitalist market imperatives, that drove French industrialisation.

As we just saw, after the signing of the 1786 commercial treaty with Britain, French merchant manufacturers had no incentive and no structural obligation to compete with immensely more efficient British producers, and could in fact benefit from access to cheaper yarn acquired from Britain. Only when entrepreneurs had already invested in factory facilities and equipment – capitalising on profitable opportunities over a period of several decades – would they be compelled to react to a renewed exposure to capitalist competition by attempting to safeguard their accumulated capital stock. Only at this point would they engage in systematic price competition and undertake investments with the aim of enhancing labour productivity. This did not take place in the wake of the 1786 Treaty – it had to wait for a new Anglo-French commercial treaty, signed in 1860; an intensification of international competition; the integration of the French national market; and the state's active destruction of normative regulations of the economy, all of which amounted to the imposition of capitalist social property relations (a new mode of exploitive production), and all of which date to the final third of the nineteenth century.[162]

During the revolutionary decade and under the First Empire, French merchant-manufacturers understood the opportunity offered by British technology, and a new protectionist context now made it possible to seize it. They could learn from the British case without suffering from the effects of British competition, and it was only in this setting that it became rational for them to begin to engage in mechanised cotton production on a large scale. In this much safer context, 'if one could just get a set of the new spinning machines into operation, one was assured a handsome profit'.[163] From the late 1790s through the first two decades of the new century, cotton-spinning capacity grew very rap-

---

159   Polanyi 1957.
160   Reddy 1984, p. 74.
161   Reddy 1984, p. 83.
162   These issues will be discussed in detail in Chapter 5.
163   Reddy 1984, p. 74.

idly. The number of mechanised spindles in France grew from 300,000 in 1800 up to close to a million by 1810.[164] For entrepreneurs, these initial investments were relatively light but yielded elevated profits.[165] Yet, because these were opportunity-driven investments, they remained much less impressive than the competitively-driven developments taking place in English cotton facilities.[166]

The expansion of cotton productive capacities in France was sustained by a rapid inflation of the demand for cotton products during the first decades on the nineteenth century. Elite consumption was still driving much of this expansion. Nobles and rich bourgeois consumption established fashion standards that one had to conform to in order to remain respectable. Elite consumption was constantly renewed, and its total increased steadily over the eighteenth century and into the nineteenth.[167] Lower bourgeois families also tried to mimic the outfits of elites and, from the turn of the century, they were increasingly able to do so due to decreasing prices brought about by the labour-saving effects of new machines.

Using profit-enhancing technologies, French cotton manufacturers now had greater latitude to reduce prices. This in turn fuelled the expansion of popular consumption of coarse cotton products across the period.[168] Hau asserts that consumption of (mainly cotton) textiles increased at a rhythm of three to four percent a year between 1820 and 1840;[169] from the Restoration to the end of the Second Empire, it increase approximately sixfold.[170] Calicoes became increasingly popular, and, by the end of the Restoration and during the July Monarchy, their consumption was well established among the working class.[171] The increased interest in cheaper cotton goods resulted in a reduction of the consumption of traditional textiles such as linen, hemp and wool among the rural and urban working classes, as these products were increasingly confined to luxury and semi-luxury production. This did not yet amount to a broader 'consumer revolution' of the type that had accompanied and sustained the British industrial revolution of the eighteenth century. Nevertheless, it was a significant development that did support further mechanisation of the cotton trade.

---

164   Reddy 1984, p. 75.
165   Bergeron 1978, p. 57.
166   Crouzet 1989, p. 1197. Crouzet notes that there were five million mechanical spindles in England in 1810, compared to a million in France.
167   Kasdi 2014, pp. 26–33.
168   Kasdi 2014, pp. 23–5; Reddy 1984, p. 91.
169   Hau 1987, p. 2.
170   Beltran and Griset 1994, p. 100.
171   Fohlen 1956, p. 54; Reddy 1984, p. 99.

As prices decreased due to labour productivity enhancing machinery, demand elasticity increased and cotton producers were provided with expanding market opportunities, which stimulated further mechanisation. This expansion of market opportunities was also tied to growing wealth and access to protected colonial markets in North Africa. That opportunities, not market compulsion, was driving this process is in part demonstrated by the fact that, when demand contracted and opportunities evaporated, as was the case during the slumps of 1811–12 and 1814, producers were not compelled to react in typical capitalist fashion by attempting to improve their competitiveness and efficiency but rather responded by putting an halt to their investments or withdrew from production.[172] Increased profits, though supported by price reductions, did not derive from, nor were they led by, price competition, and 'most profits were [still] taken immediately out of circulation'.[173]

In the absence of market compulsion to do so, manufacturers did not engage in cost-conscious management. They made no sustained efforts to take control of processes of production nor to impose a labour discipline that would allow them to optimise their labour/output and cost/price ratios. Factories and workshops were often still small, and, more importantly, except in Alsace, but certainly in the North department and in Normandy, the usage and layout of factory equipment was suboptimal.[174] Moreover, the rhythm of the adoption of English technologies was vastly diverse between, as well as within, the different producing regions.

The growth and mechanisation of the cotton trade continued apace from 1810 to the mid-1820s. But this growth still involved highly divergent levels of productivity among firms, with some investing more rapidly and showing impressive improvements, and others that were still able to lag far behind as a result of loose market structures. By the end of the decade, the mechanisation and concentration of cotton manufacturing had substantially expanded. The trade was harshly hit by an economic crisis from 1826 to 1832 that, according to Reddy, brought stiffer price competition and the first signs of an emerging cost-conscious management in some cotton mills.[175]

However, a close analyse of this slump in fact reveals it to be more indicative of the persistence of non-capitalist institutions and practices than of a transition away from them. The crisis was caused by bad harvests in 1825 and 1826, which hiked grain prices, reduced demand for textile products, and

---

172   Reddy 1984, p. 77.
173   Ibid.
174   Reddy 1984, pp. 76–7, 99.
175   Reddy 1984, p. 87.

decreased cotton good prices and firms' profits.[176] Demand and growth were back up in 1829, but another bad harvest in 1830 caused a new dip until 1831. Grain prices decreased again from 1832, and this launched a recovery that led to rapid and sustained growth until the late 1830s.[177] Moreover, the effects of the crisis were not synchronised, and producers were affected differently depending on which markets they were involved in. Firms producing luxury and semi-luxury goods for well-to-do consumers, whose consumption was less directly affected by higher grain prices, could be sheltered from the worst effects of the crisis. This is probably a key factor in explaining why a limited number of firms invested in the building of new factories in this very period.

According to Reddy, some manufacturers reacted to contracting demand and plummeting prices by improving their plants. In some towns, such as Roubaix in the North, this involved mill owners attempting to impose formal work rules on their employees. Reddy also proposes that, even though the willingness to do so varied greatly from region to region, some owners intensified their investments in equipment so as to enhance their competitiveness, buying new looms and installing an increasing number of steam engines.[178]

But as Charles Engrand's careful analysis of the unfolding and impacts of the crisis in the North demonstrates, investment efforts to improve equipment actually came to a halt right at the outset of the slump.[179] Engrand explains that these efforts were momentarily resumed during the short-lived recovery of 1829, but that sustained progress only really occurred with the end of the crisis in 1832. For instance, whereas only six steam engines had been set up in the city over six years, from 1826 to 1831, 12 new engines were installed in Lilles' spinning mills over the three years stretching from 1832 to 1834.[180] From 1832, with the return of profitable market opportunities, a new phase of industrial development began.[181] In the North department, available data points toward

---

176   Broder 1993, p. 25; Hau 1987, p. 70; Reddy 1984, p. 101.
177   Engrand 1981, pp. 239–40, 242, 245.
178   Reddy 1984, pp. 105–6.
179   Engrand 1981, p. 244. It should also be noted that Reddy's data could also be interpreted in a way that supports the argument that I am offering here. The evolution of the deliveries of new textile machinery by a Parisian firm presented by Reddy shows a substantial drop right at the onset of the crisis, as well as a substantial upturn at the end of it. Moreover, the analysis of the adoption of new steam engines he offers covers the period going from 1827 to 1834. The crisis was in fact over by 1832, and most of the new engines were installed from this year on, when market opportunities were flourishing anew.
180   Engrand 1981, p. 245.
181   Engrand 1981, p. 246; Hau 1987, p. 70.

an increase of 70 percent in investment in new machinery during the years that followed the crisis.[182]

Much more than new investments to improve efficiency, the most wide-spread reaction of cotton producers during the economic downturn appears to have been to rein in, or even to simply stop, production. Bankruptcies did occur, and some firms remained afloat only by securing substantial loans.[183] But Kasdi explains that, more than the number of insolvencies, what characterised this crisis was the high number of firms that paused their production.[184] In many cities, production was slowed down or stopped, and mills that had just been built were sometimes disassembled in response to contracting demand.[185]

This was in sharp contrast to the way cotton manufacturers reacted to the crisis that also hit Britain from the mid-1820s. North of the English Channel, capitalist manufacturers were compelled 'to seek every means possible to reduce the costs of production. This was done chiefly by speeding-up machinery and by adding power-loom weaving to spinning'.[186] Because of limited demand, no new mills were built in Manchester from 1825 to 1833. Yet, instead of causing a sharp deceleration of investment in equipment, as was the case in France, the contraction in demand actually forced owners hastily to invest in, and maximise the productivity of, already existing mills, in order to secure market share.

Finally, as Reddy himself explains – and as will be discussed in detail in the following chapter – efforts by some mill owners to develop a new labour discipline were only half-hearted, and in the end completely unsuccessful.[187] These new disciplinary measures were in fact 'not aimed at increasing productivity so much as at ensuring quality and uniformity of an article whose success depended heavily on appearance'.[188] In any case, spinners retained their autonomy at work and capitalist entrepreneurial control of the type existing in the British factory system remained nowhere to be found in France.

But even if we were to acknowledge the (as we saw, very doubtful) occurrence of notable improvements in French cotton factory equipment during the 1826–32 crisis, and to relate these to the (just as doubtful) emergence of market competitive imperatives, we should do so, as Reddy himself does,

---

182   Kasdi 2014, p. 288.
183   Hau 1987, p. 70.
184   Kasdi 2014, p. 249.
185   Kasdi 2014, p. 250.
186   Collier 1964, p. 12.
187   Reddy 1984, pp. 106, 111.
188   Reddy 1984, p. 99.

without losing sight of 'just how weak the force of competition was and how much real diversity the price-clearing mechanism of the yarn markets tolerated throughout this crisis'.[189] This 'price-clearing diversity' would in fact remain in place for decades to come.

Lowering prices expanded demand. But 'slight decreases in price brought large increases in consumption',[190] and increased opportunity through the adoption of cost-cutting machines did not lead to systematic price competition. Claude Fohlen shows how the cost price was a 'peripheral' consideration for French cotton manufacturers. As he explains, reading inquiry reports produced in the mid-nineteenth century, 'one is struck ... by how little the notion [of cost price] is present in employer's declarations. Never do they provide the slightest information concerning production in their firms, not by omission or out of discretion, but because the prosperity of their business was measured by earned money, not by quantities being produced'.[191] French entrepreneurs produced annual or bi-annual balance sheets in which 'production did not enter into consideration'.[192]

Even as late as the turn of the 1860s, profits were mainly taken out of circulation, and the reduction of production costs brought about by the use of new mechanical technologies often fuelled enormous profits rather than resulting in price cuts for consumers. Fohlen quotes a report produced by a state official in 1863 in the midst of the 'cotton famine' caused by the American Civil War – a shortage that would sharply slow down European cotton manufacturing in the years before British competition began to exert its full effects on the French cotton industry. Following years of inquiry, the report showed that Normand cotton producers had been 'only preoccupied by retaining or accumulating unbelievable profits, maintained or increased yarn and fabric prices, while they obtained raw materials for almost nothing ... This or that manufacturer earned two million francs per year while people did not pay a dime less for the clothing that they bought'.[193] In an inquiry produced in 1855, Jean Doll-

---

189   Reddy 1984, p. 100.
190   Reddy 1984, p. 91.
191   Fohlen 1956, p. 90: 'On est frappé ... du peu de place que tient la notion de production dans les déclarations concernant la production de leurs usines, non par oubli ou discrétion, mais parce que la prospérité des affaires se mesure à l'argent gagné et non pas aux quantités produites'.
192   Ibid.: 'la production n'y entre pas en ligne de compte'.
193   Fohlen 1956, p. 91: 'uniquement préoccupés de maintenir ou d'accumuler d'incroyables bénéfices, maintenaient ou haussaient le prix des filés et des fabriqués, alors qu'ils obtenaient pour presque rien la matière première ... Tel ou tel fabricant gagnait par an deux millions de francs sans que le peuple payât un centime moins cher le vêtement qui le couvrait'.

fus, a leading Alsatian manufacturer, declared that French spinning enterprises were at times generating profits that were 25 to 40 percent higher than those of foreign firms.[194]

The market in which they evolved was such that French cotton producers were, as a rule, making profits without having to pay any kind of sustained attention to the way that their facilities and the labour power they hired were organised. Nor, relatedly, did they have to attend to the level of their production costs. They did not face systemic price competition, and so they did not have to concern themselves with cost prices to ensure the survival of their enterprise, or even to make a profit. As Charles Noiret, a handloom weaver of Rouen, put it in 1836, 'the profits of the producers were such that they did not bother to count them: they bought, they produced, and sold according to habit and their capital quintupled in a single year ... They got rich without knowing why'.[195] French cotton producers could decrease selling prices to enlarge sales just as they could raise them if they perceived that this could lead to higher profits. In other words, price competition was not a requirement to secure profits, and maximising profits was not a prerequisite for survival.

This appears to have been true even for the much more productive firms of Alsace. Manufacturers from around Mulhouse played a central part in the rapid industrialisation of the region. These manufacturers refrained from monopolising technical advances and developed an active cooperation in order to emulate English technological developments. They did so through the *Société industrielle de Mulhouse*, which allowed them to set common objectives, to compare and learn from different individual experiences, and to share scientific and technical information.[196]

While Alsatian mills were rapidly mechanised, high quality luxury and semiluxury production was prioritised from the onset of this process. In Mulhouse, the major cotton center of the region, 'the industry grew out of cotton printing; the finished product was of high quality, competitive in foreign markets'. This capacity of Mulhousien cotton firms to successfully export on foreign markets – an exceptional case in France – added to domestic demand provided larger market opportunities and explains the much more rapid mechanisation of cotton production in this town. These firms did not access foreign markets through price competition, but fundamentally thanks to superior product quality. In Mulhouse, firms developed by producing 'finer fabrics' and 'what the French

---

194   Ibid.
195   Quoted in Reddy 1984, p. 113. Noiret added to this: 'Once their fortunes were made ... they bought land and retired' (Ibid.).
196   Hau 1987, p. 386.

call *tissue de fantaisie*. As Landes explains, 'the enterprise aimed at diversific-
ation and flexibility rather than specialisation; the result was short runs that
helped raise unit costs substantially above those of comparable mills in Britain'.[197] Clearly, profits depended more on the quality and reputation of printed
Alsatian calicoes than on the ability to decrease costs of production.[198]

The entrenchment of this way of doing things was demonstrated by the
insertion of the Alsatian cotton trade into the German economic space in the
wake of French defeat in the war of 1870. The German economy had engaged
in a rapid process of capitalist industrialisation,[199] and cotton and other manufacturers were competing for market share in an expanding national market
characterised by the rise of mass consumption among the working classes.
Alsatian producers rapidly lost ground to more competitive and dynamic firms
from Bavaria, Saxony, and elsewhere. Inserted in new value chains, they had
to adapt and to compete less on the basis of the quality of their products than
on their prices. Alsatian manufacturers had entered a new type of market, and
while some remained active on international markets, many now had to engage
in a 'permanent price competition',[200] which implied systematically improving
labour productivity through industrial investments not only to make profits,
but also to stay afloat by reducing costs.

Exposure to German and foreign competition would eventually contribute
to capitalist transformations in France during the second half of the nineteenth century. Until then, price competition remained limited or non-existent
in France. One reason for this, as we saw, was the poor quality of the country's
transportation networks. The outcome of the lacunas in these infrastructures is
well illustrated, for instance, by the fact that, until 1852, raw cotton and cotton
goods were still transported between Le Havre to Mulhouse in horse carts, in a
trip that lasted from 20 to 25 days. Alternatively, transportation could be made
by river from Le Havre to Paris and then by cart to Mulhouse – a journey that
would last six weeks.[201] The opening of canals did not modify transport conditions as far as cotton was concerned, and a railroad connecting Le Havre, Paris
and Strasbourg was not in function until 1852, while the railroad connecting
Paris to Mulhouse had to wait until 1858.[202]

The persistence of traditional forms of sale and marketing of textile products
was related to these lacunas in transportation networks. Until the Second

197   Landes 1969, p. 160, 163.
198   Hau 1987, p. 240.
199   Kocka 1978.
200   Hau 1987, p. 241.
201   Fohlen 1956, p. 139.
202   Fohlen 1956, p. 140.

Empire, several layers of middlemen served as intermediaries between manufacturers and consumers, and efforts to make products easily accessible and to stimulate consumption remained very limited.[203] As was mentioned above, profits largely depended on merchant-manufacturers' ability to succeed in the sphere of circulation. Lower prices, and even higher quality, did not guarantee commercial success. To prosper, merchants had to devote much of their energies to obtaining *préférence* among commercial networks, as a way of gaining privileged accesses to supplies of raw material or to markets on which to unload their final products. Such privileges were obtained through constant efforts to develop connections during fairs, at the stock exchange or within *chambres de commerce*.[204] Rather than price competition, it was practices such as these that played the central part in framing markets, setting prices, and making profits. As a rule, textile producers had secured access to specific markets. For instances, Norman cotton producers from Rouen had privileged access to markets in the West and in the Centre, while producers from the North department benefited from a 'comfortable' position on the Algerian colonial market.[205]

The fragmentation of markets is clearly demonstrated by the pace at which the major cotton-producing regions of France developed. Alsace, as was mentioned, was home to the most productive cotton mills of the country.[206] The concentration of production in factories was much more advanced there than it was in Normandy: during the first half of the 1860s, the average number of workers per mill reached 280 in the Haut-Rhin while it remained a mere 80 in the Seine-Inférieure.[207] During the 1840s, the most efficient Norman mechanised loom spindles could not go beyond 4,000 turns per minute, while Alsatian looms reached 5,500 turns per minute.[208]

Together with product quality, greater productivity did contribute to the ability of Alsatian manufacturers to gain market share at the expense of neighbouring regions. The proportion of the total number of spindles in use in France that belonged to Alsace went from seven percent at the end of the First Empire up to 23.8 percent in 1844.[209] Yet, after this date, the proportion stagnated until the late 1860s, in spite of the much greater productivity of the region's mills. But

---

203   Fohlen 1956, pp. 149–51.
204   Hirsch 2008, p. 72.
205   Broder 1993, p. 62; Kasdi 2014, p. 256.
206   Asselain 1984, p. 145; Beltran and Griset 1994, p. 96; Woronoff 1994, p. 234.
207   Beltran and Griset 1994, p. 100.
208   Hau 1987, p. 371.
209   Hau 1987, p. 88. Because demand was also growing, a reduction of the number of spindles in other regions would not necessarily have been necessary for the share of spindles belonging to Alsace to grow.

even more revealing is the fact that, even during its great period of expansion, the Alsatian cotton trade did not develop as fast as did its much less productive and less dynamic Norman counterpart. From 1812 to 1844, the additional number of cotton spindles put into use reached 745,000 in Alsace, whereas in Haute-Normandie that number jumped to 1,221,000. Haute-Normandie thus remained the first cotton-producing region of the country, ahead of Alsace, in spite of the fact that producers in the former region invested significantly less to mechanise their facilities and reached lower levels of labour productivity.

These regional disparities were certainly in part related to the disparate types of cotton goods produced in different manufacturing centres – which implied a reliance on different clienteles – but they also had to do with the fragmentation of markets, which was in turn largely due to the persistence of commercial practices of profit-making. The industrialisation of the cotton trade had been undertaken by 'commercial capital'. Emerging manufacturers were for the most part successors of earlier generations of merchants, from which they inherited business practices.[210] Until the very last decades of the nineteenth century, and even beyond, merchants acted as inexorable intermediaries between atomised producers and consumers. The crucial role of merchants was maintained in Rouen, Lyon, Lille, and Roubaix-Tourcoing, but also in Mulhouse (the residence of some of the most innovative industrialists of the country) and in every major industrial centre of the country.[211]

Over the first half of the century, many so-called cotton *fabricants* were in fact *sans fabrique* – they were mere merchants without mills. Merchants began to invest in factories only gradually, and old habits were retained for a long time.[212] In Lille and the surrounding locality, for instance, merchants remained dominant, and, among the industrial milieu of the city, productive tasks and interest in technical matters remained subordinated to a commercial perspective focused on exchanged and trade networks.[213] Merchant-manufacturers often had a *rentier* attitude towards their mills, which they perceived more as an interest-bearing placement than as a productive industrial activity and obligation.[214] Though it was less the case in Alsace, investing in industry was also very often undertaken as a means of social ascension to an aristocratic life-style and prestigious public administrative functions.[215]

---

210   Chassagne 1991, p. 661; Bergeron 1978, p. 56; Woronoff 1994, p. 263.
211   Hirsch 1985; Lambert-Dansette 1991, p. 169.
212   Lambert-Dansette 1991, pp. 155–6, 170.
213   Hirsch 1985, p. 28.
214   Bergeron 1978, pp. 53–4; Chassagne 1991, p. 629.
215   Bergeron 1978, pp. 52–3; Chassagne 1991, pp. 94, 253.

Crucially, as a rule, French textile manufacturers did not wish to put an end to the existence of fragmented markets and related practices of commercial profit-making. As Jean-Pierre Hirsh explains, assessing the period stretching from 1780 to 1860, 'the logic of an ongoing decompartmentalising of circulation, of a levelling of costs and prices did not exist in the attitudes of the vast majority [of] merchants, or even in the declarations of their representatives. Above all, *as years passed, nothing indicated an evolution toward a less "imperfect" market, nor a will to reduce the number of filters through which supply and demand were at play*'.[216] If French merchant manufacturers happily adopted the technology developed and used by British industrialists, they strongly rejected their profit-maximising strategies based on *systematic and constant* cost-cutting. Lille's chamber of commerce, rooted as it was in one of the main industrial centres of the country, for instance, 'did not have words harsh enough to describe the industrial policy practiced by English producers, the "progressive debasement" of their prices, their "bankruptcy prices", a "state of over-production that had become the normal state of the country"'.[217]

Because of social property relations existing in France at the time, and even as a town like Mulhouse experienced rapid industrial growth, '[i]n general, the French cotton industry continued to lag far behind that of Britain. Plants were smaller; machines were older, less efficient ... It profited in the first half of the century from growing wealth and population at home and the opening of overseas markets like Algeria. But its expansion, which rested on the exclusion of competition, was paid for in slower overall economic growth'.[218]

The nature of the market for, and the developmental logic of, French metallurgy was similar to what had prevailed in the cotton trade – a fact that had a profound effect on the development of this industrial branch. Annual French production of pig iron did grow from 100,000 to 600,000 tons from 1815 to 1847. But this was still much less than British production, which attained a level of five million tons in 1847.[219] Even more revealing of the pattern of development of French metallurgy is the way in which it lagged behind Britain in terms

---

216   Hirsch 1991, p. 392, emphasis added: 'La logique de décloisonnement continu de la cir-
      culation, d'un nivellement des coûts et des prix ne s'imposait ni dans les attitudes de la
      très grande majorité [des] marchands, ni même dans les propos de leurs représentant. Et
      surtout, les années passant, rien n'indiquait qu'on fit route vers un marché moins "impar-
      fait", qu'on voulût réduire les filtres à travers lesquels s'exerçait le jeu de l'offre et de la
      demande'.
217   Hirsch 1991, p. 396.
218   Landes 1969, p. 164.
219   Beltran and Griset 1994, p. 108.

of technological innovations. In Britain, from the middle of the eighteenth century, sustained demand for machinery originating from the rapid mechanisation of textile production, as well as the competitive nature of the national market, led to the rapid diffusion of more efficient techniques for iron production. Coke smelting represented one of the crucial innovations of the period and greatly improved iron production. By the turn of the nineteenth century, its usage in the production of pig iron had become universal in Britain.[220] This and other innovations were diffused in France only decades later, and, in spite of efforts to catch up, Barjot estimates that the technological level reached by the French metallurgic sector in 1870 was approximately similar to the level that had been attained in Britain in 1835.[221]

Attempts to transfer British techniques into France took place from the 1820s. At first, specific techniques and processes were borrowed from Britain and successfully implemented into French facilities. Large enterprises mobilising British high-technology and opting for 'global innovation' were also founded.[222] These developments were influenced (albeit relatively weakly) by the mechanisation of textile production and also, more importantly, by canal building and other infrastructure developments. They also took place under the umbrella of highly protective trade policies, notably with the adoption of what were in effect prohibitive tariffs for metal imports in 1822. But, as Gille explains, beyond the pressure of market demand, another crucial stimulant for the development of these large facilities was 'also the English example, the existence of a developed industrial world, and a certain fashion'.[223] Just as for cotton production, the French metal trade was modernised under sign of market opportunities and the emulation of British successes, in the context of a protected and non-competitive market.

However, market opportunities for metal production were still too limited in France at the time to support the 'global innovation' strategy of the most ambitious entrepreneurs. Very large enterprises were established in Alais, Decazeville, Le Creusot, and Terrenoire during the 1820s. But they were badly hit by the economic crisis of the 1820s and, except for Terrenoire, all of these firms were bankrupted by 1829–30.[224] These firms could not compete with their British counterparts on international markets, and, before the large-scale

---

220   King 2006, p. 264.

221   Barjot 2014b, p. 404.

222   Gille 1968, p. 48.

223   Gille 1968, p. 47: 'aussi l'exemple Anglais, l'existence d'un monde industriel développé, et une certaine mode'.

224   Caron 1995, pp. 136–7; Gille 1968, p. 50.

development of railroads, which at this time was still to begin, the narrow demand for domestic capital goods in France was not sufficient to sustain them.[225]

As a result, in 1830, only nine percent of pig iron was produced using coke fuel in France, and most enterprises remained small operations relying on traditional techniques and equipment.[226] Usage of old techniques of smelting continued to increase until 1839. In 1840, only 41 blast furnaces in France used coke, against 462 using charcoal.[227] As late as 1845, 60 percent of French pig iron was produced using charcoal fuel.[228] During the second half of the 1840s, a boom in railway construction accelerated the development of large-scale enterprises using modern English technologies. But even then, traditional consumption – mostly of agricultural metal tools – remained largely dominant, while small workshops that had avoided the transition to modern technologies were still widely present across the country.[229]

As we will see in Chapter 5, the disappearance of tariff protection and the emergence of capitalist imperatives under the Second Empire rapidly transformed French metallurgy. Until then, French producers were shielded from foreign and domestic competition, and this explains the sluggish modernisation of their industrial branch. Within France, markets for metal goods were regionally isolated, and much of the production was done in response to the traditional needs of agriculture and peasant communities. High transportation costs and dispersion ensured that many traditional producers remained largely insulated from price competition, even as large-scale modern production was beginning to emerge. In 1831, transportation costs could represent as much as a third to a half of the production costs of coke pig iron.[230]

Parisian metal merchants dominated the trade, playing a central role in mediating between hierarchies of largely disconnected markets.[231] Merchants had privileged access to specific markets and, with the resurgence of large-scale modern metal production from the 1830s, practices of price fixing and partition of markets became the rule. In such a context, as contemporaries observed, 'competition was only a fiction'.[232] In 1860, Émile Péreire, the president of the board of directors of the *Compagnie des chemins de fer du Midi*, declared that,

---

225   Beaud 2010, p. 134.
226   Caron 1995, pp. 136–7; Gille 1968, p. 51; Perez 2012, p. 5.
227   Sée 1926, p. 158.
228   Asselain 1984, p. 144.
229   Gille 1968, pp. 59, 62.
230   Gille 1968, p. 56.
231   Gille 1968, pp. 53–4.
232   Gille 1968, pp. 66–7: 'la concurrence n'est qu'une fiction'.

between 1845 and 1858, the rail production market, which was so crucial in the development of a modern French metallurgy, had not been a free market, and that concerted market control and price fixing had been generalised practices.[233] From the mid-1850s, railroad companies actively tried to counter these practices and to impose a competitive framework on French metal producers. Yet, from the 1820s until decades later – until, that is, the concerted efforts by railroad companies, the integration of the French national market, and the coming of free-trade and associated foreign competitive pressures – 'the rail market was not a free and competitive market'.[234]

5   Opportunity-Driven Growth in Non-competitive Markets

Many of the most important sectors of French industry did not mechanise or barely did during the first two-thirds of the nineteenth century. Cotton weaving, as we saw, was performed mainly using handlooms until the 1870s. Wool and silk cloth were the two most widely exported French products.[235] Yet, in spite of limited mechanisation of wool spinning in some regions, the quality of these goods called for artisanal expertise, and their production remained only weakly mechanised.[236] As late as 1873, out of the 120,000 looms in use in Lyon's silk industry, only about 5,000 to 6,000 were power-looms.[237] Together with Lyon's silk, *produits de Paris* were another vital force of quality French exports. Parisian industry remained very feebly mechanised and was in general characterised by an absence of sustained technological progress.[238] In short, processes of industrialisation and technological innovation were only marginally present in most sectors of the French economy. Still in the 1850s, small and scattered artisanal production was largely dominant.[239]

As the previous section demonstrated, even the most mechanised sectors of the French economy were not driven by a capitalist logic of development. Market demand did grow, and this resulted in substantial industrial development. Cotton clothes became accessible to new social layers of consumers. Likewise, machine-building, and especially the state-supported development of railways,

---

233   Gille 1968, p. 67.
234   Gille 1968, p. 75: 'le marché des rails ne fut pas un marché libre et concurrentiel'.
235   Verley 1997, p. 46.
236   Asselain 1984, p. 145; Broder 1993, p. 71.
237   Lambert-Dansette 1991, p. 173.
238   Broder 1993, p. 74.
239   Berenson 1984, pp. 26–7; Sée 1926, p. 159.

stimulated the modernisation of metallurgy. This swelling of market demand was not as sustained as that experienced in England with the rise of agrarian capitalism, and it did not lead to a capitalist process of industrialisation.

Rapidly expanding demand has occurred on countless occasions in diverse historical settings without causing capitalist transitions. No one would deny that the presence of sufficient market demand is necessary for a capitalist process of industrialisation, entailing sustained investment, to take place. Markets must have sufficient depth for development-driving investments to be profitable. This is, however, only a necessary, not a sufficient, condition. For capitalist development to occur, a competitive market must exist. This is a market that, in addition to offering opportunities, compels entrepreneurs to follow new rules of reproduction: systematically reinvesting surplus, securing control over labour processes, and constantly improving labour productivity.

Searching for signs of a capitalist transition, we should not simply be looking for the removal of obstacles to growth in demand, or for situations where entrepreneurs can respond to expanding opportunities. The point is rather to identify configurations that exercise positive compulsion on these entrepreneurs to act as capitalists. Such compulsion is a very rare occurrence that emerged for the first time in history out of an endogenous and unintended process in the early modern English countryside. In most other world regions, and certainly on the European continent, it first had to be actively and consciously built from above. As we saw in the preceding chapter, the first attempts to do so in France took place in the second half of the eighteenth century. As will be discussed in Chapter 5, it was only in period of the Second Empire and the Third Republic that such efforts were successful in imposing capitalist social property relations.

Capitalist market compulsion remained absent in France during approximately the first two-thirds of the nineteenth century. This obviously does not mean that French merchants and industrialists were not confronted with competitive pressures during this period, but merely that competition took a different form (often tied to product quality or commercial network control) and had different results. Industrial growth was propelled by market opportunities, and the emulation of British technological developments – not by market coercion. The development and ebbing of the productive forces and processes of specialisation in response to expanding and contracting market opportunities was nothing new, and had on occasion been tied to substantial, even if fragile and relatively fleeting, economic development. Dealing with one of the most impressive cases of pre-capitalist economic development, Wood has convincingly argued that the remarkable specialisation and investment in agricultural production that took place in the early modern Low Countries 'represents an opportunity-driven commercial economy taken to its utmost limits'.[240] Early nineteenth-century France offers another such case of pre-capitalist economic growth, this time mostly located in parts of its industrial sector, under the influence of the historically unprecedented dynamism of the British industrial revolution.

This thesis will no doubt be controversial – especially for those who tend to assume the presence of capitalism without *historically* explaining its coming into existence. But even if we were to concede that there existed in France during the first decades of the nineteenth century *incipient* market competition of a capitalist nature, it seems quite clear from the available evidence that this would at best be confined to specific and limited branches and regions.

The sluggishness of French industrial development was not merely caused by the presence of 'imperfect' forms of competition. 'Real competition', under capitalism, is different from the 'perfect competition' of neoclassical economics and its spontaneous equilibrium. Capitalist competition is by nature turbulent and leaves room for agency, power wielding by economic actors, oligopolistic tendencies, and 'imperfections' that have always been present right from capitalism's inception.[241] These 'imperfections' in the actual functioning of capitalist competition were at play in England during its industrial revolution and did, for instance, cause regional disparities in mechanisation levels. Yet, for all its 'imperfections', real competition under capitalism does not rule out, but in fact implies the existence of, a solid core of 'laws of motion' or 'rules of reproduction', which impose the adoption of cost-cutting and profit-maximisation strategies for the survival of enterprises, leading to uneven, but nonetheless quite material and inescapable tendencies toward the levelling of prices and of rates of profits, and the abstraction (i.e. alienation) of labour as a consequence of its 'subsumption' under capital.

My argument is that the form of competition associated with capitalism was not present in France before around the last three or four decades of the nineteenth century. Mechanisation did provide the leeway to reduce prices and expand market demand in some textile branches (mostly cotton production), *but cost-cutting was not yet mandatory for survival*. The non-competitive character of markets had empirical and observable consequences. It explains, for instance, why, even with a much larger population, France's steam engines where producing less than ten percent of the horsepower produced by the engines in use in Britain in 1840. Again, this cannot simply be explained by

---

240   Wood 2002b, p. 66.
241   Shaikh 2016.

smaller consumer demand in France – we have to also consider the non-capitalist nature of French markets. The proof of this, as will be in detail in Chapter 5, is that French industrial firms began to systematically and more rapidly invest in labour productivity enhancing machinery from the 1860s and 1870s, as they began to be exposed to market imperatives, *even in the absence of significantly larger market opportunities.*

Because these markets were not capitalist, French industrialisation lagged far behind British industrialisation. Before the last third of the nineteenth century, in the absence of market compulsion, French entrepreneurs had neither the will nor the capacity to compete domestically or on international markets and to eventually grab market share from British industrialists, in the way in which incipient capitalist German manufacturers were able (and indeed compelled) to do over the second half of the nineteenth century. Likewise, the absence of competitive imperatives explains why France was so shockingly easily overtaken by continental rivals – most importantly Germany – once they had engaged in a capitalist process of industrialisation.

Finally, this absence of competitive markets explains why there were no widespread and sustained efforts by French employers to seize control over labour processes and to impose the new form of capitalist discipline that had emerged with the rise of the English factory system from the second half of the eighteenth century. For decades following the 1789 Revolution, the French economy remained socially embedded, and workers actually gained greater autonomy that prevented the alienation of their labour. It is to these issues that we now turn.

CHAPTER 3

The French Revolution and the Customary Regulation of Labour

The last chapter showed that, until the closing decade of the Second Empire, the French economy was not organised on the basis of capitalist markets. Economic units were not subjected to the law of value and, consequently, economic development fell well short of the levels established in Britain. This assessment, of course, is at odds with a still widely-accepted reading of the French Revolution.

For a long time the Revolution of 1789 has been perceived as a gateway to a liberalised economy on its way to capitalist industrialisation. This, as will be discussed in what follows, has been challenged by a 'revisionist' trend of historians, but the conception of the Revolution as a period in which obstacles to capitalist development were cleared away is still probably accepted as a truism by many today. Against the latter interpretation of the Revolution, the present chapter shows how social relations of production remained embedded in normative regulations during the revolutionary period and for decades afterward.[1]

The present chapter begins with a reconsideration of the historiography of the French Revolution. Building on contributions made by 'political Marxists', it offers a class understanding of the Revolution as bourgeois but not capitalist. The French bourgeoisie was not attempting to initiate a capitalist transition, but rather to insert itself in politically constituted channels of surplus appropriation. In parallel, French workers waged important struggles that played a central part in the abolition of guilds in 1791. Contrary to a widespread conception, this abolition did not announce the triumph of economic liberalism in labour relations nor the rise of a capitalist industrial economy – just like it consolidated small peasant property and customary regulations of agrarian labour, the Revolution also preserved and actually expanded the *bon droit*, or moral economy of the working class. French workers actually gained signific-

---

1 Following Zmolek 2013 p. 28, who himself takes his cue from Polanyi's anthropological usage of this notion, I use the concept of 'normative regulations' to refer to '"economic" relations directly governed by social conventions, mores and customs, typically of a local origin.' The term will be used interchangeably with such other phrases as 'customary regulations', 'moral economy', or '*bon droit*'.

ant new rights during the revolutionary period, which prevented the alienation of their labour and its subsumption by capital.

1 Reassessing the French Revolution

The literature on the French Revolution is immensely vast. Two main schools of interpretation have been central in this literature in the post-war period. The first is the 'social interpretation' of the Revolution, which can be traced to the early twentieth-century work of Jean Jaurès[2] and is inspired by Marx's discussion of the 'bourgeois revolution' in the *Communist Manifesto*. It was dominant until the 1960s and its leading exponents, George Lefebvre, Albert Mathiez, and Albert Soboul, present the Revolution as led by a bourgeoisie liberating itself from the shackles of feudalism, thus allowing capitalism to blossom fully in France.[3] Here, the development of capitalism is connected with the fate of a bourgeoisie formed of merchants, manufacturers or capitalist yeomen arising from the interstices of feudal society. As it matures in the interstices of the absolutist regime, the bourgeoisie overcomes feudal obstacles, eventually engaging in a decisive revolutionary struggle and leading the popular masses to overthrow a retrograde aristocracy. This political victory of the bourgeoisie propels the development of capitalism as well as the emergence of a liberal democracy and public sphere.[4]

Beginning with Alfred Cobban in the 1950s, and continuing with influential figures such as François Furet from the early 1970s, the social interpretation was radically questioned by a trend of 'revisionist' historians.[5] The latter stressed that no capitalist development had taken place under the Old Regime, where industrial production had overwhelmingly involved small non-mechanised units. On the eve of the Revolution (and for decades afterward), commercial and financial wealth was not derived from the extraction of surplus value. Commerce and finance did not stand in opposition to, but in fact

---

2 Jaurès 2014–15 [1901–8].
3 Lefebvre 2015 [1947]; Mathiez, 1964; Soboul, 1975.
4 Teschke 2005, pp. 4–5 While often associated with Marxism, this paradigm actually has liberal origins and was rapidly put forth in the wake of the Revolution by Antoine Barnave and later by Toqueville (Minard 2007b, p. 22). The impact of Turgot's and Smith's liberal eschatologies of civilisational development (conceived as a progression of stages) on Marx's first conception of historical materialism, systematised in the *German Ideology*, has been convincingly demonstrated by Comninel (1987) and Brenner (1989).
5 Cobban 1964; Furet 1978. Skocpol (1979) and Minard (2007) offer excellent summaries of the revisionist assessment of the Revolution.

coexisted 'symbiotically' with, 'proprietary' – as opposed to capitalist – wealth tied to land, venal offices or annuities.[6] The rare cases of large-scale industrial enterprises were generally initiated and owned by aristocrats, not by bourgeois.[7] The bourgeois that led the revolutionary process 'came primarily from the ranks of professionals (especially lawyers), office holders, and intellectual leaders'.[8] Those 'that dominated France after the Revolution were not industrialists or capitalist entrepreneurs but primarily bureaucrats, soldiers, and owners of real estate'.[9] Quoting Cobban, Skocpol asserts that 'the economically relevant reforms enacted during the Revolution were either spurred by revolts from below or else were the culmination of "... the century old movement for the abolition of the internal customs ... [a movement] led throughout, and ultimately brought to success, not by the representatives of commercial and industrial interests, but by reforming officials" of the French state'.[10]

Some Marxists responded to the 'revisionist' historiography by sticking to the classical social interpretation,[11] others fell back on a 'consequentialist' perspective.[12] This new Marxist perspective made substantial concessions to revisionists, toning down the importance of the nature of the revolutionary agent – it is no longer important whether a capitalist bourgeoisie leads the revolution, as long as it eventually benefits from it. Likewise, the state no longer has to be 'bourgeois' (directly seized by the bourgeoisie) in order for the Revolution to qualify as 'capitalist'. What matters are outcomes, and the fact that the Revolution eventually led to the development of capitalism by establishing a socio-legal context that was conducive to it.[13] This consequentialism had in part already been anticipated by Lefebvre's and Soboul's reply to revisionists from the late 1950s to the 1970s.[14] Soboul stressed that the 'essential fact' was that the Revolution had destroyed feudal land property as well as guilds and state regulations of industry, thus establishing unrestricted freedom of enterprise and paving the way to capitalism.[15]

---

6   Skocpol 1979, p. 176. We will come back to the notion of 'proprietary wealth' in more detail
     in Chapter 4.
7   Minard 2007b, p. 27.
8   Skocpol 1967, p. 176.
9   Ibid.
10   Ibid.
11   Heller 2006.
12   Davidson 2012.
13   These 'consequentialist' concessions to 'revisionists' are dicussed in Teschke 2005, pp. 5–6.
14   Minard 2007b, p. 25.
15   Soboul 1974.

Consequentialism rescues the notion of capitalist bourgeois revolution only by emptying it of much of its content. This perspective also tends to fall back on teleological assumptions that tie the unfolding of history to an unexplained trans-historical development of forces of production, which amounts to a retro-projection of specifically capitalist tendencies onto past historical developments. More to the point, consequentialism is empirically flawed: as this chapter will demonstrate, the outcomes of the Revolution actually reproduced in fundamental ways non-capitalist land tenure *and* customary regulations of industrial trades – a fact that is still too little known. Moreover, one of its important outcomes was the expansion of the state apparatus as a mean of surplus appropriation (a point which will be addressed in Chapter 4). Crucially, capitalist social property relations did not simply arise mechanically from revolutionary processes – they actually had to be established by conscious and sustained state interventions under the Second Empire and the Third Republic (as will be discussed in Chapter 5). Without this intervention from above, capitalism would not have emerged in France, notwithstanding the political, social-legal or ideological transformations induced by the Revolution.

This argument is developed by building on an alternative Marxist interpretation of the French Revolution. 'Political Marxists' (or '*Capital*-centric' Marxists)[16] George Comninel, Robert Brenner, Benno Teschke, and Ellen Meiksins Wood reject the liberal and dominant Marxist readings of the Revolution as capitalist.[17] While revisionist historiography has clearly demonstrated the non-capitalist character of the Revolution, it also departed from class analysis, stressing that bourgeois and aristocrats were not economically distinguishable and shared the same sources of revenue. Political Marxism, on the contrary, sticks to a class analysis of 1789 and of its causes while disentangling the concepts of 'bourgeoisie' and 'capitalist class'.[18] Agreeing with revisionists that the bourgeoisie and aristocracy both reproduced themselves on the basis of non-capitalist land-tenure and politically constituted property, this Marxist assessment points to the fact that bourgeois and aristocrats had differentiated access to state offices and privileges. Bourgeois and many lesser nobles remained excluded from special privileges of noble status, and the aristocracy, the 'highest and most exclusive inner circles of the nobility', monopolised the

---

16   For a presentation of 'political' or '*Capital*-centric' see Lafrance and Post 2018.

17   Brenner 1989; Comninel 1987; Wood 1991, and 2012; Teschke 2005.

18   Comninel (1987, p. 180), explains that members of 'the bourgeoisie were understood to be those persons not having noble status who owned sufficient property – or in rare and usually marginal cases, had sufficient "talent" – not to be obliged to engage in demeaning manual labor (which included retail trade)'.

highest and most prestigious positions in the state apparatus; it was thus the chief beneficiary of its surplus extractive capacities.[19] Calling for state positions to be 'open to talent' and for liberal reforms of the state administration, the bourgeoisie did not attempt to overthrow the existing mode of exploitation but actually to improve its position in its midst. The Revolution should be understood as an intra-ruling class conflict opposing bourgeois and aristocrats over access to politically-constituted property, flanked by a popular movement of exploited artisans and peasants, in a context of intensifying geopolitical pressures experienced by the French state.

As we saw in Chapter 1, absolutist France's hegemonic aspirations were increasingly challenged by the geopolitical rise of Britain over the eighteenth century. The British state benefited from a much more successful economy that fuelled an ongoing improvement of labour productivity and efficient administrative and fiscal apparatuses that secured the confidence of financiers and allowed parliament to borrow at relatively advantageous rates in order to fund its military ambitions. In France, by contrast, agrarian capitalism was absent and taxation represented a key dimension of an extra-economic mode of exploitation of the country's massive peasantry. The expansion of the French state's tax base was dependent on a logic of 'geopolitical accumulation' that implied 'the predatory accumulation of territories and control over trade routes'.[20] This foreign policy was financially draining. It required an ongoing intensification of the taxation of a stagnant peasant economy and 'during every war, French kings were obliged to resort to the artificial creation and then the sale of more and more offices in order to raise money. They effectively mortgaged the extractive powers of the state to private financiers and tax-farmers. This led to the Byzantine and hopelessly bloated nature of the French semi-private/semi-public state apparatus'.[21] Fiscal policies were highly politicised and conflictual because they were internally related to class politics. The intricate particularistic channels of interest through which wealth was appropriated and distributed frustrated the attempts by French monarchs to directly and efficiently tax the peasantry and, in turn, to borrow sufficiently to support colonial ventures.[22]

The Seven Years' War that opposed it to France demonstrated the superior power of the British state. After its defeat in 1763, France came out of the conflict heavily indebted. It took its revenge on Britain by allying with the Thirteen

---

19   Comninel 1987, pp. 197–8.
20   Teschke 2005, p. 19.
21   Teschke 2005, p. 20.
22   Shilliam 2009, p. 39.

Colonies during the American War of Independence, but had to assume a financial burden comparable to that of Britain in order to do so. This was added to the debts already incurred over the previous war and led to a major state financial crisis around 1786, which forced the King to initiate fiscal reforms and to call the Assembly of Notables in 1787 and the Estates-Generals of 1789. As is well known, this signalled the outbreak of the Revolution.

The attempt to reform the fiscal and administrative apparatuses of the state exposed and intensified elite dissensions and led to the declaration of a National Assembly by representatives of the Third Estate. Horizontal intra-elite conflicts created a new terrain for vertical class struggles between exploiters and direct producers and fuelled popular movements that played a crucial role in the development and deepening of the Revolution. Without forceful peasant struggles and the politicisation and widespread mobilisation of Parisian crowds, most notably through the *sans-culottes* movement, the Third Estate would certainly have been defeated and republican ambitions associated with the revolutionary process could not have hatched. As Comninel puts it, 'inherent to the overall politics of the Revolution, therefore, is not merely the opposition of aristocracy and liberalism, but also the radical promise of democracy and social justice'.[23] Assessing the socio-economic impact of the Revolution, we need to recognise that both bourgeois liberal *and* popular movements made significant imprints on the revolutionary process and its outcomes.

The political, judicial and economic changes brought about by the Revolution were considerable. The abolition of privileges by the Constituent Assembly on the night of 4 August 1789 brought to an end the preferential fiscal, judicial, and political treatment that the French nobility had enjoyed. With the end of privileges came the termination of provincial particularism, replaced in 1790 by departments that were subject to the authority of a central state. And the making of a unified, judicially and administratively integrated national territory, was further promoted by the suppression of internal custom barriers as well as by the standardisation of weights and measures. Ending privileges also implied the dissolution of intermediary bodies that had until then represented constitutive parts of the state. A nation formed of formally equal individual citizens now replaced the divine monarchy as the source of legitimate political sovereignty. Representative parliamentary institutions emerged but remained subject to executive and administrative powers. Beside the liberal ideology of political leaders, much of these state building efforts and adminis-

---

23   Comninel 1987, p. 201.

trative reforms were in fact shaped by 'the exigencies of war and coping with their domestic political repercussions', not by an agenda of capitalist reform.[24] Mobilisation from below was also a determinant factor.

Many at the time actually believed that the abolition of the privileges in August 1789 had implied the eradication of guilds.[25] Trade corporations had long served as disciplinary tools wielded by the state and employers, however, and this played no small part in the reluctance of the new regime's leaders to abolish them. After long and agonising debates, the National Assembly finally abolished guilds, as well as privileged industrial enterprises, by adopting the d'Allarde decree of 1791. A few months later, the Le Chapelier decree prohibited both workers' and employers' associations or coalitions. Also in 1791, the Goudard decree obliterated fabrication rules and sacked the royal inspectors that had been enforcing them.[26]

These decrees have been presented by many as the triumph of 'liberal individualism', announcing the arrival of capitalist labour relations in France.[27] Indeed, at first glance, these judicial and administrative innovations would appear to have framed the emergence of a free and competitive market where incipient capitalist enterprises would meet free wage-labourers. As will been seen in detail below, this was not the case. Yet, a number of social historians of the French working class and labour relations have offered just such a reading of the socio-economic impact of the revolutionary period and have suggested that a widespread capitalist transformation of French artisanal production began to take root under the Restoration and the July monarchy.[28]

According to William H. Sewell, one of the most influential of these historians, the 1789 Revolution brought 'a radical transformation of the entire social order'.[29] Adhering to a revisionist reading of modern French economic history,[30] and building on this argument to develop an original thesis on the making of the French working class (to which we will come back in the following chapter), Sewell asserts that the d'Allarde and Le Chapelier decrees brought

---

24   Skocpol pp. 178–9.
25   Kaplan 2001, p. 500.
26   Minard 2008, p. 78.
27   See for instance Chassagne 1989, Kaplan 2001, Kaplan and Keopp 1986, pp. 22–5, McPhee 2013, pp. 455–7. The prevalence of this interpretation is noted by Hirsch 1989, who offers a much more nuanced perspective.
28   Aminzade 1986; Berenson 1984; Bezucha 1983; Johnson 1975; Sewell 1980.
29   Sewell 1980, p. 62.
30   I am referring here to the revisionist historiography of the modern French economy, not to be confused with the revisionist trend in the historiography of the French Revolution discussed in this chapter.

a 'radical redefinition of the very nature of property'. Sewell explains that 'property was no longer, as under the Old Regime, to be subject to manifold public regulations bringing its use into harmony with a preestablished public order'. The end of corporate policing of the trades would provide owners of the means of production with 'the "natural and inalienable and sacred right" to dispose of their property as they wish'.[31]

This rise of unfettered capitalist property is presented as the cause of a thorough transformation of the French economy. In accordance with the thesis put forward by revisionist economic historians of nineteenth-century France, and in line with the general argument offered by Sewell, Berenson suggests that the relatively limited domestic market, as well as the relative abundance of cheap and skilled labour that could be found in France, focused capitalist transformation on the already existing artisanal sector – as opposed to sustaining the rise of large-scale industrial enterprises as was the case in England.[32] Controlling the marketing of goods, merchants forced down wholesale prices, forcing master artisans to cut unit costs of production by using their newly acquired powers as capitalist proprietors.[33] A capitalist reorganisation of production, based on the exploitation of cheap labour, often through the use of putting-out work, ensued in some branches such as confection, shoe-making, furniture-making and in the building trades, where practices of *tâcheronnage* or *marchandage* were spreading.[34]

This artisan capitalism represented an extension of a process that had already emerged with the putting-out system in textiles, centuries before the Revolution of 1789. The Revolution had now transformed property relations in a way that eliminated obstacles for entrepreneurs who sought to divide labour and to increase productivity, and whose aim was to seize opportunities offered by broadening markets and rising demand.[35] As a consequence, wages were lowered and working conditions were homogenised and degraded.

In classical Smithian fashion, the 'artisan capitalism' thesis put forth by Sewell, Berenson, Johnson, and others, assumes that the removal of regulatory obstacles automatically led to the adoption of capitalist patterns of cost-cutting and profit-maximisation, in response to (specifically French) market opportunities. In the absence of competitive markets, however, such pat-

---

31   Sewell 1980, pp. 114–15, 135, 139–40.
32   Berenson 1984, p. 28.
33   Berenson 1984, p. 29.
34   Johnson 1975.
35   Sewell 1980, p. 159.

terns remained absent in France. Moreover, these historians are wrong to assume that the 1791 decrees amounted to the disappearance of customary regulations in the French economy. Such regulations were kept alive, and actually thrived during and after the Revolution, albeit at the local level and without official state approval and support. In order to recognise this, it is useful to reassess from below the process that led to the disappearance of guilds.

2   Guilds and Workers' Struggles under the Old Regime

In spite – and in part because – of the abolition of guilds, the normative regulations of industrial trades were preserved and indeed developed in post-revolutionary France. The regulations and institutions that flourished during and after the Revolution, discussed in detail in the next section of this chapter, were the outgrowth of the moral economy of Old Regime workers. Recognising this is key to understanding how artisan guilds came to be abolished during the Revolution and how this abolition actually contributed to empowering labourers against their employers. Trade corporations were not the only institutions regulating artisanal and industrial production. Workers did not simply depend on guilds to maintain the moral economy that safeguarded their material interests. Moreover, workers actually engaged in ongoing acts of resistance against guilds under the Old Regime not in opposition to the normative regulations of their trades *per se*, but against their own subordination to the masters who controlled the guilds.

Rural industrial production remained outside the reach of trade corporations. Although the state actively supported their formation, guilds were absent in several urban artisanal trades, which nevertheless maintained normative regulations, often under the supervision of municipal governments. A very intricate institutional network of high and low courts, parliaments, *mairies*, *bureaux de marque*, and police offices established a jurisprudence and rules that would then be followed, and sometimes challenged, by corporations. Corporate rules were indeed often quite broad and vague, and civil courts and municipal governments routinely oversaw contracts, tariffs and piece rates, or apprenticeship rules. These regulations, whether stemming from trade corporations or from judicial and political institutions, were not universally followed – far from it. Attempts by employers to get around existing rules to exploit underpaid workers or to produce cheap and low-quality goods were frequent, and merchants and workers *sans qualité*, who had not completed an apprenticeship and who worked without guild approbation, were numerous and active throughout the country, including in urban centres.[36] Consequently, regulations routinely had to be enforced through popular vigilance and mobilisation.

Under the Old Regime, guild and state regulations set boundaries and exercised pressures on what Michael Sonenscher has dubbed a 'bazaar economy'. The phrase refers to the large number of productive activities and economic exchanges that took place at a distance from – and that were often only remotely affected by – guild regulations. The existence of these activities and exchanges that took place outside of guild control represented a problem in the eyes of guild officials, who were continuously trying to reassert their regulatory authority. Parallel to guild rules, informal normative regulations existed, which were embedded in kinship and acquaintance networks, and which often suited the merchants' desire to maintain good reputation based on product quality. All this amounted to an unwritten *bon droit*, existing in parallel and often in opposition to various entangled sets of laws. The social norms of the bazaar economy, on the one end, and the formal rules of guilds and of state authorities, on the other, thus existed at a distance. These sets of rules reciprocally affected one another in a dense and sometimes conflicting relationship.[37] Yet, in spite of the density of this regulatory web, the 'bazaar economy' still comprised a more strongly regulated core flanked by a less ordered periphery, where workers routinely had to organise in order to defend their material interests against cheating employers and to ensure the enforcement of the *bon droit*.

The operation of the informal *bon droit* even in the absence of guilds is well illustrated by the case of the Parisian Saint-Antoine *faubourg*. A letter patent emitted in 1657 bestowed to artisan workers of this area of the capital the privilege to work without *lettres de maîtrise* ensuring that they had been through the prescribed apprenticeship to exercise their trade. In essence, artisans were formally given the right to work outside of any control exercised by trade corporations. Different authors, such as Kaplan and Horn, have tied this experiment to the rise of an incipient capitalist organisation of economic activities in the *faubourg*.[38] These authors tend to take at face value the guilds' complaints against 'false workers' lacking proper training to exercise a trade. Guild masters denounced these workers' freedom and insisted that it was causing deterioration in product quality, leading to a race to the bottom – one that would upset all Parisian trades.

---

36   Kaplan 2001, p. XIII. We have evidence of encroachments upon trade usages occurring in the sixteenth century, and these were certainly common before this date – see Guicheteau 2014, p. 62.

37   Cottereau 1993, p. 133; Sonenscher 1989, pp. 5, 28–9, 30, 33, 280.

38   See Kaplan 1988 and Horn 2012.

These alarmist discourses in fact had little material basis, as has been shown by the work of Alain Thillay. The intent of the 1657 letter patent was to provide work to poor workers who were otherwise forced into mendicity by restrictive and exclusive guild regulations preventing them from practicing their trade. Thillay shows that artisanal labour in the *faubourg* Saint-Antoine did not fundamentally diverge from labour performed in other parts of Paris.[39] Workers continued to apply and to follow different rules that were also routinely enforced by police officers. Though not as lengthy as in other parts of the capital, apprenticeships were maintained, and securing a *maîtrise* was also possible in the *faubourg*. Contracts between employers and employees were very similar to those of other areas and entailed comparable obligations. Many guild-trained and guild-endorsed masters settled in the neighbourhood, and their number continued to increase throughout the eighteenth century. In spite of guild disapprobation, many master-artisans from all over Paris routinely engaged in commercial transactions with artisans from the neighborhood.

It is true that from the 1690s corporations increasingly targeted the *faubourg* and attempted to reassert their authority so as to curb workers' insubordination – an insubordination which was by no means limited to this area of the capital. Workers mobilised, fought back, and were able to limit guilds' interventions in their neighborhood and to preserve their freedom. But if they rejected corporate subordination – just as a mounting number of workers did in Paris and elsewhere in France – it does not in any way follow that Saint-Antoine artisans accepted unregulated competition. Quite the opposite was true.[40]

Rules proscribed attempts to undersell other shops in one's trade, for instance. When these rules were infringed upon, transgressors were denounced and could be apprehended by the police. Illicit merchandise that was not produced according to customary norms was also often confiscated during attempts to smuggle it out of the *faubourg*. Artisans crossing the line of healthy competition around product quality were sanctioned, and raids cracking down on cheating artisans were organised under the supervision of police authorities. Some employers did encroach on existing norms, of course, but here as elsewhere, they often had to face the consequences of their acts, as members of the trade community mobilised against them.

Competition was also limited by informal and customary practices, and attempts to undersell competitors decried through acts of public shaming that

---

39   Thillay 2002.
40   Thillay 2002, pp. 250–7.

brought professional dishonour to infringers. In enforcing these customary rules, workers had guilds regulations in mind. These regulations, while not as strongly enforced in the neighborhood, continued to serve as flexible benchmarks. Because of these formal and informal regulations, artisan activities in *faubourg* Saint-Antoine were not nearly as different from those occurring in other parts of the capital as the inflammatory discourses of corporate leaders would tend to suggest. Indeed, these regulations upheld by trade communities showed that, in spite of their relative freedom, artisans were not tempted by the prospect of a capitalistic transformation of their social relations of production.[41]

We need not assume, then, that the abolition of guilds would automatically pave the way for the rise of a liberal, capitalist economy. The social embeddedness of economic activities was not simply hanging by the thread of guild regulations. With this in mind, we need to go a step further and to recognise that the abolition of guilds during the Revolution derived less from the liberal intentions of certain parts of the ruling class than it did from workers' struggles.

No doubt, a considerable number of liberals belonging to France's political elite were in favour of abolishing guilds. But simply focusing on this factor leaves us, at best, with a one-sided explanation. As Liana Vardi puts it the abolition of corporations 'was not, as is usually thought, an outgrowth of the commitment of the revolutionary bourgeoisie to the principle of economic freedom'.[42] An analysis of the *cahiers de doléances* and petitions demanding the eradication of guilds addressed to the National Assembly from 1789 reveals that journeymen (and, more broadly, craft workers who were not guild masters) formed the core of the movement that demanded their abolition. A substantial proportion of the handicraft workers' *doléances* called for the abolition of all masterships.[43]

Workers decried guilds as serving the privileges of the master-artisans who controlled these institutions. Kaplan has shown how one of the central function of guilds was to act as a *police du travail* to maintain the subordination and the servility of workers.[44] Sponsoring artisan corporations, the state aimed to maintain workers in a condition of domesticity to their masters. Backing the guilds' authority, a 1749 royal edict condemned insubordination and general-

---

41   Thillay 2002, pp. 13, 181, 255.

42   Quoted in Fairchilds 1988, p. 691.

43   Vardi 1988, pp. 708, 712.

44   Kaplan 1979; see also Guicheteau 2014, p. 54.

ised to all trade the practice of the *billet de congé*, which precluded workers from leaving their master before the work that they had been hired for was completed.[45] State authorities also often acted directly to prevent workers from unilaterally leaving their employers.[46]

The full meaning of these workers' calls to abolish guilds is only revealed when it is treated as the culmination of a protracted cycle of resistance. Sonenscher presents instances of artisans resisting 'servitude' imposed through guild provisions going back to the seventeenth century.[47] Rejection of subordination by craft workers became widespread, and deeply penetrated urban and sometimes rural popular cultures during the eighteenth century.[48]

Certainly, artisan workers – masters as well as journeymen – clashed with *négociants* and *marchands-fabricants* throughout the eighteenth century, as they had done at earlier times and would continue to do into the nineteenth century. At least from the seventeenth century, large merchants attempted to impose their domination upon the different regional and local manufacturing networks of France. Muscling in on these networks, these merchants acted as suppliers of raw material and marketers of final products, and formed their own guilds in order to establish their full control over the marketing of products.[49] Such endeavours proved successful in some trades, while failing in others.[50] As they increasingly came to assert their dominance over some trades, merchants gained the ability to fix product prices – and consequently workers' incomes. Merchants did not wish to extinguish all trade regulations, which guaranteed quality standards, nor necessarily always to eliminate artisan guilds, which could be relied upon to discipline workers. Yet, the traders' control over product marketing represented a major encroachment upon the prerogative of artisan corporations. While they were not systematically propelled by market imperatives (as they become with the rise of capitalism), such an encroachment still entailed significant downward pressures on workers' incomes and had important consequences for their material well-being. In the face of the growing power of merchants, masters and journeymen did use artisan guilds as instruments of resistance, not least by imposing or maintaining existing tariffs, fixing the prices at which merchants bought manufactured goods from workers in a given region.

---

45   Guicheteau 2014, p. 81.
46   Chassagne 1991, pp. 171–2.
47   Sonenscher 1989, p. 16.
48   Kaplan 1979; Cottereau 2002, p. 1534.
49   Guicheteau 2014, pp. 26–8.
50   Faure 1986.

Yet, within trade communities, journeymen and apprentices also actively resisted the subordination imposed by guild masters and decried their control over the granting of *maîtrise*, which precluded many workers from freely exercising their trade. As merchant corporations became more successful in imposing their dominance over product marketing in some trades, many artisan guilds responded by further restraining their granting of mastership, so as to preserve the privileges of masters in a context where tariffs and incomes were being forced down.[51] This reaction by privileged guild leaders only exacerbated unemployment issues. To cope with this problem, state authorities and masters established employment offices that provided guilds with powers to coerce journeymen into the jobs on offer. Workers had to comply or else move to a new city. Sonenscher explains that 'not surprisingly, journeymen could easily equate the creation of a *bureau de placement* with slavery'.[52] Against this 'slavery', workers claimed their autonomy, and defiant artisans unilaterally set up their own unauthorised workshops.

Workers often collectively defended their autonomy and material interests by forming associations that were independent of state-sponsored guilds. These organisations resisted guild subordination, and enforced formal and informal regulations against masters and merchants who did not respect the price-fixing tariffs on which incomes were dependent.[53] Upholding a moral economy against both guild-imposed subordination, state authorities and the infringement of normative regulations, many French workers came under the influence of Enlightenment philosophers and reclaimed 'rights' as a way of defending their material interests and well-being.[54] Denunciations of 'slavery' and 'dependence' and claims of 'natural rights', 'natural liberty', and of a 'right to work' (*droit au travail*) were used throughout the century in ordinary speeches as well as in legal arguments against artisan and merchant guild officials.[55]

The 1760s brought about an intensification of the workers' insubordination and a period of widespread conflicts between urban workers and guild officials.[56] Resistance to subordination at work intensified, while masters attempted to reassert their authority through different guild provisions. Workers continuously asserted their refusal to be 'domesticated' and reduced to 'slavery'.[57]

---

51   Guicheteau 2014, p. 47.
52   Sonenscher 1989, p. 285.
53   Guicheteau 2014, p. 62.
54   Guicheteau 2014, pp. 99–105.
55   Sonenscher 1989, p. 332.
56   Kaplan 1979, p. 70; Nicolas 2002, pp. 291–3.
57   Guicheteau 2014, p. 113.

Clashes arising from the vehement assertion by workers of their right to unilaterally leave their employers also intensified. These struggles, however, generally developed out of trade-based solidarities – a class-outlook was still absent among French workers.

From the late 1770s, following their reinstatement after their short-lived abolition by Turgot, artisan guilds were rationalised.[58] The number of guilds was reduced, with many of them merged as part of an attempt to reinforce the repressive powers of masters. A primary and explicit objective was to eradicate insubordination and job desertion. This process of rationalisation served as a backdrop to the proliferation of conflicts and the denunciation of corporate 'servitude' during the 1780s, which reached a climax during the Revolution.[59]

From the outset of the Revolution, and especially from 1790, resistance from below intensified. Assemblies sprouted across the country, growing numbers of workers formed associations, demonstrations multiplied and petitions received an immense number of signatories.[60] Workers fought for better wages. While refusing the liberalisation of the grain trade and upholding the moral economy of their trades, they also demanded the dismantling of the guilds. Engaged in the broader popular movement that was propelling the radicalisation of the Revolution, workers put forward their own demands while incorporating revolutionary principles and values into their struggles.[61] Before the emergence of the *sans-culotterie* in 1792, left democrats and workers' organisations converged around different journals and clubs in Paris and other cities.[62] Prefiguring the popular republican alliance that would be key to the making of the French working class in the aftermath of the 1830 Revolution, democrats and workers refused to separate political and social demands, asking for male universal suffrage while also defending the material conditions of labourers.[63] State repression from 1791 halted this major labour offensive, but struggles from below continued, and important gains were made in the sphere of labour relations that would endure for decades to come.

Workers interpreted the Revolution as a complete reversal of the situation of labour in the Old Regime. For them, the Revolution announced the end of subordination to masters and the abolition of the guild privileges that subtended it. The Revolution was also seen as an opportunity to defend and expand tra-

---

58   Kaplan 2001.
59   Cottereau 2002, pp. 1534, 1536; Kaplan 1979, p. 22; Sonenscher 1989, pp. 13, 23.
60   Guicheteau 2014, pp. 132–3; Kaplan 2001, p. 424.
61   Guicheteau 2014, p. 141.
62   Guicheteau 2014, pp. 137–8.
63   Guicheteau 2014, p. 141.

ditional trade regulations that were threatened by liberals. The application of revolutionary principles to labour relations was at stake. During the first years of the new regime, workers consciously led their struggles as part of a broader movement against privileges that also included the peasants' fight against seigneurial powers.[64]

On the night of 4 August 1789, the Constituent Assembly abolished privileges. Artisan workers were well aware of the emancipatory potential of this decision and firmly believed that the revolutionary rupture also applied to labour relations.[65] Between September 1789 and March 1791, the Assembly received around one hundred petitions regarding guilds, most denouncing the arbitrary powers of guild masters. Meanwhile, the guild system's advanced stage of decomposition became increasingly obvious, as a growing number of workers were by then overtly and unilaterally refusing guild rules, leaving their masters, and ignoring the consequences. This process of decomposition was well encapsulated by Paris mayor Jean Sylvain Baily's recollections of the period: 'the decrees of August had a strong effect on the corporations: all people rebelled against the privileges of masters. The National Assembly, however, had not legislated on the guilds ... But there was widespread resistance; the forces at our disposal were inadequate and difficult to deploy; and license and violations grew apace'.[66]

This statement also illustrates the fact that, however vocal it might have been in its assertion of liberal principles, it was not the Constituent Assembly, which was largely overtaken by the pace of events, nor its bourgeois and noble liberal constituency that led the forces that were eventually responsible for the fall of the trade corporations. Their disappearance was more strongly related to popular resistance from below. As Vardi explains, 'until the Assembly abolished the guilds, the authorities persisted in these half-hearted attempts to shore-up the corporatist system, but they proved incapable of arresting defections within individual guilds. Journeymen were quick to act. Irrespective of the deputies' ultimate decision, the guilds were slowly disintegrating ... many workers were establishing themselves without mastership'.[67]

While, as discussed in Chapter 1, liberal reformers had been active within the state – with mixed results – for nearly half a century, no army of merchants or industrialists stormed the gates of the archaic feudal guilds, and the impetus for their abolition finally came mainly from below. In 1791, the Assembly at last

---

64   Guicheteau 2014, p. 135.
65   Guicheteau 2014, p. 131; Kaplan 2001, p. 611.
66   Quoted in Vardi 1988, p. 711.
67   Vardi 1988, p. 712.

moved to abolish guilds with the d'Allarde decree. This was celebrated as a triumphed by workers, and the government rapidly attempted to repress their collective power by means of the Le Chapelier decree that prohibited coalitions.[68] Adopting the Goudard decree, it also eradicated state-enforced manufacturing rules. Le Chapelier promoted his decree with a strongly individualist discourse,[69] but the liberal intentions of the Constituent Assembly should not be overstated. Indeed, the liberalisation ensuing from these decrees was not as potent as it might appear at first glance. Breaking the guilds' monopolies, these laws formally instated the freedom to form new enterprises in France, and granted the payment of a new tax – the *patente*, which was decried by many workers. But, for all this, economic rules and regulatory institutions were not altogether wiped out – far from it. If setting up enterprises had been liberalised, once founded, these enterprises continued to evolve in a regulatory framework that had little to distinguish it from the customary rules of the Old Regime.[70]

The oft-cited Article 7 of the d'Allarde decree stipulated that 'Any person will be free to choose the trade, profession, art or occupation he wants ...' Yet this was supplemented by a much less often mentioned, though crucial amendment that specified '... as long as he follows the various regulations that may be adopted'.[71] This seemingly not very liberal amendment begins to make sense if we let go of teleological assumptions about the Revolution as a gateway to a new capitalist society and begin to consider that the d'Allarde and Le Chapelier decrees had less to do with economic than with *political* liberalism.[72] The main objective of these reforms was to break with guilds that stood between individuals and the state within the field of labour relations, and was part of a broader process aimed at redefining political sovereignty by rooting it in a nation formed of individual citizens, instead of in the principle of a monarch overseeing a series of intermediate bodies. The main target of the Assembly was not so much economic regulations *per se* as it was the guilds that administered them. Guilds and coalitions, and also corporate bodies more generally, had become associated with privileges and were perceived as dividing the citizenry. Hence, the Le Chapelier decree mentioned that, since 'there no longer are corporations within the state', citizens belonging to a specific trade 'should not be

---

68   Kaplan 2001, p. 614.

69   Kaplan 2001, pp. 501–2.

70   Moreover, we should not overestimate the restrictions on the establishment of workshops that had existed under the Old Regime. Artisans routinely established workshops and practised their trade without formal permission from guilds, as has been demonstrated by Sonenscher, 1989.

71   Quoted in Hirsch 1989, pp. 1286–97. See also Hirsch 1991, p. 53.

72   Hirsch 1989, p. 1286; Minard 2008, pp. 89–90.

allowed to coalesce in order to promote their so-called common interests'.[73] No common interests existed besides the national interest safeguarded by the state – guilds and coalitions needed to go.

Likewise, the liberalising intentions of the Goudard decree should not be overblown. Goudard had in fact no intention of supressing all manufacturing rules, but wished to relegate the responsibility for establishing, administering and enforcing these rules to local and regional authorities.[74] As stated by Minard, Goudard's aim was not to establish laissez-faire but rather *laissez-régler-ailleurs*.[75] In this, he was following the opinion already expressed in 1789 by some of his fellow assembly members in favour of local regulations of trades, and article 8 of Goudard's projected bill following his first decree stated that 'the policing of manufactures will be entrusted to municipalities in order to maintain, as in the past, good order and good faith'.[76] Being drafted on the eve of new elections, however, this projected bill was never adopted. As Hirsch explains, '[o]verworked and with many unsolved questions before them, the deputies simply approved the articles that abolished the old system. They expected their successors to discuss a new one'.[77]

As legislative debates around the reestablishment of an official national administration of trade stalled, the institutional void that was left was rapidly filled by new judicial and regulatory institutions that kept the old subterranean regulatory practices of the bazaar economy alive, and also instated new ones. As envisioned by Goudard and others, these institutions acted on a local and regional scale. They were also instrumental in the partial emancipation of labour in France that occurred in the wake of the Revolution.

3   The Persistence of Customary Regulations and Aspects of Labour Emancipation in Post-revolutionary France

Gerard Noiriel has warned us against an inclination to see the French Revolution as paving the way to capitalism.[78] He stresses that the gigantic social upheaval that began in 1789 brought crucial popular gains that were not con-

---

73   Quoted in Hirsch 1989, p. 1286 and Minard 2008, p. 89.
74   Minard 2008, p. 90.
75   Minard 2008, p. 369.
76   Quoted in Minard 1998, p. 353: 'la police des manufactures sera confiée aux municipalités pour y maintenir, comme par le passé, le bon ordre'.
77   Hirsch 1989, p. 1287; see also Guicheteau 2014, p. 140.
78   Noiriel 1986, p. 265.

ducive to capitalist development. In addition to the consolidation of small peasant rural property, he also points to the tradition of struggles launched by the *sans-culottes* and the acquisition of citizenship rights and of male universal suffrage, all of which were used by workers in their struggles against capital. These are indeed important points, but Noiriel leaves out other revolutionary gains made by workers that had an emancipatory impact that cut right to the heart of the social relations of production.

There is a widespread consensus that the Revolution consolidated the French system of small peasant land tenure.[79] For decades after the Revolution, church and émigré properties that had been taken over by the state were sold to land-hungry peasants. Miller notes that 'the peasants' landownership varied from region to region but probably increased from about 30 to 40 per cent of the national total to about 50 per cent as a result'.[80] The rural population continued to increase over the first half of the nineteenth century and, until well into the twentieth century, self-subsistence agriculture remained a major feature of the French countryside.[81] Small peasant proprietors practising self-subsistence agriculture 'dominated the countryside in the nineteenth century and became the chief props of all subsequent regimes, none of which had any interest in enclosing, and evicting them from, the land'.[82]

Inheritance patterns induced by Napoleon's Civil Code, however, accentuated the partition of land that was already common under the Old Regime and, from 1815 to 1870, the number of landowners increased by 55 percent.[83] As plots were pulverised and many became insufficiently large to ensure survival, considerable numbers of peasant families had to fall back on alternative strategies of reproduction. Some produced for markets as an ancillary activity, marketing part of their harvest and engaging in labour-intensive production such as viticulture, potatoes or maize.[84] Peasants often engaged in rural proto-industrial production to supplement their incomes. A recurrent pattern led them to offer their labour at cheap rates, working as wage-labourers on large landed estates, often during harvest times. Their precarious situation also compelled peasants with insufficiently large plots to accept leases through which landlords were

---

79   Crouzet 1989, p. 1201. See also Comninel 1987, p. 202; Crouzet 2003, p. 235; Démier 2000, p. 44; Guicheteau 2014, p. 189; Jessenne 2006; Noiriel 1986, p. 265; Perrot 1986, p. 72; Price 1981, pp. 55, 68, 94, 167.
80   Miller 2015, p. 244.
81   Asselain 1984, p. 138; Broder 1993, p. 48; Miller 2015, p. 241.
82   Miller 2015, p. 245.
83   Moulin 1991, p. 57.
84   Ibid.

able to impose on their dependants all sorts of harassing stipulations and obligations to perform services on their land and to make payments in kind.[85]

Landowners and merchants could tap into a large pool of cheap rural labour, but they did not exploit it in a capitalist manner. Landlords, just like merchant-manufacturers overseeing proto-industrial networks, 'could count on profits from the peasants' toil without having to invest in labour-saving capital ... Large landowners did not respond to market opportunities by producing more efficiently but rather by taking advantage of the unequal distribution of land, the opportunities for unequal exchange, and redistributing income and wealth from others'.[86] Hence, the 'technical cul-de-sac' that could be witnessed on the land of peasant owner-occupiers practising self-subsistence agriculture also 'applied with equal force to the large landowners, many of whom sought only to maximise short-term rental income to the detriment of any long-term improvements in the conditions of estates'.[87] Most large landowners actually represented a conservative force, restraining the development of agricultural practices and productivity.[88]

Thousands of revolutionary peasants rising up over a period of five years 'had devastated tax offices, intimidated seigneurs and fiscal agents, and destroyed their titles and properties'. And it was this that 'eventually drove the government to definitely abolish the seigneurial regime',[89] in 1793. The seigneurial regime had been abolished by an intense process of struggles from below – not by capitalists from above – and, as has already been made clear, it was not replaced by agrarian capitalism. Peasants reproduced their village solidarities, and customary regulations of agrarian labour remained strong. It is certainly true that liberal views on the economy became increasingly entrenched among sections of the French elite during the revolutionary period. Yet, as Price explains, 'there existed a gulf between official conceptions, between lib-

---

85   Miller 2009, p. 5.
86   Miller 2009, pp. 5–6.
87   Moulin 1991, p. 43.
88   Price 1981, p. 71. From the 1815 Restoration to the coming of the Third Republic, France experienced an important increase of its agricultural output. This growth however, was not in any fundamental way propelled by a transformation of farming systems and practices. It was largely related to an intensive use of large reserves of cheap rural labour. The growth of agricultural output stemmed from an intensification of existing traditional practice. Most importantly, it came out of a steady and massive expansion, by 20 percent over the period, of land under cultivation, and a related massive input of human labour, all of which tended to provide diminishing returns. See Moulin 1991, pp. 48–54 and Broder 1993, pp. 49–51.
89   Miller 2015, p. 244.

eral economic theories, and the realities of rural life. Attitudes in the village remained dominated by the spirit of the *Ancien Régime*'.[90] Traditional leases, ways of life, and methods of production were largely preserved; sharecropping, too, remained widespread.[91]

In 1792, the central government proclaimed the right for landowners to use their land as they wished. But a 1791 decree had already given recognition to customary collective practices. The latter came to prevail. Peasants preserved their collective rights and 'instinctively rejected the theory that a proprietor had absolute rights in his property. There was an intense consciousness of the common interests and customary rights of the community',[92] and leases would often include instructions to 'cultivate in accordance with local customs'.[93] Moreover, central state authorities repeatedly allowed municipal control of bread and meat prices until the second half of the nineteenth century. Price ceilings and restrictions on trade (ensuring prior access to local consumers) were maintained, and guaranteed the reproduction of a 'moral economy' enforced by sporadic riots.[94]

A similar gap between elite liberal discourses and actual practices was also characteristic of French industry, where traditional regulations of economic activities remained vibrant. Over the nineteenth century, the official interpretation of the d'Allarde, Le Chapelier and Goudard decrees that had been adopted in 1791 was of course often coated in an economic liberal discourse. Yet this discourse did not result in changes to commercial practices, which 'had in fact changed very little'.[95] Customary regulations persisted and had practical effects that could hardly be distinguished from those of Old Regime guilds' guidelines and prohibitions.[96] An important transformation did take place in the wake of the Revolution: the state would no longer officially and actively back normative regulations of labour relations and of economic activities as it used to do under the Old Regime's system of trade corporations. This, as will be seen in the next chapter, had important repercussions on the development of a republican and socialist labour movement under the July monarchy. This did not mean that a laissez faire system had been established, however, and normative regulations of trades still flourished on a local level for decades to come.

---

90   Price 1981, p. 68; see also Moulin 1991, p. 29.
91   Broder 1993, p. 49.
92   Price 1981, p. 70.
93   Price 1981, p. 71: 'cultivater [sic] selon les usages du pays'.
94   Bourguinat 2002; Judt 2011, p. 56; Price 1981, p. 61.
95   Hirsch 1989, p. 1284.
96   Hirsch 1991, p. 56.

While liberalism was promoted by different sections of the ruling class, following the Revolution, 'many regulations were re-established or created (mainly at the municipal level) and constituted as "exceptions" to a general system of laissez-faire'.[97] These 'exceptions', however, rapidly became the rule, and soon formed local regulatory sub-systems. Regulations were sometimes hidden but also often known and tolerated – or else ignored – by complacent state officials. No longer officially backed by the central state, though in practice often upheld by prefects, traditional usages and coordinating practices retained a strong and widespread presence in trade communities.

The French Revolution brought about a transformation of labour relations that had substantial emancipatory effects. No doubt, poverty and the threat of unemployment remained pressing issues for many workers, but the fact remains, as stated by Alain Cottereau, that the Declaration of the Rights of Man and of the Citizens, the abolition of privileges, and the erosion and eventually the formal eradication of guilds 'were intensely lived as an effective workers' emancipation, as a triumph of old moral struggles, and as the consecration of an effective capacity to fairly negotiate with employers. These were not only new formal civil rights, but indeed new real possibilities, massively used'.[98] A vast majority of workers were freed from subordination to their employers in their workplace. Moreover, every category of workers, including domestics and apprentices, were now allowed to leave their employers without the threat of having to face legal prosecutions for work desertion. And, as Sonenscher puts it, because of 'practical limitations upon [their] powers' that had been imposed by workers' struggles over the revolutionary period, 'it was not particularly easy to be an employer in early nineteenth-century France'.[99]

Already before the Revolution, there had been a difference between work contracted as a *louage d'ouvrage* and work contracted as a *louage de service*. The first type of contract established specific tasks and results to be delivered. Work was performed autonomously by the worker, according to established usages in a given trade, and did not imply obedience to a master. A worker could organise his labour as he saw fit or do so together with his employer, as an equal. The second type of contract concerned work bought by an employer for a given

---

97   Hirsch 1989, p. 1287.

98   Cottereau 2006, p. 104: 'furent vécus intensément comme une émancipation ouvrière effective, comme un triomphe des anciennes luttes morales, et comme la consécration d'une capacité effective de négocier équitablement avec les employeurs. Il ne s'agissait pas seulement de nouveaux droits civils formels, mais bien de nouvelles possibilités réelles, massivement utilisées'.

99   Sonenscher 1989, p. 367, 368.

period of time. It was closer to a relation of domesticity and implied submission to a master's directives. The new labour rights conquered during the revolutionary period materialised through an immediate and massive expansion of the number of workers – soon a vast majority – that were entering *louage d'ouvrage* contracts, which became widely known as *vrai louage*. Indeed, even at the end of the Second Empire, around 90 percent of workers performed jobs under *louage d'ouvrage*. Fines and retribution for insubordination were repealed and this now dominant form of work agreement was emancipated from old corporate rules and status – while still being regulated by customary social and legal norms, as will be seen below. Most workers could now freely and legitimately discuss the organisation and execution of work with an employer to whom they were no longer subordinated.[100]

At first, these new rights were not always formalised. As was mentioned in the preceding section, by invoking the Rights of Man and newly declared rights of liberty, workers spontaneously considered themselves to be freed from the guilds' hierarchical structures and subordination. As these structures were eroded, a new set of norms began to emerge, and artisan workers made sure to maintain 'vigilance against despotism at work'.[101] This vigilance – and the egalitarian principles that corresponded to it – was soon embedded into new usages which were eventually validated by tribunals.

Concretely, these principles and norms were made part of a *bon droit* – to use Cottereau's expression – that existed at the margin of, and sometimes in opposition to, the dominant judicial system, through local jurisprudence, and that was reminiscent of the moral economy of the Old Regime. These legal norms were primarily elaborated and administered by justice courts such as the *justices de paix* and *conseil de prud'hommes* – which will be discussed in more detail below. During the first months of their existence, from 1791, *justices de paix* made decisions that concretised the emancipation of 'citizen-workers' from subordination to their employers.[102]

The Civil Code, promulgated in 1804 but elaborated from 1793, also embodied some of these emancipatory principles. This was noted by nineteenth-century commentators and legal treatises, but is often forgotten today. Many historians take for granted that the abolition of guilds, and subsequent adoption of the Civil Code, introduced economic laissez-faire in France. According to this view, the Code introduced absolute private property and made clear that

---

100   Cottereau 2002, pp. 1530, 1546; and 2006, pp. 113–14.
101   Cottereau 2002, p. 1537: 'vigilance contre le despotisme au travail'.
102   Cottereau 2002, p. 1528.

no power or form of arbitration could interfere with labour relations established through purely private contracts. This liberal conception of labour relations had in fact already been put forth during the 1880s by the jurist Ernest Glasson, who maintained that 'the Civil Code is but the legislation of capital; it does not deal with the legislation of work; it is a bourgeois code and not a popular code; our code is the law of a bourgeois society and of families that own a more considerable capital, but it is not the code of labour or of the worker'.[103] However, as we will see in Chapter 4, Glasson's statement entails a studied ignorance of – indeed it actively participates in an effort to put an end to – decades of non-capitalist jurisprudence. It was only after the new judicial doctrine promoted by Glasson and other jurists – with the support of top state officials and judges – was embedded in law that the myth of a liberal Civil Code granting unilateral powers to employers and disallowing any kind of social regulation of economic relations came to be accepted as a given truth.

Still today, many believe that the often-cited article 1781 of the Code instituted an unequal relationship between employers and workers, asserting: 'The master is believed on his own statement ... for the payment of the wage of the past year and for the down payment of the current year'. On its own, this article seems to suggest that only employers were considered trustworthy and so could arbitrarily determine if contractual obligations had been met or not. Yet until the last third of the nineteenth century, jurisprudence considered that this article only concerned domestics and workers entering *louage de service*, and did not apply to workers engaged in *louage d'ouvrage*.[104]

The Code recognised the difference between types of *louage* and the fact that it could include or exclude a relationship of subordination. As noted by Raymond Théodore Troplong, an eminent jurist and commentator on the Civil Code:

> workers are divided between two classes: those that rent their services for a given price by the day ... and those with whom one establishes the work to be accomplished, in exchange for a set price. The latter enter a *lou-*

---

103   Quoted in Portis 1988, p. 19: 'le Code civile n'est que l'ensemble de la législation du capital; il ne s'occupe pas de la législation du travail; c'est un code bourgeois et non un code populaire; notre code est la loi d'une société bourgeoise et des familles qui possèdent un patrimoine plus considérable, mais ce n'est pas le code du travail ou du travailleur'.

104   Cottereau 2006, p. 114. See also Sonenscher 1989, p. 367, who explains that decisions by the courts following the adoption of the Civil Code made clear that, except in specific cases, 'in disputes over daily and monthly rates in the urban trades, the courts expected more than an employer's affirmation before they were satisfied'.

age d'ouvrage, called *marché*, and is covered by the article 1787 and those that follow. The former, ordinarily known under the name of *journaliers*, enter a *louage de service* rather than a *louage d'ouvrage*. Their condition is inferior.[105]

The recognition of this difference between forms of labour contract, and the fact that the vast majority of French workers entered reciprocal employment relationships excluding relationships of subordination, led Charles Renouard, another jurist and commentator on the Civil Code, to note in 1854 that it 'clearly established that the renting of one's labour is not an alienation of the capacity to work, and that this faculty, inherent to human activity, remains the property of the worker'.[106] The Code, in other words, precluded the alienation of labour and, as we will see, the related subsumption of labour to capital, which is a functioning requirement of capitalism. It prevented the differentiation of labouring individuals from their labour-power which, under capitalism, is reduced to a commodity, bought and used like any other factor of production by employers. From the Revolution and until the last third of the nineteenth century, the vast majority of French workers remained largely in control of their labouring activities and faced their employers as equals in a relation of genuine and substantive reciprocity.

Article 1134 of the Code is also routinely cited as a proof of its liberal character. Claiming that 'contracts freely established have force of law to those who established them',[107] it appears to suggest that labour relations are to be determined only through private contracts between individuals meeting on unregulated markets. Yet, Article 1135 gives it a wholly different meaning, specifying that 'contracts compel not only to what they express, but also to every follow-up that equity, usage or the law pose as an obligation according to its nature'.[108] Equity and usage, positively recognised by a legal code that thus can-

---

105   Quoted in Cottereau 2002, p. 1543: 'Les ouvriers se divisent en deux classes: ceux qui louent leurs services à tant par jour, ... et ceux avec qui l'on convient d'un travail à faire, moyennant un prix fait. Ceux-ci contractent un louage d'ouvrage, appelé marché, et réglé par les art. 1787 et suivants. Ceux-là, ordinairement connus sous le nom de journaliers, contractent plutôt un louage de services qu'un louage d'ouvrage. Leur condition est inférieure à celle des premiers'.
106   Quoted in Cottereau 2002, p. 1553: 'il a marqué nettement ... que la location du travail n'est pas une aliénation de la puissance de travailler, et que cette faculté, inhérente à l'activité humaine, demeure la propriété du prestateur d'ouvrage'.
107   Ibid.: 'les conventions librement formées tiennent lieu de loi à ceux qui les ont formées'.
108   Ibid.: 'les conventions obligent non seulement à ce qui y est exprimé, mais encore à toutes les suites que l'équité, l'usage ou la loi donnent à l'obligation d'après sa nature'.

not simply be presented as unequivocally liberal, were components of a *bon droit* that was administered and enforced by a set of institutions that we will now consider.

Over the last three decades, a new historiography has emerged that challenges the interpretation of the 1791 decrees (and revolutionary reforms more broadly defined) as announcing the triumph of economic liberalism in France.[109] This literature underlines the important role of a set of institutions – including *justices de paix, conseils de prud'hommes, chambres de commerce, tribunaux de commerce*, as well as municipal governments – in regulating economic activities in post-revolutionary France. It allows us to see that, if French workers were freed during the Revolution from control and subordination exercised by trade corporations, then this did not mean that they were simply tossed into unregulated markets and social relations of production. If they could now freely decide to take and to leave a job, workers were also in a position to negotiate their working conditions with their employers, and to do so as equals, in a regulated, 'socially-embedded' normative context.

As a major contributor to this literature, Alain Cottereau explains that the Revolution announced not only the advent of formal law (as embedded in different codes) but also the institutionalisation, within trades, of the popular 'natural justice', *sens du juste* or *bon droit*, that had existed under the Old Regime, in part through a jurisprudence produced by different courts of justice and through municipal rules. During the first two-thirds of the nineteenth century, this customary *bon droit*, often unwritten (even when supported by court decisions), repeatedly contradicted the official liberal discourse of political leaders.[110]

This *sens du juste* manifested itself in every trade through sets of rules, or *usages*, concerning hiring, departures and dismissals, sick pay, wages and piece tariffs, schedules, apprenticeship, work methods, or subcontracting.[111] These were often enforced by different informal popular practices. In many trades, for example, hiring was done in public, in squares or at cabarets, so that negotiations over pay and tasks could be witnessed by everyone. Workers accepting contacts in secrecy were put on blacklists and would lose the respect of their fellow workers. This bargaining also took place within a framework defined by municipal policies and the decisions of *conseils des prud'hommes*, establishing

---

109   Lemercier 2005, and 2008, p. 62.
110   Cottereau 2002, p. 145.
111   Cottereau 2011, p. 17; Lemercier 2009b.

minimum wages and tariffs; and whenever the *bon droit* was infringed upon, discussions, arguments and (sometime violent) conflicts emerged.[112]

Trade regulations were thus crafted and enforced by different judicial and political institutions. We already noted the enduring and crucial regulatory role of municipal governments. This would continue even after the Revolution, most importantly through the setting of tariffs and the monitoring of collective negotiations of tariffs for different trades.[113] The *justices de paix*, created by the Constituent Assembly in 1790, also played a fundamental role in this process of regulation.[114] Justices of the peace were instrumental in the establishment of a simplified, rapid and free form of justice that would be more accessible to regular citizens than the parallel and more formalised, classic form of justice that came to be embedded in the Civil Code. They dealt with a vast range of day-to-day disputes while adopting a conciliatory approach, but also intervened in conflicts related to labour and commercial relations, and were solicited by both employers and employees.[115] Justices were elected, and no specific qualification was requested for the position. The justices' success was immediate. They arbitrated hundreds of thousands of legal conflicts in 1791, and between two and four million each year during the eight decades that followed. This, explains Cottereau, was a clear indication of a new role for citizens in the administration of their community life. It signalled a durable institutionalisation of *bon droit*, which had a major impact on labouring activities.[116]

First appearing in Lyon in 1806, *conseils de prud'hommes* were conceived as industrial justices of the peace that also developed a conciliatory approach while specialising in the regulation of economic activities. Proposals to establish such councils had already been formulated in the context of eighteenth-century conflicts between artisans and guild officials, in order to cope with the issue of subordination in labour relations.[117] The need to establish local institutions to monitor labour relations had also been noted by the Constitu-

---

112   Cottereau 2002, p. 1549; and 2011, pp. 6–11.
113   Cottereau 2002, p. 1531. It should be stressed that these tariffs were not negotiated by a
        single employer and his employees – they were not the collective agreements over which
        British trade unions started to bargain with specific employers around the same period.
        They were often negotiated by trade assemblies that gathered employers' as well as work-
        ers' delegates, applied for a trade as a whole, and were enforced by municipal govern-
        ments, justices of peace, *prud'hommes*, and commercial tribunals.
114   The mission and methods of these justices of the peace differed from that of their British
        equivalents, as noted by Cottereau 2006, p. 116.
115   Guicheteau 2014, p. 173.
116   Cottereau 2002, p. 1545.
117   Sonenscher 1989, p. 284.

ent Assembly in 1791. But the creation of *conseils de prud'hommes* also resulted
from powerful struggles led by workers over the revolutionary period. As noted
by Guicheteau, it represented the outcome of multiple experiments led by different actors, most notably in Lyon, with the aim of applying revolutionary
principles to the field of labour relations.[118]

The councils' officials were representatives elected from within trade communities – merchants, master-artisans and eventually also workers. Their success was also impressive, and new councils were soon created in other cities, so
that by the end of the century they had spread throughout the country. In cities
where *prud'hommes* remained absent, justices of the peace continued to deal
with labour conflicts.[119] Though at first also created to deal with commercial
matters such as brand and quality control, *prud'hommes* rapidly narrowed their
focus down to labour relations. It is crucial to note that, though they were ruling
on individual disputes, their decisions had crucial collective implications.[120]

Prud'hommes pronounced judgements and gave conciliatory advice on
every aspect of labour relations, and thus played a pivotal role in the structuring
of social relations of production.[121] In doing this, they systematically refused to
grant arbitrary powers to employers or to let unfettered market competition
determine working conditions.[122] A close analysis of *prud'hommes*' decisions
conducted by Cottereau clearly and amply confirms this.[123] Whenever they
felt that their rights were not respected, workers would appeal to these courts.
Employers were not granted the right to define individual tasks or the organisation of work. Methods of production could only be established by workers
alone or jointly with employers, according to local trade usages, but could not
simply be imposed from above by employers. Until the last third of the nineteenth century, *prud'hommes* objected to the establishment of all internal factory or workshop regulations that did not respect customary trade customs.[124]
In this, they were often backed up by municipal and regional political authorities. For example, refusing the creation of internal regulations in his town's
numerous textile factories, Roubaix's mayor issued a decree in 1837, which was
then approved by the department's prefect, explaining that unilateral rules set
by employers 'injure distributive justice and natural equity, since they concede

---

118   Guicheteau 2014, pp. 174, 176.
119   Guicheteau 2014, p. 174.
120   Cottereau 1987b, pp. 33–8; and 2006, p. 116; Kieffer 1987, p. 22.
121   Kieffer 1987, p. 22.
122   Delsalle 1987, p. 69; Lefebvre 2003, p. 98.
123   Cottereau 1987b.
124   Cottereau 2011, p. 10; and 2002, pp. 1547–9; Delsalle 1987, p. 69.

to masters rights it refuses to workers'.[125] Lefebvre explains that the 1803 law that allowed employers to establish internal workshop rules had rapidly fallen into disuse.[126] The state council continuously postponed proposals for legislation that would grant employers the unilateral power to implement workplace rules, until judicial decisions and new labour legislations finally did so from the late 1860s.[127]

The point is not simply that the employers' powers were importantly circumscribed. Over the first two-thirds of the nineteenth century, such powers, at least in a unilateral form, were nowhere to be found. *Prud'hommes* and local or regional authorities justified their decisions and interventions by stressing the fact that issues pertaining to labour relations and the organisation of production were 'public matters'.[128] The separation of 'economic' and 'political' spheres specific to capitalism, which implies the privatisation of political powers to organise production, and their confinement to an 'economic' sphere, simply did not exist in France until the last decades of the nineteenth century.[129] An authentic relationship of reciprocity characterised labour relations and was largely accepted, and sometimes even actively defended, by most employers, as well as by workers. As Cottereau explains, *justices de paix* and *prud'hommes* enforced, and helped to define the contours of, a moral economy, and this economy was at times also upheld by collective struggles.[130]

The notices and decisions delivered by *prud'hommes* were informed by customary usages, and also by the new rights gained during the revolutionary period.[131] They also established precedents and created new norms. *Prud'hommes* were law-producing entities in an era of underdeveloped official labour legislation.[132] These new norms were widely recognised as valid in local communities and were taken over and enforced by justices of the peace and commercial tribunals. In effect, *prud'hommes* councils established and enforced a kind of virtual local labour legislation.[133] New regulations emerged by trial and error and as part of a dialogue among the members of the trade com-

---

125 Cottereau 2002, pp. 1549–50: 'blesse la justice distributive et l'équité naturelle, en ce qu'elle concède aux maîtres des droits qu'elle refuse aux ouvriers'.
126 Lefebvre 2009, p. 52.
127 Fombonne 2001, p. 97.
128 Cottereau 2002, p. 1552.
129 On the separation of the 'economic' and the 'political' in capitalism, see Wood 1995, pp. 19–48.
130 Cottereau 2006, p. 118; Reddy 1979.
131 Fombonne 2001, pp. 53–5.
132 Kieffer 1987, p. 22.
133 Cottereau 1987b; Guicheteau 2014, p. 177.

munity by whom the councils' officials had been elected. To secure agreements within trade communities, these officials would often summon general assemblies where heads of workshops or workers' delegates would meet in order to discuss and harmonise existing regulations, and to develop new ones. These meetings were sometimes presided over by local mayors.[134] Rules were emerging not out of a judicial hierarchy but from local consent and dialogue. This method for overseeing trade communities and customs leads Sonenscher to note that *prud'hommes* can be considered as extensions of Old Regime guilds. They were, however, much more democratic institutions, and they developed in a context in which the subordination of workers had been swept away.[135]

Importantly, these trade communities were also no longer backed by the central state. Sets of customary norms represented a kind of local and semi-clandestine legislation. Consequently, *prud'hommes* made sure not to over-publicise some of their decisions, as many could have been – and were, in fact, on relatively rare occasions, until the last third of the nineteenth century – recognised as illegal by superior law courts and high state officials and politicians.[136] This partly explains why their crucial regulatory role within the nineteenth-century French economy has been so often ignored by historians.[137]

It is true that employers often attempted, and were sometimes able, to escape these webs of customary regulations overseen by *prud'hommes*, justices of the peace, and municipal governments. Ready-made clothing, or confection, was one of the trades where such attempts were frequent, and *marchandage* – which implied practices of subcontracting – was a widespread practice in construction trades and many other industrial sectors. But this in no way amounted to a transition to 'artisan capitalism', as Sewell, Johson and others would have us believe.

Subcontracting – which should be sub-divided between regulated and legitimate *marchandage*, on the one hand, and illicit *mauvais marchandage*, on the other – as well as the presence of 'dishonourable' producers in different trades such as confection, were nothing new, and did not stem from the d'Allarde and

---

134   Cottereau 1987b, pp. 39, 53; 2011, p. 18; and 2002, p. 1549.
135   Sonenscher 1989, p. 369.
136   Cottereau 2011, p. 17.
137   Thus, for instance, after the central state's intervention to abolish the tariffs set by Lyon's municipal government for the silk industry in 1831, and following the popular revolts that ensued that same year and in 1834 (which will be discussed in the next chapter), the city's *prud'hommes* continued to administer and to enforce piece rates clandestinely, with the support of the trade community and in direct opposition to the official liberalism. See, Cottereau 2006, p. 118.

Le Chapelier decrees. An issue of the *Gazette des Tribunaux* published in 1840 noted that the subcontracting of jobs 'has been customary from time immemorial in the professions connected with construction'.[138] It did not originate with the abolition of guilds and was not intensified by it either; and, as Sonenscher has shown, in post-revolutionary France, 'there was nothing new about sub-contracting work and the system of payment that came to be known as *marchandage*'.[139] Nor was confection new under the Restoration or the July Monarchy – it had already been present, and circumscribed by the Paris Parlement, during the eighteenth century.[140]

Again, the social embeddedness of economic activities never meant that all production and exchange relations were regulated at all time. Under the Old Regime, many practices were not completely in keeping with the norms established by guild, government, and court officials.[141] Production often took place at a distance from these regulations and was influenced by them to various degrees.[142] The same was true during the nineteenth century: the core of every trade remained organised and institutionally regulated, while ongoing labour vigilance and periodic mobilisation to enforce normative regulations took place in the periphery.

'Over-competition' – not to be confused with systemic capitalist competition – and 'dishonourable' employer practices had been a threat to the workers' well-being for centuries under the Old Regime – and had led to sporadic collective mobilisation in defence of the *bon droit* –[143] and continued to be so in post-revolutionary France. Though trade corporations were no longer there to tone down this threat, new regulatory institutions had emerged. Through various informal practices, labourers also acted so that subcontracting and *marchandage* practices would not result in a race to the bottom. They developed 'solidarity within work gangs to eliminate inter-exploitation: workers with different levels of skill refused to compete with each other. They harmonized their rates of production and established more or less egalitarian rules for the sharing-out of subcontracted wages'.[144] Moreover, 'frequently the subcontractors themselves played along with this. Sometimes they took charge of a workers'

---

138   Bezucha 1983, p. 472.
139   Sonenscher 1989, pp. 30–1.
140   Sonenscher 1989, p. 372.
141   Gerstenberger 2009, p. 456.
142   Harold D. Parker explains, for instance, how many textile merchants refused to bring their products to brand offices during the eighteenth century, and how inspectors had to constantly discipline 'cheaters'. See Parker 1993, p. 33.
143   Nicolas 2002, pp. 317–32.
144   Cottereau 1995, p. 279.

counter-subcontracting system on an egalitarian basis'. Such collusion and solidarity between workers in order to avoid excessive levels of competition was reminiscent of practices that had also existed under the *Ancien Régime*.[145] These practices of solidarity often transmuted into formalised rules. Already from 1791, in spite of the proscription of coalitions under the Le Chapelier law, employers and workers of different trades often got together to work out agreements around tariffs setting the workers' pay. These tariffs were validated and publicised by municipal authorities.[146]

Moreover, *prud'hommes* did actively clamp down on confection and *mauvais marchandage* tied to illicit and inequitable forms of hiring (as opposed to licit *marchandage*, which respected customary regulations, implied a relationship of reciprocity and was actually perceived by workers as a condition of their autonomy). For instance, in 1847 a Parisian council judged that wages paid by some *confectionneurs* were derisory and ordered an increase. Explaining its decision, it declared that the issue was a 'public matter' and that such low wages were unjust and counter to usages. The decision was opposed by the liberal *Cour de Cassation*, the country's highest court of justice, which cancelled the wage increase. This intervention from the top of the judicial hierarchy, however, had no immediate consequence. The *prud'hommes* council reaffirmed their decision and made sure to no longer appeal to civil law to back its decisions.[147] In part due to this regulatory framework, confection remained a small sector of the economy – one which had still barely encroached on the activities of Parisian master tailors in 1850.[148]

Hence, relations of production and labour relations remained socially embedded in ways that were strikingly similar to those that had had currency before the Revolution. Hiring contracts had to abide by existing usages, employers did not gain the capacity to unilaterally organise production, and workers were actually empowered by new rights that turned their relationship to their employers from one of subordination to one of reciprocity. What *did* change during and after the revolutionary period, was that the local norms and institutions that regulated artisanal and industrial trades no longer benefited from strong official support from a central state, since the state was no longer erected on a series of entangled intermediate bodies. Thus, if *prud'hommes* councils did represent an extension of old guilds, insofar as ensured the regulation of trade communities in a more democratic way, they did not benefit from the

---

145   Thillay 2002, pp. 250–4.
146   Lefebvre 2009, p. 52.
147   Cottereau 2002, p. 1552.
148   Faure 1986, p. 544.

same positive support from the central state. Normative regulations persisted and indeed even thrived over the first half of the nineteenth century, but did so in a less formalised way than under the Old Regime.

Commerce also remained socially embedded. In the wake of the elimination of state-sponsored regulations enforced by state inspectors and bureaus in 1791, many merchants were in disarray, asking how product quality would be guaranteed, and demanded the re-establishment of regulations, while others seized what they perceived as an opportunity to self-manage their trade and regional economy.[149] Over the revolutionary period, the First Empire and after, the void left by the Goudard decree of 1791 was filled by local and regional trade actors and institutions. In the absence of disembedded and self-regulated markets, commercial tribunals and chambers of commerce safeguarded customary practices and collective rules that acted as the armature allowing production and trade to proceed more or less smoothly. In this way, trade regulations remained alive.[150] Even in the late 1850s, commercial law treatises were filled with specific regional regulations.[151] Tribunals and chambers maintained, developed and enforced a 'local self-discipline' of commerce in the different regions of France.[152] They participated in local arbitrations of disputes between merchants on different issues, including branding and product quality. Through these institutions, in different French regions and municipalities, such as Lyon and Roubaix, 'stable networks formed by the great merchant families ... organized durable agreements' to monitor the different activities related to their trade.[153] Merchants and entrepreneurs were thus demanding, but also directly creating laws and regulations.[154] Beside participating in tribunals and chambers of commerce, they established many more *ad hoc* organisations and associations across the country that had a wide range of purposes, from verifying the reliability of suppliers to ensuring the quality of materials used in production.[155]

Following in the footsteps of similar institutions going back to the sixteenth century, commercial tribunals were established in 1790. Judges in these tribunals were merchants elected by their peers. Their authority derived from their expertise as practitioners. Though they could request the use of pub-

---

149   Hirsch 1989, pp. 1285, 1287; Minard 1998, p. 360; and 2008, pp. 88–9.
150   Hirsch 1991, p. 56.
151   Minard 1989.
152   Lemercier 2008, pp. 62–3.
153   Hirsch 1989, p. 1285.
154   Hirsch and Chassagne 2012.
155   Sonenscher 1989, p. 370.

lic coercion to enforce their decisions, these tribunals mostly favoured conciliation and reconciled common law with the revolutionary principles that were mentioned above, and which acted as vectors of reciprocity and equality among economic actors.[156] Commercial tribunals were widely successful and their number, already reaching 120 in 1795, went up to 220 in 1815.

Chambers of commerce were reinstated from 1801 under the aegis of Jean-Antoine Chaptal, Napoléon's Minister of the Interior.[157] By 1803, the government had adopted a law that 'reestablished the major part of the regulatory framework of manufactures'.[158] Still, many merchants and industrialists remained dissatisfied, and soon established chambers of commerce in different municipalities. While some of their officials had sympathies for liberalism, most chambers of commerce had the explicit intention of eradicating forgery and 'over-competition' and developing a 'family spirit' and an 'industrial confraternity' between their members. Chamber officials also actively participated in commercial tribunal activities as *arbitres rapporteurs* – experts that were consulted and granted power to produce judgements on specific issues. Making these judgements, chambers of commerce representatives regularly produced *parères*, which were expert opinions that formalised local and professional customary practices. The provision of *parères* provided real and ample powers to chambers in the regulation of trading activities; this had important implications for the organisation of production, and for the control and enforcement of product quality standards.[159]

Chambers of commerce were indispensable actors in the establishment of economic norms.[160] They rightly perceived efforts at regulating brands and product quality as essential for the success of French luxury products on international markets. The chambers' archives clearly show that these institutions largely maintained their Old Regime practices. They established regulations and often appeared to have been 'engaged in activities closer to co-management [of their regional trade] than to the simple provision of advice'.[161]

An illustration of this form of co-management is provided by Lyon's silk industry. Like most craft trades across nineteenth-century France, silk production in Lyon was organised on the *fabrique* model, which implied an elaborate

---

156 Guicheteau 2014, pp. 175–6.
157 Minard 2008, p. 91.
158 Hirsch 1989, p. 1287.
159 Hirsch 1991, p. 108; Lemercier 2003, pp. 61, 64, 66; 2008, pp. 64–6, 73–4; and 2009a, pp. 326–7.
160 Lemercier 2003.
161 Hirsch 1991, p. 104: 'engage dans une tâche plus proche de la congestion que de la simple fourniture d'avis'.

division of labour involving a multitude of small workshops specialising in specific tasks.[162] The model of development adopted by the city's silk producers was a controversial issue that sparked sometimes violent disputes within the trade. Yet in the end, the activities of the myriad small enterprises, and also their mutual relations, remained collectively organised and coordinated, and artisanal production continued to thrive until the late 1870s. Unlike in London, where the silk industry had been liberalised in the wake of the abolition of the Spitalfield Acts,[163] the development and diffusion of technological innovations and new fashions were cooperatively managed in Lyon, as opposed to being organised through decentralised and individualised market exchanges. This collective supervision of the trade, which also involved matters such as tariffs and quality concerns, was undertaken by an intricate institutional network that involved the *prudh'hommes* council as well as the municipal government. This was a democratically inspired mode of regulation that had matured in the wake of the Revolution; it incorporated principles of reciprocity and equity, and ran counter to economic liberalism.[164] Until the closing decades of the nineteenth century, silk products remained luxury goods, and superior quality provided a critical competitive advantage over other producers engaged in this branch.[165] The British government's decision to force London's silk producers to emulate the capitalist cotton industry proved to be ill-advised. Relying on institutions that ensured the quality of their products, Lyon's silk merchants conquered the world market, while London's industry was only able to grow on the basis of internal demand.

The impressive success of Lyon's silk industry during most of the nineteenth century clearly did not stem from a capitalist transformation of production. On the contrary, market exchanges remained deeply socially embedded and regulated, as did relations of production in workshops. Similar strategies of regulation also ensured the (often more modest) success of trades in other French regions during this period.[166] Hirsch, for instance, studied the collective administration of textile trades by merchants in Lille and in Roubaix.[167] Alsa-

---

162   On the *fabrique* model of industrial production, see Faure 1986, p. 531. We will come back to this point in more detail in Chapter 4.

163   The Spitalfields Acts, enacted between 1765 and 1801, regulated wages and working conditions and protected London's silk industry from overseas competition.

164   Cottereau 1997, pp. 78, 81, 89–93, 109, 127–8, 137, 142; Guicheteau, 2014, p. 135; Frobert 2009, 17–19; Lequin 1977.

165   Cottereau 1997, p. 102.

166   Cottereau 1986; Didry 2001, p. 1261.

167   Hirsch 1991.

tian industrialists around Mulhouse also collaborated to develop, share and diffuse technological innovations in the decades following the First Empire. While commercial exchanges and merchant interactions were regulated through the delivery of *parères* and other means of coordination, French labour relations were characterised by the absence of the subsumption of labour by capital, in sharp contrast to the capitalist transformation of production taking place in England.

4   The Absence of Labour Subsumption by Capital in Post-revolutionary France

Comparing the French and English cases will here again be helpful. In France, as we just saw, an intricate set of local institutions actively ensured the regulation of social relations of production until the last third of the nineteenth century. In England, by contrast, the corrosive effects of agrarian capitalism on industrial labour relations had long been felt. The development of agrarian capitalism implied the dispossession of a large and growing mass of customary tenants and the consequent rise of national labour and consumer markets. This in turn entailed emerging price competition between employers that had access to ever-larger pools of cheap labour, and put guild and customary regulations of markets and labour relations under increasing stress. Fearing the social unrest that could ensue from these developments, the Tudor state reacted with the adoption of the Statute of Artificers in 1563, thereby elevating the normative regulation of trades (regarding wage-fixing, training, etc.) enforced by guilds to the status of a national policy.[168]

Very soon, however, the Statute of Artificers came under attack. The first decades of the seventeenth century already saw the adoption of a series of provincial liberal by-laws that challenged the regulations enforced by guilds.[169] These legal reforms launched a protracted process of liberalisation that culminated with the abrogation of the Statute by the British Parliament in 1813. But even as legal regulations were eroded, customs survived, protecting trade traditions and ensuring that the old moral economy still largely prevailed. Although with decreasing success as time passed, labourers were still often able to appeal to justices of the peace in order to enforce normative regulation within their respective trades. As late as the eighteenth century, wages

---

168   Zmolek 2014, p. 102.
169   Zmolek 2014, pp. 106, 137–8.

remained stable over long periods, as they continued to be largely governed by non-market factors. Workers also largely retained control over labour processes.[170]

This began to change swiftly, especially during the second half of the century, as a capitalist industrial revolution took off.[171] Under the whip of competitive market imperatives, English employers began increasingly to disregard customary regulations: the labour market and labour processes were 'in the process of being dis-embedded from the age-old economy dominated by custom'.[172] Pointing to the economic advantages of market-driven agriculture, English justices of the peace began to rule against the enforcement of customary regulations within industry. 'By the 1790s probably a majority of judges in England had conformed to the outlook of the political economists', and became active agents of a capitalist transformation of labour relations.[173] In parallel, and as a consequence, a new relationship of exploitation was developing, pitting employers against employees and acknowledging 'no lingering obligations of mutuality'. Henceforth, there was 'no whisper of the "just" price, or of a wage justified in relation to social or moral sanctions, as opposed to the operation of free market forces'. And, systematically fuelled as it was by new market forces and imperatives, antagonism was now 'accepted as intrinsic to the relations of production'.[174]

This unfolding process was 'in a very real sense one of local custom being supplanted by state law'. Zmolek goes on to explain that, by extinguishing customary trade regulations, capitalists and their allies within the British state were 'asserting absolute property rights under the common law'.[175] In essence, they were subsuming and dissolving under the central state's common law 'a wide variety of normative modes of organising labour, many that had existed since time out of mind'. In France, by contrast, and as we have discussed above, local regulations remained untouched, and in fact continued to thrive for decades, even as an official liberal discourse was embraced by the central state. As a consequence, while the expansion of 'dishonourable' trades was contained in France, the same trades boomed in capitalist England, where their methods eventually became the new norm.[176]

---

170   Zmolek 2014, pp. 356–7.
171   Rule 1981.
172   Zmolek 2014, p. 358.
173   Zmolek 2014, p. 531.
174   Thompson 1968, p. 222.
175   Zmolek 2014, p. 555.
176   Thompson 1968, p. 278.

As markets were liberalised and customary regulations eroded, English employers gained the opportunity – even as they were also compelled by price competition – to seize control over the organisation of production and to impose a new and productivity-enhancing division of labour within the workplaces that they owned. As Thompson has brilliantly shown, the industrial revolution cannot in any way be reduced to a technological transformation. It represents a fundamentally *political* change – the imposition of a 'new system of power' (both in workplaces and on a broader social scale) attached to a new set of property relations. It entailed a transition not to 'industrialism *tout court*', but to 'industrial *capitalism*', and called for radical and profound social and cultural transformations.[177] New time and work disciplines had to be imposed on labouring people in order to break their old customary habits. Religious figures and organisations eagerly embarked upon an ideological campaign. They published pamphlets and pronounced sermons that condemned 'laziness' and 'indolence'. Schools became places where punctuality, frugality, order and regularity were inculcated in pupils, with the intention of moulding disciplined future workers.[178] It became 'a matter of public-spirited policy' for landowners to drive out smallholders so as to reinforce the market-dependence of labourers. Employers saw that wages remained low – not simply to maximise their profits, but also as a means to 'pare away at supplementary earning' of workers, with the aim of reinforcing social and time discipline.[179] Workers resisted what was for a long time perceived as a deeply alien mode of labouring and of living. They still valued the limitation of their work time and the maximisation of leisure. Yet, according to Thompson, after a few generations, 'they had learned their lesson, that time is money, only too well'.[180]

The British state also played a crucial part in imposing new social property relations and the new labour discipline that came with it. It exercised its coercive powers to sustain the development of the private coercive power of employers in their workshops and factory realms. In Britain, the state acted decisively to maintain and intensify a subordination of labourers that had become intolerable and inapplicable in post-revolutionary France.

In the wake of the Revolution, as we saw, French workers gained new rights: contract breach was decriminalised and subordination at work prohibited. This can be further illustrated by considering the transformed use of the *billet de congé* across the revolutionary divide. Under the Old Regime, the *billet de congé*

---

177 Thompson 1993, p. 382, my emphasis; and 1968, p. 214.
178 Pollard 1965, pp. 192–6; Thompson 1968, pp. 441–56; and 1993, pp. 383–94.
179 Thompson 1968, pp. 243–4.
180 Thompson 1993, p. 390.

was a document used as an instrument of control by employers. Workers had to hand over this document to their employer in order to be hired. Holding on to this document until a job had been completed to their satisfaction, employers made sure that workers could not leave them at will. The *billet* was a tool of subordination, since it allowed employers to write down an assessment of their employees that would be considered by the next person to hire them. Falling into disuse during the revolutionary decade, this practice became the object of a widespread debate that led workers, but also bosses and state administrators, to agree that Old Regime rules would not be restored.[181] When the *billet de congé* was reinstated as the *livret ouvrier* by the Napoleonic state in 1803, its function was radically transformed by the application of revolutionary principles of reciprocity and equality to labour relations, under the auspices of tribunals and local authorities.[182] The document had thus lost its disciplinary power, and the law that re-established it was in any case largely ignored by employers and labourers alike.[183] *Prud'hommes* ensured that employers could not retain the *livret*, even in case of conflict with their employee, and labourers no longer faced criminal charges when unilaterally leaving their bosses. Moreover, according to 'a frequently reprinted circular by the Minister of the Interior, Montalivet, in 1809, [employers] were expressly prohibited from making any comment about a worker's performance or ability on the *livret* itself'.[184] Far from restricting it, by acting as a way to establish private contracts (in accordance with customary usages), the *livret* had in fact become a means to facilitate the worker's mobility.[185]

This contrasted sharply with the intensification of penal sanctions imposed on workers by the British state during the industrial revolution. The adoption of the Black Act of 1723 and the rapid growth of a body of criminal law had sustained the sacralisation of private property and the imposition of capitalist landholding that accompanied the peak of Parliamentary enclosures during the last decades of the eighteenth century.[186] The state was by then similarly committed to wielding its coercive powers to back the imposition of capitalist property in industry. From 1766 to 1823, jail sentences and measures against insubordination, along with restrictions on workers unilaterally leaving their employers, were gathered under the *Law of Master and Servant*. These were

---

181   Cottereau 2006, p. 106.
182   Guicheteau 2014, p. 172.
183   Fombonne 2001, pp. 58–60.
184   Sonenscher 1989, p. 368.
185   Cottereau 2006, p. 108.
186   Hay et al. 2011; Thompson 1975; Zmolek 2014, pp. 520–8.

further reinforced and perpetuated until their final abolition in 1875, after decades of struggles waged by labour unions. As explained by Robert J. Steinfeld:

> [u]nder the 1823 Master and Servant Act, English employers could have their workmen sent to the house of correction and held at hard labor for up to three months for breaches of their labor agreements. Actions that exposed a worker to criminal sanctions included not only quitting before one had served out one's term or one's notice but also temporarily absenting oneself from work for a day or an afternoon or merely being neglectful or disobedient at work. Other statutes subjected cottage workers to fines or imprisonment for failing to finish work timely. The 1823 act contained broad language that could be read to cover the overwhelming majority of manual wage workers.[187]

The rise of free markets in England did not entail free labour. Justices of the peace routinely imposed sanctions to undisciplined labourers. Upper echelons of the judiciary system also played their part. As Douglas Hay explains, '[t]he triumph of free market ideology in the high courts in the early nineteenth century also seems to have increased the importance of master and servant at this time'.[188] As capitalist industrialisation unfolded, a strengthening of the judiciary control of the labour force took place and,

> between about 1750 and 1850 there was a marked change in the application of the law. Sentences became longer, and were increasingly likely to be served in the prisons and jails of the new carceral regime prescribed by reformers of criminal punishments. Between about 1790 and 1820 there was a marked per capita increase in the use of penal sanctions, probably followed by stability (with fluctuations around the trend) for much of the rest of the century.[189]

Employers benefited from these restrictions on labour mobility that allowed them to retain workers at a cheaper rate during periods of low unemployment and tight labour markets.[190] But even more fundamentally, restricted mobility,

---

187   Steinfeld 2001, pp. 47–8.
188   Hay 2004, pp. 114–15.
189   Hay 2000, pp. 263–4; see also Hay 2004, p. 115.
190   Steinfeld 2001, pp. 57–72.

punishment of labour insubordination, and legal injunctions to accept time-discipline at work supported the employers' exertions to take over the organisation of labour processes.

British industrial employers were compelled to become *capitalist* entrepreneurs as they increasingly became 'acutely conscious of the dangerous competitive environment within which they operated'.[191] To improve their competitiveness, they devised divisions of labour that enhanced the productivity of the labour they hired. Workers, however, fiercely resisted the new time discipline imposed upon them by incipient capitalists. In the face of this resistance, the coercive support of the state came in handy, sustaining the employers' endeavour to develop their own disciplinary institutions within their workplaces. To stay afloat in his competitive environment, a British industrialist had to become a 'disciplinarian' and 'a supervisor of every detail of work'. This amounted to acquiring 'new powers which were of great social significance'.[192]

During the second half of the eighteenth century, Josiah Wedgewood famously introduced a sophisticated division of labour in his pottery workshops. For this, without relying on any substantial mechanical innovation, Wedgewood had to impose a rigorous discipline, detailed instructions on how to perform different tasks, and fines in case of violation.[193] Likewise, Richard Arkwright, best known for the invention of the water frame, considered as his greatest accomplishment the development of the first 'factory system', involving the development of a 'rational' organisation of labour and the adoption of disciplined work habits by workers.[194] Cotton factories in the Midlands rapidly implemented many of the labour-discipline techniques designed by Arkwright and others.[195] Competitive imperatives ensured that Wedgewood's innovative labour management methods also spread rapidly within the pottery trade. Similar labour management systems were diffused in many other trades over the first phase of the industrial revolution, including iron-making, coal-mining, glass-making, the brewing industry, button-making, engine-making, and so on.

This diffusion signalled 'the beginnings of scientific management and cost accounting' in England.[196] The new capitalist management called for the development of hierarchical supervisory structures within workplaces. The intro-

---

191   Pollard 1965, p. 258.
192   Pollard 1965, p. 185.
193   Pollard 1965, p. 265; Zmolek 2014, pp. 409–12.
194   Pollard 1965, p. 184.
195   Zmolek 2014, p. 451.
196   Pollard 1965, p. 261.

duction of managers and of wage-earning and loyal foremen by capitalist bosses became essential and widespread.[197] Meanwhile, these supervisory structures – contributing significantly to the subsumption of labour by capital – remained absent in France.

Until the end of the nineteenth century, French workers preserved their autonomy and largely controlled the organisation and rhythm of their labour, not only in their houses (as domestic outworkers) and in small workshops, but also in larger workplaces. As Philippe Lefebvre points out, to the strong autonomy of workers corresponded the very feeble hierarchy of workplaces.[198] The fact that French workers had so successfully opposed insubordination left very limited room for manoeuvre to employers when it came to designing supervisory structures. This was true in urban artisan workshops.[199] Domestic workers, whether weavers, blacksmiths or other trades people, also remained in control of the organisation of their tasks and production techniques.[200] Indeed, until the coming of a sweating system in weaving during the last third of the nineteenth century, domestic weavers experienced a 'golden age'. They welcomed the so-called 'proto-industrialisation' of the countryside as a way to supplement their family income and, while remaining 'their own masters with respect to the means of production, [they] sought to maintain a moderate rate, preferring leisure to additional income'.[201]

This was true in big mechanised factories too. Indeed, the depiction of pre-Third Republic factories as places of bondage is a myth.[202] In France, factories remained spaces where workers, sometimes involved in different trades, were brought together for the fabrication of a product without their labouring activities – previously performed at home or in smaller workshops – being much affected by this new setting. Textile weavers, for instance, remained largely in control of their labour, and their commercial relationship with merchants were in many cases similar to that which existed in the context of rural putting-out systems.[203]

Traditional work methods and forms of apprenticeship were reproduced and adapted in a situation of relatively slow technological change.[204] Until the late nineteenth century, elaborated divisions of labour remained unheard-of

---

197   Pollard 1965, pp. 266, 270.
198   Lefebvre 2009, p. 54; see also Fureix and Jarrige 2015, p. 82.
199   Cottereau 1986, pp. 132–3; Perrot 1986, pp. 81–2.
200   Lequin 1983, p. 423.
201   Perrot 1986, p. 75.
202   Cottereau 1986, pp. 133–4; Jarrige and Chalmin 2008, p. 55; Lefebvre 2003, p. 16.
203   Reddy 1979.
204   Lefebvre 2003, pp. 102–3; Lequin 1983, pp. 424–5.

in large factories.[205] This was true for weaving as well as for metal production, mining, mechanical construction factories, and other industrial sectors,
where workers performed what often remained quasi-artisanal labour, either
individually or as part of a team.[206] The division of labour brought about by
England's capitalist industrial revolution was still absent in France, where the
relatively few factories that were built did not bring about a transformation of
work, but instead (as a rule) only a concentration of labour, as workers were
massed together under one roof to perform the same tasks in parallel.

In larger factories, smaller workshops, or domestic work, hierarchical supervisory structures remained weak. *Contre-maîtres*, or foremen, hired by merchants were few and far between. Foremen had to oversee the work of a great
number of workers. For instance, the thirty-four foremen of St-Quentin's textile branch, in northern France, had to provide raw materials to, and to collect woven pieces from, nearly four thousand looms dispersed throughout the
countryside.[207] Even when attached to specific plants, foremen were acting
less as disciplinary figures at the behest of facility owners than as 'engineers',
ensuring machine maintenance and trying to plan the disposition of machines
in the factory space.[208] They were not disciplinary figures seeking to control
labour so as to enhance its productivity. On occasion, foremen even sided with
workers in rejecting internal factory rules that had been unilaterally initiated by
owners.[209] They were generally hostile to the adoption of new production processes, and, when trying to impose such transformations, they often faced fierce
resistance from workers.[210] Overall, French factories were not rationalised and
compartmentalised working spaces until the turn of the twentieth century.[211]

In the absence of top-down supervisory structures, workers essentially self-
managed their labour. As a rule, a more experienced or accomplished worker
selected by his or her peers led teams of workers.[212] Here again, these individuals were not serving the workshop or factory owner's interests. On the

---

205 Lefebvre 2009, p. 54.
206 To be sure, sophisticated divisions of labour between workshops existed in many *fab-
     riques*, such as in the Lyon silk trade. These networks, however, were not organised through
     market competition, nor did they entail the development of supervisory and disciplinary
     structures of a capitalist type. They were as a rule coordinated through collective, if often
     tense, efforts facilitated by different regulatory institutions.
207 Jarrige and Chalmin 2008, p. 48.
208 Lefebvre 2003, pp. 61, 63, 99; Lequin 1983, p. 425.
209 Jarrige and Chalmin 2008, p. 56.
210 Lefebvre 2003, pp. 63, 130.
211 Perrot 1983, p. 5.
212 Lequin 1983, p. 425.

contrary, they were the guardians of their fellow workers' autonomy. Illustrating this point, a textile factory investigator noted around the mid-nineteenth century that 'the great organizing autonomy of workers: they establish rules themselves, enforced them and designate their chiefs themselves'.[213] The same investigator described textile factories in the Rouen region, reporting that 'each room, whatever the number of looms, has a chief which is always the oldest worker, is called the *curé*. The authority of this chief, which expires at the factory door, consists in maintaining order as the workers have conceived it, to ensure the execution of diverse measures determined by them'.[214] Similar structures of self-regulation of labour were the rule across French industry throughout most of the century.[215]

French workers had not yet internalised capitalist time-oriented work-discipline.[216] Nor had they developed an 'acquisitive mind' – as they would under capitalism. Most were paid by the task, controlled their own work schedule and level of income.[217] Absenteeism was widespread (even among foremen) and many contemporary witness accounts noted the time spent by workers away from work, 'apparently doing nothing, at the coffeehouse, in the street'.[218] Moreover, French industrialisation largely took root in and spread across the countryside, and factories and workshops hired workers who were also peasants. These would also have to engage in farm labour, which they typically prioritised. Yearly industrial work schedules were thus deeply affected by harvest cycles, and were punctuated by numerous holidays.[219] As mentioned earlier, idleness on 'Saint Monday' was also a quasi-universal practice in most trades.[220]

Workdays were long, often stretching up to 12 to 16 hours in most branches.[221] Such extensive workdays had also been the rule in medieval times and over the

---

213   Quoted in Lefebvre 2003, p. 60: 'la grande autonomie d'organisation des ouvriers: ils établissent eux-mêmes leurs règles, se chargent de les faire respecter et *se dotent eux-mêmes de leur chef*'.

214   Ibid.: '*chaque salle*, quel que soit le nombre des métiers, *a un chef qui est toujours l'ouvrier le plus ancien et qu'on appelle le curé*. L'autorité de ce chef, qui expire au seuil de la fabrique, consiste à maintenir l'ordre tel que les ouvriers l'ont conçu, à assurer l'exécution des diverses mesures arrêtées entre eux'.

215   Lefebvre 2003, p. 102.

216   Fombonne 2001, p. 87. On capitalist work-discipline, see Thompson 1993, pp. 352–403.

217   Noiriel 1986, pp. 55, 60; Perrot 1986, p. 75.

218   Jarrige and Chalmin 2008, p. 58; Lequin 1983, p. 423: 'en apparence à ne rien faire, au café, dans la rue'.

219   Bourdieu and Reynaud 2004, p. 21; Fombonne 2001, p. 86.

220   Fombonne 2001, pp. 87–8.

221   Bourdieu and Reynaud 2004, p. 20.

early modern period.[222] The persistence of long workdays into the nineteenth century was not evidence of the establishment of factory discipline. Working exceedingly long hours was in fact characteristic of self-exploiting domestic outdoor workers – more than it was of factory workers – who used weaving or other crafts as ways of supplementing their family incomes.[223] In the factory as in the cottage, however, workers tolerated long hours because they controlled the pace of their labour. Breaks were frequent and often lengthy.[224] Factories were fence-free, open spaces, where workers could enter and exit at will.[225] The workplace was overall a congenial environment.[226] Commenting on early nineteenth-century factory life, the worker Norbert Truquin noted in his *mémoires* that workers 'told stories and performed theatre plays; jokers improvised religious sermons; time went by cheerfully'.[227] By the mid-nineteenth century, the most forward-thinking French employers and entrepreneurs were perfectly conscious of the contrast with English factories, in which strict order and silence reigned.[228]

This extensive autonomy at work, even in the larger mills, was associated with the preservation of *merchant relationships* between factory owners, *négociants* and their agents, on the one hand, and the direct producers, on the other.[229] Hiring generally took the form of a *marchandage*. Factory textile workers, for instance, would rent access to a loom and other tools in a mill owned by a merchant, perform their work, and then resell their products to the foremen. Hiring entailed negotiations, either with a leader or a whole team, to establish fees for using machines, tasks to be accomplished, as well as piece rates (within a regulatory context policed by *prud'hommes* and municipal authorities). This commissioning of labour by merchants had not changed in any fundamental way since the development of the commercial putting-out system under the Old Regime – it had simply been transferred to larger mills.

---

222   Martin Saint-Léon 1922, pp. 136–40.
223   Bourdieu and Reynaud 2004, pp. 29–30.
224   Reddy 1984, p. 118.
225   Perrot 1983, p. 6. Perrot mentions that women and children freely entered factories to deliver their lunches to workers. Vagabonds also entered the factory walls to escape cold temperatures and to warm up by the ovens.
226   Lequin 1983, p. 423.
227   Quoted in Noiriel 1986, p. 38: 'on racontait des histoires, des pièces de théâtre; des loustics improvisant une chaire s'amusaient à prêcher; le temps passait gaiement'. See also Perrot 1986, p. 83.
228   Perrot 1983, p. 6.
229   Lefebvre 2003, p. 65, emphasis added: 'continuaient de s'en tenir à des rapports marchands avec les ouvriers'.

Furthermore, these had not displaced widespread cottage production, which had survived the arrival of steam-powered looms, and remained in place until the last decades of the nineteenth century.[230]

Through their foremen, merchants were also still dealing with individual domestic workers or groups of labourers within small urban workshops. Similar systems of hiring were also in place in other industrial sectors and in mining. All of this was in keeping with *louage d'ouvrage*, discussed above, which prevented subordination at work and was intended to preserve a relationship of reciprocity between employers and workers. Reddy notes that the standard practice was 'to treat spinners as if they were independent operators who sold the *product* of their labor, not labor itself'; and he adds that 'nowhere [was] there any actual buying or selling of "labor" as so obviously happens in the present day when one punches a time clock'.[231] With the intention of defraying what had sometimes been quite heavy investments in equipements, employers did develop systems of fines, and on occasion different 'incentive pay schemes', to encroach on this pattern of employment and remuneration (as they did in Rouen during the early 1830s). Yet, notwithstanding these – often fiercely resisted – efforts, merchant-industrialists continued to pay not for labour but for its outcome until very late in the century.[232] As Lefebvre explains, the collection of fees for equipment usage by factory owners was not *in itself* perceived as a form of exploitation by workers – though, of course, conflicts could and did frequently occur if, for instance, specific fees were deemed too high.[233] Workers understood that these fees were an irritating sign of their independence.

Factory owners, then, did not control the organisation of production. They could not – nor did they wish to – appropriate surplus value (either 'absolute', by intensifying and lengthening the workday and systematically limiting or reducing wages, or 'relative', by increasing labour productivity). As Lefebvre explains, in order for merchant-industrialists to reproduce and to accumulate wealth, 'to organize work was not economically relevant ... In the end, the idea of organizing work was not even envisaged'.[234] Technological innovations did take place, albeit at a relatively slow pace. But, overall, merchant-industrialists did not attempt to develop their productive forces by reorganising work and adopting new technologies in order to increase productivity – at least not as

---

230   Reddy 1979.
231   Reddy 1979, p. 207.
232   Reddy 1984, p. 119, 124, 136.
233   Lefebvre 2003, p. 65.
234   Lefebvre 2003, pp. 130–1: 'organiser le travail n'était pas économiquement pertinent ... Au total, l'idée d'organiser le travail n'était même pas envisagée'.

systematically as British industrialists did. Indeed, Perrot notes that French factory and workshop owners possessed no 'true productivity policy' during this period.[235]

Commenting on the behaviour of steel mill owners, Achille Chaper – himself the son of an industrialist, but also a polytechnician and 'enlightened administrator' – asserted that they had 'no theory to guide them', and that they 'bought ore and coal at the lowest price possible, sold the iron back at the highest price possible, and that was all'.[236] This was also true in other industrial sectors. French industrialists remained essentially merchants – they had a 'mercantile and speculative vision of profit',[237] which they did not associate with control over the organisation of work. Their success was still overwhelmingly rooted not in production, but in commodity circulation – in the art of buying and selling.[238]

Lefebvre relates this lack of concern with the organisation of production among French employers to a corresponding lack of 'sufficient competition forcing owners to pay attention to production costs'.[239] Merchants and industrialists did not face the imperatives of market competition, and they did not need, in order to stay in business and to socially reproduce themselves, to systematically maximise their profits through constant reorganisation of production. This absence of capitalist market imperatives is related to factors discussed in the previous chapter – the lack of an integrated competitive national market; protection from British capitalist competition – as well as to the persistence of normative social regulation of production in post-revolutionary France. These normative regulations remained necessary, as they played a crucial role in coordinating economic activities in the absence of 'self-regulated' markets. Normative regulations and the institutions that supported and enforced them are probably better described as alternatives rather than as obstacles to capitalist social relations of production.

In the absence of capitalist markets and price competition, and with the perpetuation of normative regulations of social relations of production, employers were not compelled – and in any case were not able – to act as capitalists overseeing the production of surplus-value by directly organising the work process.

---

235   Perrot 1974, p. 275.
236   Quoted in Lequin 1983, p. 209: 'aucune théorie pour les guider'; 'achetaient des minerais et du charbon au meilleur marché possible, revendaient la fonte et le fer au plus haut prix possible, et c'était tout'.
237   Lefebvre 2003, p. 132: 'une vision marchande et spéculative du profit'.
238   Hirsch 1985, p. 28; Lefebvre 2003, p. 132.
239   Lefebvre 2003, p. 131: 'concurrence suffisante pour devoir prêter grande attention aux coûts de fabrication'.

Surplus extraction took a non-capitalist, mainly extra-economic form, and this shaped the making of the working class in France in fundamental ways.

The Rise of the French Working Class: Republican and Socialist Struggles against Extra-Economic Exploitation

How does the formation of the French working class fit into the social and economic context described in the preceding chapters? We are facing an apparent paradox identified long ago by Ernest Labrousse. How is it, Labrousse asked, that, while industrial development had been relatively slower in France – where, he maintained, an 'ancient regime economy' remained in place until the mid-nineteenth century – it was nonetheless in this country that the working class had been most vibrant and politically radical throughout the nineteenth century?[1] Taking note of this paradox, two types of explanations of the making of the French working class have become dominant in recent years and will be discussed below. While some authors borrow from both explanatory strategies, the first one focuses on the effect of a transforming political culture, while the second emphasises a material context characterised by the rise of artisan capitalism, out of which there developed class-based solidarities.

In this chapter, I offer an alternative perspective on the making of the working class in France that derives from the argument developed in the preceding chapters. While recognising the crucial causal importance of the 'political culture' and institutions developed by French workers before and during the French revolution, I refuse to follow the 'discursive' or 'cultural' turn that has led many historians and social scientists to perceive language and culture as the disembodied creators of class and other social identities.[2] I remain faith-

---

1　Labrousse 1954. As noted by Tombs (1996, p. 267), it is true that historians now accept that deriving the emergence of a self-conscious and organised working class from the development of large-scale factory production is also unsatisfactory in the British case. In his classic study of the making of the working class in England, E.P. Thompson (1968) had already noted how this process was underpinned by a *capitalist* transformation of English society that included the rise of factory production, but also had much wider effects on the artisanal and agrarian sectors of the economy and had a broader social, cultural and political impact. Still, the pace of economic change in France was remarkably slower, and this implies specific problems for the study of the working class in this country.

2　Patrick Joyce (1991), Joan W. Scott (1988) and Gareth Stedman Jones (1983) are influential advocates of the linguistic turn. For a discussion of theoretical debates in the fields of social and labour history in the wake of the linguistic turn, see Berlanstein 1993; Eley and Nield 2007.

ful to the approach developed by E.P. Thompson, who studied working classes as processes and relationships actively made by workers experiencing a given material context – fundamentally characterised by a given mode of exploitive production – that exercises pressures and imposes (potentially contested) limits on their agency.[3] Even in the absence of sustained industrial development, the material context in which French workers united to defend their collective interests still matters, just as it would in any other time and place. The question is then to identify the nature of this material context and to observe how workers reacted to, and were in turn influenced by, the nature of the material constraints that they faced. To provide an answer to this question is the aim of this chapter.

The main argument will be that the material context in which French workers came to think of themselves and to act as a class was not capitalist in nature. This new class-consciousness developed in opposition to a ruling class of notables – which included merchant and finance 'capitalists'[4] – that relied on non-capitalist modes of surplus extraction, appropriated mainly 'proprietary' wealth, and monopolised access to the state as a direct lever of exploitation. What had changed was neither the mode of exploitation nor the mode of production but rather, first, the relationship that workers established between themselves within the 'intermediary publics' of their trades in the wake of the Revolution, and, second, their perception of what the state was (a tool of exploitation) and especially of what it ought to be (a democratic vector of solidarity). From the 1830s, undergoing a deep process of politicisation, French workers adopted a republican agenda and struggled for a democratic and social republic, seeking to rip the state out of the notables' hands and to use it to consolidate and expand the gains made during and following the 1789 revolution, in terms of normative regulation of their social relations of production. It was in facing a class of *notables*, whose existence was premised on non-capitalist strategies of reproduction, and in trying to take over the state that they controlled, that French workers discovered their shared interests beyond trade-based solidarities.

To support this argument, this chapter will first portray the composition of the French working class during the first half of the nineteenth century

---

3   Thompson 1968; 1978.
4   I use 'capitalist' in quotation marks here for two reasons. First to reflect the fact that workers (and others) did refer to the owners of financial capital and to large merchants as 'capitalists' at the time. But also to underline the fact that these economic actors were *not* the profit-maximising capitalists described by Marx (or indeed by Weber, in his analysis of *modern* capitalists).

and will offer an explanation of the first emergence of working-class solidarities in France. Then a section will discuss the perpetuation of non-capitalist patterns of surplus extraction in post-revolutionary France, while insisting on the crucial role of the state in the reproduction of relations of class exploitation. To highlight its specificities, the French mode of exploitation will again be contrasted with the British case. We will then see how workers perceived this class exploitation and identified their class antagonists. The analysis will set the scene for a discussion of the first manifestations of working-class consciousness in the wake of the revolution of July 1830 and in relation to the rapid growth and evolution of the republican movement. We will then conclude with an assessment of the maturation of this class-consciousness, which was expressed through efforts to transform the state from below in order to consolidate and to develop institutions that upheld the moral economy of the working class under the Second Republic.

1   The Composition and the Making of the French Working Class

Whatever meaning we want to assign to the French Revolution of 1789, it is beyond doubt that it did not give birth to a modern working class tied to large-scale factory production.[5] The Revolution actually rooted the French people in the countryside for over a century.[6] On the eve of 1789, British agronomist Arthur Young was shocked by the vast number of small agricultural producers toiling on miniscule plots across France, in sharp contrast to his native England, where agrarian capitalism had made small landowners a much rarer occurrence. The sale of *biens nationaux* (church, royal and noble land properties confiscated during the Revolution) only strengthened this phenomenon. The confiscated land was mostly bought by rich urban investors and large landowners, but considerable amounts were eventually resold to small peasant farmers over the following decades.[7]

No rural exodus took place in the wake of the Revolution. The number of rural workers permanently moving to towns and cities remained limited until the late nineteenth century, and the absolute size of the rural population continued to increase.[8] It is probable that the population movement from rural to urban settings had in fact been faster over the eighteenth century than during

5   Noiriel 1986, p. 60.
6   Calhoun 1983, p. 495; Guicheteau 2014, p. 189; Tombs 1996, p. 269.
7   Tombs 1996, p. 269.
8   Marchand and Thélot 1991, p. 23.

the first part of the nineteenth century. Even though the urbanisation rate grew slowly from 19 percent in 1806 to 24 percent in 1846, the rural population actually increased in absolute terms over this period. So did the agricultural labour force, which numbered 900,000 new individuals by the mid-1840s.[9]

This consolidation of the rural population in the wake of the Revolution had important consequences for nineteenth-century French social structures. The weight of peasants in the overall labour force was much more important in France than it was in Britain, and eventually in Germany.[10] Another crucial and related consequence was that the French working class largely developed in a rural setting. Until the last decades of the century, industrial French workers and peasants did not form neatly distinguished social groups. They were part of a broader labouring class that, even as late as the 1860s, comprised a majority of about 7.3 million primarily agricultural workers.[11] A census realised in 1866, which, according to Noiriel, is considered the most accurate of the nineteenth century, suggests that there were around 4.1 million French industrial workers, including 1.3 million master-employers, out of a total population of around 38 million.[12]

These figures however, must be taken with a grain of salt. And not only because nineteenth-century censuses are often unreliable and their professional categories blurry, but also, indeed mostly, because vast numbers of agricultural labourers were also part-time industrial workers, while most industrial workers could be found toiling on the land during at least part of the year. Many peasants possessed holdings that were too small to sustain their families, and consequently had to work as wage labourers on larger domains for some portion of each year. Most agricultural wage labourers, as well as farmers and sharecroppers, possessed at least a small plot of land of their own.[13] Yet, 'the smallness of holdings meant that much farm work was only part-time: women and men had other occupations to keep the "household economy" functioning'.[14] This versatility of French peasants and workers was a key characteristic of their class.[15]

---

9   Ibid.
10   Marchand and Thélot 1991, p. 26.
11   Tombs 1996, p. 269.
12   Noiriel 1986, p. 13. According to the 1851 census, however, 4.7 million industrial workers in France – including 1.5 million masters – belonged to small artisanal enterprises, while 1.2 million workers belonged to larger industrial enterprises of 10 employees or more (Guicheteau 2014, p. 189).
13   Marchand and Thélot 1991, p. 89.
14   Tombs 1996, p. 269.
15   Guicheteau 2014, p. 191.

There was a deep interpenetration of agricultural and industrial activities.[16] Peasants routinely engaged in industrial activities, either at home or in rural factories and workshops. The case of the thousands of Massif Central inhabitants that left their region for a few months at the beginning of each year, to be hired as construction workers in Paris or Lyon, is illustrative of the broader pattern of seasonal migration in which many French agricultural workers engaged at the time.[17] For most of the nineteenth century, the industrialisation of France took place through the extension of industrial activities in the countryside.[18] This was the case, of course, for the dominant industrial activity of the period, textile production, which produced around fifty percent of the national industrial added value, and in which around sixty percent of industrial workers were engaged.[19] The same was true in the case of metal production, which was scattered across the countryside and often involved small independent rural black-smiths.[20] Even large workshops and metal factories mostly hired peasants.[21]

For industrial workers in general, factory labour was often only a complementary activity, in which they engaged exclusively during the off-season.[22] As a rule, most workers hired by large-scale industrial enterprises were peasants.[23] When hands were needed on the land, workers left the manufactures. Factory production peaked when harvests were done and workers were no longer on the land, and, as a result, the monthly labour force of factories fluctuated greatly, by an average of 38 percent, until the last decades of the nineteenth century.[24]

Factory workers wanted to preserve their access to the land and, as a rule, had a strong 'hunger to buy land that industrial earnings helped to feed'.[25] As a result, 'landownership among industrial workers actually increased over the century'.[26] Working in a factory 'was not a permanent condition or one that separated industrial workers from the rest of the rural community as an indus-

---

16   Marchand and Thélot 1991, pp. 136–8.
17   Marchand and Thélot 1991, p. 136; Noiriel 1986, p. 51.
18   Noiriel 1986, pp. 33–5.
19   Guicheteau 2014, p. 191; Marchand and Thélot, p. 45.
20   Guicheteau 2014, p. 196.
21   Noiriel 1986, pp. 34, 52.
22   Noiriel 1986, pp. 39, 49.
23   Tombs 1996, p. 270.
24   Marchand and Thélot 1991, p. 139; Noiriel 1986, p. 65.
25   Tombs 1996, p. 270.
26   Ibid.

trial "working class".[27] For most of the nineteenth century, women and men active as industrial workers 'were determined to preserve their ways of working that allowed them to keep their ties with the land ... Time and again, the offer of higher wages did not change their minds; nor did the threat of lay-off or dismissal'.[28] French workers had not yet evolved an acquisitive mindset. Their popular culture valued multi-activity and led them to seek self-subsistence on the land.[29]

The most important division that existed among labouring people did not oppose a proletariat and a peasantry, but rather urban and rural workers. Yet, our appreciation of this division should be nuanced. Firstly, as mentioned above, considerable numbers of urban workers were in fact seasonally migrating from the countryside. Secondly, the industrial networks or *fabrique* overseen by *négociants* across the different regional economies of France occupied both urban and rural workers.[30] While they offered cheaper labour, rural producers relied on *prud'hommes* and other institutions to preserve the normative regulations of their industrial activities, just as did their urban counterparts.

Still, it is true that urban workers were as a rule qualified artisans, often engaged in small-scale skilled industrial work. As Tombs notes, 'urban crafts *métiers* had strong corporate identities, developed by heredity of occupation (in Paris in the 1860s, in several trades over 70 per cent of sons followed their father's footstep), geographical concentration, long apprenticeships, rituals, oral traditions, lavish collective festivities, a high degree of literacy and politicization, self-help organizations and distinctive costumes'.[31] Because of these relatively stronger trade-based collective identities, urban craft workers were often at the vanguard of political struggles and played a key role in the making of their class. But these strong identities also divided urban workers from rural workers and implied divisions between urban trades. French workers developed class solidarities by overcoming both types of division.

Just as divisions among trades remained strong before the rise of broader working-class solidarities at the turn of the 1830s, no permanent or systematic opposition existed between employers and employees *within* trades during most of the nineteenth century. Employers and employees laboured side by side in small workshops and 'as in the case of rural workers, wage earning was

---

27   Ibid.
28   Tombs 1996, pp. 270–1.
29   Noiriel 1986, pp. 61–2.
30   Guicheteau 2014, p. 190.
31   Tombs 1996, p. 271.

(or was intended to be) a periodic condition, often a stage in a craftsman's career, or a necessity imposed by hard times'.[32] In 1831, there were 2.6 million independent artisan workers in France, amounting to 48 percent of all non-agricultural workers. Their number grew by 0.6 percent on a yearly basis until 1866.[33]

Only a minority of these industrial workers were grouped in factories, while most belonged to *fabriques* – a very old way of organising an industrial trade by connecting dispersed and specialised small workshops and domestic workers in a regional or municipal division of labour that continued to flourish in post-revolutionary France. These networks often spilled into the countryside (even in the case of Parisian trades) and were organised by *fabricants*, who placed orders, sometimes with a large number of workshops and individual producers; bought manufactured products at a given rate set by tariffs; and controlled their marketing. *Fabricants* were thus merchants who exercised more or less unrestrained power over chains of production and distribution.[34]

These local and regional networks of production were hierarchically organised. Occupying a position of power, *fabricants* were sometimes small artisans who exercised collective control over the *fabrique*, but were also sometimes large merchants, or *négociants*, who were tied to finance capital and had gained control over a trade in a given region. *Façoniers* were workshop heads who sold products to merchants and hired journeymen and women as well as apprentices. Clashes between workshop owners and their employees were frequent but not yet propelled by systematic market competition.[35] Conflicts between workers (workshop masters and their employees) and merchants were also recurrent and revolved around tariffs (and their enforcement) and credit provided by *fabricants* to chronically indebted workers. These conflicts, however, were not capitalist in nature and did not revolve around the production and appropriation of *surplus value* – a point to which we will come back in the next section.

On the basis of what experience, then, did French workers feel the need to unite as a class during the 1830s and 1840s? Again, in France, at least until the last decade of the Second Empire, there was no massive rural exodus.[36] French workers did not experience what Marx dubbed the 'so called primit-

---

32   Ibid.
33   Marchand and Thélot 1991, p. 96.
34   Faure 1986, pp. 531–5.
35   Focusing on craft production, Harvey (2005, p. 151) notes that 'there was little basis within the small enterprises for strong class antagonisms'.
36   Marchand and Thélot 1991, p. 94.

ive accumulation' that had implied the violent uprooting of English labourers from their land. For decades after the Revolution, France did not go through the 'great transformation' that, according to Polanyi, involves a large-scale commodification of labour (among other processes of commodification). For most of the nineteenth century, no self-regulated labour markets could be found in France.[37]

In the same vein, French workers did not experience any rapid process of deskilling, nor were they rapidly and massively hoarded into large factories until very late in the nineteenth century and the first decades of the twentieth.[38] This was, once more, in sharp contrast to their British counterparts.[39] As an illustration of this disparity, Tombs reminds us that 'the demise of handweaving, which took only ten years in Britain, took 70 in France'.[40] Far from going downhill, scattered rural handweaving actually developed until well past the mid-century mark in France.[41] Broadly speaking, highly-skilled urban craft trades rapidly vanished in Britain from the 1820s, while in France the world of urban workers was dominated by artisanal forms of labour until the 1880s and beyond.[42]

Recognising the blatantly low level of French industrial development during the first half of the nineteenth century, many students of the emergence of the French working class have come to assign much heavier explanatory weight to the impact of a changing political culture, often moving away from a materialist theoretical perspective.[43] The most common argument along these lines is that it was the transformation of politics in the wake of the French revolution, rather than an industrial revolution, that propelled the rise of the labour movement. Thus, as Perrot explains, there now exists 'at least among historians, a fairly high degree of agreement to the effect that, at least in the French case, "class consciousness" has been largely independent of economic structure'.[44] In a country that experienced a relatively slow industrialisation process, the

---

37   Noiriel 1986, p. 60.
38   Guicheteau 2014, p. 216.
39   The point made here is obviously not that all, or even a majority, of British workers entered
      large-scale factory production. It is rather that, from the last decades of the eighteenth
      century, rapidly increasing numbers of workers experienced processes of de-skilling and
      new forms of time-discipline related to a capitalist transformation of the economy even
      outside of large-scale factory production.
40   Tombs 1996, p. 272.
41   Guicheteau 2014, p. 192.
42   Calhoun 1983, p. 490; Lequin 1983; Noiriel 1986, p. 35.
43   See for instance Sonenscher 1989; Judt 2011; Rancière 1981.
44   Perrot 1986, p. 93.

French working class made a relatively early appearance due to 'the impact of political factors and events, more particularly of the revolutions of 1830 and 1848'. Artisans played a crucial role in these political events, and did so in the tradition of *sans-culottisme* that had developed during the first half of the 1790s.[45] The introduction of a new political culture in the wake of 1789 becomes the fundamental factor behind the rise of the working class. Adopting a similar interpretation, Tony Judt insists that the evolution of the French labour movement is 'only contingently identifiable with the overall pattern of employment and industrialization' of post-revolutionary France.[46] No rapid transformation of the country's economic life had taken place, and so the formation of the working class 'can so much better be understood as a response to the *political* history of France'.

Refusing to confine the incubation of the French working class to the political sphere, a number of historians have proposed an alternative explanatory strategy that retains economic transformations as a fundamental causal factor.[47] This economic change, however, was identified not with the emergence of mechanised factories, but rather with a capitalist transformation of small-scale craft production. This is the 'artisan capitalism' thesis that was discussed in the previous chapter.

It is worth considering in some detail the contribution of William H. Sewell, an influential and strong proponent of the artisan capitalism thesis who also took seriously the impact of the new political culture that emerged within the labour movement after 1789. In his *Work & Revolution in France*, Sewell mobilises the work of revisionist economic historians of nineteenth-century France in order to relate the country's specific path of economic development to the particularities of the making of the French working class. He comes to the conclusion that 'class consciousness emerged in France as a transformation of the artisans' corporate understanding of labour under the twin impact of capitalist development and revolutionary politics'.[48]

As we have seen, Sewell believes that the abolition of guilds in 1791 introduced capitalist property of means of production and a liberalised economy in France. In this new economic context, employers could reorganise production in order to seize market opportunities and a radical capitalist transformation of labour processes ensued. Sewell maintains that this transformation created

---

45   Ibid.
46   Judt 2011, pp. 51, 60.
47   See for instance Bezucha 1974; 1983; Johnson 1974; 1975; Sewell 1980; 1986; Aminzade 1993.
48   Sewell 1986, p. 53.

a new class antagonism that divided individuals as property owners, on the one hand, and propertyless 'proletarians', on the other.[49]

According to Sewell, this evolution in production relations was a necessary, but insufficient, condition in the making of a self-conscious working class. Indeed, for several decades following the Revolution, trade divisions remained strong and workers did not immediately develop class solidarities in order to resist the new capitalist form of exploitation that was emerging. The emergence of a working-class consciousness had to wait for the July Revolution of 1830. The latter revived the political discourse of the 1789 Revolution, including the key republican notion of a free association of citizens. As this process unfolded, a self-conscious working class began to flourish. Mobilising the notion of association, workers went beyond a conception of their trades as self-enclosed entities and began to see themselves as citizens that could unite beyond trade boundaries. As Sewell puts it, 'the creation of a class-conscious proletariat ... was a projection to a higher level, of the loyalties that workers in a given trade had long felt for each other. But it was not until workers' corporations were themselves seen as free associations of productive laboring citizens, rather than as distinct corporations devoted to the perfection of a particular craft, that the wider fraternity of all workers became thinkable'.[50]

The explanation of the making of the first version of a self-conscious French working class presented in this chapter diverges from Sewell's on important points. Sewell is certainly right to signal the importance of republicanism and of the concept of citizenship in this process of working-class formation, but his depiction of the context in which these ideas were put forth by workers is misleading. As preceding chapters made clear, there was no capitalist transformation of the French economy – including artisanal production – during the first half of the nineteenth century. As we saw, over this period, French markets were not competitive and French employers did not face capitalist imperatives that would have led them to transform production in the ways suggested by Sewell and others. Moreover, as was amply demonstrated in the previous chapter, 1791 did not at all introduce absolute private property over the means of production as described by Sewell. Normative regulations of trades, and of industrial production more broadly, remained in place. French employers did not gain arbitrary powers over labour processes. French workers actually made new gains during and following the Revolution. They continuously, and often

---

49   Sewell 1980, p. 139.
50   Sewell 1986, p. 63.

successfully, attempted to apply newly acquired rights to their labouring lives in the decades that followed. In the absence of competitive markets, economic activities and trades continued to be organised on the basis of non-capitalist, traditional modes of regulation.

No radical economic transformation, then, can explain the rise of the working class. What had changed, and what explains the emergence of working-class solidarities as well as republican ideas, was the relationship of workers to an exploitive state in an evolving political context characterised by the – highly contentious – development of a public sphere in France in the wake of the Revolution. As has been emphasised by Judt, Perrot, Sonenscher, and others, it is true that the coming of a self-conscious working class had much to do with politics. But we also need to register the fact that post-revolutionary French politics continued to be directly enmeshed in relationships of class exploitation (only not of a capitalist nature). Put another way, superior social status and surplus appropriation by one class at the expense of another was still deeply enmeshed with privileged access to state power in nineteenth-century France. This specific form of politically mediated class antagonism gives us a key to understanding the republican tone of the first self-conscious manifestation of the French working class. And the other key factor is the age-old exploitation of workers by big merchants and financiers – more often than not one and the same – which was now contested in a context where workers had gained new rights and attempted to make social relations of production public and democratic, by consolidating the existing normative regulations of their trades.

The contentious debates around the political economy of the state that emerged in France from the mid-eighteenth century prefigured the country's incipient public space, which would more fully emerge in the first decades of the nineteenth century.[51] As we saw in the first chapter of this book, in reaction to the threat posed by the rising might of Britain, liberal reformists attacked Colbert's heritage and insisted on the benefits of free market mechanisms, while also promoting the rationalisation of the state's administrative structures. The stimulation of public debates emerged in France 'as a political invention appearing in the context of a crisis of absolute authority in which actors within an absolute political system appealed to a "public" beyond as a way of reformulating institutional claims that could no longer be negotiated within the traditional political language'.[52]

---

51   Tucker 1996, p. 76.
52   Baker 1992, p. 192.

Physiocrats, whose reformist initiatives were, as we saw, largely frustrated, played a key part in these debates, and Jürgen Habermas explains that they 'spoke out in favour of an absolutism complemented by a public sphere that was a place of critical activity'.[53] In the last decades of the old regimes, 'pamphlets proliferated on all sides', disseminating (often illegally) both conservative and liberal criticisms of the absolutist monarchy.[54] Yet, 'the literary public sphere of the Enlightenment remained more closely tied to aristocratic society, while the development of a public sphere in the political realm remained relatively rudimentary for much of the century'.[55] While debates raging within this incipient and mostly secretive Old Regime public sphere covered a wide range of economic and administrative matters, they eventually came to revolve fundamentally around issues of taxation and representation that were linked to skyrocketing state debt. An important threshold was crossed with the publication of Necker's *De l'administration des finances de la France* in 1784. Submitting the unknown details of the French state debt to public discussion, Necker breached the absolutist principles of secrecy. As Baker explains, the subsequent convening of the Estates General finally brought about a revolution that would radically open up French public debates during the 1790s.[56]

This deepening of the public sphere – as well as efforts to rationalise the state's administrative structures – largely stemmed from liberal ideology and policies that originated in elite circles, but also from peasant revolts from 1789 to 1793 and the ongoing pressures from below exercised by the *sans-culotterie* of the first republic from 1792 to 1794.[57] Liberal and republican values slowly took root over the following decades, contributing to the expansion of public debates.[58] This public sphere, emerging in the wake of 1789, was importantly circumscribed by severe restrictions on freedom of expression and assembly imposed by the authoritarian government which took power following the Restoration of 1814–15.[59] Still, 'the experience of the Revolution diffused the ideals of equality, justice, nationalism, and appealed to the people as the basis of political sovereignty throughout the population'.[60] Within a cir-

---

53   Habermas 1989, p. 99.
54   Baker 1992, p. 191.
55   Baker 1992, p. 190.
56   Baker 1992, pp. 190–1.
57   Miller 2015, p. 246.
58   Tucker 1996, pp. 77–8.
59   Démier 2000, p. 18.
60   Tucker 1996, p. 75.

cumscribed public sphere, lively debates opposed liberal constitutionalism to notions of active citizenship that were put forward by radical and socialist republicans.[61]

As these transformations unfolded, the private activities of aspiring citizens, and 'the reproduction of their material existence', which had been politically and legally overseen by guilds and parliaments under the Old Regime, 'became publicly relevant' in a new and much expanded way.[62] As asserted by Miller, 'the administrative contact between the state and the economy became a subject of national interest in the nineteenth century. Even some peasants began to evaluate state policy, with regards to taxes, the grain and other issues affecting consumers, in broader terms'.[63] Issues concerning direct producers – including artisans and industrial workers – were also brought under public scrutiny in a much more democratic way.

Cottereau explains how, as trades were 'disincorporated' following the elimination of guilds in 1791, they reconstituted themselves into what he calls 'intermediary publics'.[64] As we saw in the preceding chapter, through institutions such as *prud'hommes* councils, workers established and maintained local usages that regulated their productive activities. Trades were thus collectively administered by workers. *Prud'hommes* (or, where such councils had not yet been created, justices of the peace) established local jurisprudence by means of their conciliatory activities. Their decisions stimulated a collective evaluation of labour (and also broader economic and political) issues. These decisions and debates were guided by principles of justice, brought forward by the Enlightenment, that had been widely diffused during the Revolution, and that were instrumental in the formation of public opinion within each trade. Workers debated decisions and the evolution of their trade's regulation and the local press routinely commented on these decisions and debates.[65]

These usages, and the jurisprudence that concerned them, however, were only locally sanctioned – often by mayors. Unlike eighteenth-century guilds, who were directly part of the corporatist structure of the monarchical state and whose rules were routinely revised and authorised by regional *parlements*, the 'intermediary publics' of nineteenth-century trades were not institutionally backed by authorities reaching beyond local government.[66] Trades, as we saw,

---

61   Tucker 1996, p. 82.
62   Miller 2015, p. 246.
63   Miller 2015, pp. 246–7.
64   Cottereau 2004.
65   Cottereau 2004, p. 60.
66   Cottereau 2004, p. 60; Sonenscher 1989, pp. 370–1. When prefects did intervene, they were

were constituted by a strongly regulated core and by peripheries where workers had constantly to remain vigilant and to organise in order to restrain the
behaviour of malevolent employers and compel them to respect regulations.
As workers organised and struggled to consolidate, expand and to guarantee
the application of their trades' usages over the first decades of the nineteenth
century, they often began to reach out to the state. These collective attempts
to institutionalise normative regulation of productive activities from the bottom up played a key role in the first making of the French working class. As
Sonenscher explains,

> what changed between 1748 and 1848 was not so much the relation-
> ship between workers and employers, or the immediate circumstances in
> which production was carried out, as the identity of the public to which
> actors in conflicts appealed and the manner in which those appeals were
> couched. Instead of lawyers and magistrates, nineteenth-century workers
> and employers addressed other workers or employers and, increasingly,
> their own political intermediaries or representatives.[67]

Over the first half of the nineteenth century, French workers increasingly politicised their struggles to regulate their trades and to improve their working lives.
Trade communities and the 'intermediate publics' to which they gave birth
were thus ends in themselves, but also communities on which workers could
rely to confront the ruling class and its state. As they politicised their struggles,
workers came to confront political leaders and, in the process, developed new
ideas regarding the state and how it ought to be constituted – increasing numbers of workers adhered to republican ideas and developed a class consciousness.

All of this was not simply a matter of 'political culture' – workers had a material class interest to defend here. Their class consciousness did not develop in a
vacuum or out of 'discursive' thin air. It was deeply rooted in a specific mode
of class exploitation in which the French state played a key role, side by side
with big merchants and finance 'capitalists'. As we will now see, the French ruling class relied directly on the state to maintain its status and class privileges.
Its capacity to extract surpluses from the direct producers partly depended on
its capacity to keep exclusive control over the state. Thus, 'government leaders

---

unreliable, and could either upheld normative regulations and usages or decry them from
a liberal perspective.
67   Sonenscher 1989, p. 375.

feared that expanded [electoral] participation might open the way to a republic of the Jacobin sort dreaded since 1793'. As Miller goes on to explain, 'this
rigidity created an explosive political context and openings for further popular
involvement'.[68]

It was largely as a result of experiencing a common state-mediated economic exploitation that workers eventually acquired their particularistic trade
mentality and developed class solidarities. Engaging in this turbulent and politically loaded class struggle, workers adopted a republican ideology. In doing
this, they aimed to take over and to transform the state so that it would no
longer be a tool of class exploitation. They were also planning to use the state
to consolidate and expand the normative regulations of their trades, and to
enforce the rights acquired in the wake of the Revolution in order to circum-
scribe or (in the case of more radical workers) overthrow the power of merchants and financiers. Doing this, they had to fight notables whose vital class
interest it was to maintain their privileged access to the state.

2   Notables, the State, and the Perpetuation of Non-capitalist Surplus
       Appropriation

> Il signifia sa résolution formelle d'habiter Paris.
> – Pour quoi y faire?
> – Rien!
> Mme Moreau, surprise de ses façons, lui demanda ce qu'il voulait devenir.
> – Ministre! répliqua Frédéric.
>
>   FLAUBERT, *L'Éducation sentimentale*

∴

The Revolution of 1789 brought down the curtain upon the Old Regime, but
did so without fundamentally altering social property relations. The Revolution
abolished the fiscal immunities and legal privileges of the nobility, and ended
the venality of offices, while the Declaration of the Rights of Man stated that
all men were equally admissible to public offices. The political regime brought

---

68   Miller 2015, p. 248.

about by the 1814 Restoration, a constitutional monarchy, confirmed these principles. Yet, the eradication of seigneurial rights and new principles of equal access to public employment and 'openness to talent', did not translate into fundamental transformations with regards to class exploitation. In spite of these changes, rentier and state-mediated forms of surplus appropriation that had characterised the Old Regime remained firmly entrenched, and guaranteed the reproduction of a ruling class of *notables*.

We saw in Chapter 1 how the ruling class of the Old Regime favoured what Taylor calls a 'proprietary' kind of wealth embodied in investments in land and urban property, venal offices, state bonds, and annuities, which were often derived from loans to private individuals who were then forced to pay back interest in the form of what was commonly called a *rente*. This proprietary, as opposed to capitalist, wealth (capitalist wealth being derived from the accumulation of surplus value), was linked to patterns of investment that guaranteed relatively low but secured revenues that supported elite families and enshrined their social standing. Taylor explains that 'both before and after the Revolution, the social values of the old elite dominated the status conscious men and women of the wealthy Third Estate. Avid for standing, they had little choice but to pursue it as the aristocracy defined it, and the result was a massive prejudice that diverted *roturier* as well as noble wealth into comparatively proprietary investments'.[69] For decades following the Revolution, most rich bourgeois did not seek to indefinitely increase their fortunes, and in any case preferred safe and steady incomes to risky investments. Social property relations did not compel members of the ruling class to seek endless capital accumulation as an end in itself. Wealth was a means of social standing and of political influence, which was in turn itself a source of wealth.[70]

Tombs explains that 'the very term *bourgeois* was frequently taken to mean only *rentiers* living off their property, not *négociants* engaged in business'.[71] But even rich merchant-bankers, who controlled the country's financial capital, and factory owners were part of, or aspired to join, the select club of notables. Just like the latter, they possessed or sought state position for themselves or for their offspring. They also remained very fond of landholding.[72] Their capital did not stand apart, but was in fact an integral part of the property wealth described here.

---

69   Taylor 1967, p. 472; see also Zeldin 1993, p. 113.
70   Daumard 1993d, pp. 916–17.
71   Tombs 1996, p. 282.
72   Barjot 1995, p. 122; Démier 2000, pp. 48–9.

While until the last decades of the nineteenth century, the French ruling class in general favoured the acquisition of landed property other important forms of proprietary investments also existed. Around 1848, rich French families

> invested about 43 per cent of their wealth in land or houses (two-thirds of it in Paris, one-third in the provinces), they placed about 18 per cent in state bonds, safest after houses, and they lent 15 per cent to individuals. They put only 3.7 per cent in company shares, and 4.5 per cent in the shares of the Bank of France. Retired members of the liberal professions, on average, lent 25 per cent of their wealth to individuals and put 53 per cent in land and houses. Those who were pure *rentiers* with no immovable property at all, lent 44 per cent of their wealth to individuals, put 33 per cent in state bonds but only 5 per cent in company shares.[73]

The proportional weight of land and rentier investments (land rents, private loans to individuals, the acquisition of state bonds, etc.) actually substantially increased in Paris from the Restoration until at least the late 1840s, but overall, the national pattern of wealth investment presented by Zeldin was not fundamentally altered until the last third or even the last two decades of the century.[74]

A striking characteristic of this investment pattern is how little was invested in commercial and industrial enterprises. These enterprises, while not capitalist in nature, offered riskier investment opportunities that were generally avoided by members of the ruling class. Wealthy individuals and families remained, essentially, rentiers, and could expect steady and often bountiful revenues in cash or in kind from *fermages* and *météyages*. Land remained a steady source of income for French elites, and Tombs notes that, 'in 1840, of 57 men nationwide who paid over 10,000 francs in tax, 45 were landowners, six merchants or bankers, and three industrialists'.[75] Land bestowed revenues, but also status: throughout the century, a relationship of dependency similar to that which had existed under the Old Regime was maintained between farmers and sharecropping, on the one hand, and landlords, on the other.[76]

---

73   Zeldin 1993, p. 60.
74   Barjot 1995, p. 121; Daumard 1993c, p. 884; Zeldin 1993, pp. 59–62. By contrast, in Britain, investment related to the development of industrial capitalism became dominant during the second third of the century (Beaud 2010, p. 144).
75   Tombs 1996, p. 281.
76   Daumard 1993b, pp. 834–5.

Lending to individual was also a widespread investment practice, and a lucrative one. But here again, it was also a matter of status. By lending to individuals, one could build up a clan of dependents and develop his social and political influence.[77] Throughout France, the tyranny of usurers was strongly resented by needy peasants and workers, as a form of exploitation quite as severe as that which was associated with the taxation imposed by the state.[78] These two forms of exploitation were in fact often intertwined, and both directly involved governmental agents. Money-lending in the countryside was in large part offered by *trésoriers généraux* – state officials in charge of collecting taxes 'who did more private than public business'.[79] These state-officials 'had a massive amount of business, because they specialised in mortgages on land, long considered the safest of investments, and involving some 500 million francs each year in the 1840s, at a time when the Bank of France was discounting only about 150 million francs of commercial paper'.[80] Since 'the Bank of France refused to give credit beyond three months', and the French banking system was still largely underdeveloped and inadequate, peasants and workers had to rely on *trésoriers généraux* and notaries practising loan sharking in order to satisfy their financial needs.[81]

Trésoriers généraux offered a palpable example of state officials using governmental resources to secure private gains, but they were far from being alone in this position. The French ruling class as a whole still relied on the state for a substantial share of its revenues. Figures presented above show that a considerable share of wealth was invested in state bonds, which yielded interest that was paid by governments out of tax revenues. High state offices were still also highly sought-after and offered superior social ranking and important income sources. The continuity with the Old Regime is here again obvious, and reliance on these forms of extra-economic revenues and marks of social ranking compelled the post-revolutionary French ruling class to assert its exclusive control over state institutions.

A crucial way to assert this control was to limit the franchise. It was not the least of the paradoxes of post-revolutionary French political regimes that, even though both the 1814 and 1830 Charters acknowledged the equality of subjects (under the Restoration), and then of citizens (under the July Monarchy), before the law, political privileges linked to gender and wealth remained well

---

77   Zeldin 1993, p. 60.
78   Zeldin 1993, p. 80.
79   Zeldin 1993, p. 81; see also Pinaud 1990.
80   Zeldin 1993, p. 81.
81   Ibid.

entrenched.[82] Women were altogether excluded from the legally defined body politic. A tax quota limiting the franchise opposed a majority that was excluded from state power, which was monopolised by a tiny minority of rich male proprietors who were entitled to vote. This minority included an even smaller group of individuals who possessed the privilege to run as electoral candidates.[83]

A law adopted in 1817 limited the vote to men paying 300 francs per year in direct tax. Most of these privileged electors, around 89,000 in total, were large landowners. The property qualification to exercise the right to vote was cut down to 200 francs in the wake of the 1830 Revolution, and the electorate swelled to 166,000 – out of population of some 33 million – as a result. Further reforms and the growth of personal fortunes had enlarged the electorate to around 248,000 by the late 1840s, but this still represented only a tiny minority of the country's population. Peasants and workers were of course excluded from the electorate, but significant layers of the middle and lower middle class were also left disfranchised.[84]

The Revolution did not promote the rise of capitalists, but rather that of a new ruling class of *notables* whose members, as we just saw, reproduced themselves in ways strikingly similar to the methods of the Old Regime's elites.[85] The notability mingled a minority of (preeminent) nobles with the high bourgeoisie, who formed the majority of the ruling class.[86] *Notables* controlled the state and used it to reproduce their class domination.

Under the First Empire, Napoleon established a list of 70,000 individuals belonging to the higher bourgeois ranks of the Third Estate in order to create a new stratum of state notables. A high notability gravitated around the central state, above a series of regional and local notabilities articulated with 83 newly instated prefectures as well as local *mairies*. Building this notability,

---

82   Daumard 1993a, pp. 138, 144, 147.

83   Charle 1991, p. 27.

84   Tombs 1996, pp. 102–3.

85   Démier 2000, p. 49; Price 1987, p. 113. As will be explained below, French workers did decry the behaviour of 'capitalists' during the first half of the nineteenth century, but their targets were in fact bankers and *négociants* (large merchants) who controlled the financial resources of the nation. These owners of 'capital' (understood as a stock financial assets) were still very similar to Old Regime bankers and 'merchant capitalists', and had very little to do with *capitalism*, understood as a system where entrepreneurs are compelled by market imperatives to supervise the production of surplus value as a source of unending capital accumulation.

86   Daumard 1993, pp. 942, 955.

Napoleon explicitly made a point of selecting large landowners.[87] Purges performed in the wake of the 1814–15 Restoration made nobles the dominant group of notables, and ensured that they regained control over the top administrative and political functions of the state. New purges following the 1830 Revolution greatly improved the position of the high bourgeoisie within the state. But old nobles retained their preeminent social status and remained a majority among the wealthiest notables of France, with their way of life, their speech and dress mimicked by members of the bourgeois milieu.[88] As official control over noble titles eroded and eventually disappeared, rapidly growing numbers of bourgeois made up titles for themselves, which they paraded in Parisian high society.[89]

Notwithstanding this ascendancy of nobles, the indicator of notability was less *lettre de noblesse* – though the latter still commanded social and political privileges – than land ownership. In addition to being the most important source of notable income, land was a gateway to state power and high office holding. Together with landownership, this privileged access to state power was in fact the fundamental distinguishing characteristic of notables in post-revolutionary France during much of the nineteenth century. Notables established their monopoly over the state through their control of representative institutions and the administration, where they appropriated high offices for themselves.[90] Referring to the work of Charle,[91] Tombs explains that 'those who were important in this society were those "closest to the power of the State"; to be or become a *notable* meant the "seizure of the State and private use of its sovereign power"'.[92]

The basis of the notability's class power was thus its privileged access to, and control over, the state. The venality of offices might have been formally eliminated, but the extra-economic form of surplus appropriation enabled by the state remained. The hunger for positions in the civil service actually became even greater after the Revolution than it was under the Old Regime. Until the end of the nineteenth century, these positions were frantically sought after by individuals from the upper and middle social strata.[93]

---

87   Mooers 1991, pp. 74–5.
88   Daumard 1993b, p. 833; Tombs 1996, p. 284; Zeldin 1993, pp. 17, 19.
89   Daumard 1993e, p. 933; Zeldin 1993, p. 16.
90   Charle 1991, p. 43.
91   Charle 1991.
92   Tombs 1996, p. 99.
93   Zeldin 1993, pp. 113–14.

To be a high-ranking state official conferred power and influence over sub-ordinate public employees, as well as social prestige, exhibited in the form of uniforms, medals and the granting of public honours.[94] It also bestowed exor-bitant stipends. The salaries of high officials were arbitrarily set and tended to vary greatly, but were generally large by any standards. Hence, 'at the end of the July Monarchy, the rewards for those who reached the top were outstanding and placed them among the richest men in the country. Four ambassadors were paid over 150,000 francs a year, 102 civil servants earned over 20,000 francs, and 1,009 over 10,000 francs ... The finances paid best: the director in charge of indirect taxation in a department got between 7,200 and 12,000 francs'.[95] Besides salaries, office-holders could count on other lucrative rewards such as fees levied from the public and different types of bonuses.[96] It was also under-stood that individuals entering higher ranks of the civil service had to be able to rely on other sources of revenues, and so the combined public and private incomes of upper state officials easily dwarfed the average 700 francs earned annually by married workers. Exorbitant public remunerations were not sub-stantially reduced before the coming of the Third Republic. Large and growing numbers of intermediary office-holders also earned relatively high wages and frequently received public honours.[97]

Many top bureaucrats were paid astronomical sums, while junior officials performing similar tasks earned derisory amounts. Some of these high offi-cials pocketed their salaries while hiring substitutes to take charge of their responsibilities. Zeldin notes, for instance, that 'the chief tax-collectors had the privileges of delegating their duties, so that a *receveur particulier des finances*, earning between 15,000 and 20,000 francs (side by side and covering the same area as a sub-prefect earning 3,000 to 4,000), would often appoint a substitute at 1,800 or 2,000'.[98] Many high-ranking officials were thus getting rich without really working, 'but work was not what they were really paid for. This was still a spoil system'.[99] These high-ranking officials were living the life of Parisian leisure sought after by Frédéric Moreau, the central character of Flaubert's *Édu-cation sentimentale*, who, as indicated by the epigraph at the beginning of this

94   Charle 1980, pp. 26–7.
95   Zeldin 1993, pp. 116–17. On the staggering salaries of high-ranking state officials, see also Chagnollaud 1991, p. 66; Daumard 1993c, p. 883.
96   Zeldin 1993, p. 117.
97   Le Bihan 2008, pp. 61–98.
98   Zeldin 1993, p. 117.
99   Ibid.

section, wished to live in the capital doing 'nothing' – which, according to Moreau, could apparently eventually lead to becoming a minister.

Political patronage reminiscent of the Old Regime was still alive and kicking. The distribution of lucrative administrative positions was a key tool for the government, who used it as a way to pacify the parliament and to preserve the loyalty of administrative apparatuses.[100] Arbitrary appointments and favouritism were common practices that played an integral part in the stabilisation and functioning of the political system. Far from being stopped by the 'bourgeois' revolution of 1830, these practices, and the multiplication of positions, actually intensified afterwards, demonstrating once again that the bourgeoisie was much less interested in demolishing the remaining elements of the Old Regime than in integrating the extra-economic channels of enrichment provided by the state.[101]

Daumard states that the mode of office transfer that was in place at the time was one of the clearer indicators of continuity with the pre-revolutionary era.[102] A law adopted in 1816 authorised ministerial officers or their heirs to choose their successors, on condition they could obtain the king's approbation. This practice was denounced – most vehemently in the wake of the 1830 Revolution – as a revival of office venality. Yet, in spite of many press campaign and boisterous parliamentary debates, no reform was adopted, and the practice remained in place. Within the state administration, widespread nepotism and patronage were routinised, and amounted in practice to a revival of the venality of offices.[103] Social connections and networks were by far the most important factor for obtaining higher positions, and office-holders frequently bequeathed these jobs to their relatives.[104] *Grands corps* of state officers and prefectures were filled with sons, nephews and other dependants of politicians. Intermediate and lower-ranking officials also jealously defended their privilege of handing over their offices to their sons.[105] These practices of patronage radically perverted, and in fact made obsolete, the principles of competence and equal access put forth by the Declaration of the Rights of the Man.[106] Meritocracy remained a dead letter – careers had not been opened to talents in the wake of the Revolution.[107]

---

100   Dreyfus 2000, pp. 134–6.
101   Mooers 1991, p. 77.
102   Daumard 1993b, p. 832; see also Charle 1980, p. 12.
103   Daumard 1993b, pp. 832–3.
104   Chagnollaud 1991, pp. 96, 103; Charle 1980, pp. 27, 31, 34–5; Daumard 1993b, p. 837.
105   Kingston 2012, pp. 142–3.
106   Charle 1991, p. 44.
107   Charle 1980, pp. 29, 39; Zeldin 1993 pp. 116, 118.

The consequences of the formal abolition of venal offices, then, should not be overblown. From small localities, all the way up to the apex of the central state, being a notable implied the accumulation of offices. The connection between processes of 'political accumulation' identified by Brenner[108] – the processes in which feudal lords and monarchs were engaged, and which had propelled the development of the French absolutist state – on the one hand, and persisting practices of nepotism and patronage allowing powerful notables to cumulate offices, on the other, is hard to miss. Indeed, it was noted by many contemporaries. As part of their 'politically constituted property', nineteenth-century notables often combined elective offices and administrative positions. This was true at local, regional and national levels, and, in 1840, high office holders occupied 175 out of the 459 seats in the Chamber of Deputies.

Together, the logic of patronage in post-revolutionary French politics and the class interest of notables fuelled a considerable swelling of the state. During the revolutionary period, 'the bureaucracy expanded five times its size ... During the Directory, the bureaucracy as a whole had grown to between 130,000 and 250,000 employees'.[109] The administrative apparatus continued to grow steadily under the Restoration and the July Monarchy, 'both in size and in terms of the resources it consumed. By 1845, the bureaucracy is estimated to have grown as large as 670,000 and to have devoured roughly 20 per cent of the royal budget'.[110] The state's budget grew massively in parallel. Total expenditures reached 900 million francs during the decade following the Restoration, and then rapidly increased, fluctuating between 1,350 and 1,700 million francs during the last five years of the July monarchy.[111] The salaries of bureaucrats greatly contributed to this expansion of the budget. According to Zeldin, around 1848, 'France's financial administration was the largest item in its budget: 89 million went to pay the salaries of financial officials, as against only 62 million for the army, 26 for the navy, 30 for religion, 15 for justice, 7.6 for the ministry of the interior, about 5 each for the foreign office, public works and education, 1.7 for agriculture and commerce, plus 11 million for central administration. This gives some idea of the spoil'.[112]

Observing this expansion of an 'immense bureaucratic and military organisation', Marx recognised it as a crucial nexus of class exploitation in nineteenth-century France, and characterised the state as a 'frightful parasitic

---

108   Brenner 1987a; 1987b; see also Teschke 2003.
109   Mooers 1991, p. 73.
110   Mooers 1991, p. 83.
111   Bonney 1995, p. 359; Bonney 1999, p. 167.
112   Zeldin 1993, p. 117.

body'.[113] He added: 'the *material interest* of the French bourgeoisie is most intimately imbricated precisely with the maintenance of that extensive and highly ramified state machine. It is that machine which provides its surplus population with jobs, and makes up through state salaries for what it cannot pocket in the form of profit, interest, rents and fees'. Crouzet, for its part, speaks of a 'state bourgeoisie' that developed from the revolutionary and imperial era. This bourgeoisie was 'not entrepreneurial' and enriched itself by way of 'privileged relations with the state'. Crouzet adds that, compared to this 'state bourgeoisie', cotton industrialists were no match, in spite of the expansion of their businesses.[114]

The growth of the parasitic state was sustained by efforts that had begun under the *Directory*, and that were continued under the First Empire, to rebuild an efficient and more centralised system of tax collection. This would replace the one that had been left in a state of disarray during the first year of the Revolution.[115] The revolutionary period brought important popular gains on fiscal issues, and a programme of direct taxation that would increase the fiscal contributions of richer citizens was proposed.[116] Indirect taxes on consumer goods were, however, reintroduced by Napoleon as early as 1804, and were renewed after 1815 and again under the July monarchy. This represented a fiscal reaction launched by the ruling class that successfully imposed a regression to Old Regime-like taxation patterns. Again, this was noted by contemporaries, and, in his encyclopedic three-volume *Histoire de l'impôt en France*, published at the end of the Second Empire and during the first years of the Third Republic, the historian Jean Jules Clamageran notes the striking similarity between pre- and post-revolutionary fiscal structures.[117] Asserting their class power during the First Empire and after the Restoration, notables prevented the implement-ation of a direct income tax (which remained absent until the First World War) and were able to limit the size of other direct taxes, thus successfully alleviating their tax burden.[118] The resulting loss of tax revenues was compensated for by the steady increase of indirect taxes on consumer goods over the first half of the nineteenth century. The intended effect of this increase in indirect tax was to force peasants and workers to bear the larger part of the French fiscal burden. In this, the ruling class was very successful: the share of indirect taxes in the

---

113   Marx 1954, p. 104.
114   Crouzet 1989, p. 1200.
115   Miller 2008, pp. 200–2.
116   Frobert 2009, p. 52.
117   Clamageran 1867–76; see also Delalande 2011.
118   Delalande 2011, p. 40.

state's total tax revenues more than doubled from 1816 to 1847.[119] By the end of the July Monarchy, the French state mostly collected indirect taxes, while direct taxes represented only 30 percent of its revenues.[120]

The expansion of the state and its high cost was denounced at the time in political pamphlets and by many novelists, playwrights and caricaturists. Illustrative of the rise of a literary sub-genre, Ymbert's *L'art d'obtenir des places* (1816), *La bureaucratie* (1825), and *Moeurs administratives* (1825), and Balzac's *Les Employés* (1837) and *Physiologie de l'employé* (1841) decried the way in which ministers acted as 'manufacturers' of positions, with which they 'basted' their protégés. From 1815 to 1848, moderate as well as radical republican political pamphlets recurrently denounced the swelling of the state administration. A recurrent argument suggested that this phenomenon – which was widely described as a remnant of the Old-Regime – stemmed from the distribution of positions, aimed at controlling the parliament and at buying votes among a highly restricted electorate. According to many pamphleteers, universal suffrage was the only way to put an end to this institutionalised clientelism.[121]

A radical enlargement of the franchise, however, did not occur again before the Second Republic. In the meantime (and again under the Second Empire and beyond), nepotism and patronage placed important limits upon the rationalisation of the French state. For most of the nineteenth century, the state was clearly lagging behind other modernising European powers.[122] In France, 'no government, and no regime, was willing to rationalize and professionalize the bureaucracy, which despite its Napoleonic reputation and the thorough training of its technical branches (bridges and highways, and mines) was far less well organized by the mid-nineteenth century than that of Germany or Britain'.[123] True, the revolutionary decade of the 1790s had brought enhanced scrutiny of state administrators and the elimination of some of the privileges of administrators that had been enjoyed by aristocrat office-holders under the Old Regime.[124] These developments had stemmed from efforts to rationalise the state bureaucracy, which had been launched under the Old Regime and had been taken over by the deputies of the National Assembly. But it appears, as Rosanvallon suggests, that the Revolution and the First Empire were more suc-

---

119   Caron 2002, pp. 74–5.
120   Bonney 1999, pp. 165–6; Delalande 2011, p. 39.
121   Rosanvallon 1990, pp. 58–60.
122   Charle 1980, p. 12; Rosanvallon 1990, pp. 63–4.
123   Tombs 1996, p. 100.
124   Kingston 2012, p. 149.

cessful in centralising than in rationalising the state administration.[125] Kingston explains that the Revolution led lower and middle-ranking administrators
to assimilate prevailing values of civic professionalism.[126] They also secured a
system of promotion based on seniority. In doing so, however, they obtained
the right to see their sons inherit their offices. Moreover, programmes to regulate the length for which offices could be held, and to improve administrative
performance, which were initiated by some bureau chiefs, proved in the end to
be largely ineffective. Under the First Empire, and for decades afterward, modern standards for recruitment and assessment of employee competence were
absent. Hiring and advancement remained essentially discretionary, and incid-
ental to social and family connections.[127]

Middle and lower-ranking state employees had an ambivalent attitude
toward state modernisation. As much as they might have been enthusiastic
about new civic virtues and notions of careers open to talent when it benefited
them, the majority of these employees often saw measures aimed at rationalising the bureaucracy as a threat to their own advancement and to their capacity to pass on their offices to their sons.[128] The will of leading political figures
to professionalise the bureaucracy was in any case lacking, because the ability
of ministers to keep it under their control depended upon the perpetuation of
old practices of favouritism and arbitrary appointments.[129]

The contrast with Britain is once again evident. The divergent modes of surplus appropriation of England and France had given rise to the gradual emergence of different types of modern states.[130] In England, the rise of agrarian
capitalism saw landlords rely on a new form of absolute private property supporting an 'economic' form of exploitation. As a mode of exploitation, absolute
private property served as an alternative to an absolutist monarchy and its
tax/office structure. Contrary to their French counterpart, 'the English landed
classes had no need to recur to direct, extra-economic compulsion to extract a
surplus. Nor did they require the state to serve them indirectly as an engine of

---

125   Rosanvallon 1990, p. 63.
126   Kingston 2012.
127   Dreyfus 2000, pp. 118, 120.
128   Middle- and lower-ranking employees, for instance, successfully forced the government
      to close the *École d'administration*, just over a year after its opening. This short-lived insti-
      tution, which selected students exclusively among notable circles, had originated out of
      calls to reform the administration that had become frequent from the 1830s (Kingston
      2012, pp. 142–3).
129   Tombs 1996, p. 100.
130   Wood 1991; 2012.

surplus appropriation by political means (tax/office and war)'.[131] While absolutism thrived in France, English monarchs faced stubborn opposition from
capitalist landlords and were frustrated in their attempts to emulate the absolutist state structures of their southern neighbours.

The separation of moments of coercion and of appropriation that characterised the capitalist mode of exploitation prevailing in England announced a
new form of modern sovereignty, as 'Parliament became the locus of centralized state power' in the wake of the 1688 Revolution that put a definite end to
the crown's absolutist aspirations.[132] This process of modernisation entailed a
de-privatisation of state offices and of the civil service, which became responsive to processes of rationalisation. From the end of the seventeenth century and
across the eighteenth century, under the leadership of a Parliament controlled
by landlords, a rapidly modernising administrative edifice was put together. An
increasing number of full-time employees received salaries instead of fees and
standardised patterns of advancement were adopted. The examinations of candidates and the development of training schemes also became frequent. Office
rules and daily and weekly routines were formalised in different departments.
Systems of punishment and rewards were put in place, and it became a frequent practice to resort to parliamentary commissions and inquiries in order
to monitor department performance.[133]

Archaic and modern practices continued to exist side by side within and
across bureaus, and the British state remained 'a mixture of medieval and modern institutions'.[134] This mixed character of the state implied that sinecures
and ineffective officers also remained in place as a result of state patronage.
Favouritism, partisan appointments and administrative purges remained common practices, and were severely disruptive of good government.[135] While it
had lost much of its powers to Parliament, the Crown continued to influence
the latter through political patronage, and 'Old Corruption' grew apace under
the Whig supremacy of the first half of the eighteenth century. Yet, a growing consideration for efficiency progressively took roots in parallel, and would
eventually contribute to severely constrain these practices. Overall, compared

---

131   Brenner 1987b, p. 298. As we saw in Chapter 1, the argument here is not that the Old-Regime
      French ruling class relied primarily on offices as a source of income. Landholding was
      more lucrative. But the state still played a crucial role in the reproduction of the ruling
      class. It offered positions that upheld social status, but also served as a direct nexus of
      extra-economic surplus extraction, through state offices and interests on state loans.
132   Techske 2003, pp. 252–5.
133   Brewer 1989, pp. 53, 57, 69–70.
134   Brewer 1989, p. 58.
135   Brewer 1989, pp. 60–1.

to France and continental Europe, 'politically constituted property' was a much less important dimension of the strategy of reproduction adopted by the British ruling classes, who could rely on an 'economic' form of surplus appropriation on the basis of its capitalist land tenure. Consequently, already during the 1780s, the overall cost of the privileges, sinecures and prerequisites from which inefficient office-holders benefited was at least four times higher in France than they were in Britain.[136] Thereafter, this gap would rapidly widen.

While the post-revolutionary French state quickly swelled, a new wave of rationalisation of the state took place north of the English Channel. In France, the granting of offices and favouritism aimed at controlling legislative assemblies and the bureaucracy intensified under the July Monarchy and reached its apex under the Second Empire.[137] The British state evolved following a visibly different logic over the nineteenth century.

Public spending had actually risen very substantially in Britain over the eighteenth century – by 'some 400 per cent between the Peace of Utrecht (1713) and the Congress of Vienna (1815)'.[138] This increase accompanied the rise of what Brewer has called the 'fiscal-military' state, which allowed Britain to expand its imperial and commercial power so impressively over the period (and largely at the expense of France).[139] This imperial success stemmed from the immense wealth created by agrarian – and from the mid-eighteenth century, industrial – capitalism, but also from the British state's unmatched capacity to collect this wealth and to channel it so as to efficiently support its military enterprises.[140] In other words, as Brewer explains, the 'fiscal-military' state was built on a public administration that was the first to approach (even if in a patchy way) Weberian standards of rationality. Still, as public expenditures and indebtedness peaked as a result of the war for American Independence, and then the Napoleonic wars, dissatisfaction grew and calls to reduce the size and cost of the state were made in both popular and elite milieus.

During the 1780s, an 'Economical Reform' of the state was launched as part of a broader struggle against 'Old Corruption'.[141] This implied a system-

---

136 Brewer 1989, p. 60.
137 Mooers 1991, pp. 77, 181.
138 Harling 2003.
139 Brewer 1989.
140 Its improved capacities to collect wealth also meant that it was much easier and cheaper for the British state to borrow: 'The side-effect of systematized public tax collection and fiscal control was the creation of a superior public credit system. Precisely because tax returns were predictable and secure, creditors had greater incentives to provide loans to the government' (Teschke 2003, p. 253).
141 The 'Old Corruption' denounced by both elite and popular radicals at the turn of the

atic revision of the state administration in order to root out sinecures, reversions (promise of a future sinecure) and inefficient offices, to replace fees
with fixed and standardise salaries, to cut back pensions, and to put an end
to the granting of contracts and of other privileges that aided political patronage. The two main and interrelated objectives of this initiative were to
curb the political patronage that allowed the Crown to maintain an influence
over Parliament, on the one hand, and, on the other, to reduce the cost and
enhance the efficiency of government and of its officials. Again, the desire
to reform the British state along these lines was not new and can be traced
back to 1688 and even earlier.[142] It also needs to be located in the broader
context of the specific mode of *economic* – as opposed to extra-economic,
state-mediated – exploitation that had been developing in early modern England. Still, at the turn of the nineteenth century, the rationalisation of the state
was pursued with renewed urgency in the face of soaring military expenditures.

Commissions were established, reports produced and several pieces of legislations were adopted over the 1780s and 1790s, all contributing to the 'zeal for
retrenchment' that characterised the period.[143] The assault on 'Old Corruption'
continued in the wake of the Napoleonic wars – even as state expenditures
were massively increased by military needs – and over the following decades.
By the late 1820s, achievements were substantial:

> The number of MPs who held places, pensions, and/or sinecures fell from
> some two hundred in 1780, to eighty-nine in 1822, and to sixty in 1833, by
> which time virtually all placemen held efficient offices. The number of
> unregulated sinecures in the central establishment was cut from around
> six hundred in 1780, to some two hundred and fifty in 1810, to ten in 1835.
> While there were about a hundred claims to reversions to civic offices in
> 1809, no new reversions were granted after 1814. The annual cost of pen-
> sions on the various civil lists fell from almost £200,000 in 1809 to £75,000
> in 1830. As sinecures and reversions were gradually abolished or reformed

nineteenth century referred to sinecures and reversions (and other forms of illegitimate
enrichment that represented 'a charge on the public purse') as well as to 'the "political
influence of the crown" – the patronage which the government continued to have at its
disposal to bribe or reward members of parliament, voters, municipal corporations and
the like' (Rubinstein 1983, p. 57). The popular understanding of the phrase tended to be
broader. While also referring to the aforementioned processes, it was used to decry 'systematic political oppression' (Harling 2003, p. 99).

142   Brewer 1989, p. 71.
143   Brewer 1989, p. 71; Dreyfus 2000, pp. 104–8; Ertman 2010, pp. 1003–4; Harling 1996.

from the late 1790s onwards, fees in many of the major departments of the state were pooled together into central funds from which officers were paid strict salaries.[144]

Over the two decades following 1815, as peace returned, but also in considerable part as a result of this process of rationalisation, public spending was cut by 25 percent.[145] Britons were still heavily taxed in absolute terms. But sustained capitalist industrialisation also meant that much more wealth was available for taxation. As a result of both rapid wealth creation and drastic retrenchment in public spending, the proportion of the national product captured by the British state decreased drastically over the nineteenth century. As Harling explains, 'the British central government had absorbed some 30 per cent of gross national product at the height of the Napoleonic War; it was absorbing only 8 percent of it by the 1870s, compared with 13 per cent in France and 12 per cent in the German states'.[146]

The settlement of the 1688 Revolution and the transformation and rationalisation of tax-raising and collection – including the introduction of landlords' self-taxation through Parliament and the abandonment of tax-farming (which had previously led the Crown to sell the right to collect tax) – had turned British fiscal policies into a 'national and relatively conflict-free affair'. As Teschke explains, 'Britain faced neither bankruptcy nor major tax riots during the entire eighteenth century' (in sharp contrast with France).[147] However, at the beginning of the nineteenth century, Bonaparte's extraordinary military might – stemming from levée en masse, which helped build conscript armies out of a patriotic French citizenry – imposed an unprecedented charge on British public finances. State expenditures and indebtedness soared and a highly unpopular income tax was introduced. A petition campaign contributed to the end of income tax shortly after the war. Over subsequent decades, the further economies and retrenchments mentioned above contributed decisively to shifting the nexus of surplus appropriation away from the state and into the 'economic' sphere, and this allowed Peel to reinstate income tax by 1842 (over seven decades before its original introduction in France).[148]

The British state monopolised a lesser part of the national wealth. It also used this share more efficiently, and less of it was earmarked to serve the private

---

144   Harling 2003, pp. 100–1; see also Harling 1996, pp. 16, 20–1, 109–10.
145   Harling 2004, p. 111.
146   Harling 2003, p. 101.
147   Teschke 2003, pp. 261–2.
148   Burg 2004, pp. 323–6.

interests of rich individuals. The sale and purchase of offices was legally banned from 1809.[149] Taken together, reforms aimed at rooting out Old Corruption contributed to 'the gradual acceptance of the notion that public office was not the private property of the officer-holder, but a public trust that should be carried out in person, compensated by strict salary, and superannuated according to an authorized scale of retirement provisions'. In the Victorian era, when the success of these reforms was becoming increasingly evident, if 'politicians had wanted to gorge themselves on the fruits of office, the decline of patronage gave them few chances to do so. But few of them would have wanted to, anyway'.[150]

Rubinstein notes that the number of government bureaucrats and other individuals benefiting from fees, pensions and grants, and building their wealth at the expense of the state, 'decreased strikingly between the early and middle nineteenth century'.[151] The mid-century 'marked the virtual cessation of this type of top wealth-holder in the British élite structure'[152] – at a time when the number of such figures was still increasing in France. Corruption remained a major fact of British political life, and many pre-modern forms of favouritism and patronage endured. But they were remarkably mitigated, and became increasingly regulated by strict rules.[153]

By the 1830s, the political influence of the crown and of the prime minister over the parliament had been reduced to a very considerable extent. Rubinstein notes that 'when Wellington said in 1830 that he commanded, as prime minister, virtually no patronage, his statement was not refuted; crown influence was widely regarded – in the words of one "Old Whig" of 1831 – as having been "completely destroyed"'.[154] To speak of complete destruction might have been an overstatement. Again, corruption remained, but it was soon to be alleviated still further. Up until then, British elites had focused on administrative reforms to tackle 'Old Corruption', wisely preferring to leave aside the issue of electoral reforms. But mounting economic distress during the final years of the 1820s, the French and Belgian revolutions of 1830, and intense popular agitation at home in 1831 forced the government to reorient its strategy and to finally address the electoral issues.[155]

---

149   Dreyfus 2000, p. 118.
150   Harling 2004, pp. 113–14.
151   Rubinstein 1983, p. 56.
152   Ibid.
153   Harling 2004, p. 112.
154   Rubinstein 1983, p. 57.
155   Ertman 2010, pp. 1008–9; Smith 2004, p. 159.

The adopted solution, the Reform Act of 1832, only very modestly expanded the electorate, which grew from 3.2 to 4.7 percent of the population.[156] This expansion allowed for the inclusion of significant layers of the new middle class, which had been surging with the rise of industrial capitalism. It contributed to making the British electorate considerably larger than it was in France, where only about 0.5 percent of the total population could vote. On its own, this increase amounted to little in terms of democratisation of the political system. Yet, this seemingly limited change significantly contributed to the autonomy of Parliament from the government, since the number of electors was now much too large for the rapidly decreasing quantity of positions available for ministers to distribute. The offer of patronage could no longer follow the clients' demand and, as influence through favouritism waned, the electorate could now select its representatives much more freely without – or with considerably less – undue interference.[157]

Meanwhile, the French state remained unable to integrate and accommodate the middle classes in the same way.[158] Frightened by the 1830 French Revolution, the class of capitalist landlords in control of the British state had been able to expand the electorate in 1832, in a successful attempt to preserve its hegemony by shutting out a potential alliance between the rising industrial capitalist class and the working class.[159] Such manoeuvring proved impossible in France, where not only the political system, but also, and even more fundamentally, the class system rested on the limited character of the suffrage, political patronage and an ongoing expansion of the number of state offices. Here, limited suffrage allowed governmental rulers to exercise efficient political patronage and, in the process, to continuously expand the number of positions that notables – and would-be notables – were so fond of.

It should also be stressed that, because of its capitalist character, the British middle class was not as anxious as its French counterpart to join the body politic. Hence, in the wake of the 1832 Reform Act, 'even the industrialists who remained under-represented there over the Victorian decades "saw nothing much wrong in leaving the details of government in aristocratic hands, provided that the government created a suitable framework for the promotion

---

156   Ertman 2010, p. 1008.
157   Dreyfus 2000, p. 133. The recasting of electoral counties and boroughs, and especially the elimination of 'pocket borough' with very small electorates that could easily be controlled by patrons, also contributed significantly to the decline of the political influence exercised over the Parliament by the executive power (Ertman 2010; Smith 2004).
158   Charle 1991, p. 41.
159   Zmolek 2013, pp. 703–10.

of economic growth and pursued congenial economic policies"'.[160] Not having
the luxury of an alternative, capitalist mode of exploitation, the French middle
class did not adopt such a relaxed attitude in relation to electoral and constitutional issues.

Since the state was a crucial nexus not only of political power, but also of
class exploitation, the bitterness of the social conflict over its control that raged
in nineteenth-century France need not surprise us.[161] Notables were divided
into political factions, and these partly overlapped with hierarchies within
which rank resulted from one's property value and one's position within the
state.[162] The ubiquitous conflict between factions over state power and offices
made successive regimes remarkably unstable. With the 1830 Revolution, the
ruling notable faction of the Restoration was ousted by liberal Orleanists, who
proceeded to modestly expand the electorate and grab their own share of high
offices. To stabilise their regime, Orleanists were ready to accommodate Legit-
imists who had lost their former hegemony. Both factions, however, refused
the inclusion of *capacités* – educated bourgeois, often belonging to the liberal
professions, who were unable to join the ruling class of notables via the pro-
curement of prestigious state offices.[163]

The number of state offices was growing, as ruling factions consolidated
their political base by granting jobs to their dependants. But this inflation was
not rapid enough to accommodate *capacités* – nor was this the aim that ruling
notables, imbued with the values of patronage networks, had set for themselves. Promises of meritocracy made during the Revolution remained a dead
letter. As favouritism grew stronger, large numbers of educated younger men
remained excluded from office, and lower rank employees saw their careers
stagnating and their hopes for advancement shattered.[164] Le Bihan shows how,
during the first half of the nineteenth century, the vast majority of intermediary office holders issued from the middle or upper socio-economic layers.[165]
Intermediary functionaries, however, faced a promotion ceiling that prevented
them from reaching the apex of their professions.[166] The social malaise that
ensued intensified during the 1840s, as the overproduction of young graduates

---

160   Harling 2004, p. 113.
161   Charle (1991, p. 43) and Tombs (1996, p. 123) insist on the intensity of this conflict over the
      control of the state.
162   Charle 1991, p. 43.
163   Charle 1991, p. 41.
164   Charle 1991, p. 49; Kingston 2012.
165   Le Bihan 2008, pp. 99–107.
166   Le Bihan 2008, pp. 226–31.

fuelled repeated student agitation in Paris and elsewhere. The declared intention of the authorities to solve this issue by increasing the selectivity of the great
schools only made matters worse.[167] The political disaffection of the middle
class was heightened, during the 1840s, by the stubborn refusal of Guizot's
government to increase the electorate to include significant layers of *capacités* by reducing the tax qualification. As Tombs sums up, '[t]his refusal left
unenfranchised a considerable middle and lower-middle class, literate, politicized and dangerously disaffected; and this helped bring about revolution in
1848'.[168]

The rigidity of the 'regime' of notability in post-revolutionary France created an explosive political context, pregnant with opportunities for popular
involvement. For it was not just the middle class that was interested in reforming the state – so was the working class, whose members were heavily taxed
and repressed by this humongous and growing 'frightful parasitic body' decried
by Marx, over which they had no control. Notables aggressively defended their
monopoly of the state because it was, after landholding, an important source
of their material wealth, and the base of their social standing. Peasants and
workers wished to take over the state to put an end to this parasitism. The state
continued 'to be a primary extractor of direct producers through the medium
of taxation for the benefit of office-holders'.[169] It was only natural, then, that it
would be a focal point of class struggle: just as exploitation took a non-capitalist
form and was partly facilitated by the state, so was class struggle expressed in
a directly political fashion.

This point is aptly stated by Tombs when he asserts that what gave France
its specificity during the nineteenth century was 'the importance of the role
of the state and of the ideological inheritance of the Revolution in the development of class identities'.[170] During at least the first half of the nineteenth
century, France did not experience the differentiation of 'political' and 'economic' spheres that characterises capitalist societies and that was taking form
in Britain at the time. To quote Tombs again, 'France held back the development of autonomous institutions by which civil society might have regulated itself'.[171] What should be added here, is that this absence of a resolutely
autonomous civil society *vis-à-vis* the state stemmed from the fact that the
latter remained an important nexus of surplus appropriation in the absence

---

167   Charle 1991, pp. 48–9.
168   Tombs 1996, p. 103.
169   Wood 2012.
170   Tombs 1996, p. 299.
171   Ibid.

of capitalist absolute private property and disembedded self-regulated markets.[172] In the absence of capitalist channels of surplus appropriation, social conflicts were 'inevitably politicized because of the involvement of the state' – an involvement not merely in the running of civil society, as implied by Tombs, but also specifically in the operation of class relations of exploitation. Tombs goes on to suggest that classes did not make themselves through their relationship with one another, but through their relationship with the state. As he puts it: '[t]he theorizing, organising and action of various groups was above all focused not on influencing each other but on influencing the state'.[173] A more apt appreciation of processes of class formation in post-revolutionary France might be formulated thus: while the ruling class reproduced itself partly through – and in this sense fused with – the state, the labouring classes made themselves in large part through their opposition to the state.

3   Pinning Down Social Ills, Naming the Antagonists

Within the regulatory context that was stabilised in the years and decades following the 1789 Revolution, relationships between small employers and employees were characterised by conciliation. Guilds, and the subordination at work that they entailed, had been abolished, and no entrenched division existed between masters and workshop heads, on the one hand, and journeymen and companions, on the other. Tensions, sometimes leading to intense conflicts, were certainly part of the scenery, but, as workers experiencing very similar working conditions and frequently interchanging positions, generally within very small workshops, masters and journeymen generally cohabited in a peaceful way. They frequently belonged to the same organisations, took action side by side, and often shared a common perspective on the organisation of their trade, and on broader economic and political matters. Conflicts between these workers and *marchands-fabricants* and big *négociants* were more frequent and more deeply entrenched. Large merchants and factory owners often controlled supplies necessary for production, and the marketing of finished goods that had been produced by workers in workshops, factories, or at home; furthermore, they regularly attempted to impose pay rates that departed from existing usages and that were detrimental to workers. Other sources of con-

---

172   Wood 1995.
173   Ibid.

flict were related to the merchants exercising control over the credit that many small producers needed in order to finance their activities.

Yet, for reasons already addressed in previous chapters, these conflicts did not stem from a systemic *capitalist* class antagonism. Because of their limited orderliness and fragmented nature, French markets did not distribute competitive pressures as capitalist markets would do. Though fluctuations in demand might force individual enterprises to engage in punctual adjustments (as would be the case in any non-capitalist commercial system), French employers – whether workshop heads or *négociants* – did not face *systematic* and *continuous* imperatives to control production costs, to improve productivity, and to maximise profits. Moreover, extricating themselves from under the guilds' yoke during the Revolution, French workers had gained new rights that severely limited their employers' power and prevented the alienation of their labour power. The application of revolutionary principles of equality and freedom to the sphere of labour was overseen by institutions such as *prud'hommes* councils, which administered the application of usages among the different trades and localities of France. For these reasons, there was no room in post-revolutionary France for the capitalist social property relations and artisan capitalism described by Sewell, Johnson and others.

For all that, the life of labourers was not an idyllic one. As a rule, and excluding domestics, workers did not have to subordinate themselves to their employers, they were often shielded by regulations from the worst types of economic abuses, and many had access to a parcel of land. In good times, this organisation of labour relations 'clearly gave immense satisfaction, social, cultural, and even economic' to considerable layers of the French working class.[174] Yet, it is also true that many were poor and led 'a hard, insecure and unstable existence'.[175] Unemployment was an ongoing problem in different sectors, and many workers experienced recurrent 'fluctuations of overwork and lay-offs'.[176] In this context, workers expanded their *compagnonnage* during the 1810s.[177] Also from the 1810s, and even more over the following decades, workers formed an increasing number of mutual aid societies.[178] These societies provided resources to workers and their families in case of illness, injury or death, but were also import-

---

174   Tombs 1996, p. 271.
175   Tombs 1996, p. 271; see also Guicheteau 2014, p. 222.
176   Tombs 1996, p. 271.
177   Faure and Rancière (1976, p. 146) report that *compagnonnage* then rapidly receded from the 1830s. New forms of working-class solidarity and struggle were emerging during this decade.
178   Guicheteau 2014, p. 180; Rougerie 1994, pp. 494, 503, 507.

ant incubators of resistance through which workers defended their material interests.[179] Workers involved themselves in strike activities and in political actions. As we will see in more detail below, from the 1830s many also began to adopt Republican ideas, and eventually came to combine these with aspects of different socialist doctrines that had been developed by wealthier and more comfortable intellectuals. We thus return to this recurring question: How are we to explain these developments while also asserting that workers were not at the time wrestling with an emerging capitalist system?

As Sonenscher explains, 'much of the environment in which [workers] lived and worked was not very different from that of the eighteenth century'.[180] The operation of trades still entailed its own set of challenges and problems, linked to the enforcement of usages and tariffs, the quality of materials, the development and diffusion of technical and design innovation, the assessment of the capacity of partners, clients and sub-contractors to honour their debts and other financial obligations, and so on. As we saw in the previous chapter, different institutions had been established during and after the Revolution to manage the manifold economic transactions that kept trades going. Yet, the 'local self-discipline' that commercial tribunals and chambers of commerce attempted to maintain across France could often prove insufficient, and, in addition to participating in these institutions, employers regularly had to form informal and voluntary associations in order to check the solvency of potential partners or to enforce product quality control.

The same was true for labour relations. Workers could and did massively rely on justices of the peace and *prud'hommes* councils to uphold tariffs and usages, but a number of malevolent practices nonetheless escaped these institutions' scrutiny, and, as a consequence, employees who found themselves at the less strictly regulated peripheries of their trade faced greater precariousness. Again, conflict could often be avoided, and the carpenter Agricole Perdiguier, for instance, recalled in his memoirs, published in 1854, how masters and companions would methodically favour conciliation whenever issues emerged in a workshop. Yet, when conciliation proved impossible, or when

---

179   While Hunt and Sheridan (1986) suggest that mutual aid societies 'were associated with protest activity only exceptionally', Rougerie (1994, p. 507) insists that there are multiple examples of the active engagement of these societies in campaigns of resistance. Whichever might have been the case, it seems clear that workers did engage in numerous cabals over the period, and that mutual aid societies were part of their movement's 'infrastructure of dissent' (Sears 2014), which also comprised spaces of socialisation such as cabarets, taverns, churches, etc. For an overview of mutual aid society in post-revolutionary France before 1848, see Pilbeam 2000, pp. 135–51.

180   Sonenscher 1989, p. 370.

merchant-manufacturers or *négociants* disregarded tariffs, it became necessary for workers to engage in collective action in order the safeguard the moral
economy of their trades.[181] In so doing, workers recurrently insisted on the
need to root out 'bad' or 'excess' competition, confronted 'dishonest' employers who did not respect tariffs and tried to escape usages, and denounced their
'regrettable abuses'.[182] The existence of *prud'hommes*, then, did not rule out
'abuses'. Yet, while they engaged in collective action in order to eliminate these
abuses, workers often focused their efforts on consolidating and reforming the
prud'hommes to their advantage,[183] thus expressing their fundamental trust in
this regulatory institution.

These struggles against cheating employers were nothing new. Numerous
cases of sometimes violent cabals against dishonest employers that took place
under the Old Regime have been listed by historians.[184] These historical
instances can be traced back to the sixteenth century, and probably earlier.
Workers denounced employers who did not respect trade rules and hired
employees at lower rates. Workshops of dishonest masters were targeted and
closed down and disobedient workers were molested. Legal recourse to parliaments as well as other courts and political authorities to enforce normative
regulations were also very frequent.[185] Journeymen and companions formed
diverse illegal organisations that imposed fines on unruly workers and confronted masters in charge of guilds to force them to preserve and enforce the moral
economy of their trade in a way that served their interests and well-being.[186] As
we saw in the previous chapter, bad *marchandage*, other subcontracting practices, and resort to cheap and underqualified labour did not emerge in the early
nineteenth century. These practices had been occurring for centuries, in a non-
capitalist context, and so had the workers' vigilance against them.

Nineteenth-century workers still denounced these practices as 'abuses', precisely because they were not normal and widespread in the way that they would
become under capitalism. This non-capitalist context is in part reflected by the
overall relatively limited growth of French mutual aid societies. While these
societies' membership reached about 83,000 in 1843, British trade-unions had
already acquired over 925,000 members by 1815.[187] Likewise, if the amount of

---

181   Guicheteau 2014, p. 227; Reddy 1984, pp. 127–9.
182   Faure and Rancière 1976, p. 27.
183   As did Lyon canuts during the early 1830s (Frobert 2009, pp. 56, 59–60).
184   See Nicolas 2002.
185   Sonenscher 1989.
186   Guicheteau 2014, pp. 55–62.
187   Rougerie 1994b.

collective action in opposition to the mechanisation of industry was growing in France, the extent of the phenomenon remained limited in comparison to Britain.[188] Different modes of exploitation nurtured different practices of resistance (we will come back to this point in a moment).

What *was* new – and explains the growth of resistance, organisation, and the republican and socialist ideas of the working class after the Restoration – was the absence of state-backed regulatory institutions. As we saw, trades under the Old Regime were formed of strongly regulated cores and more permissive peripheries, and they preserved this form after the Revolution. Yet, whereas under the Old Regime normative regulations had been enforced by guilds incorporated by the state and regional parliaments, the post-revolutionary *bon droits* was locally anchored and upheld by justices of the peace, *prud'hommes* and mayors. As representatives of the central state, prefects intervened in labour relations only erratically and their decisions were sometimes informed by the official liberal spirit of the time. The informal character of workers' mutual aid societies did not have the formally recognised authority and powers of pre-revolutionary guilds. As Sonenscher puts it, 'the voluntary character of collective association in the early nineteenth century was a significant departure from the obligatory associations attached to the *métiers jurés* of the Old Regime'.[189]

As has already been made clear, local usages did have significant weight, and *prud'hommes* did play a key role in the life of nineteenth-century French trades. Yet, workers had to be on their guard in a legal and ideological context in which regulations were no longer formally and actively backed by the central state, and where different French elites were flirting with liberalism (as they had been doing for many decades). Here lies an important factor behind the rise of the French labour movement over this period: the need to fight abuses by formally consolidating their usages and regulatory institutions. Sonenscher thus explains that 'the resonance of socialism may, therefore, be more intelligible in a legal and institutional context than one defined principally in terms of unregulated markets and capitalist development'.[190] 'In this context', he goes on, 'the antithesis between competitive individualism and collective association that was made so frequently during the early nineteenth century was

---

188   Guicheteau (2014, p. 219) mentions that, out of the dozens of strikes that took place in Paris in 1830–3, only six stemmed from opposition to machines. Acts of machine breaking took place elsewhere in France, but nothing came close to the extent of the English Swing Riots that took place north of the Channel. On machine-breaking in France and Britain from the 1780s to the 1860s, see Jarrige 2009.

189   Sonenscher 1989, pp. 170–1.

190   Sonenscher 1989, p. 371.

less a judgement upon the noxious effects of unregulated markets than it was a response to the absence of any formal injunctions compelling artisans to associate as they had done before the Revolution'.[191]

As we saw, different historians have clearly shown that the abolition of guilds in 1791 did not leave a regulatory void. Usages prevailed, and local institutional networks flourished. But the state was no longer part of the equation in the way it had been before. A debate between liberalism and corporatism was raging among elites and, for decades after the Revolution, many were still arguing for the reinstatement of guilds. Socialists thinkers, who were mostly petit-bourgeois intellectuals and rarely workers, engaged in this debate.

Many influential socialist figures, such as Victor Prosper Considerant, the leader of the Fourierist movement that became increasingly significant from the mid-1830s, or Louis Blanc, who played a leading role in the Provisional Government of 1848, put forth a hyperbolic discourse about the threat of competition. Thus, according to Considerant, because of 'free and anarchic competition', the workshop was becoming a 'battlefield', and labour and capital were engaged in a 'permanent state of war'. Also because of competition, one could witness 'the gradual crushing of small and middle-sized property, industry and commerce under the weight of big property, under the colossal wheels of big industry and commerce'.[192] Similarly pessimistic assessments can be found in Blanc's influential *Organisation du Travail*, where the 'unlimited competition' existing in France is presented as a 'system of extermination' of the people that 'systematically reduces wages' and leads to the elimination of small and middle-size enterprises.[193] Such condemnation of competition as the source of all misery was a recurrent theme of early French socialists.[194]

What are we to make of such statements? As should be clear by now, though they were certainly not free of conflicts, early nineteenth-century French workshops and factories hardly resembled 'battlefields', and wages were not subjected to 'unlimited' competition. Moreover, in blatant contradiction of the assertions made by Considerant, Blanc, and others, one of the most noticeable traits of the French economy of the period was not the dissipation of small enterprises but rather their enduring presence and even their growth, as the proportion of industrial firms employing a single person reached 62 percent of the total in 1860, up from 50 percent in 1847–8, and the proportion employing

---

191   Ibid.
192   Quoted in Beecher 2001, p. 132.
193   Blanc 1847, pp. 27, 31–2, 84.
194   Bouchet et al. 2015, p. 9.

more than ten actually fell from 11 to 7 percent over the same period.[195] Things might become clearer if we approach the kind of catastrophic discourse put forth by Considerant, Blanc, and others as rhetorical devices. The latter were mobilised by early socialists against liberals as part of an ongoing debate that very much revolved around Britain and its economic model.

In his *Principes du Socialisme*, Considerant asserted that France and Belgium were following the example set by England. Yet, he also claimed that French workers would never tolerate the sort of treatment that their English and Irish counterparts were enduring. As Considerant puts it, 'before our working classes would reach such a degree and reaction and animosity' as the one caused by the English economic model, 'there would have been in our country ten revolutions'.[196] France was in fact not experiencing the ruthless capitalist industrialisation that was taking place in Britain, and Considerant wanted France *to avoid it*. Likewise, in his *Organisation du Travail*, after presenting the harmful consequences of competition, Blanc, 'who was the most-read publicist of this viewpoint',[197] devotes a full chapter to the ways in which 'competition is condemned by the English example' (followed by another one explaining how competition will necessarily lead to a war to the death between France and England). The main point asserted by the author is that France must avoid the path taken by England.

Considerant (as well as Fourier, his *maître à penser*), Blanc, and other early socialists were clearly obsessed with English capitalism and wanted France to keep away from it. This implied confronting thinkers who promoted capitalism, and 'French socialism at its very inception was a methodical refutation of the economic doctrines of David Ricardo, Thomas Malthus and Adam Smith'. Corcoran explains that '[i]t was the reaction to British classical economics' that 'provided the socialist movement with its theoretical rigour and moral fervour'.[198] French socialists also fought French liberals who, since the mideighteenth century, had been promoting ideas and policies that were often directly inspired by the British example. While the Restoration had been considerably less supportive of liberal political economy, research chairs and different authors actively promoted its ideas from the late 1810s. Jean-Baptiste Say, the leading figure of liberal political economy in France at the time, was made professor at the College de France under the July monarchy. Backed by

---

195   Harvey 2005, p. 153.
196   Considerant 1847, pp. 11, 13: 'Avant que nos classes ouvrières arrivassent à ce degré de réaction et d'animosité, il y aurait eu chez nous dix révolutions'.
197   Pilbeam 2000, p. 23.
198   Corcoran 1983, p. 2.

his disciples, Say used this prestigious position to promote liberal ideas, fought normative regulations of industrial trades, and championed international free trade.[199]

Pierre Leroux, one of the most influential and popular socialist thinkers of his time, opposed socialism to 'individualism', which was threatening 'the unity of the reciprocal relations of all the parts of the social body'. Leroux developed his socialism, which proved to be 'enormously influential', in direct opposition to English political economy, which was being popularised in France by Jean-Baptiste Say. Constantin Pecqueur and Pierre-Joseph Proudhon, other influential socialists, also built their ideas out of a critique of liberal economics.[200] In his *Organisation du Travail*, Blanc scornfully refers to Smith, Say, and their disciples and condemns liberal journals such as *Le Constitutionnel* and *Le Courrier Français* for their promotion of the 'absolute liberty of industry'.[201] In an appendix to the fifth edition of his book, entitled 'response to diverse objections', Blanc presents and comments in detail on an exchange that opposed him to Michel Chevalier, and which was published in the journal *Débats* during the mid-1840s. Chevalier, as we will see in the following chapter, was a liberal who oversaw the negotiations that led to free trade between France and Britain in 1860. Here, we find the leading republican-socialist of the Second Republic engaged in a debate with a liberal who played a key role in expediting the transition to capitalism in France under the Second Empire.

In engaging in these debates with liberals – and even though many of their ideas eventually penetrated the labour movement – early French socialists of the 1830s and 1840s were mostly attempting to secure the support of members of the privileged class. In so doing, and while their political perspectives were remarkably diverse, French socialists were ultimately less interested in exposing the faults of British capitalism than in defining new principles that would hold French society together, after the evaporation of the corporatist paradigm in the wake of 1789. This is the reason why Beecher presents them as 'romantic socialists' who 'were writing out of a broader sense of social and moral disintegration'.[202] Their main concerns were social and political, rather the economic: 'their ideas were presented as a remedy for the collapse of community rather than for any specifically economic problem'.[203] In this respect,

---

199   Etner and Silvant 2017, pp. 25, 36–7.
200   Corcoran 1983, pp. 3, 4, 20; Roberts 2017.
201   Blanc 1847, pp. 76, 80.
202   Beecher 2001, p. 2. A long list of authors share Beecher's characterisation of early French socialism – on this point see Corcoran 1983, pp. 4–7, 21.
203   Ibid.

their thought was rooted in a long-standing debate in French political thought. The debate had evolved for centuries under the Old Regime, revolved around the challenge of integrating 'a fragmented social order ... a network of corporate entities', and was informed by 'a conception of society in which the totality of social relations, including economic transactions, was subsumed in the *political* community'.[204] Romantic socialists were deeply concerned by the fact that, within the post-revolutionary society, 'individuals were becoming increasingly detached from any kind of corporate structure, and that society as a whole was becoming increasingly fragmented and individualistic'.[205] To solve these issues, they proposed models of social organisation based on a new 'science' of society that mixed Christian principles of fraternal love with the rational worldview of the Enlightenment.

In Britain, a nation of 'desocialised' individuals had been increasingly (if turbulently and conflictually) integrated on the basis of a 'self-regulated' economy. No such integrating mechanism had existed in early modern France and, after the Revolution – and with the official repudiation of corporatism and the embrace of individualistic liberalism by sections of the French ruling class – the challenges of social and political unity became more acute than ever. Accordingly, '[t]he conception of a society as a *political community* remained a recurrent theme' in French social and political thought.[206] During the 1830s and 1840s, French socialist thinkers – and through collective struggles and the mobilising of socialist ideas, eventually workers too – created their own solutions, not simply to the alleviation of economic misery, but also, more fundamentally, to the reformation of a French political community.

While growing numbers of workers engaged in these political debates and often adhered to socialist ideas in the two decades that followed the 1830 Revolution, they did so with the intent of defending their material interests – and this implied fighting the ruling class that exploited them. During this period, French workers routinely denounced the power that 'capitalists' had over them. In doing this, they targeted bankers and big merchants (*négociants*). They denounced the 'feudality of finance' and the 'tyranny of usurers'.[207] Larger merchants were simultaneously bankers, and many *négociants* belonged to the

---

204   Wood 2012, p. 170. As Wood explains, '[t]his constellation would continue to dominate French social thought up to the Revolution and beyond'.

205   Beecher 2001, p. 2.

206   Wood 1991, p. 88.

207   Harvey 2005, p. 119; Zeldin 1993, p. 80.

Parisian *Haute Banque* in which was concentrated the country's largest financial fortunes. Workers deeply resented their exploitation by merchant-bankers.
The latter encroached on tariffs and attempted to reduce prices paid for final
products (often by imposing fines if product quality was judged unsatisfactory
or for other reasons). Merchant-bankers also fleeced workers by charging exor-
bitant interest on loans used to acquire workshops, tools or raw material.[208]
Many industrial workers were also peasants who, in attempting to acquire land
to consolidate and expand their family holding, found themselves at the mercy
of usurers.

It is crucial to underline, then, that when French workers spoke of 'capitalists', they had in mind the owners of monetary wealth – bankers and big
merchants – not the 'captain of industry' who emerged with the coming of
a capitalist mode of production. As Marx explains, 'capital is not a thing, but
a social relation between persons which is mediated through things'.[209] This
implies that '[i]n themselves, money and commodities are no more capital than
the means of production and subsistence are'.[210] The creation of the 'capital-
relation' that compels capitalists to exploit workers by systematically enhancing their labour's productivity necessitates a process of radical transformation
of social property relations – one that had not yet taken place in France. Consequently, French 'capitalists' were named as such because they happened to
be in possession of 'capital' (monetary wealth), not because they were accumulating capital by way of producing *surplus value*.

According to Marx, '[i]nterest-bearing capital, or, to describe it in its archaic
form, usurer's capital, belongs together with its twin brother, merchant's capital, to the antediluvian forms of capital *which long precede the capitalist mode
of production* and are to be found in the most diverse socio-economic forma-
tions'.[211] Indeed, 'the less developed production is, the more monetary wealth
is concentrated in the hands of merchants',[212] and '[u]surer's capital, as the
characteristic form of interest-bearing capital, corresponds to the predominance of petty production, of peasants and small master craftsmen working for
themselves'.[213] Direct producers are here in possession of means of production
and are exploited by merchant-bankers, from whom they are forced to borrow

208   Tombs 1996, p. 271.
209   Marx 1990, p. 932.
210   Marx 1990, p. 874.
211   Marx 1991, p. 728.
212   Marx 1991, p. 444.
213   Marx 1991, p. 729.

in order to pursue their activities as independent producers.[214] Marx stresses that 'it lies in the very nature of the matter that interest-bearing capital should appear to the popular mind as the form of capital *par excellence* ... it also happens that even a section of political economists, particularly in countries where industrial capital is not yet fully developed, as in France, cling to interest-bearing capital as the basic-form [of capital]'.[215] Until the end of the nineteenth century, most French industrial workers indeed belonged to small craft workshops, and perceived capital in these interest-bearing and merchant forms.

The author of *Capital* also explains that, even as it exploits independent direct producers, the 'usurer's capital impoverishes the mode of production, cripples the productive forces instead of developing them, and simultaneously perpetuates the lamentable conditions in which the social productivity of labour is not developed even at the cost of the worker himself, as it is in capitalist production'.[216] This form of financial capital, which is anterior to capitalist production, 'does not change the mode of production, but clings to it like a parasite and impoverishes it. It sucks it dry, emasculates it and forces reproduction to proceed under ever more pitiable conditions. Hence the popular hatred of usury, at its peak in the ancient world'.[217] Once again, this applies remarkably well to the French context during the first half of the nineteenth century, where workers perpetuated this age-old hatred of interest-bearing and commercial capital precisely for the reasons identified by Marx.

In the eyes of early nineteenth-century French workers, capitalists were the opposite of captains of industry. They were consistently depicted as 'idle' and 'unproductive'.[218] The criticism of 'capitalists' put forth by the French working class was systematised by democratic-socialists (the 'democ-socs', or *Montagnards*), who secured growing popular support under the Second Republic. Berenson explains how, 'according to the democ-socs, the capitalist class did not consist of those who directed industrial enterprises ... [R]ather it comprised those who controlled the nation's purse strings'.[219] Capitalists monopolised the financial resources of the nation and made investment decisions

---

214 This is in sharp contrast to the capitalist mode of production, where dispossessed *wage-labourers* are exploited. As Marx (1991, p. 729) explains: 'Where, as in the developed capitalist mode of production, the conditions of production and the product of labour confront the worker as capital, he does not have to borrow any money in his capacity'.

215 Marx 1991, p. 744. Note that Marx wrote *Capital Volume III* from 1863 to 1883.

216 Marx 1991, pp. 730–1.

217 Marx 1991, p. 731.

218 Faure and Rancière 1976.

219 Berenson 1984, p. 109.

that served their own private interests rather than public need. Hence, 'the barons of the Bank of France and other capitalists subjected the prosperity of the nation's productive citizens to the requirements of their own self-serving greed'.[220] Workers understood that 'the capitalists' autocratic control over the economy not only caused misery and suffering, but it blocked industrial and agricultural development as well'.[221] The Saint-Simonian vision of a society divided between producers (including workers and farmers, but also workshop and factory owners) on the one hand, and idle rentier capitalists on the other, was widely accepted among proletarian milieus during the 1830s.[222]

French labourers understood that the lack of productive capital investment was responsible for the unemployment and precariousness that plagued large sections of the working class. Accordingly, the Montagnard's electoral platform, which would gain increasing popular support at the end of 1848 and in 1849, 'denounced the exigencies and timidities of capital, the two great obstacles to industrial progress'.[223] There was not much new about this 'timidity' of capital or the exploitation decried by French workers. The profits earned by bankers and merchants were created in much the same way as they had been under the Old Regime. What *was* new was the workers' will to take over the state, and to turn it into a republic that would allow them to redirect financial wealth in ways that would serve their interests. In parallel, socialists such as Proudhon gained popularity by developing non-statist (or 'mutualist') schemes to democratise the workers' access to credit.

Though designated as 'capitalists' by republican-socialists, bankers and *négociants* thought of themselves as landholder notables.[224] They also battened on state financial resources.[225] French workers were well aware of the fact that 'capitalists' belonged to the notability, and they identified the state as a nexus of exploitation and a central antagonist in their struggle to defend their class interest. The tailor Aguier echoed a widespread sentiment when he denounced the 'state employee paid a fortune for doing nothing' in a letter published by the journal *Le Père Duchêne* during the spring of 1848.[226] But the labour movement of the period did not simply depict deputies and high

---

220   Ibid.
221   Berenson 1984, p. 111.
222   Tombs 1996, p. 274.
223   Ibid.
224   Bergeron 1978, p. 41.
225   Bergeron 1978, pp. 9–11.
226   Faure 1974, p. 90: 'l'employé de gouvernement gagnant des prix fous à ne rien faire'.

officials as 'idlers' – it also recognised that, via their privileged access to the state, they were directly exploiting workers who paid for their salaries with their taxes.[227]

As Faure stresses, a large and growing number of workers agreed with the tailor Grignon when he declared in an open letter published in 1833 that

> we must raise our views to new ground, reach back to the cause of the evil, and prepare ourselves to destroy it. It is less the masters for which we are working than our country's laws that are opposed to the betterment of our condition; it is the taxes on essential goods that are taking away the largest share of our wages; it is these monopolies that are forbidding us to enter the most lucrative professions. We must consequently not forget that only the rich make the law, and that we will only be able to definitely free ourselves from the yoke of misery by exercising, as they do, our rights as citizens.[228]

Denunciations of laws made for and by the rich, of indirect taxes on consumer goods, and of the grabbing of lucrative government positions by notables – these were recurrent themes within working-class circles.

Iorwerth Prothero's work on nineteenth-century radical artisans shows how French republican workers repeatedly condemned idle rich landowners who monopolised access to state positions. Prothero reports how workers denounced 'the personal rewards, favours, honours, patronage, and incentives that were crucial constituents of politics; the jobs for friends, relatives and clients'.[229] Workers understood that, 'intrinsic to this corruption of the political establishment was its cost, as radicals condemned high salaries, sinecures, and pluralism (*cumul*), and the creation of posts simply to support members of upper-class families at public expense'.[230] It follows that a central theme put forth by French republican workers concerned 'the high burden of taxa-

---

227   Hayat 2014, p. 296.
228   Quoted in Faure and Rancière 1976, pp. 60–1: 'Il faut porter nos vues plus haut, remonter à la cause du mal, et nous préparer à la détruire. Ce sont moins les maîtres pour lesquels nous travaillons que les lois de notre pays qui s'opposent à l'amélioration de notre état; ce sont ces impôts sur les objets de première nécessité qui nous enlèvent la plus forte partie de nos salaires; ce sont ces monopoles qui nous interdisent l'entrée des professions lucratives. N'oublions donc pas que les riches seuls font la loi, et que nous ne pourrons nous affranchir définitivement du joug de la misère, qu'en exerçant, comme eux, nos droits de citoyen'.
229   Prothero 1997, p. 22.
230   Prothero 1997, p. 23.

tion' that was understood as 'a cause of distress and the result of government extravagance, waste, incompetence and indebtedness that involved high taxes to pay interest to idle speculators. Taxes should therefore be reduced by reducing government expenditure and personnel'.[231] Furthermore, French workers demanded a shift from indirect taxes on consumption – an important burden upon artisan living standards – to direct taxes targeting the wealth of idle notables.[232]

Denunciations of parasitic appropriation of state resources surfaced consistently during the first cycle of self-conscious working-class struggles that took place in France from 1830 to the Second Republic. Nathalie Jakobowicz relates, for instances, a popular song railing the 'feast of offices' that took place following the July 1830 Revolution and from which future officials would benefit.[233] During his trial after a failed Parisian insurrection in 1832, another tailor named Victor Prospert, presenting himself as 'a representative of the working class', insisted on making a speech in which he demanded political equality, universal suffrage, and the suppression of useless jobs and of indirect taxes on food on which poor people depended.[234]

In its *Exposé des principes républicains*, the *Société des Droits de l'Homme et du Citoyen*, which played a crucial part in the making of the French working class in 1832–4, explained that 'the association will mainly count on the support of those who, deprived of political rights, barely protected by civil laws, made by the rich and for the rich, succumb under the excess of work and the burden of public offices'.[235] Also in 1832, the jurist Marius Chastaing published a series of articles in the journal *L'Écho de la fabrique*, which was instrumental in the organisation of the working class of Lyon from 1831 to 1834. Chastaing noted the injustice stemming from the fact that, within the tax system then in place, the majority of the tax burden was borne by those who were excluded from political citizenship. He also decried the unjust indirect tax that 'crushes the indigent, brushes the better-off, and spares the rich'.[236] Tax revenues, Chasta-

---

231   Ibid.
232   Ibid.
233   Jakobowicz 2009, p. 263.
234   Guicheteau 2014, p. 239; Zancarini-Fournel 2016, p. 254.
235   Quoted in Hayat 2014, p. 53: 'L'association comptera principalement sur l'appui de ceux qui, déshérités de leurs droits politiques, à peine protégés par les lois civiles, faites par les riches pour les riches, succombent sous l'excès du travail et le fardeau des charges publiques'.
236   Quoted in Frobert 2009, p. 52: 'il écrase l'indigent, il effleure l'homme aisé, il épargne l'homme riche'.

ing went on, were monopolised by the rich when they should have served social solidarity and been used to finance much needed infrastructure that would benefit the poor.[237]

Such examples could be multiplied, and the republican movement continued to denounce fiscal injustices during the 1840s. These were still burning issues in 1848, under the Second Republic – as will be discussed in the closing section of this chapter – and beyond.[238] Republicans and socialists opposed tax increases that served not the public but rather the private interests and caprices of the imperial court under the Second Empire, and tax reforms were also a priority of the Parisian *Communards* in 1871.[239]

Besides speeches and pamphlets, collective actions also took place. Opposition to taxation had been the most widespread motive of popular rebellious action under the Old Regime.[240] After the Restoration, the state continued to be perceived as a predatory institution, and fiscal issues remained subject to social conflicts and violent confrontations until at least the middle of the nineteenth century, with peaks in 1814–16, at the beginning of 1830, in 1841, and under the Second Republic.[241] Tax agents were repelled and attacked, registers were burned and tax collection gates surrounding cities were knocked down.[242] Most of these actions were undertaken in opposition to indirect taxes, which were highly detrimental to the poor. Associations against taxes began to appear from 1829 and rebellion erupted in 1830. Until 1835, intense anti-fiscal agitation took place and ran throughout the country.[243] After new rebellions in the West, the Massif Central and the Berry in 1840, a widespread and intense movement of opposition emerged across Southern France in 1841, when the Minister's announcement of a census of doors and windows sparked rumours of new taxes.[244] Clearly, fiscal issues and denunciations of state parasitism were at the heart of the class struggle that raged in France at the time.

It is true that the British labour movement also formulated many of their class grievances in political terms and took the state as a target. From the early 1810s to the late 1840s, British workers engaged in class struggles of unparalleled scale.[245] As Thompson has shown in his classic study, the English working

237 Frobert 2009, p. 53.
238 Delalande 2011, pp. 44–8.
239 Delalande 2011, pp. 50, 61.
240 Guicheteau 2014, pp. 44–5.
241 Guicheteau 2014, p. 41.
242 Delalande 2011, p. 41.
243 Caron 2002, pp. 50–1; Zancarini-Fournel 2016, p. 275.
244 Caron 2002; Zacarini-Fourel 2016, pp. 276, 280–1.
245 Phillips 1989, p. 25.

class was first made in the 1830s out of the experience of 'an intensification of two intolerable forms of relationship: those of economic exploitation and of political oppression'.[246] Through Chartism, class conscious English workers increasingly expressed demands for universal manhood suffrage, confronting a state that was still under the control of a restricted elite. The British labour movement also had to deal with another urgent issue: the rapid development of industrial capitalism. Whereas French workers railed against 'capitalists' as 'idlers', their British counterparts were facing capitalists that had been asserting their power over the organisation of production for decades, and with increasing success. These capitalists were castigated by British workers as 'petty monarchs' who thought of themselves as 'the lords of the universe'.[247]

The class consciousness of British workers thus stemmed from an experience of the intensified state repression of movements demanding electoral reform; but it was also developed through the formation of trade unions and by demanding a reduction of workdays. It also became increasingly evident that by actively eroding trade regulations, the state was instrumental in the development of the new, 'economic' form of exploitation that they faced and that pitted them against their employers.[248] As Gareth Stedman Jones explains, eventually,

> less emphasis was placed upon the state as a nest of self-interest and corruption – 'old corruption' in Cobbett's phrase; instead, it increasingly came to be viewed as the tyrannical harbinger of a dictatorship over the producers. As the 1830's progressed, the predominant image was no longer merely of placemen, sinecurists and fundholders principally interested in revenues derived from taxes on consumption to secure their unearned comforts, but was something more sinister and dynamic – a powerful and malevolent machine of repression, at the behest of capitalists and factory lords, essentially and actively dedicated to the lowering of the wages of the working classes through the removal of all residual protection at their command, whether trade societies, legal redress, poor relief or what survived of the representation of the interests of the working classes in local government.[249]

Eventually, political corruption unequivocally receded into the background, and dealing with capitalist employers became the main concern of British

---

246 Thompson 1968, p. 217.
247 Thompson 1968, pp. 218, 221.
248 Phillips 1989, p. 24.
249 Stedman Jones 1983, pp. 173–4.

workers. After reaching its apex from 1839 to 1842, and in spite of a temporary revival in 1848, the vitality of the Chartist movement was on the wane.[250] The decline of Chartism represented an important moment of discontinuity, and the British labour movement became much more moderate from the middle of the nineteenth century.[251] Republicanism, as well as cooperatism – which had in any case always secured much less support than the fight for the expansion of the franchise – faded away.[252] Past the mid-century point, the British labour movement was centred on the trade unions.[253] Chartism had been the last working-class movement in nineteenth-century Britain in which political and economic issues could not be separated.[254] As Wood explains, 'economic' surplus appropriation had been present in Britain for a long time,

> but once the 'real subjection' of labour to capital by the industrial transformation of production had been assured, once industrial capitalism had made the processes of appropriation and production inseparable, working-class structures were, inevitably, concentrated on the 'economic' terrain and enclosed in the workplace. While 'economistic' struggles were to erupt regularly into the political arena, there was no longer the same immediacy in the connection between economic and political issues. The defeat of Chartism ... was an epochal watershed in the transformation of working-class militancy from political to an 'economistic' consciousness which was grounded in the transformation of British capitalism, together with a degree of adaptation and accommodation on the part of the ruling class.[255]

The concentration on the 'economic' terrain of the British working-class might not have been as inevitable as Wood would have it. The reconfiguration of class exploitation did directly impact employer-employee relations, increasingly confining them to an economic sphere. But as robust as this tendency might have been, it remained a process that could be contested. Yet, this capitalist reconfiguration also implied two important phenomena that contributed

---

250 Calhoun (2012, pp. 213–14) explains that, 'during the crisis of 1846–1848, [Chartism] seemed momentarily to take on a new life, but this was an illusion; while millions would sign petitions, very few were interested in risking much in an insurrectionary mobilization'.
251 Phillips 1989, p. 13.
252 Phillips 1989, p. 31.
253 Phillips 1989, p. 36.
254 Wood 1991, p. 73.
255 Wood 1991, p. 74.

to the greater quiescence of the working class. First, British workers had discovered that they could make 'incremental but certainly not negligible gains'
within capitalism and developed a 'consciousness of the effectiveness of trade
unionism and political reformism, not of a need for radical, transformative
struggle or revolution'.[256]

The second phenomenon had to do with the 'degree of adaptation and
accommodation on the part of the ruling class' that Wood alludes to. As discussed in the previous section, efforts to retrench sinecures and to staunch corruption and patronage had been a highlight of early nineteenth-century British
political life. Through these efforts and a series of economic reforms, states-
men sought 'to create a neutral, passive, almost apolitical state'.[257] 'Most of the
reforming legislation of this era sought to convince an ever more diverse body
of social interests that the state was no longer in the business of privileging
some of them at the expense of others'.[258] This transforming state, of course,
was subservient to the interests of capital, but it was also increasingly becoming
formally autonomous from the ruling class. Though several decades would still
have to elapse before the coming of universal suffrage, the British ruling class
relied less and less on the state as a means of surplus appropriation – and the
credibility of the case for the neutrality of the state grew proportionally. Thus,
Tombs suggests that 'Peel and Gladstone calmed Chartist radicalism by repeal-
ing the Corn Laws and cutting taxes on workers' consumption, thus convincing
them that the State was not hostile to popular claims'.[259]

While British workers slipped towards trade-unionism and reformism,
French workers held on to their revolutionary aspirations. Observing a march
of brick-makers in Oldham in 1870, the conservative French philosopher, historian and writer Hyppolyte Adolphe Taine reflected that '[i]t is a remarkable fact
that these unions do not deviate from their original object: they have no other
aim but wage increases, and do not think in terms of seizing political power,
which they most certainly would do in France'.[260]

Class struggles in France remained a deeply political affair. Rougerie asserts
that during the 1830s and 1840s, 'the proletarian [was] first that which is
deprived of political rights'.[261] Complaints that 'the rich are making the laws'

---

256   Calhoun 2012, p. 215.
257   Harris, quoted in Harling 2004, p. 113.
258   Harling 2004, p. 113.
259   Tombs 1996, p. 274. Developing a similar argument, Phillips (1989, p. 36) tells us that Shaft-
      esbury announced in Manchester in 1851 that 'Chartism is dead in these parts, the Ten
      Hours Act and cheap provisions have slain it outright'.
260   Quoted in Phillips 1989, p. 12.
261   Rougerie 1997: 'le prolétaire est d'abord celui qui est privé des droits politiques'.

were recurrent in the documents, letters, and testimonies produced by workers during this period.[262] Struggling for electoral reforms, French workers had come to believe that, fundamentally, they were poor *because* they were not represented, rather than the other way around.[263] From 1830, they began to speak of exploitation and of classes, and made themselves into a class by adopting and developing a republican ideology.

4   The Revolution of 1830 and the Rise of a Republican-Socialist Working Class

In spite of the constitutional concessions it had introduced, the Bourbon Restoration always stood on shaky political and social ground. Disputes between ultra-royalists and liberals over royal and parliamentary prerogatives contributed to the instability of the regime.[264] Liberals organised banquets to underline the importance of the *Chartes* and of the constitutional limits they believed it ought to impose on the monarch's powers. In 1827, they gained greater parliamentary weight – a victory celebrated with the erection of barricades by Parisian workers.[265] Tensions intensified rapidly during the spring and summer of 1830. After a renewed electoral victory for the liberals, the King released six orders that included the suspension of freedom of press, the dissolution of the Chamber of Deputies, and the tightening of the franchise. This act of force was met with widespread popular outrage. During the 'Three Glorious Days' of 27, 28 and 29 July 1830, the people of Paris rose and overthrew the Bourbon monarchy.

All commentators agreed that the workers played an absolutely central part in toppling the regime.[266] Yet the revolution did not serve their class interests. The new monarchical regime reduced the *cens* and opened up the political body to broader bourgeois layers, while the workers' demands were ignored. As Mooers explains,

> [o]ne of the chief tasks of the Orléanist regime was ... to attempt to redress the career grievances of this section of the ruling class at the same times as it smashed the wave of popular insurrection unleashed by the

---

262   Faure 1974, p. 90.
263   Hayat 2014, p. 59.
264   Bourguinat 2005, pp. 63–4; Zancarini-Fournel 2016, pp. 233–7.
265   Guicheteau 2014, p. 226.
266   Bruhat 1972, p. 360; Faure 1974, p. 53.

July Days. The monarchy moved quickly on both these fronts. Ninety-five percent of the prefects appointed under the restoration were purged from the administration. Worker and peasant grievances over wine taxes, communal rights, grain prices and unemployment, were dealt with through savage repression.[267]

Leading the July revolution, workers had acquired a greater awareness of their collective power. Yet, they also resented their political exclusion from the new regime. It was out of this sense of exclusion that workers discovered their common class experience and developed new forms of solidarity.[268] From 1830 to 1834, workers engaged in a sustained cycle of mobilisation that blended economic and political issues and culminated in insurrectionary episodes in Paris (in 1832 and 1834) and Lyon (in 1831 and 1834). These mobilisations launched an intense and protracted period of politicisation of French workers that eventually led to the Revolution of 1848 and the political and social struggles of the Second Republic.[269] Through this process of politicisation, workers barged into the official public space that notables attempted to restrict to themselves. They also developed their own alternative and oppositional public spaces in cabarets, theatres or in the streets, and via customary rituals such as charivaris, banquet and funerals.[270] Workers launched strikes, joined electoral reform campaigns, participated in municipal electoral politics, and erected barricades.[271] While some workers retained royalist inclinations, a republican, and eventually socialist, political culture grew steadily within proletarian quarters. Intense organisational efforts also took place, as the labour movement forged its own class organisations and developed its own press.

Following the 1830 Revolution, an 'explosion' of working-class self-expression took place.[272] One could witness the 'singular effort of a class to name

---

267 Mooers 1991, p. 77.
268 Hayat 2014, pp. 48–50; Tombs 1996, p. 274.
269 There is a vast literature on the politicisation of the French working class over this period. Maurice Agulhon's *La République au Village* (1979) has been a pioneering work on this issue. Agulhon, who describes this process of politicisation as one of 'descent of politics towards the masses' under the aegis of local elites, has been criticised for his top-down approach. For critical assessments of Agulhon's work and alternative understanding of popular processes of politicisation in nineteenth-century France, see Rougerie 1997, Soulet 2004, Guionnet 1997. For a general assessment of these historiographical debates, see Fureix and Jarrige (2015, pp. 233–44).
270 Fureix and Jarrige 2015, pp. 238–9.
271 Faure 1974; Moss 1976, p. 40.
272 Guicheteau 2014, p. 244.

itself, to expose its situation and to answer to the discourses that took it as a subject'.[273] From August to September 1830, workers' demonstrations continued to be organised on a trade by trade basis. Yet, by the end of September, as the government's refusal to consider working-class political and economic demands became clear, a minority of workers began to formulate their grievances in terms that transcended trade barriers.[274] This new political outlook was conveyed by the creation of working-class journals. In Paris, *L'Artisan, journal de la classe ouvrière*, *Le Journal de ouvriers*, and *Le Peuple, journal général des ouvriers, rédigé par eux-mêmes* first came out in September and were published until the end of the autumn of 1830.[275]

These journals insisted on the fact that the working class had been used and betrayed by the bourgeoisie during the July Revolution that had just taken place. The role of the proletarian press was to denounce those who spoke in the name of workers and to provide them with an authentic tool with which to express themselves. *Le Peuple* and *L'Artisan* both made a point of redefining the notion of 'the people', which, they said, was composed of 'the most laborious, the poorer and the most useful part of a nation'.[276] The people was in fact the working class, and this class was divided. *Le Journal des Ouvriers* and *Le Peuple* called for 'the cooperation of all professions'.[277] This unity was envisaged as a way to emancipate the working class from the exploitation it was experiencing.[278] These journals proved ephemeral, and they reached only a limited audience.[279] Yet they played a crucial role in launching an active and multifaceted process of class formation that took place over the following two decades and culminated under the Second Republic.

This incipient self-conscious working class made itself by adopting a Republican ideology and adapting it to its own class interests.[280] The liberal move-

---

273 Faure and Rancière 1976, p. 10: 'effort singulier d'une classe pour se nommer, pour exposer sa situation et répondre aux discours tenus sur elle'.

274 Hayat 2014, p. 51.

275 In Lyon, *L'Écho de la fabrique* was published from 1831 until 1834 and played a similar role in the making of the local working class. See Frobert 2009.

276 Quoted in Jakobowicz 2009, pp. 259–60: 'la partie la plus laborieuse, la moins riche et la plus utile d'une nation'.

277 Quoted in Jakobowicz 2009, p. 273: 'la coopération de toutes les professions'.

278 Ibid.

279 The last issue of *L'Artisan*, of *Le Peuple*, and of the *Journal de Ouvriers* appeared on 17 October, 10 November, and 12 October of 1830, respectively. The circulation of an issue rarely exceeded a thousand copies.

280 Aminzade 1993, pp. 45–8; Faure 1974, p. 76.

ment had developed out of a confrontation with ultra-royalists during the 1820s. Its membership had been variegated and represented a broad coalition amalgamating bourgeois elements and politicised urban artisans. The liberals' main purpose had been to defend the *Chartes* against the *utlrasroyalistes* – the issue of knowing which type of political regime to support (whether a monarchy or a republic) had not been a central preoccupation. This issue, however, was brought to the fore in 1830, and the Revolution led to a scission of the liberal movement and to the emergence of multiple republican associations.[281] These included the *Société des amis du peuple*, a political club that brought together much of the leading intellectual left of the time.[282] Republican associations distinguished themselves from the liberal movement by calling for the establishment of a republic, but also by embracing the *question sociale*, especially in the wake of the *canuts* revolt of 1831, which led the *Société des amis du peuple* to engage in efforts to recruit workers.[283]

The failed republican insurrection, demanding universal male suffrage and the abolition of indirect taxes, that took place in Paris in 1832 led to a reshuffling of the republican movement.[284] The *Société des amis du peuple* vanished, and republicans joined the ranks of the *Société des droits de l'Homme*, which had been founded back in 1830 and came to play a major role in the organisation of the working class from 1832 to 1834.[285] The *Société* was at first the site of a confrontation between moderate *Girondins* and radical *Montagnards* that advanced a much more far-reaching social agenda. As growing numbers of workers joined the organisation, *Montagnard* rapidly got the upper hand, and this led the organisation to extol the social measures of the 1793–4 Convention and the radical ideas of Marat, Hébert and Babeuf.[286] Thus one of the brochures published by the *Société* claimed that 'each property owner is ... properly speaking, only the depository of a share of the national wealth, entrusted to his administration'.[287]

---

281 Bouchet et al. 2015, p. 28; Hayat 2014, pp. 26–36.
282 Bourguignat 2005, p. 65; Huard 1996, p. 67.
283 Bourguignat 2005, p. 66; Hayat 2014, p. 43.
284 Guicheteau 2014, p. 239.
285 Bruhat 1972, p. 363; Huard 1996, p. 67.
286 Guicheteau 2014, pp. 240–1.
287 Quoted in Bruhat 1972, p. 363: 'Chaque propriétaire n'est ... à proprement parler que le dépositaire d'une partie de la fortune nationale, confiée à son administration'. The extent to which the *Société des droits de l'Homme* promoted a socialist ideology is debated. Bruhat (1972) maintains that, in spite of a strong will to tone down social inequalities, the society was not socialist. Moss (1976) claims that its socialist aspirations were straightforward.

Though most of its leadership was formed of intellectuals and middle-class professionals, three-quarters of the society's membership were workers.[288] The organisation had 3,000 formal adherents in Paris and around 300 affiliated groups in about 40 cities across the country.[289] It was, however, a male organisation. The republicanism that was being reloaded and appropriated by workers tended to repress the self-activity of women, who had irrupted into the French public sphere in the wake of the 1789 Revolution.[290] If republican 'fraternalism' was crucial in the making of the working class, it was indeed a 'brotherhood' – one that preserved the masculinist heritage of the First Republic.[291]

The rapid influx of workers led the *Société* to reorganise its sections by associating them with existing trades. Much energy was devoted to providing workers with a solid political education in a republican spirit.[292] Organising and mobilising the trades were also priorities. The society helped place workers in workshops, collected money for mutual aid funds, and led the organisation of work stoppages.[293] This mobilisation of trades was done with a class solidarity outlook. The *Société des droits de l'Homme* wanted to improve labour conditions while also seeking the republican emancipation of workers as class. As such, it operated at the crossroad of economic struggles and political agitation. As Faure puts it, the *Société*'s evolution led to 'a total fusion of professional action and political action, and made [it] a society of resistance and of mutual aid, and a workers' war machine against the monarchy'.[294]

The politicisation of workers over this period was thus accomplished in close connection to struggles revolving around socio-economic issues.[295] The *Société des droits de l'Homme* was part of this pattern that had deep roots in the class context and political economy of the period. Defending their material interests, workers always kept an eye on public authorities. Attempts to constrain 'unscrupulous' employers and 'bad' competition led workers to appeal to municipal authorities and to ask for 'regulation of the industry to limit com-

---

288   Faure 1974, p. 80.
289   Huard 1996, p. 72.
290   On the political irruption of women into the French public sphere, and efforts to exclude them from this sphere over the period covered in this chapter, see Zancarini-Fournel 2005, pp. 23–41.
291   Aminzade 1993, pp. 33–4.
292   Huard 1996, p. 69; Rougerie 1997.
293   Guicheteau 2014, p. 241.
294   Faure 1974, p. 87: 'une fusion totale de l'action professionnelle et de l'action politique, faisaient de la Société républicaine une société à la fois de résistance et de secours mutuels, et une machine de guerre ouvrière contre la monarchie'.
295   Guicheteau 2014, p. 241.

petition and to prevent abuses either by more active government intervention or by means of an industrial council of workers' and masters' representatives (such as the *conseil des prud'hommes*) ... For them the *prud'hommes* would serve in conjunction with their resistance association as a mean of defending their interests'.[296] Acting against employers who were trying to escape it, workers endeavoured to expand an already existing set of normative regulations by soliciting political interventions that would enforce and increase tariffs, as well as alleviate the effects of unemployment by constituting public workshops.

Workers were evolving in a non-capitalist setting where there was no 'economic' sphere abstracted from political institutions. Securing economic gains called for directly political struggles – a confrontation with the state, at its different levels.[297] This was true for the skilled crafts of major urban centres just as much as for rural textile production, where weavers appealed to mayors and prefects to enforce tariffs. This political process of resistance, and attempts to consolidate and expand trade regulations directly and naturally, contributed to the formulation and adoption of a republican agenda by French workers.

One of the best illustrations of this phenomenon is provided by the struggles led by the *canuts* of Lyon, which are worth considering here in some detail. As we saw in the previous chapter, Lyon's silk *fabrique* was composed of a multitude of small workshops that coordinated their activities not via market competition but through an intricate network of regulatory institutions. Under the Old Regime, the supervision of these regulatory functions was undertaken by a guild, the control of which remained a subject of conflicts that opposed artisans and merchants throughout the eighteenth century.[298] 1789 marked a major turning point in the evolution of the *fabrique*. In that year, silk workers waged a successful struggle against a 1786 edict that had established the free negotiation of prices between *canuts* and merchants. The tariff was reinstated in 1789 and administered via the creation of a joint commission of artisans and merchants.[299]

Following this initial success, workshop heads (the *canuts*) and journeymen acted as 'citizen-workers' engaged in a renewal of the *fabrique*. This implied a deep process of democratisation, with a *Tribunal des arts et métier* created to regulate silk production, prefiguring the first *prud'hommes* council established

---

296   Hunt and Sheridan 1986, p. 828.
297   Bruhat 1972, p. 362; Faure 1974, p. 66; Faure and Rancière 1976, p. 25; Moss 1976, p. 21.
298   Guicheteau 2014, pp. 69–70.
299   Guicheteau 2014, p. 131.

in 1806. As their employers, however, merchants did not welcome this application of revolutionary citizenship principles to labour relations. Contrary to French cotton producers, Lyon's silk merchants sold most of their high quality goods on international markets. When the abolition of the Spitalfield Acts put an end to the regulation of piece rates and liberalised London's silk industry, a number of Lyon's merchants and notables became scared that this might lead them to lose much of their international market share. In 1829, they addressed a letter to the king announcing their intention to initiate a profound reorganisation of the *fabrique*, following the model provided by English cotton manufactures that was now being adopted by silk producers in London.[300] Against these liberal merchants, *canuts* responded that both the workers' well-being and the economic prosperity of the city depended on the amelioration and extension of the democratic procedures that regulated the life of the *fabrique* and allowed it to adapt to the specific issues that a industry for high-quality products, such as silk production, was then facing.[301]

The merchants' first move to carry out their plan was an attempt to abolish the existing tariff that fixed the remuneration of workers. In October 1831, workshop heads had massively mobilised and obtained the fixing of a new tariff, established by a joint commission (in which merchants enjoyed representation) that had been organised under the aegis of the prefect. In early November, however, 104 out of the 400 silk merchants of the city announced that they refused to abide by the tariff. By mid-November, the prefect's initiative was gainsaid by the central government and the tariff abolished. This decision deeply shocked the 8,000 *canuts* and 20,000 journeymen and companions of the silk industry – after all, the tariffs had been revised and approved by the central state in 1807, 1811, and 1817.[302] Workers claimed that they would 'live working or die fighting' and organised a major demonstration on 21 November that quickly turned into an insurrection and a military victory that allowed them to take control of the city.[303] Workers handed power back to the mayor and prefect on 28 November. The government pronounced a general acquittal,

---

300   Frobert 2009, p. 21; Zancarini-Fournel 2016, p. 244.
301   Frobert 2009, p. 22.
302   Frobert 2009, p. 57.
303   Frobert 2009, pp. 28–30; Guicheteau 2014, pp. 238–9; Zancarini-Fournel 2016, pp. 243–9. The Lyon-based working-class journal *L'Écho de la fabrique* commented that the events of 1831 had not been caused by the existence of a systemic antagonism opposing workers and merchants but rather by some merchants who had been acting in bad faith. The journal insisted that compromises were possible and rejected the justification offered by merchants, according to which they had been facing an intensification of international competition (Frobert 2009, p. 40).

but confirmed that the tariff would not be applied.[304] Calls for the reinstatement of the tariff were made over the following months and years. Yet, it was
the workers' intention not simply to ensure that the tariff would be respected,
but also to consolidate and to expand the normative regulation of their trade so
as to curtail abuses. During the winter of 1831 and 1832 the city's working-class
press put forth a plan to reform and improve *prud'hommes* councils by making
them more democratic.[305]

The government's liberal stance set the stage for a renewed insurrectionary mobilisation. Work stoppages demanding the reinstatement of a tariff took
place on July 1833. On 14 February 1834, workers assembled and voted in favour
of another strike, again in favour of a fixed tariff, that lasted until 24 February and was successful in exacting gains from some merchants. A new general
strike was initiated on 9 April under the banner 'the republic or death' and
turned into another major insurrection that lasted until 14 April, when it was
violently repressed by government troops.[306]

A very important point to underline, here, is the politicisation of Lyon's
working class, which took place between the first and second *canuts* insurrections. Attempts to uphold the moral economy of their trade involved workers
in a directly political struggle and led them to confront different levels of government. Facing the stubbornness of a violent monarchical regime, workers
were logically steered to consider, and increasingly to adopt, republican ideas.
As Cottereau explains,

> the second and more violent revolt of 1834, though still more directly
> political and republican and in certain respects close to the spirit of Eng-
> lish Chartism, was a logical outcome of the event of 1831: since a man-
> datory official *tariff* had proved impossible to impose, there was nothing
> for it but to band together and impose an unofficial one. However, the
> freedom of association had been abolished by the July monarchy and so
> the need to guarantee such a price list led to the call for a republican
> regime.[307]

Since the current regime would not defend the interests of workers, their economic well-being called for a new political regime – the republic. And, indeed,

---

304   Only an indicative tariff – a 'mercurial' – would remain in place (Frobert 2009, p. 59; Gui-
        cheteau 2014, p. 243).
305   Frobert 2009, pp. 59–60.
306   Guicheteau 2014, p. 243; Zancarini-Fournel 2016, pp. 255–7.
307   Cottereau 1997, p. 115.

by the time of the second *canuts* revolt in 1834, the influence of republicans within Lyon's labour movement had become overwhelming.[308]

In the end, by leaning on the *prud'hommes*, and by exercising constant vigilance, Lyon's working class was able to enforce an 'unofficial' tariff, independently of the central state and in collaboration with municipal authorities and most members of the trade community. For decades to come, Lyon's silk trade prospered by sticking to a non-capitalist model of organisation.[309] But the insurrections of 1831 and 1834 served to highlight the relevance of a republican ideology – an ideology that radiated much beyond Lyon and across France. To consolidate and secure a normative regulation of the economy, a new political regime was needed.

On 13 and 14 April of 1834, Paris was the scene of an insurrection in support of the working-class struggle waged in Lyon.[310] This renewed insurrectionary effort was, however, once again crushed and a period of severe political repression ensued that lasted throughout the year. This political defeat led to a break-up followed by a recomposition of the republican labour movement that perpetuated the process of politicisation of the working class. Regular municipal elections contributed to this process. Following a law adopted in March 1831 – a delayed consequence of the 1830 Revolution[311] – city councillors were elected instead of being nominated by the state.[312] The *cens* for these local elections was considerably lower than for national elections and the result was that nearly 3 million male citizens could now exercise their right to vote. This permitted a certain polarisation of citizens and nourished the ongoing process of republican politicisation.[313]

Working-class republicanism was also nurtured by a major campaign in favour of an electoral reform that took place from 1838 and 1841.[314] This campaign saw the creation of newspapers, the organisation of banquets and intense popular agitation around the election of *Garde Nationale* captains. The demand for universal male suffrage was advanced with the purpose of emancipating the people. From the spring of 1840, the call to enlarge the franchise was increasingly linked to socio-economic issues in a way that was clearly reminiscent of the social and political struggles of the early 1830s.[315] Thence-

---

308   Bruhat 1972, p. 362.
309   Cottereau 1997.
310   Zancarini-Fournel 2016, p. 258.
311   Agulhon 1979, p. 17.
312   Mayors were selected by the municipal council, but designated by the king.
313   Guionnet 1997; Hayat 2014, p. 56.
314   Hayat 2014, pp. 57–9.
315   Bourguignat 2005; Hayat 2014, p. 59.

forth, workers invaded banquets organised to promote electoral reform, and the composition of the campaign's organising committees was modified in order to welcome a growing number of labourers.[316] Here again, political and economic struggles appeared side by side and tended to intersect: also in 1840, a movement of work stoppages that had begun the year before in the provinces reached Paris, and a major strike wave erupted in the capital. Workers struck for better wages and against different abuses such as bad subcontracting practices. To support their demands, strikers invaded public space. At the end of August, around 5,000 workers occupied the streets and organised periodic assemblies to discuss demands and select representatives. Authorities feared a republican contagion of the movement that would endanger the regime, and rapidly moved to repress it.[317] This sort of direct democracy was prefigurative of the republic that growing sections of the French working class were aiming for at the time.

In part because of divergences within the parliamentary left, the campaign for electoral reform went out in 1841; but it had significantly marked the labour movement. From the beginning of the 1840s, the fight for an electoral reform (which was resumed in 1847) was intractably linked to the demand to organise work in a planned and democratic way, and this imbrication became key in the making of a republican working class.[318] Put another way, the republicanism of the working class was a socialist republicanism.

The *canuts* insurrections and the great Parisian strikes of 1840 were only a spectacular illustration of a widespread pattern: to defend their material interests, workers felt the need to consolidate the existing normative regulations of their trades, and this put them on the path to republicanism. Republican principles were to be implemented within trades. In some instances, workers wrote down their republican ideas on the walls of their workshops.[319] The implementation of these principle also had a deeper and more practical consequence. According to the socialist Étienne Cabet, working-class actions naturally led to republican politics.[320] Pointing to the example of the Saint-Antoine *faubourg* carpenters, he noted that when workers associated to defend

316   Hayat 2014, p. 62.

317   Zancarini-Fournel 2016, p. 277.

318   Hayat 2014, pp. 61, 63. This interlacing of politics and economics in the programme of the working-class republican movement was summarised by the journal *Le Peuple* who wrote in 1847 that 'economic science teaches us that to organize work and to organize the government are one and the same' (quoted in Judt 2011, p. 72).

319   Guicheteau 2014, p. 208.

320   Rougerie 1994, p. 507.

their interests, when they formed a mutual aid or a resistance society (which were often one and the same), when they discussed their interests and elected representatives, they not only became imbued with a republican political culture, they were also already concretely building the republic. Discussing how the wallpaper workers and the hat makers of Paris associated to democratically organise their trades and to share available work before and during 1848, Rougerie offers further support to Cabet's assertions.[321] Other examples abound, and these practices became quasi-universal in Paris and widespread in many other towns of France from February 1848, in the wake of a new revolution.[322]

If republican principles became part of the lifeworld of trades, workers, as we saw, also massively joined the republican movement, and did so with the aim of giving a social consonance to the new political regime they aimed to build. Hayat explains that workers saw the monarchy as the regime of the exploiters and of the rich, while they presented the republic as the regime of the poorest class, who formed the majority of the population.[323] The republic was a political regime that would hand over power to the exploited and would thus put an end to their exploitation. Workers had to take over the state and turn it into a republic so that it would no longer be a tool of exploitation in the hands of the ruling class, and could instead be wielded by the working class to accomplish a socialist transformation of society.

The republican socialism of the French working class of the 1830s and 1840s revolved around the notion of *association*. The notion remained vague during this period. Associations could be producer cooperatives, but also mutual aid societies and resistance societies. The producer cooperative was a cornerstone of the dominant socialist project of the period, which Bernard H. Moss has called 'trade socialism'.[324] Republican socialists envisaged the creation of a democratic republic that would emancipate workers by funding producer cooperatives within each trade. This 'pragmatic socialism' had first been put forth by the socialist Philippe Buchez. It was also formulated by Blanc in his highly influential *L'Organisation du Travail*, first published in 1839, and was a crucial aspect of the political programme put forth by the democratic-socialists of the Second Republic.[325] Since, as workers complained, capital was not dir-

---

321   Rougerie 1994, pp. 508–9.
322   Gossez 1964.
323   Hayat 2014, pp. 46–7.
324   Moss 1976; see also Bruhat 1972, p. 385.
325   Berenson 1984, pp. 113–24.

ected toward industrial development and since banks and financiers refused to provide credit to fund cooperatives, a republican state would act in order to redirect financial resources by taxing capital and creating public banking institutions that would provide cheap credits.[326] State funded cooperatives would in turn allow workers to seize control of means of production and to eliminate internal trade hierarchies. This scheme would gradually eliminate the 'wage system' as well as 'usury capital' and 'parasitic intermediaries' who represented merchants and *négociants*. The payment of interests to financiers (*négociants*-bankers who advanced funds necessary to buy raw materials and tools) would stop, and producers would directly undertake the distribution of manufactured goods. As a result, workshop heads and their companions would be reaping the full fruit of their labour.[327]

The notion of association was also closely related to that of the guild and to the organisation of trades.[328] Republican socialists, however, had in mind a transformed and democratised version of guilds. These transformed trade corporations would ensure 'self-regulation within craft communities'.[329] Already in 1833, the tailor Grignon, as a member of the *Société des droits de l'Homme*, suggested that a republican 'popular governement' should put in place a 'permanent commission' that would ensure the organisation of all matters pertaining to a specific trade. The idea proved widely popular and was still discussed during the last decade of the Second Empire.[330] Functioning on the basis of a participatory democracy, such a 'permanent commission', representing a new form of guild, would be fixing tariffs, upholding usages, placing workers looking for jobs and administering mutual aid funds. It would act as an 'arbitrator' that would help or even replace the *prud'hommes* council.[331] Ultimately, the notion of association also implied regulating the economy as a whole through the federation of the different trades. This idea had already been formulated by

---

326   This plan was an important part of the democ-socs' programme under the Second Republic. The state would establish public banking institutions that would lend at 2.5 to 3 percent interest instead of the 8 to 10 percent offered by existing banks (Berenson 1984, pp. 111, 118). Besides supporting cooperatives, public banking institution would also provide credit to peasant, thus freeing them from the hold of usury and helping them to become independent landowners (Berenson 1984, p. 118).

327   Berenson 1984, p. 117.

328   Sewell 1980.

329   Calhoun 2012, p. 219.

330   According to Moss (1976), this kind of trade socialism remained dominant within the labour movement until the coming of the Third Republic.

331   Grignon in Faure and Rancière 1976, pp. 58–60.

members of the *Société des droits de l'Homme* in the early 1830s.[332] And it was this republican socialism that the labour movement of the Second Republic endeavoured to put into practice.

5 The Revolution of 1848 and the (Interrupted) Rise of the Democratic and Social Republic

The electoral reform campaign was resumed in July 1847, against the backdrop of a major subsistence and economic crisis that had begun the previous year and led to an acute unemployment problem.[333] An initial banquet was held in Paris, followed by several others across the country in the following months. The campaign was at first under the control of the royalist opposition, but a split took place over the autumn as republicans decided to organise their own *Montagnard* banquets. When a planned banquet, to be held again in the capital on 22 February, was prohibited by the government, the people of Paris took to the streets in opposition to the regime – the 1848 Revolution had begun. On 23 February, the National Guard defected to the opposition, forcing Louis Philippe to flee the capital, leaving a political void behind him.

A Provisional Government was formed at the City Hall to fill this void in preparation for the election of a Constitutional Assembly to be held later that spring. The new executive power was born out of a compromise between the liberal republicans linked to the journal *Le National* and the moderate democrats of another journal, *La Réforme*. Counting eleven members, the government was formed of a moderate liberal majority flanked by a socialist minority of two: the socialist Louis Blanc and the worker Alexandre Martin, often referred to as 'Albert'.[334] The government's majority intended at first to leave aside for later the issue of the nature of the new regime to be built. However, sustained popular pressure and mass demonstrations in the streets of Paris, but also in many other provincial cities, constrained the new political leaders of the nation to proclaim the Republic on 25 February. Governmental decrees adopted on 2 and 5 March ensured that representatives to the Constitutional Assembly would be elected on the basis of male universal suffrage.[335]

---

332   Hayat 2014, p. 54.
333   Bezucha 1983, p. 470; Hayat 2014, pp. 64–8.
334   Agulhon 1973, pp. 31–2; Zancarini-Fournel 2016, p. 289. Martin signed governmental decrees as 'Albert, worker'.
335   Zancarini-Fournel 2016, p. 301.

The question of the class nature of the republic, however, remained open before the promulgation of the constitution (which would only take place in November of 1848).[336] Most notables and many active politicians had come to accept the republic only insofar as they perceived it as a transitory regime in the temporary absence of a credible figure who could seriously aspire to restore the monarchy. If popular pressure from below had been instrumental in establishing the republic, the new regime was also an outcome of the fact that notables were torn apart by their allegiance to three rival dynasties (the Bourbon, the Bonapart, and the Orléans).[337] But the republican camp was also deeply divided. Hayat claims that the revolution had given birth to 'two republics' embodied in two opposed political sides.[338] Liberal, moderate and conservative republicans, forming the *parti de l'ordre*, had no intention of reforming the social basis of the nation and were content with a liberal form of representative democracy, often even if it fell short of ensuring universal male suffrage. They faced the partisans of a social and democratic republic, who were leaning towards a direct form of democracy that was reminiscent of the *Jacobin* tradition of the First republic, and had an eye on major socialist reforms.[339]

An isolated minority within the newly formed executive power, Blanc and Martin could count on the support of a mobilised and armed people, permanently present outside the walls of the Parisian City Hall. In the first days and weeks of its existence, the government was routinely visited by diverse popular delegations presenting demands and submitting petitions. Ideas, slogans and demands floating in the public domain were then distilled in the journals and clubs that multiplied rapidly in the wake of the Revolution: 739 journals and 440 other publications appeared, and 450 clubs were formed in Paris

---

336   Agulhon 1973, p. 27.
337   Agulhon 1973, pp. 3, 8–9.
338   Hayat 2014, pp. 11–24.
339   Left republicans held different attitudes towards the issue of the political representation of the people. Agulhon (1973, p. 16) claims that they saw the Republic and universal male suffrage as a 'social panacea' that would serve to emancipate the people. However, pointing to the constant vigilance of the people of Paris right from the outset of the new regime, embodied in continuous mass mobilisations meant to pressurise the government, Hayat (2014) explains that large sections of the republican working class, in the capital and elsewhere, believed that only direct democracy could ensure the sovereignty of the people. Though many took greater interest in a more direct form of democracy towards the end of the Second Republic, the *Montagnards* (democ-socs) accepted existing rules and attempted to capitalise – with impressive success – on universal male suffrage, in the hope of implementing a socialist programme of reforms, in 1849 and 1850 (Berenson 1984; Hayat 2014, pp. 340–1).

alone – many of which were linked to the labour movement.[340] In the absence of an elected assembly, much of the government's legitimacy depended upon its ability to read and to satisfy demands emanating from the street. However, although the working class was constantly mobilised and contributed to pushing the government to the left, political signs coming from the streets could be contradictory. On 16 March, between 30,000 and 60,000 elite troops demonstrated in the streets of Paris in opposition to the democratisation of the National Guard that had been decreed by the government. This was in effect a show of force by the right-wing opposition, intended to intimidate the incipient regime, and anti-socialist slogans were shouted by the crowd. On the following day, answering a call made by corporations, 200,000 marched in support of the regime and in favour of an agenda of social reforms.[341]

A class struggle was being waged out in the streets, but also within the state. While the republican-socialist minority attempted to capitalise on all the support it could gather from the streets, the moderate majority within the government relied on the backing of the ruling class inside the state. Numerous *notables* were allowed to retain their official position in the army, the high tribunals and public administration.[342] Both in the Provisional Government, and later in the Executive Commission, moderate and conservative republicans could rely on the support of wealthy landlords and notables linked to high finance, whose interests they shielded against socialist republicans. The class character of the state did not escape workers, who placarded the walls of Paris with posters denouncing the parasitism of notables living off public positions.[343]

The ongoing influence of notables upon state power explains governmental tergiversations over taxation issues during the first months of the Republic in spite of sustained popular pressure from below. The severe economic crisis that had begun in 1846 and lingered on as a result of the revolution created severe financial problems for the new regime. To cope with this situation, a new 'forty-five centime' tax was established by decree on 16 March 1848 – amounting to a 45 percent increase in all direct taxes. This new tax-grab aroused popular anger and incomprehension. Until then, the republican ideal had been

---

340   Agulhon 1973, pp. 47–8; Zancarini-Fournel 2016, p. 292. On the Paris clubs of 1848 as a vector of mass democracy, see Amann 2015 and Hayat 2014, pp. 96–104.

341   Zancarini-Fournel 2016, pp. 296–7. The organisers of the demonstration presented a petition asking that the election of the Constitutional Assembly be delayed. This, they hoped, would provide enough time to spread progressive republican ideas among the peasantry. The government agreed to delay the election by only two weeks (Agulhon 1973, p. 51).

342   Price 1987, pp. 106–7, 116, 119–20.

343   Hayat 2014, pp. 292–4.

associated with a sharp reduction and modification of taxes (including, especially, the elimination of indirect taxation). The anger was particularly acute
among the peasantry, which was hard hit by the new fiscal policy. Revolts erupted in several villages, and a violent confrontation with the National Guard
caused the death of twelve people in Guéret on 15 June 1848. Passive resistance
and refusal to pay the new tax was also in evidence, especially in the South
West, and intensified after the election of the Constitutional Assembly and the
refusal of the new republican government to abolish the reviled tax. This policy
helped to drive large sectors of the rural population away from the republic and
towards Bonapartism. Fiscal defiance in the countryside nourished the popularity of Louis-Napoleon Bonaparte, future Emperor Napoleon III, who was
elected president by the end of the year.[344]

The 1848 Revolution and the Second Republic highlighted divergences
among republicans on fiscal issues. Conservative and moderate republicans
refused progressive fiscal reforms while socialists promoted direct income and
capital taxes and rejected indirect taxes.[345] Working-class mobilisations did
bring gains, but these remained fragile and were retracted as the Republic
became increasingly conservative. Pressed by popular effervescence, the Provisional Government announced its intention to end the salt tax and the municipal customs tax days after the fall of the Monarchy, on 29 February, before
making its decision official by way of a decree on 15 April 1848. The salt tax was,
however, reintroduced (albeit in a reduced form) in 1849. Likewise, the Constituent Assembly voted for the suppression of the drink tax in May 1849 – following a government commitment to do so made during the preceding year –
but then backtracked and re-established the drink tax on 20 December.[346]

Large sectors of the working class and peasantry, then, were engaged in
a fight against notables over fiscal issues. Workers were seeking state power
because they wanted to make the Republic not only democratic, but also social.
From day one of the new regime, this was a clear priority. On 25 February of
1848, a crowd burst into the City Hall to present a petition demanding that
the government proclaim and guarantee the right to work, which was done by
official decree on that same day. The right to work, a demand that had been
strongly promoted by Considerant and the Fourierists, and the related demand
for the organisation of work put forth by different socialist groupings, had by
1848 deeply penetrated working-class consciousness.[347] With endemic unem-

---

344 Delalande 2011, pp. 45–6.
345 Delalande 2011, p. 47.
346 Delalande 2011, p. 47; Merriman 1978, pp. xxxii–xxxiii.
347 Beecher 2001, p. 165; Tombs 1996, p. 275.

ployment cursing the labouring masses (there were about 15,000 unemployed in Paris in March 1848), these demands were at that time more pressing than ever.[348]

Addressing the unemployment issue and acting on its commitment to guarantee a job for all, the government announced the creation of 'national workshops' on 27 February 1848. In essence, this represented a plan to put the unemployed to work on different public works (road building, land levelling, etc.). Labour was organised on a strictly hierarchical basis, discipline was severe, and the whole scheme was much closer to the 'charity workshops' that had existed in 1789 and 1830 than it was to Blanc's 'social workshop', which envisaged the self-organisation of labour.[349] Though many workers hired in the national workshops – out of a total of 120,000 across France by April 1848 – came to support the new institution on which they depended, much of the labour movement sensed that their creation was a defeat.[350]

In spite – or because – of this setback, the fight for the social republic continued. On 28 February, the day after the creation of the national workshops, a large demonstration marched to City Hall asking for the establishment of a Labour ministry that would take care of the organisation of work. The moderate governmental majority refused to abide by the crowd's demand, but a compromise was reached after hours of debates: a Commission of the Government of Labour, bringing together delegates from all trades, was established under the presidency of Louis Blanc. The mission of the Luxembourg Commission, hosted in the palace of the same name, was to study the issue of the organisation of work and to submit proposals to the government. Contemporary commentators, including Marx, and different historians since, have presented the Commission as a diversion, a 'synagogue of socialism', where workers would talk about pie in the sky instead of addressing more pressing political tasks at end.[351] The narrowness of its official mandate would seem to justify such severe judgements.

Workers, however, soon gave the new institution a much more subversive character. Most delegates had no intention of restricting themselves to theoretical and innocuous discussions. The Luxembourg Commission rapidly adopted motions to reduce the workday to ten hours in the Capital (and to eleven hours in the provinces) and to abolish bad *marchandage* – decisions that were rubber-stamped via a governmental decree on 2 March 1848. The ultimate goal

---

348   Zancarini-Fournel 2016, p. 291.
349   Agulhon 1973, p. 44; Zancarini-Fournel 2016, p. 290.
350   Agulhon 1973, p. 45; Zancarini-Fournel 2016, p. 290.
351   Agulhon 1973, p. 45; Hayat 2014, pp. 145–6.

of the Luxembourg delegates, however, was to end their dependency on a government formed by a majority of moderate republicans. This implied electing a majority of working-class representatives to the Constitutional Assembly. For this, Luxembourg delegates formed committees to select candidates within the capital and surrounding departments and supported their electoral campaigns. This represented an endeavour to supervise the political participation of workers in the emerging republican institutions in a centralised way – an effort, in other words, to turn the Luxembourg commission into a workers' party.[352] This effort was reminiscent of the aim, first formulated by working-class journals in the autumn of 1830, of transcending trade-corporation divisions in order to develop class-based solidarities. What had remained a project under the July Monarchy was now being built through the efforts of the Luxembourg Commissions. In the end, the life of the Commission was too brief and the electoral timeline did not allow the kind of mobilisation that would have been necessary – especially in the countryside – to make substantial gains at the polls. Still, this represented an original and rich popular experiment. As Hayat explains, beyond electoral participation, the aim was to forge a perennial and autonomous organisation capable of providing a political direction to the working-class, in order to ensure the development and defence of a truly social and democratic republic and to defend the workers' material interests.[353] Emerging out of workers' struggles, the Luxembourg Commission came to organise and to constitute the 'working class as a public force'.[354] It stimulated and structured political debates and mobilised workers, coordinating political actions and strikes.[355]

The Luxembourg Commission did not only organise the working class, it also began to regulate social relations of production. Its creation consolidated the revival of trade corporations, and did so from a class perspective. The Commission was an assembly of representatives from all different trades; its very creation by the government implied the organisation of trades in order to select delegates and to assign mandates.[356] The organisations being formed were reminiscent of Old Regime guilds, but were much more democratic. The new guilds internalised the revolutionary principles that had been nurtured by workers since 1789 and were developed as an outgrowth of the *prud'hommes*

---

352   Hayat 2014, pp. 142, 147, 149–51.
353   Hayat 2014, p. 153.
354   Sewell 1980, p. 252.
355   Moss 1976, p. 42.
356   Sewell 1980, p. 252. The classic reference on the organisation trade communities under the auspices of the Luxembourg Commission is Rémi Gossez's *Les ouvriers de Paris* (1964).

councils that had emerged from the turn of the nineteenth century. They were, in effect, an embodiment of the republican-socialist call for self-regulation that had been heard within trade communities over the previous two decades.[357] Holding regular internal general assemblies, Parisian trades sent delegates and proposals to the Luxembourg Commission. The organisation of trades also took place in the provinces and petitions were sent to the Commission from all over the country.[358] Bodies similar to the Luxembourg Commission were created in other French cities, with great success in Lyon.[359]

From the outset, the Luxembourg Commission solved conflicts between workers and employers in a conciliatory fashion, and this became a fundamental task that the new institution assigned to itself. Tariffs were also established at the Luxembourg Palace and enforced by the police prefecture in the name of the Commission. A back and forth was taking place between internal trade assemblies and meetings at the Commission, where workers' and employers' delegates would establish tariffs. This regulatory function was not part of the original mandate of the Commission, but was imposed by the workers themselves. As Hayat puts it, these practices gave new amplitude to the *prud'hommes* tradition, which was itself rooted in the corporative culture of the trades.[360] Contemporary commentators presented the Commission as a 'high court of *prud'hommes* [exercising] a sort of moral government by the free wish and express appeal of workers and of heads of enterprises'.[361] Corroborating such statements, the Commission itself declared that it was 'transformed incontinently, by the logic of things, into a high court of arbitration and exercises a sort of moral government by the free will and the express call of laborers and heads of establishments'.[362] Delegates determined the tariffs and usages that they considered most equitable, and new ones were elaborated, thus consolidating and expanding gains made by workers over previous decades.[363]

Through the activities of the Luxembourg Commission, republican principles penetrated trades more concretely and more deeply than ever before. In the spring of 1848, work was becoming a 'public activity'. Workers approached their trade organisations as public institutions and referred to their delegates, whose mandate they democratically controlled, as *fonctionnaires*.[364] These

---

357 Calhoun 2012, p. 219.
358 Zancarini-Fournel 2016, p. 295.
359 Bruhat 1972, p. 503.
360 Hayat 2014, pp. 147–9.
361 Hunt and Sheridan 1986, p. 829.
362 Quoted in Sewell 1980, p. 259.
363 Cottereau 2011, p. 18.
364 Sewell 1980, p. 263.

developments had the potential powerfully to extend the democratisation of social relations of production initiated in 1791, with the abolition of authoritarian guilds and their replacement by new and more democratic regulatory institutions. The 'intermediary publics' that had since been developing within trade communities were now being connected with one another under the supervision of the delegates sitting at the Luxembourg palace. While republicanism permeated trades, the federation of trades was foreshadowing a potentially radical reshaping of the republic: 'the Luxembourg Commission became something much grander than an advisory study commission; it became a kind of prototype of the future republic', claims Sewell.[365]

In addition to strengthening and expanding the normative regulation of trades, leaders of the labour movement wanted to build a socialist republic that would rest on the rapid development of producer cooperatives. For this, too, they leaned on the Luxembourg Commission. In only a few months, over a hundred producer cooperatives were established with the active support of the Commission.[366] These cooperatives were democratically organised and brought together workers and their former employers. Thus Blanc claimed at the time that numerous 'workshop heads came [to the Luxembourg Commission] to offer their mills to the state, and put at its disposal their means of production [for the formation of cooperatives], some out of generosity, others out of an intelligent calculus, others out of despair'.[367] This initiative, launched under the auspices of the Luxembourg delegates, persisted after the Commission's disappearance and the number of associations grew very substantially between 1848 and 1851.[368] By the end of the Second Republic, there were approximately 800 producer cooperatives in the provinces and more than three hundred in Paris, bringing together 50,000 workers from 120 trades.[369]

In spite of these significant accomplishments, delegates to the Luxembourg Commission experienced a series of political setbacks that eventually led to the Commission's disbanding.[370] The failure of working-class candidacies for the 5 April 1848 National Guard elections was followed by an unsuccessful demon-

---

365   Sewell 1980, p. 253.
366   Hayat 2014, p. 154.
367   Blanc 1849, pp. 85–6: 'Les chefs d'ateliers viennent ... offrir leurs usines à l'État, et mettre à sa disposition leurs instruments de travail, les uns par générosité, d'autres par un calcul intelligent, d'autres par désespoir'.
368   Judt 2011, p. 78.
369   Berenson 1984, p. 120.
370   Hayat 2014, pp. 233–6.

stration organised by trade corporations in Paris on 16 April, during which workers were vilified as 'communists' by national guards.[371] The demonstration exposed the strength of reactionary forces, but also the depth of divisions within the republican camp. A week later, the Constituent Assembly elections proved disastrous for the labour movement. Only eight socialist republicans were elected on 23 April, out of an assembly counting 900 members. The electoral efforts of the Luxembourg Commission delegates proved insufficient – socialist republicans lacked a single list and programme – in a context where peasant and rural workers had been alienated from the republic by a tax-surcharge. Moderate and conservative republicans formed a majority determined to end socialist experiments.[372]

During the week following the announcement of the election results, political deception was expressed through demonstrations and acts of violence in Limoges, Rouen, Rodez and various other towns and regions.[373] Such shows of discontent, however, proved entirely insufficient to halt a reaction that was already firmly underway. On 15 May 1848, the Executive Commission that had been formed by the Constituent Assembly permanently shut down the Luxembourg Commission. On 21 June, the new government announced the closing of the national workshops, which employed nearly 120,000 workers. Two days after, barricades were erected by Parisian workers and four days of violent clashes ensued. The insurrection, reaching civil-war proportions, was repressed in a bloodbath, causing over 5,000 deaths, with traumatic repercussions for the labour movement.[374]

As a result of this trauma, many socialists turned away from the state. They hoped to emancipate the working class through a process of self-organisation taking place underneath the state institutions, which federated trade communities would eventually displace.[375] Producer cooperatives continued to be established and ideas like Proudhon's bank of exchange (which proved unsuccessful), formed with the purpose of lending to cooperatives at minimal interest rates and without state support, became increasingly influential within trade communities.

Parallel to these development, however, working-class electoral mobilisation in support of the democratic and social republic continued apace with, in fact, much greater success than before. After the Parisian June days

371 Agulhon 1973, pp. 51–2; Hayat 2014, pp. 211–12; Zancarini-Fournel 2016, p. 297.
372 Zancarini-Fournel 2016, p. 302.
373 Agulhon 1973, pp. 54–7; Zancarini-Fournel 2016, pp. 303–5.
374 Zancarini-Fournel 2016, pp. 306–9, 313.
375 Hayat 2014, pp. 341–9.

Montagnards actively sought the electoral support of peasants. Coated in a religious discourse, the democ-socs' programme stuck to a socialism that assigned a key role the republican state in providing financial aid to producers' cooperatives.[376] The democ-socs also fought for the abolition of all indirect taxes and proposed to withdraw and to reimburse the recent forty-five centime tax by cancelling the compensation that had been offered to rich nobles for the sale of 'national goods'.[377] These proposals had a large echo among popular communities and active electoral mobilisation of democ-socs was a major cause of the substantial rural swing to the left that took place in many regions in 1849.[378] The May 1849 legislative elections turned out to be a significant electoral success for the *Montagnards*, who garnered 35 percent of the vote and won 200 seats. This electoral support was especially strong in rural areas of the South and Center, and the democ-socs won an absolute majority in 16 departments (out of 86).[379]

Yet, in spite of these impressive electoral results, the labour movement of the Second Republic had never fully recovered from the election of a right-wing Constitutional Assembly in April 1848 and from the trauma of the June days that followed. After the failure of an ultimate Parisian insurrection on 13 June 1849, Louis-Napoleon Bonaparte, who had been elected president in December of the preceding year, engaged in a systematic repression aimed at destroying the *Montagnards*. The resilience of the democ-socs was impressive, and new electoral gains were made during the by-elections of March 1850, but a thousand 'little events' of repression paved the way to the coup of December 1851, which rapidly turned the president into the Emperor Napoleon III and put an end to the Second Republic experiment.[380]

As noted by Calhoun, had it come to maturation, the Revolution of 1848 would have decisively taken France away from capitalism.[381] Bonaparte's coup, however, and the repression that ensued, brought labour quiescence 'for nearly a generation'.[382] The notables' class interest had been safeguarded, and this lull

---

376   Berenson 1984, p. xxii.
377   Delalande 2011, p. 47.
378   Berenson 1984, p. xix.
379   Berenson 1984, p. xiii; Bouchet et al. 2015, p. 272; Merriman 1978, p. xvii.
380   Merriman 1978. The fact that the coup sparked an uprising of some 100,000 peasants and workers in defence of a democratic and social republic is, however, a spectacular indicator of the depth of the republican and socialist politicisation of the popular masses that had been taking place over the preceding years and decades (Berenson 1984, p. xiii).
381   Calhoun 1983, p. 502.
382   Tombs 1996, p. 275.

in working-class militancy offered an opportunity to the new imperial regime to engage in reforms that finally announced a clear transition to capitalism in France.

The State-Led Capitalist Transformation of French Industry

Capitalism was imported into France on the state's initiative, in a process that spread over the second half of the nineteenth century. We saw how France's effort to reform its economy to cope with an increasingly powerful capitalist Britain largely failed during the second half of the eighteenth century. In the decades that followed Napoleon's debacle, old-regime agriculture endured, while industrial firms developed by seizing opportunities in a protected and fragmented non-competitive market – a process that remained non-capitalist. The capitalist restructuring of the French industrial sector was begun under the Second Empire and the Third Republic. While state interventions established its prerequisites from the 1850s, this restructuring really gathered steam from the 1860s and unfolded over following decades.

French politicians and officials were reluctant to impose a modernisation of agriculture that would upset the peasantry, since they understood that it was this class that had formed the linchpin of successive regimes since the Revolution.[1] However, the maturation and consolidation of British *industrial* capitalism over the second third of the nineteenth century compelled continental states to engage in capitalist transitions 'from above', in order to maintain their geopolitical standing. France was no exception. Not all sectors of the French elite agreed with this project, however, and many were still attached to their ideal of a rural and non-industrialised France.[2] Conflicts over the need to imitate English capitalism raged outside and within the state well into the Third Republic, and were still very much active in the early decades of the twentieth century.

In the wake of the 1851 coup that made the French President an Emperor, a new regime was able to override some of this resistance on crucial occasions, and to introduce structural economic changes. In spite of its ostensibly democratic (but in fact tightly controlled) electoral processes, the Second Empire imposed a personalised dictatorship that was largely freed from the parliamentary control that monarchs had had to concede after the Restoration.[3]

---

1   Kemp 1971, pp. 228, 232.
2   Verley 1997, pp. 27–8.
3   Plessis 1985, pp. 15–18.

Sharply breaking with the economic policies of the July monarchy, the new regime was the first to give a clear priority to industrial growth.[4] Under the influence of high-ranking liberal servants, economic advisors, and bankers – Saint-Simonian in tendency, and all fascinated and inspired by the British experience – Napoleon III made industrial growth a top priority right from the start.[5] Economic welfare was to stabilise the regime domestically by reducing unemployment and increasing popular consumption, while it would also empower France geopolitically.

In what follows, we discuss the processes through which the French state implemented capitalist social property relations in France, and demonstrate how this implied the making of a competitive national market that was in turn inserted into an emerging world market. The state-led creation of a new mode of industrial production implied the erosion of customary regulations as well as competitive imperatives that compelled firm owners to seize control of production and to engage in capitalist patterns of investment. The absence of agrarian capitalism in France slowed down the ensuing process of industrialisation, and yet, by the turn of the twentieth century, and as a result of the capitalist transformation of French society, one can witness the consolidation of a new mode of surplus appropriation. We begin our account of these changes by focusing on the international context of the second half of the 'long nineteenth century', in which their first stirrings can be identified.

1   Geopolitical Competition and Capitalist Industrialisation

At first a localised English phenomenon, capitalism emerged on the continent out of *geopolitical* pressures originating from Britain. While commercial rivalry among states eventually fuelled processes of capitalist investment on the continent, it did not induce the international spread of capitalism on its own. For this to happen, new social property relations first had to be implemented by states. Continental ruling classes that reproduced *in and as* the state,[6] via politically constituted modes of surplus appropriation, were forced to adapt to the increasingly threatening military might of Britain, which relied on a capitalist economy, a modernising state, and incomparable access to financial resources. In order to develop the military power that upheld their geopolitical standing,

4   Kemp 1971, p. 161.
5   Perez 2012, p. 14; Plessis 1985, p. 65.
6   Teschke 2005, p. 93.

'state-classes' engaged in a series of 'revolutions from above', pursuing political, legal and economic renewal from the late eighteenth century and throughout the nineteenth.[7] The nature and outcomes of these state-led transformations varied according to the class resistance with which they were met by elites and from below. Moreover, even when these modernising processes were capitalist in intent and result, the logic of the old regime tended to persist for decades after the inception of a capitalist transition in a given state: politically constituted property remained crucial for the reproduction of large sectors of continental ruling classes even as alternative 'economic' modes of surplus appropriation were developing. This had consequences for class and political relations at both the domestic and international level. Hence, the geopolitical accumulation that had been pursued by absolutist states seeking to preserve and expend their tax-base lingered on throughout the nineteenth century and into the twentieth. The dynastic policy of 'territorial equilibrium, partitions, and compensations'[8] was still in fashion, wars and contentions over dynastic successions still occurred, and the European inter-state system continued to be dominated by a logic of predation.[9]

It is true that treaties negotiated at the Vienna Congress in 1814–15 were consciously aimed at restraining the 'cannibalism that had characterised the balance of power in the eighteenth century'.[10] A quarter century of revolution and ongoing wars in which France had occupied centre stage had left their mark. After being played against one another by Napoleon, Britain, Prussia, Austria and Russia finally pledged to an alliance to contain France's imperial ambitions.[11] The emperor was defeated and ousted, and the monarchy was restored. France retained its territorial integrity, but it would no longer be permitted to act as a continental hegemon. The five great powers instituted a Concert of Europe as a system of dispute resolution designed to check each other's territorial aspirations and to contain revolutionary and nationalist movements. Central Europe was (temporarily) stabilised with the creation of a German Confederation under joint Austro-Prussian leadership. Behind the scenes, Britain pursued its policy of active balancing so as to prevent the emergence of hegemons. All of this contributed to the often-noted relative decline of military conflicts and the overall stability of the nineteenth-century European balance of power.

---

7   Skocpol 1979.
8   Teschke 2003, p. 260.
9   Lacher 2006, p. 90.
10   Gildea 2003, p. 59.
11   Gildea 2003, pp. 57–61; Schroeder 2000, pp. 158–62.

The Vienna system, however, rapidly eroded around the mid-nineteenth century. The bloody repression of the 1848 revolutions only highlighted the fundamental logic of this system: the interests and power politics of monarchs were to prevail over the rights of peoples to self-government and of nations to self-determination.[12] From the 1850s, geopolitical tensions intensified, and great powers began once again to engage in military conflicts against one another. First France, in 1851, and then Germany, in 1871, declared themselves empires. Wars were waged, and European geopolitical competition was soon projected on the world stage more than ever before, as states engaged in intense campaigns of colonial expansion in new regions from the closing decades of the century, during what became the 'classic age' of imperialism.[13] While economic competition between industrialising states intensified, it had not yet replaced the primacy of great power military rivalries, which culminated in a horrific bloodbath during World War I.

An early military manifestation of the demise of the Vienna system came with the Crimean War in the mid-1850s – the first major war between great powers since the fall of Napoleon. The nephew of the fallen Emperor, Napoleon III, now himself at the head of an empire, was the first French head of state since 1815 who was resolved to break out of the straightjacket imposed by the Vienna Congress. Officially championing the principle of national self-determination, the new French Emperor was determined to alter the existing equilibrium and respective zones of influence of the great powers. Conscious of Britain's desire to attenuate Russian influence over the Ottoman Empire, the French Emperor extended its sway over Constantinople at the expense of Saint Petersburg. He thus stirred up a crisis that eventually led to a war that France intended to exploit, in order to gain prestige and reassert its leadership over the continent.[14] Napoleon III won his wager. He secured an alliance with Britain, the Kingdom of Sardinia and the Ottoman Empire against Russia, which was decisively defeated by a war effort overwhelmingly carried by France. Russia partly withdrew from European affairs in order to implement internal reforms, while France was able to recover the status of first continental power – thus forcing Britain to focus on containing France in order to maintain equilibrium between powers.[15] In the late 1850s, the Second Empire set its sights on Italy, where it provoked a new crisis aimed at challenging Austria's influence over the peninsula. In 1859, France defeated Austrian troops in Lombardy, forcing

---

12   Gildea 2003, p. 59; Schroeder 2000, p. 167.
13   Wood 2003, pp. 124–30.
14   Gildea 2003, pp. 178–83; Schroeder 2000, pp. 168–9.
15   Anceau 2012, p. 286; Gildea 2003, pp. 183–9; Schroeder 2000, p. 171.

Emperor Franz Joseph to accept a truce. In the process, Paris gained Savoy and Nice and, more importantly, confirmed its geopolitical leadership.[16]

France's newfound hegemony, however, was fragile – as was revealed by the setbacks of its Mexican colonial adventures from 1862 to 1866[17] – and would not last. Its Italian intervention had isolated it, nourished fears in Germany of seeing its troops crossing the Rhine, and hastened a process of German unification. Acting as Minister-President and Foreign Minister from 1862, Otto von Bismarck had long 'advocated expanding Prussia's territory and power to fit its great power needs and role, absorbing or subordinating smaller states and ousting Austria from at least north Germany and possibly the south as well'.[18] France actually supported Prussia's growing influence over central Europe at the expense of Austria over the first half of the 1860s, hoping that mounting conflicts would weaken the two leading German powers.[19] French perceptions changed, however, when Prussia inflicted military defeat upon Austria and formed and controlled a North German Confederation from 1866. It soon became clear that the annexation of the remaining independent South German states – which had historically been used by France as a buffer against Prussia and Austria – into the Prussian controlled confederation would imply military conflict with France.[20] Conflict did ensue a few years later when Bismarck attempted to place a Hohenzollern prince upon the vacant throne of Spain. In response to Bismarck's endeavour, Napoleon III rashly declared war on Prussia in 1870, but French armies were rapidly routed by their opponents' superior strike force. This military blow led to the collapse of the French Empire, while his victory allowed the Prussian Minister-President to engage in negotiations with southern German states that would pave the way to William I's proclamation as Emperor of the Second German Reich in Versailles in mid-January 1871. Germany had now displaced France as the leading military and diplomatic power in continental Europe.[21]

Of course, it was not simply Bismarck's astute diplomacy that had allowed Germany to overtake France. Fundamentally, Prussia's military and diplomatic successes had been supported by the country's 'economic miracle', while France's debacle in 1870 underlined its relative industrial weakness.[22] The

---

16   Anceau 2012, pp. 381–7; Schroeder 2000, pp. 171–3.
17   Anceau 2012, pp. 391–3, 429–31.
18   Schroeder 2000, p. 175.
19   Marcowitz 2008, p. 17.
20   Gildea 2003, p. 40; Marcowitz 2008, p. 13; Schroeder 2000, p. 179.
21   Orgill 2008, p. 50.
22   Kemp 1971, p. 218.

imperial ventures of the Third French Republic over the decades that followed can be seen as an attempt to reverse its relative decline and to keep up with Britain and Germany. But France was not simply dealing with one established and one aspiring imperial state – it had to cope with one industrialised (Britain) and one very rapidly industrialising (Germany) capitalist economy. The international context of the second half of the nineteenth century was thus marked by three important interlaced phenomena: the unification of powerful and modernising polities, most notably in Germany, in Italy, in the United States and in Japan;[23] the imperial partition of what is called today the 'Global South'; and, crucially, the emulation of British industrial capitalism by European, North American and Japanese states. In this rapidly evolving and hostile context, the French state – and the ruling class that controlled it – had no choice but to follow suit and to initiate a transition toward industrial capitalism, if it was to maintain its geopolitical standing. Napoleon III had already understood this. For him and for his councillors, 'the nation's greatness depended – no less than on military victory – on the success of an "industrial revolution", in the broadest sense, that would hoist France to the level already reached by England'.[24] In order to safeguard the interests of the regime 'in relation to foreign powers', the Emperor recognised 'that national power was bound up inextricably with industrialization' and the necessity 'to impel manufacturers into improving their technical efficiency in the cause of national power'.[25]

2   Building Foundations: the Making of a Competitive Market

Acting as Foreign Minister in Louis-Philippe's government, François Guizot had told the French in 1843: 'Enrich yourself, improve the material and moral condition of your country'.[26] This, however, had remained a mere incantation, and had in fact been gainsaid by the government's own economic policy. Only under the Second Empire did Guizot's call become a real leitmotiv that materialised in concrete governmental initiatives.

---

23   These processes of state building were associated with the aforementioned German leadership under Prussian leadership, the Italian *Risorgimento*, the Northern victory in the American Civil War, and the Meiji Restoration in Japan. The Russian state also undertook major internal reforms from the 1860s.

24   Plessis 1985, p. 62.

25   Kemp 1971, pp. 172–3.

26   Quoted in Plessis 1985, p. 62. See also Kemp 1971, p. 159.

Louis-Napoléon Bonaparte had spent years in exile in London, the effervescent capital of a rapidly modernising capitalist society. Upon becoming an emperor, Napoleon III surrounded himself with liberals such as Michel Chevalier, the key architect of the 1860 commercial treaty with Britain, the Pereire brothers, and other prominent businessmen such as the banker Paulin Talbot. The regime established closed ties between business and politics; rich businessmen were introduced into the Legislative Body and gained strong influence over executive power and high-ranking civil servants.[27] In spite of this penetration of state institutions by business and liberals, the Emperor often had to fight conservative figures within his government in order to impose reforms conducive to a capitalist reconfiguration of the French economy. This was clearly illustrated, for instance, by the Council of State's strong opposition to the liberalisation of company law during the early 1860s.[28] Nevertheless, Napoleon III and his liberal supporters were able to implement decisive transformations in the French economy.

The imperial government adopted the novel idea of making use of credit to propel development by investing in public works. The ensuing deficit would eventually be eliminated, debts reimbursed, and interest paid for, while the stimulation of economic development would lead to increased government revenues. This strategy partly supported both Haussmann's transformation of Paris – which was reproduced on a smaller scale in cities across the country – and the state's encouragement of railroad building. But this was not a socialist regime. Though it often came at the price of bitter internal strife, Bonapart's government was the first to actively engage in a capitalist transition. In point of fact, direct state investment in public works was rather modest, and remained of far less importance than military expenditures.[29] The government's fundamental goal – not least in order to support military expenditures, by increasing national wealth and thus state revenues – was in fact to introduce structural changes that would foster private investment of a capitalist type.

The Emperor outlined his economic programme in his Bordeaux speech of October 1852, and in a more detailed manner in a letter to his Minister of State Achille Fould, published in January 1860 by the journal *Le Moniteur universel*.

---

27   Plessis 1985, p. 80.
28   Dougui 1981, p. 281. By contrast, magistrates of the *Cour de cassation*, the highest tribunal in the country, intervened publicly to back liberalisation. As will be discussed below, the *Cour* played a crucial role in the implementation of capitalist social property relations in France.
29   Plessis 1985, pp. 64–5.

For Napoleon III, industrial development was key, and without it agriculture would remain in its infancy. To build an industrial sector that could cope with British competition, trade needed to flourish, and this called for the prompt development of a modern transport network as well as the liberalisation of international trade. It was also necessary to provide industry with low-interest capital loans that would enable the upgrading of plants.[30]

The new regime acted rapidly to reform the French financial sector, which had retained a conservative rentier attitude in the 1840s. In 1852, the Pereire brothers received the support of the Emperor to create the *Crédit Mobilier*, a joint-stock company that raised finance for investment by selling bonds and attracting deposits. The *Crédit Mobilier* became the key player of the investment banking that emerged under the Second Empire. The intention of the regime was to support men willing to develop innovative and unorthodox financial practices. *Crédit Mobilier*'s turbulent and adventurous existence ended in 1867, but it introduced inventive investment schemes that had a transformative impact on the old and hitherto conservative *Haute Banque* concentrated in Paris.[31] Other large credit institutions such as the *Crédit Lyonnais* (1863) and the *Société générale* (1864) were also established to favour commercial and industrial development in France. In parallel, the government pressured new and old financial institutions to open up provincial branches. Local banks multiplied, banking became increasingly specialised and detached from commerce, and the Second Empire witnessed the arrival of deposit banking – a development directly inspired by the British model.[32]

All in all, however, while important advances had been made, the modernisation of the banking system was far from complete, even in the final years of the Second Empire. Banks had only begun to develop their branch networks, and 'France still had one of the lowest "bank densities" among the developed countries of the time'[33] – a handicap that limited the possibility of tapping into the savings of the country's massive peasantry. Moreover, in spite of the Pereire brothers' stated goal of developing industrial firms and promoting their merger and consolidation, investment banks had only very limited holdings in manufacturing and mining companies, and were much less involved in the funding of industrial activities than German banks at that time.[34] Missing a base in productive industry, *Crédit Mobilier* derived much of its profits from

---

30   Teurnier 2015; Plessis 1985, p. 62.
31   Harvey 2005, p. 116; Kemp 1971, p. 163; Plessis 1985, p. 76.
32   Plessis 1985, pp. 75, 78; Plessis 1996, pp. 139, 148; Kemp 1971, p. 192; Zeldin 1993, p. 83.
33   Plessis 1985, p. 78; Asselain 1988, p. 1242.
34   Kemp 1971, p. 190.

speculation – facilitated by the frantic expansion of the Paris stock market during the 1850s – which it encouraged by manipulating and inflating the value of the corporate structures that it created via its investments in railway and public work companies.[35] Overall, French savings were invested in three sectors of roughly equal size. One-third went into French government borrowing, another third was invested in industrial activities revolving mostly around railroad building, and the final third was exported to fund foreign governments, railways and public works.[36] Since the government guaranteed the investments made in this sector, banks deployed much of their resources on railroad building. They also invested in the ongoing frenzy of urban public works. Funding industrial development remained very limited until the closing decades of the nineteenth century. Even large banks such as the Crédit Lyonais retained a conservative outlook when financing industry, favouring discount credit over long-term and substantial investment in large and modern industrial firms.[37] Yet, if the involvement of French financial institutions in the industrial sector remained peripheral, it was probably less out of conservatism (though this remained a factor) than because domestic demand for capital was still relatively weak.[38]

In addition to reforming finance, the regime needed to create a context in which firms would be compelled to invest. Napoleon III and his advisors were well aware that the key for the 'industrial revolution' that they wished to launch was to incite price competition that would force industrial firms to modernise their installations and activities. As the Emperor put it in his 1860 directives to Fould, 'without competition, industry stagnates'.[39] It was understood that to encourage competition, it would be necessary to develop transport and communication networks.[40] Roads and canals were built, and rivers were converted into navigable waterways; but this was the rail era, and train transport became the government's priority. Road and water circulation grew modestly in absolute terms under the Second Empire (road transport actually declined sharply after 1870), but rapidly lost ground to rail transport. Representing 11 percent of total commodity transport in 1851, train transportation reached 63 percent in 1876.[41] This reflected a clear policy choice.

---

35   Kemp 1971, p. 168.
36   Plessis 1985, p. 81.
37   Plessis 1996, p. 151.
38   Plessis 1985, 82.
39   Quoted in Teurnier 2015: '[S]ans concurrence, l'industrie reste stationnaire'.
40   Anceau 2012, p. 351; Perez 2012, p. 3.
41   Léon 1993, pp. 293, 295.

An 1842 law had launched the formation of a national railway network, but its construction was slow and France lagged behind several European countries. The Emperor's entourage understood that granting concessions to private companies that built and exploited railway lines was not enough, and that resolute state action was needed actually to mobilise the capital needed to develop a proper railway network. The government granted 99-year concessions to companies and authorised them to issue bonds (an initiative that had already been taken by the Second Republic). It also guaranteed the payment of four-percent interest on these bonds and on loans contracted by railway companies to finance their investments. Once the initial network was completed toward the end of the 1850s, the government directed the Bank of France to support the building of branch lines and continued to back interest payments.[42]

These efforts rapidly paid-off. Counting 1,931 km in 1850, France's railway network expanded to 4,100 km in 1860 and again to 17,400 km, before reaching 23,600 km in 1880. Already by 1869, all the main routes of the present-day network had been built and France had caught up with or surpassed most of its neighbours.[43] Rail transport quickly increased, going from 100 million tons per kilometre in 1845 to 5,057 million tons in 1870. From 1851 to 1876, rail traffic rose by 1,590 percent. Railroads introduced a spectacular 'contraction of space'.[44] By the early 1860s, for instance, merchandise was moved from Lille to Paris in three days, instead of the standard eight days by road. This general acceleration of transport throughout the country was also due to constant improvements of locomotives and the creation of rationalised rail yards, while the movement of commodities across France was facilitated by the state's construction of a national electric telegraph network, which was made available to the public by the mid-1850s and became widely used, including by private industrial firms.[45] The cost of transport fell rapidly, from 12 centimes by tonne-kilometre in 1841 to 5.88 centimes in 1881, and to 4.8 centimes in 1900.[46]

The rapid development of modern transport and communication infrastructures by the Second Empire occurred alongside a profound transformation of commercial and marketing practices. Increasingly, trade in commodities was rationalised, and the number of commercial intermediaries significantly

---

42   Anceau 2012, p. 352; Perez 2012, p. 6; Kemp 1971, pp. 170–1; Plessis 1985, p. 83.
43   Anceau 2012, p. 353; Beltran and Griset 1994, p. 90; Léon 1993, pp. 264–5, 293–5; Perez 2012, p. 7; Plessis 1985, p. 85; Woronoff 1994, p. 230.
44   Léon 1993, p. 266.
45   Anceau 2012, p. 351; Plessis 1985, p. 87.
46   Léon 1993, p. 268; Verley 1996, p. 108.

decreased. Contacts between producers and consumers became much more direct and constant, as the former began to make systematic efforts to reach the latter. The co-dependence of industry and commerce also significantly intensified, as production began to systematically follow the flow of orders that could now be placed on a daily basis and swiftly shipped. Embodying these transformations was the new figure of the commercial commissioner. Establishing themselves in all branches, commissioner houses developed a mode of distribution that allowed consumers to simultaneously have access to similar products made by different French as well as foreign firms. This induced price competition that was then further facilitated by the emergence of *grands magasins*, which made their influence felt in Paris and in other larger cities from the 1860s and 1870s especially. Whereas small traditional boutiques had been unappealing places, where price bargaining had been the rule, the emerging capitalist retail sector imposed fixed and marked prices, fluctuating according to market competition, and engaged in new and sustained marketing efforts including advertising campaigns.[47]

The development of railways in the 1860s and the concomitant transformation of the sphere of circulation led to the emergence of a national market that reached completion in the late 1870s. This was the end of the internal compartmentalisation of the French economic space. The multitude of local and regional economies that had endured into the nineteenth century were now being integrated within, and subsumed under, a national market. This represented a quantitative as well as a qualitative change – market opportunities were enlarged, but market compulsion was now also coming into play. The important inter-regional price disparities that had persisted in post-revolutionary France were rapidly eroded.[48] Price competition ensued, causing the disappearance of guaranteed incomes tied to regional monopolies, and whole regional industries were sometimes wiped out as a result. This leads Caron to suggest that the formation of a unified national market was as important a factor as the intensification of international competition in causing the economic transformation of France during the Second Empire and beyond.[49] Modern transport infrastructures were in fact also a vector of the foreign competition that began to seriously impact French firms in the wake of the signing of commercial treaties by the French state.

The national market that was forming was in turn about to be integrated into an emerging capitalist 'world market'. The government of Napoleon III played

47   Folhen 1956, pp. 149–57; Léon 1993, pp. 285–90; Plessis 1985, p. 95.
48   Beltrand and Griset 1994, p. 90, Léon 1993, p. 304; Woronoff 1994, p. 231.
49   Caron 1995, p. 120.

a central role in forging this market, signing a commercial treaty with Britain in 1860, the first of a series signed between European states in the years that followed. It did so with a diplomatic purpose, as France wanted to develop its alliance with its powerful neighbour. Modernising the economy was another central goal of the government. As Kemp explains, '[t]here is no doubt that by lowering tariffs Napoleon III hoped to stimulate material progress, after the initial dislocation'. The intent was to impose a change of context so that 'the most highly protected French industries would be forced to equip themselves to world standards on pain of losing their home market, and thus their whole basis for existence'.[50] While the emperor was opposed to complete free-trade, he had been convinced by his Saint-Simonian entourage of the need to liberalise international trade in order to stimulate economic development. Liberal *économistes* had been organising in support of free trade since the 1840s, arguing that internal competition was too limited and had to be supplemented by external competition.[51] They were backed by wine producers, silk merchants, and some luxury good producers, confident that freer trade would allow them to penetrate new foreign markets. The vast majority of French industrialists, however, were pungently opposed to any questioning of the prevailing and long-standing protectionist policy. Their strong lobbying organisations, their capacity to mobilise the support of their workers on this issue, and their numerous powerful allies within the state, including eminent ministers, had allowed them to impose and to reproduce a protectionist orthodoxy since the fall of the First Empire.

Napoleon III and his close entourage advanced with caution. Already in 1853, duties on iron and coal were reduced to support the construction of railroads, and other targeted reductions in duties were also adopted in the years that followed. The Emperor and his advisors had already prepared a plan for a far more thorough reform of tariffs, but the State Council was still divided on this issue.[52] In 1856, a bill to replace prohibitions on textile imports with moderate duties incited strong opposition in industrial circles and was repelled by the Legislative Body.[53] In spite of this rebuff, the Emperor announced that international trade would be liberalised within five years and proceeded to circumvent legislative power. Whereas under the Restoration, executive power had to secure legislative approval to modify tariffs on imports, Napoleon III had obtained the constitutional right to act unilaterally on these matters.

---

50   Kemp 1971, pp. 173, 174; see also Dunham 1930, pp. 6, 141.
51   Hirsch 1991, pp. 399–400.
52   Dunham 1930, pp. 20–1.
53   Anceau 2012, p. 377; Dunham 1930, p. 22.

As a close collaborator of the Emperor, Michel Chevalier engaged in secret negotiations with Britain to prepare a commercial treaty between the two nations. For Chevalier, the treaty would force the modernisation of industry, which would in turn be favourable 'to the increase in the power of the state'.[54] Chevalier's efforts led to the Anglo-French commercial treaty of 1860, which was denounced as a '*coup d'État douanier*' by industrialists and members of the legislative assembly. The treaty, however, did not impose free trade. While Britain would not enforce any tariffs (thus sticking to the free trade posture it had already adopted), the agreement stipulated that French tariffs could not exceed 30 percent (25 percent from 1864). Separate conventions were subsequently negotiated, also in 1860, to fix duties for specific sectors. In order to avoid the economic debacle that followed the trade treaty of 1786 and to appease industrialists, the government put in place a commission of enquiry to guide the negotiation of these conventions. It also offered low interest loans to support the modernising efforts of French firms.[55]

The Anglo-French treaty of 1860 served as a template for 14 others signed by France with European countries, including the Ottoman Empire, in the years that followed. In 1872, Thiers's government attempted to modify the Anglo-French treaty to increase tariffs, but failed to do so, and the treaty remained in force until 1881. Growing discontent forced the adoption of the Méline law of 1892, which introduced new, higher tariffs on foreign trade. These duties, however, were remarkably moderate (especially for industrial products) compared to those that had prevailed over the first half of the nineteenth century.[56] They were, moreover, mostly targeting exports of agricultural products – a sector in which price competition had proved especially harsh.

We need to situate these French developments in the context of the second half of the nineteenth century, which saw the rapid development of industrial capitalism across continental Europe. This was a 'watershed' in European economic history: whereas the average annual rate of growth of the gross national product per capita had averaged no more than 0.3 percent until the turn of the nineteenth century, the average figure rose to 1.5 percent from 1860 to 1890.[57] While the French state was building an integrated and competitive economy, other states were doing the same. Prussia was the primary initiator of the *Zollverein*, a customs union of German states that grew steadily from 1834.

---

54   Quoted in Dunham 1930, p. 148.
55   Anceau 2012, p. 379; Cadier 1988, p. 357; Dunham 1930, pp. 139–41, 146–50; Kemp 1971, pp. 175–6.
56   Barjot 2014b, p. 393.
57   Ferguson 2000, p. 83.

The Austro-Hungarian customs union was established in 1850, and a Russo-Polish union was created in 1851. An Italian single market also emerged as a consequence of the country's unification.[58] European states built the infrastructure that ensured an effective integration of these economic spaces. In 1850, Europe counted 14,500 miles of railroads; by 1880, there were 101,700 miles across the continent.[59]

From the 1860s, the rapid development of communication and transport infrastructures, combined with the signing of a series of trade treaties, facilitated the emergence of a European market. The value of total European exports, established at 1,200 million dollars in 1850, had risen to 4,050 million by 1880.[60] As summarised by Gildea, '[b]y 1880, it would be fair to say that the international economy had been integrated, that a single world market had been created'.[61] This new reality was not really altered by the return to protectionism in Europe after the 1870s. Tariffs did not return to the highs that they had reached in earlier historical periods, and 'nor did rising tariffs in Europe as a whole (and in the United States) impede the growth of trade, which was more rapid in the so-called neo-mercantilist period than in the decades of free trade'.[62]

The world market was there to stay, and this implied new competitive imperatives. Many have questioned the notion of a 'Great Depression' of the world economy from the mid-1870s to the mid-1890s, stressing that world production actually continued to rise dramatically throughout this period. Severe recessions certainly punctuated this era, but their cause, and the fundamental reason behind the profound anguish that affected contemporaries, was intensified price competition that compressed profitability margins.[63] This was an especially sensitive issue in a context where, at least until the turn of the twentieth century, the share of the population that had become market dependent was still limited (especially in France, as will be discussed below), and where aggregate demand was consequently still relatively low. Competitive imperatives incited constant development of new technologies and enhancement of labour productivity, and this in turn fuelled massive increases in output capacities, leading supply to overtake demand. As the number of capitalist economies and firms grew, and markets were flooded with commodities, prices fell –

---

58   Ferguson 2000, p. 105.
59   Gildea 2003, p. 150.
60   Gildea 2003, p. 152.
61   Gildea 2003, p. 150.
62   Ferguson 2000, p. 106.
63   Hobsbawm 1994, pp. 35–6.

especially the price of agricultural products, but of industrial goods as well. The European price of iron fell by 50 percent from the early 1870s to the late 1890s. In Britain, the overall level of prices dropped by 40 percent.[64] In France, industrial prices fell by approximately 35 percent from the late 1860s to the late 1890s.[65]

As international competition intensified, France was falling behind. Its share of world manufacturing output fell from 7.9 percent in 1860 to 6.8 in 1900. Meanwhile, Germany's share went from 4.9 percent in 1860 to 13.2 percent in 1900, while Britain remained at the head of the league even as its share went down from 19.9 percent to 18.5 percent.[66] By 1880, Germany 'had overtaken France as an exporting economy'.[67] The shares of exports in the French GDP had continued to grow until the mid-1870s, but fell afterward, and the country's commercial balance became negative during the closing decades of the nineteenth century.[68] Competition, however, forced French firms to adapt. From 1900, the shares of exports in GDP once again grew, and France was able to halt its relative economic decline. This adaptation was once again facilitated by state interventions aimed at advancing the capitalist transformation of social property relations. The French state had created a competitive national market that had been inserted into an emerging capitalist world market. The state had exposed industrial firms to new competitive imperatives, and it had also helped industrial firms to subsume labour under capital in order to cope with those imperatives.

3   The Erosion of Customary Regulations and the Subsumption of Labour

In the new context of a unified national market exposed to international competition, French industrial firms were compelled to seize control over labour processes in order to survive.[69] These efforts were assisted by important judicial transformations, as sectors of the French state sought, from the second half

---

64   Hobsbawm 1994, p. 37.
65   Caron 1995, p. 122. The prices of agricultural products fell even more sharply. For instance, the price of wheat decreased by 45 percent from 1860 to 1895 (Marchand and Thélot 1991, p. 25). However, for reasons that will be presented below, this did not incite a capitalist transition in the French agrarian sector.
66   Ferguson 2000, p. 122.
67   Gildea 2003, p. 152.
68   Verley 1989, p. 63.
69   Barjot 2014b, p. 385; Beltran and Griset 1994, p. 120; Caron 1995, p. 122.

of the 1860s, to nullify the power of proximity justice courts that was discussed in Chapter 3 and that prevented the subsumption of labour by capital. The state no longer ignored local and regional customary regulations of labour markets and processes as it had done since the Revolution. The Second Empire and, with greater and growing consistency, though often at the price of internal strife between state organs, the Third Republic intervened to eliminate these regulations. The *bon droit* that had been preserved and expanded by the Revolution now had to go, if France was to successfully undergo its transition toward industrial capitalism.

In 1866, a ruling made by the *Cour de cassation* – France's highest court of justice – invalidated a previous ruling made by a *prud'hommes* council and was widely publicised. Against the council, the high court had confirmed that an employer could retain two weeks' pay from a worker who had entered the workshop in her clogs, in violation of rules established unilaterally by her employers.[70] Similar decisions, granting arbitrary powers to employers, were issued under the Third Republic from the 1870s. In 1871, rail workers of different companies mobilised and sent a collective petition to the Minister of Public Works asking him to improve health and safety standards for them as well as for passengers. Eighty of them were dismissed and rail companies confiscated the money they had contributed to their pension funds. The Parisian *Conseil de prud'hommes pour les métaux* cancelled the companies' decisions and forced them to return the monies that had been seized, thus refusing to grant unilateral powers to employers and arguing that they could not be both judge and jury in their own case. A commercial tribunal that got involved in this case confirmed the *prud'hommes*'s decision. Following an appeal by the companies, however, these rulings were invalidated by a series of decisions delivered by the *Cour de cassation* in 1873 and 1874. These decisions confirmed the prerogatives that rail employers had bestowed upon themselves, and asserted the lawfulness and usefulness of the subordination of workers to private disciplinary agents.

For the time being, these rulings concerned only rail workers, but they were still violently decried by the press and diverse political parties, both republican and conservative. While growing sections of the French political and social elite understood the pressing necessity of nurturing capitalist industrial development, divisions and tensions were still palpable. Members of the Chambers of Deputies proposed bills seeking to overturn these rulings, which had brought widespread public outrage. These legislative efforts, however, were systematic-

---

70   Cottereau 2002, p. 1555.

ally impeded by the Senate, which sided with the *Cour de cassation*.[71] France's top judicial and legislative institutions were making progress in their efforts to abolish the reciprocity that characterised labour relations, and to extend the unilateral power of employers. In light of the posture adopted by these powerful and influential state institutions, employers' associations perceived opportunities and undertook to challenge decisions made by proximity courts on the basis of the *bon droit* claimed by employees. Meanwhile, the *Cour de cassation* issued a series of similar rulings through the end of the century, creating in the process a crisis among *prud'hommes* and leading many to resign. Some councils refused to follow rulings released by the *Cour*, while others bent and complied under pressure exercised from above.

As this process of restructuring intensified, a new legal doctrine was produced. Until then, the relatively rare scholarly analysis of commercial and civil law tended to underwrite the jurisprudence produced by *prud'hommes* as well as by the *justices de paix* concerning labour relations. From the late 1860s, this interpretative tradition began to be contested by a growing numbers of jurists. This provoked an academic debate on these legal issues that endured throughout the following half century and beyond.[72] The growing challenge to the judicial status quo was systematised into a coherent doctrine during the 1880s. In an article published in 1885, Émile Delecroix suggested as a self-evident truth that the authority of bosses over workers, who had to be reduced to obedient soldiers, automatons, was necessary for efficient production.[73] Delecroix's work inspired Ernest Désiré Glasson's *Le Code civile et la question ouvrière*, first published in 1886. This work introduced the notion of the 'labour contract' in France and confirmed the rupture with previous jurisprudence that had already begun in practice, through the rulings of the *Cour de cassation*. Ignoring decades of legal decisions following the Revolution by *prud'hommes councils*, justices of the peace, and commercial tribunals, Glasson accepted as a given that all labour contracts were in fact *louage de service*, which implied the subordination of workers to their employers.[74] Echoing Glasson's ideas, the jurist Marc Sauzet reasserted in 1890 that the labour contract necessarily implies 'a certain subordination of the worker to the employer, in the execution of the work he agreed to'.[75] Until the end of the Second Empire, and

---

71 Cottereau 2002, pp. 1522–3; Lefebvre 2009, p. 50.

72 Lefebvre 2009, pp. 56, 64.

73 Lefebvre 2009, pp. 62–3.

74 Cottereau 2002, pp. 1521, 1524–5.

75 Quoted in Cottereau 2002, pp. 1525–6: '[U]ne certaine subordination de l'ouvrier au patron, dans l'exécution du travail promis'.

during the first years of the Third Republic, all this would have been understood as a legal aberration. Yet, social-legal relations between bosses and workers were changing fast.

The assertions made by Delecroix, Glasson, Sauzet and other jurists were as a rule substantiated by references to works of liberal political economy. Thus Sauzet appealed to Bastiat, who explained that capital could legitimately expect subordination from labour, since the former assumes all the risks.[76] From the 1880s, the new liberal doctrines informed by political economists was mobilised in rulings delivered by law courts. They were embraced in a growing number of scholarly judicial publications that accepted the fairly new proposal that subordination at work, and the reduction of labour contracts to a *louage de service*, were notions embedded in the Civil Code.[77]

Meanwhile, legal rulings supporting the mounting power of capital continued to roll in. In 1886, the *Cour de Cassation* expanded the employers' unilateral right to dismiss workers – which had until then been limited to the railroad sector – to all sectors. In December 1890, a bill reforming dismissal law led to the first legislative consecration of the doctrine elaborated by Glasson and others. The new law advanced the removal of reciprocity in labour relations that had been implied by *louage d'ouvrage* contracts during the post-revolutionary period.[78]

The 1898 law on occupational injuries subsequently reinforced the power of employers over the organisation of production. Until the last decade of the Second Empire, *louage d'ouvrage* guaranteed that most workers were hired for a specific task, often renting access to machines or a workplace – they were not renting their labour power for a given period of time. They retained autonomy and control over their labouring activities and were consequently considered responsible in case of injury. The new law, however, established that, as representatives of their firm, employers were responsible in case of injuries and should contribute to a collective fund used to compensate injured workers. This had implications for labour relations, since legislators confirmed by the same token a hierarchical relationship between empowered employers and subordinated workers. As Hervé Chamerttant puts it, commenting on this law: 'it is through the same process that, on the one hand, the employer as representative of the collective entity that is the firm, assumes responsibility for occupational injuries and is bestowed with the powers to command over wage-labourers; and that, on the other hand, the wage-labourer, as member of this collective

---

76   Cottereau 2002, pp. 1525–6.
77   Cottereau 1987, p. 115; 2002, p. 1526.
78   Cottereau 2002, pp. 1523, 1555.

entity, is freed of his responsibility in occupational injuries and has to subordinate his will to that of his employer'.[79] A few years later, in 1901, a further law officially introduced the notion of the 'labour contract' and reasserted the soundness and validity of workers' subordination to their employers.[80] In parallel, and throughout the 1900s, French jurists elaborated the notion of 'renting of labour power', which they equated with labour contracts.[81] This evocative phrasing reflected and supported the alienation of labour that was part of the ongoing consolidation of capitalist industrial production in France.

The establishment and enforcement of tariffs that regulated workers' revenues was also coming under attack. Workers were now expected to rent their labour power, and to accept that market competition would fix the price of this rental. In 1893, the *Cour de Cassation* rejected the demand for the enforcement of a local tariff fixing wages that had been made by the weavers of Chauffailles. Workers had sued their employer for refusing to respect a tariff established in 1889 that fixed piece rates and work schedules for all of the town's mills. The *Cour* challenged the validity of regulations fixing wages and working conditions for an entire trade in a given region. The judgement asserted that tariffs established by justices of the peace or *prud'hommes* according to a law that had been adopted in 1892 were in no case binding.[82] This episode was part of a broader legal struggle, in which workers sometimes convinced judges to uphold local customary regulations.[83] Still, the increasingly dominant perspective within the judicial system and the French state was that wages and working conditions were to be determined by employers in single production units. In parallel, customary regulations directly enforced by workers also tended to erode. Focusing on the capital, Harvey explains that 'traditional labor market control ... tended to break down as the Parisian labor market exploded in size and dispersed in space. The centralized hiring points, still a matter of

---

79   Chamerttant 2006, p. 226: '[C]'est dans le même mouvement que, du côté de l'employeur en tant que représentant du collectif qu'est l'entreprise, il endosse la responsabilité des accidents de travail et se voit attribuer les pouvoirs de commandement sur les salariés; et que du côté du salarié, en tant que membre de ce collectif, il est déchargé de sa responsabilité dans les accidents du travail et est tenu de subordonner sa volonté à celle de son employeur'.

80   Charmettant 1986, p. 220.

81   Cottereau 2002, p. 1554.

82   Didry 2001, p. 1260.

83   This principle of jurisprudence was not universally respected during the years that followed. In 1896, weavers from Cholet sued their employer in a civil court because he refused to respect the tariffs negotiated under the auspices of a justice of the peace in agreement with the rules established by the 1892 law. The workers won their case and the judge forced the employer to respect the tariff (Didry 2001, p. 1262).

comment in the Enquête of 1847–1848 had all but disappeared by 1870. And most commentators agreed that the labor market had become characterized by a much more pervasive competitive individualism in 1870 than had existed in 1848'.[84]

The debate between supporters of subordination to employers at work and those who opposed it raged on until the adoption of the Labour Code in 1910 – which consolidated the incipient capitalist legal framework – and beyond. The new socio-legal framework imposed by legislators and magistrates, often under governments led by left republicans, especially from 1902, represented a frontal attack on customary regulations and a radical transformation of labour relations.[85] Indeed, the salient characteristic of the new model was 'to no longer treat relationships of subordination [of workers to their employers] as an annoying epiphenomenon but to move it to its centre'.[86] Whereas interpretations of the 1804 Civil Code had previously asserted that the employer 'was not a judge', the new labour law implied that the employer was in fact the 'only judge' when it came to the best ways of organising work.[87]

As *bon droit* was eroding, the state softened emerging forms of labour subordination: the Empire allowed strikes from 1864, while the formation of unions was legalised by a recently stabilised Republic in 1884. A law on conciliation adopted in 1892 stipulated that collective bargaining would be overseen by *justices de paix*, whereas individual labour conflicts would be arbitrated by the *conseils de prud'hommes* – only now not according to local *usages* but on the basis of the emerging labour law. That same year, the government took the initiative of funding *bourses du travail* as a substitute for the hated *bureau de placement*. The objective was to provide support for unemployed workers, but also to promote moderate trade unions and collective bargaining.[88] A 1919 law on collective agreements turned them into civil contracts, enforceable in law courts.[89] The state thus granted to employers arbitrary powers that were qualified *a posteriori* by regulations and collective bargaining. These legislative developments were in fact part of a broader process of dismantling of the

---

84 Harvey 2005, p. 171.
85 Salais, Baverez and Reynaud 1986, p. 65.
86 Cottereau 2002, p. 1555: '[D]e ne plus traiter le rapport de subordination comme un épiphénomène gênant mais de la situer en son centre'.
87 Cottereau 2002, p. 1555.
88 Friedman 1990, pp. 157–8.
89 Shorter and Tilly 1974, pp. 22–5.

working-class moral economy. This took place against a backdrop of intense labour mobilisation and rising strike activity. The state reacted by purposefully attempting to pacify the labour movement by facilitating conciliatory relationships between employers and workers. As we will see in the next chapter, these attempts largely failed, and strike activity increased rapidly during the closing decades of the nineteenth century.

The promotion of workers' subordination in a largely unregulated, competitive context – at the centre of which was the rise of the new labour law supporting the eradication of decades of local jurisprudence and normative regulations of social relations of production – implied the emergence of capitalist private property. This was a process of progressive privatisation of the power to organise production; it amounted to a de-politicisation of power over production and the confining of such power to a self-regulating 'economic' sphere. As this restructuring of social power unfolded, workers lost their normatively mediated access to the means of production and were abstracted from their customary trade communities.

Those outcomes of the 1789 Revolution that had been experienced as emancipatory by workers, were now being curtailed. 'French industrial labour law got closer to English law. The French worker became a kind of "servant", a status that revolutionary emancipation had rejected in horror'.[90] French workers had in fact expected these developments after the signing of the Anglo-French Free Trade treaty of 1860 and had feared the impact of international competition. During the 1867 Universal Exhibition, French goldsmiths claimed that exposure to British competition was bringing to France 'large centres of manufacture where accumulated capital, enjoying every freedom, becomes a kind of legalized oppression, regulating labour and parcelling work'. This, they claimed, 'is the English system which is threatening to take us all over by turning the worker into a labourer, subjected to mindless production which brings him no personal benefits'. This 'English system' – capitalism – was a 'major attack' on 'workers' personal freedom', and would roll back the gains made in 1789 when '[their] fathers crushed their warden and masters; by destroying privilege and proclaiming every freedom, they believed that henceforth justice and equity would control relations between capital and labour'.[91]

---

90   Cottereau 2006, p. 115: '[L]e droit français de l'emploi ouvrier se rapproche alors ... du droit anglais. Désormais, l'ouvrier français redevient une sorte de "servant", qualité que l'émancipation révolutionnaire avait rejetée avec horreur.'

91   Cottereau 1995, p. 272. See also Harvey 2005, p. 166.

While the regulation of social relations of production was transformed, commercial exchanges were also liberalised, and increasingly organised through market competition. After vacillating for a long period, Napoleon had finally discarded price controls on bread and granted freedom of trade to bakers in 1863.[92] While further historical work is needed on the evolution of trade customs over the closing decades of the nineteenth century,[93] it appears that the hitherto important regulatory role of chambers of commerce and tribunals began to fade out, as price competition came to be the central mechanism of coordination of production and exchange. Alessandro Stanziani explains that 'trades customs were increasingly challenged during the course of the nineteenth century' and, under the pressure of different trade associations, 'the ministries in charge during the Second Empire and again under the Third Republic launched major investigations in order to codify customs in a given industry'.[94] What is clear, however, is that *parères* – those expert opinions requested by commercial tribunals and delivered by experienced merchants or industrialists in a given trade, which had played a key part in formalising customary practices and orienting commercial exchanges and the organisation of production – fell into disuse during the 1860s. The legal notices produced by lawyers that replaced *parères* had much less authority and only limited impact on the general orientation of concrete economic activities.[95]

As gains made by French workers in the wake of the 1789 Revolution were increasingly imperilled, employers moved forward to assert their control over production. The inquiry launched as part of the 1860 commercial treaty revealed that managerial style had not really changed since a similar enquiry into import prohibition that had been conducted in 1834.[96] But things changed rapidly from the 1860s and over the following decades. While textile employers had – unsuccessfully – attempted to interfere with labour processes once or twice in the period since 1820, attempts to impose new modes of management became routine in the emerging capitalist context of the last decades of the nineteenth century. This new context 'required owners to interfere directly in the work process, to induce laborers to alter their habits, apply themselves more assiduously, and accept dramatic price cuts'.[97] Labour productivity was

92   Plessis 1985, p. 11.
93   Stanziani 2012.
94   Stanziani 2012, pp. 186–7.
95   Hirsch 1991, p. 108.
96   Reddy 1984, p. 237.
97   Reddy 1984, p. 241.

the employers' new obsession, and they came to realise that '[e]xactly how time was spent was often more important than how much'.[98]

The age-old merchant model, in which individuals or, as was generally the case for textile mills, teams of workers bought raw material, rented access to factory facilities (and sometimes tools as well), and sold their products back to mill owners, gave way to new hiring practices in which workers were directly engaged by employers as wage-labourers.[99] Whereas they previously had to deal with a group leader who would subsequently form their own work team, employers began to increasingly hire workers on an individual basis. This tighter control over individualised hiring processes encroached upon what had until then often been considered a family prerogative – this certainly was the rule in the textile sector. Disregarding tariffs and usages, more and more employers unilaterally fixed piece rates and often imposed performance-based pay.[100] This was a process that converted growing numbers of French workers into wage-labourers. But it did not rely simply on a new mode of remuneration – fundamentally, the process represented the implementation of a new relationship of power between factory owners and workers. It announced a 'transition from a relationship between merchants and direct producers inside the enterprise, in which the worker retained her or his autonomy (at least regarding the organization of her or his labour), to a relation of subordination in which control over the organization of her or his labour was taken away from the worker'.[101] Put another way, with the rise of this new employer-employee relationship, industrial workers began to sell their *labour power*.[102] Labour was being commodified; it was being abstracted from the individual that practised it, at the same time as this individual was abstracted from her trade community. These transformative processes paved the way to the capitalist alienation of labour that *louage d'ouvrage* contracts had until then prevented. Employers were gaining the ability to define their employees' tasks and to develop a new division of labour.

From the last decade of the Second Empire, and even more evidently during the 1870s and 1880s, industrial labour began to be divided and rationalised so as to sustain the maximisation of profits, while factory and workshop owners

---

98   Reddy 1984, p. 245.
99   Lefebvre 2003, pp. 160–1.
100   Noiriel 1986, p. 94.
101   Lefebvre 2003, p. 161: '[T]ransition qui conduit de rapports marchands dans l'entreprise, dans lesquels l'ouvrier est considéré comme indépendant (au moins dans l'organisation de son travail), à des rapports de subordination dans lesquels l'organisation de son travail échappe largement à l'ouvrier'.
102   Reddy 1984, p. 251.

developed hierarchical structures and imposed strict discipline within work-places.[103] The hitherto marginal number of companies managed not by their owners but by salaried executives was growing.[104] Foremen multiplied and were assigned a new role – they became disciplinary agents expected to over-see efficient labour processes. In order to enhance labour productivity, factory rules were enforced. In a growing number of capitalist workplaces, schedules were strictly monitored and workers were no longer allowed to chat or sing on the job or to step out of the workshop to smoke a cigarette or grab a pint at the nearby cabaret.[105] Mills were equipped with bells and whistles, and employers engaged in sustained efforts to acclimatise workers to receiving and following orders. Schools increasingly took the initiative in inculcating a new sense of discipline in future workers, 'emphasing thrift, sobriety, punctuality, hard work, and property'.[106] A new paternalism emerged in industry, illustrated by the case of the company school associated with Schneider's large-scale metal factory Le Creusot, which developed a curriculum that encouraged submission to super-iors and respect for authority, and that insisted on the natural harmony that existed between labour and capital.[107] A growing number of segments of the working class began to internalise a new time discipline. The last decades of the nineteenth century brought to France a 'gigantic mutation, the disrupt-ing rise of the notion that "time is money", this rationalization of time'.[108] This was imposed by 'market forces, [which] were pushing shop-floor practice in a similar direction. The clock became a growing preoccupation of all parties'.[109] Labourers were learning 'to think of time and effort as underlying variables in relating work to pay, instead of concentrating all their attention on the tan-gible product'.[110] More and more workers began to wear watches, and overtime labour became normal practice from the 1890s.[111] The Saint Monday was less and less observed and the English 'week-end' began to punctuate the weekly routine of many labourers.[112] Patrick Fridenson argues that a 'Taylorist turn'

---

103   Beltran and Griset 1994, pp. 120–1; Charmettant 2006, p. 215; Fureix and Jarrige 2015, p. 82; Lefebvre 2003, pp. 172, 197–8, 207, 238; Lequin 1983, p. 428; Perrot 1983, p. 6.
104   Tombs 1996, p. 289.
105   Perrot 1974, pp. 103, 299.
106   Magraw 1986, p. 218.
107   Lefebvre 2003, pp. 240–2.
108   Noiriel 1986, p. 96: 'Cette mutation gigantesque, la montée bouleversante du "time is money", cette rationalisation du temps'. See also Perrot 1974, pp. 298–9; Magraw 1992, p. 16.
109   Reddy 1984, p. 240.
110   Reddy 1984, p. 244.
111   Bourdieu and Reynaud, p. 33.
112   Reddy 1984, p. 245. Traditional communities and customary values in both cities and vil-

had already been taking place in France well before 1914.[113] New industrial sectors such as the automobile industry were directly inspired by Taylor in their efforts to reorganise factory production. Illustrating the rapid transformations that ensued, at Renault factories, the number of unskilled workers went from 85 out of 1,660 employees in 1906 up to 1,203 out of 4,220 in 1914.[114]

In sectors where industrial production was developing, small artisan workshops also engaged in processes of subsumption and the speed-up of labour.[115] Out-workers populating the countryside surrounding manufacturing centres, even as they continued to relate to their employers as merchants rather than wage labourers, were facing intensifying competition from French and foreign capitalist factories. This led them to increase their self-exploitation in a context were local customs and tariffs were increasingly infringed upon. Urban artisans were not immune to these changes. In Paris, a major centre of artisanal production of quality goods, merchants responded to international competition and the imperative to maximise profits by increasing their domination over indebted master artisans. Through vertically integrated commercial and financial networks, merchants extended divisions of labour in many trades, which resulted in the proliferation of new technologies and processes of labour deskilling.[116] Similar developments also took place in Lyon[117] and elsewhere. Urban handicraft was not transformed overnight – this was an uneven process that spread over several decades and was far from being completed on the eve of World War II. Still, the impact of the capitalist restructuring of industry on

---

lages were also greatly upset by the rise of capitalism. Social atomisation, individualism and violent crimes soared, and were accompanied by an important growth of alcoholism. Magraw (1992, pp. 11, 18) reports, for instance, that absinthe consumption rose by a factor of 2,500 percent between 1875 and 1904, while the number of *débits de boisson* in Belleville grew from 275 in 1885 to 448 in 1910. On the distortion of community life, see Noiriel 1986, pp. 95–9.

113 Fridenson 1987.
114 Charle 1991, p. 285.
115 Charle 1991, p. 311.
116 Harvey 2005, pp. 157, 158, 160–1, 164. Harvey is right to associate this evolution of artisanal production with exposure to international competition in the wake of the 1860 Anglo-French commercial treaty. However, he is wrong to present this evolution as an intensification of what had already been occurring prior to 1848 (2005, p. 161). Harvey does not see the radical gap that separated these two historical periods, because he completely ignores the literature cited above that describes the profound transformation of labour law during the last third of the nineteenth century. More than the evolution of financial networks or the emergence of a 'new merchant class', it is this transformation of labour law in the context of an emerging capitalist market that explains the transformation of artisanal production.
117 Magraw 1992, p. 49.

240

the world of the artisan was tangible, and was made still more evident by the erosion of apprenticeship.[118] While apprentices represented 18 percent of the Parisian workforce in 1860, this proportion had shrunk to five percent in 1900. The proportion of workers of the Parisian suburb of Belleville that were handicraft labourers producing quality goods went from 29 percent in 1871, down to 14 percent in 1891.[119] These figures reflect in part the evolution of French manufacturing production under the impact of new, capitalist patterns of industrial investment.

4   The Emergence of Capitalist Patterns of Investment

As we saw in Chapter 2, French textile merchants had responded to British competition in the wake of the 1786 Anglo-French commercial treaty either by decreasing rates paid to factors, and in turn to direct producers, or by buying goods directly from English producers in order to distribute them in France. The upshot was the collapse of French textile production in entire regions, as hundreds of thousands of domestic spinners were forced out of the trade. At the time, most French merchants had only limited or no fixed capital to defend against price-cutting competitors. They consequently did not adapt to foreign competition in a capitalist way, by investing in productivity-enhancing machinery. The formation of substantial fixed capital, as we also saw, had finally taken place during the first half of the nineteenth century, but this time in a protected, compartmentalised, customarily regulated, and therefore uncompetitive context. In the absence of capitalist imperatives, French industry had developed much less rapidly then British capitalist industry. Nonetheless, by the 1860s, a much larger proportion of French merchants had become actual industrialists, owning mills equipped with modern machinery – they could no longer react in the way they had after 1786. In the emerging competitive context of a rapidly industrialising Europe, access to the means of production was becoming market-dependent, and this implied that French industrialists now had to abide by new rules of reproduction.

The intensification of competition that took place from the 1860s was unprecedented. The last third of the nineteenth century was a period of declining profitability.[120] Growing international competition, impacting on a much more

---

118   Charmettant 2006, pp. 214–16.
119   Magraw 1992, p. 12.
120   Caron 1995, p. 121. Profitability began to rise again from the second half of the nineteenth century.

integrated national economy, pushed down prices and profits, and this led to a sharp increase of bankruptcy rates. Industrial growth decelerated, going from 2.5 percent per year on average from 1815 to 1854 down to 1.6 percent per year from the turn of the 1860s to the turn of the 1890s.[121]

And yet, in spite or in fact *because* of this tighter price competition, playing out in a depressed economic context characterised by falling profits and decreasing market opportunities, French industrial firms did not diminish but actually *intensified* their investments aimed at mechanising their facilities.[122] Caron stresses that industrial growth changed style during the last third of the century, becoming 'strongly capitalistic'. The deceleration of production was not tied to a deceleration of industrial investment growth. On the contrary, industrial investments accelerated until the mid-1880s. They decelerated during the second half of the 1880s – though their absolute value remained much higher than it had been at any point before 1860 – during the low-point of the depression that marked this decade, before accelerating again rapidly in the 1890s.[123] What we see, then, during this period, is a contraction of market opportunities taking place at the same time as increased investment in fixed capital.[124] This, probably more than anything else, was a clear signal of the capitalist transformation of France's industrial sector: whereas firms previously tended to pause their activities in times of economic slowdown, they now systematically invested to cope with strengthened competition in tighter markets. The last third of the nineteenth century brought a clear epochal break, as the capital factor was increasingly replacing the labour factor in different sectors of French industry.[125] Net investments in plant and equipment, which had reached 72 million francs in 1835, before decreasing to 60 million francs in 1850, skyrocketed to 164 million in 1880, and reached 310 million in 1910.[126] The overall share of investments in the country's GDP went from 12.1 percent in the 1850s, up to 13 percent from 1875 to 1889, before reaching 14.2 percent from 1905 to 1913. Meanwhile, the share of industrial investments in total investments reached 38 percent from 1905 to 1913, up from 13 percent from the mid-1840s to the mid-1850s.[127]

121   Asselain 1984, p. 130.
122   Broder 1993, p. 59; Beltran and Griset 1994, p. 125.
123   Caron 1995, p. 120.
124   Caron 1995, p. 122.
125   Caron 1995, pp. 115, 123, 129; Broder p. 59; Plessis 1996, p. 149.
126   Plessis 1996, p. 134. Taking into account amortisation costs, total firm investments are set at 153 millions francs in 1835 and 192 millions in 1850. They then rise very rapidly to 428 millions francs in 1880 and 778 millions in 1910.
127   Asselain 1988, p. 1232; Caron quoted in Broder 1993, pp. 216–17.

These investment patterns materialised in a sharp acceleration of the average annual growth of horsepower in use in industry, which went from 9,500 from 1839 to 1869, up to 32,800 from 1871 to 1894, before reaching 73,350 from 1883 to 1903, and 141,800 from 1903 to 1913.[128] French industrial growth was still largely based on luxury goods production, but the proportion of capital-intensive sectors grew over this period. In an increasing number of trades, technological backwardness, which had still been allowed by the economic context of the 1840s, was becoming crippling in the changed circumstances of the 1870s.[129] The concentration of production in factories accelerated from the 1860s, and again over the 1880s and during the opening decade of the twentieth century.[130] The diffusion of technological innovations accelerated, the time span from the discovery of a new manufacturing process to its implementation contracted, and the obsolescence of industrial equipment came about with ever-increasing rapidity.[131]

Clearly, exposed to foreign as well as domestic competition in a levelled national economic space – one where customary regulations of production and of labour markets were being rolled back – French firms were forced to adapt. New social property relations had imposed new rules of reproduction: cost-cutting and profit maximisation had become a matter of economic survival for many firms. In the wake of the trade treaty signed with Britain, imports of cotton goods increased. This incited a competitive selection of firms at the expense of those who maintained a more traditional production structure – modernising, capital-intensive firms absorbed failing firms.[132] During what Fohlen calls an 'industrial revolution', cotton weaving was rapidly mechanised and domestic hand weaving practically disappeared. Cotton spinning was also increasingly integrated into mills in urban centres.[133] From 1870 through 1914, the improvement of cotton weaving by way of mechanisation was uninterrupted. The overall productivity of this sector improved by over 52 percent from 1800–84 to 1901.[134] These productivity gains allowed French cotton firms to recapture home markets from the second half of the 1860s. Similar processes of competitive selection, concentration, and mechanisation also took place in the wool trade.[135] As was discussed earlier, French silk producers had been able

---

128   Caron 1995, pp. 120, 123.
129   Beltran and Griset 1994, p. 97; Rioux 1989, p. 89.
130   Barjot 2014b, p. 384; Beltran and Griset 1994, pp. 100–1.
131   Beltran and Griset 1994, p. 115.
132   Caron 1995, pp. 127, 129; Fohlen 1956, pp. 445, 452.
133   Fohlen 1956, pp. 441, 458, 461.
134   Caron 1995, pp. 130–1.
135   Caron 1995, pp. 133–4.

to capture foreign markets on the basis of traditional artisanal structures that ensured the quality of goods. From the mid-1870s, however, this trade was also plunged into crisis by the new international economic context. French silk production began to grow again from the mid-1880s, but this time due to efforts to penetrate entry-level markets for cheaper goods by mechanising workshops.[136] The mechanisation of production did not spare many of the old 'noble' artisanal trades in Paris and other French towns. Parisian shoemaking and tailoring, for instance, went through substantial mechanisation during this period.[137]

The targeted reduction of dues on imported iron goods by the government in 1854 had sent a clear message to iron producers: the days of protectionism were numbered and firms needed to prepare to cope with stiffer competition by adopting cost-cutting technologies.[138] Growing numbers of firms began to use coke-fired blast furnaces; by the mid-1860s, around 90 percent of French firms had been compelled to switch to this technique.[139] This amounted to 'a deep structural evolution ... that gained even further speed after the commercial treaty with Britain. By 1864, although the "industrialization" of iron- and steel-making was not yet completed (some one hundred old "Catalan forges" and 210 wood-fired blast furnaces survived), the modern mode of production had undoubtedly triumphed'.[140] Thanks to the rapid dissemination of the Bessemer process, French steel production, which did not exceed 10,000 tons in 1865, reached 100,000 tons by 1873, and 283,000 tons in 1878.[141]

As a consequence of this capitalist transformation of French industry, labour productivity growth reached 2.4 percent per year over the 1890s – twice the rate of the rest of the nineteenth century.[142] It needs to be stressed that the substantial and sustained intensification of industrial investments that made these productivity gains possible did not simply derive, in Smithian fashion, from expanding market demand. As a matter of fact, internal demand for consumer goods stagnated over the last quarter of the nineteenth century, while French firms also lost ground to international competitors in foreign markets.[143] Real incomes rose from the 1850s in the provinces and from the 1860s

---

136   Caron 1995, p. 135; Verley 1989, p. 70.
137   Charle 1991, p. 283.
138   Gille 1968, p. 69. See also Caron 1995, p. 124; Bergeron 1978, pp. 73–4; Rioux 1989, p. 89.
139   Beltran and Griset 1994, p. 96.
140   Plessis 1985, p. 90.
141   Beltran and Griset 1994, p. 108.
142   Marchand and Thélot 1991, pp. 143–4.
143   Verley 1996, pp. 96–7.

in Paris, until the 1890s. This, however, did not in any significant way affect consumption of consumer goods among the peasantry and the working class, since additional spending was overwhelmingly directed toward improving food consumption.[144] While, as we just saw, mechanisation intensified in all major textile trades, the growth of demand for French textile goods decelerated from the 1860s to the 1870s; overall demand for textiles subsequently stagnated around the level of 400 millions francs, and even went through a minor decrease in the closing decade of the century.[145] Working-class consumption of cotton textiles did increase slightly over the period, but this was achieved by price reductions arising from labour productivity-enhancing mechanisation and industrial discipline.[146] The unprecedented development of industrial capacities that was taking place in France was caused less by the quantitative expansion of markets than by their qualitative transformation.[147]

French industrial firms adopted new financing strategies to support their capital-intensive development. Self-financing by family-owned firms, which had been the dominant strategy over the first half of the nineteenth century, was no longer sufficient. A critical mass of French entrepreneurs broke with the timorous financial attitudes of their predecessors – they developed new funding strategies and borrowed more in order to invest.[148] Here, once again, the 1860s represented a transitional period during which the intensity and structure of industrial firms' financing needs were evolving, while new financing methods were in gestation.[149] Until then, limited companies – the 'cornerstone of corporate capitalism'[150] – had remained very scarce and were as a rule a façade for what essentially remained family businesses. Moreover, their creation had remained subject to official authorisation. The Second Empire proceeded to liberalise company law by easing and then completely removing governmental control over the establishment of limited companies. This was achieved by means of two laws adopted in 1863 and 1867. These legal innovations were implemented only after bitter internal governmental debates, and numerous French businessmen had in fact expressed their strong opposition

---

144 Asselain 1988, pp. 1227–8; Verley 1996, p. 102.
145 Verley 1996, p. 104.
146 Verley 1996, p. 106.
147 It is true, however, that the limited depth of the French national market did constrain industrial development in comparison with other industrial powers – a point to which we will come back in a moment.
148 Hirsch 2001, p. 9.
149 Plessis 1996, p. 129.
150 Plessis 1985, p. 74.

to the proposed reforms.[151] It is really during the 1870s that an appreciable rise in the number of limited companies could be observed.[152] This movement accelerated afterward, and the proportion of limited companies out of the total number of newly established firms went from six percent in 1875, up to 14 percent in 1913 – a substantial increase, considering that most firms in France remained small and artisanal well into the twentieth century.[153] The establishment of limited companies had become a key strategy to fund the capitalist restructuring of larger French firms.

In order to meet their growing financial needs, French firms also increasingly relied on bank loans and began to issue much more shares and bonds – tendencies that accelerated during the *Belle Époque*. From 1890 to 1913, the share of self-financing in the overall funding of French firms went down from 74 percent to 46 percent. Meanwhile, over the same period, the proportion of bank loans and of shares and bonds issuance in the funding of firms increased from 10 percent to 19 percent, and from 16 percent to 35 percent, respectively.[154] This was reflected in the evolution of the French banking sector. Though the interpenetration of finance and industry never reached the level that was attained in Germany, French banks began to issue longer-term loans supporting substantial fixed capital formation. Such loans came to represent 70 percent of the loan portfolio of *Crédit Lyonnais*, while they represented 78 percent in the case of *Société générale*.[155] New investment banks were also established, such as the *Banque française*, in 1901, and the *Banque de l'union parisienne*, in 1904. In parallel, 'the growth of a national system of deposit banking was one of the outstanding developments in the French economy during this period [1870–1914] which marked the transition to modern large-scale capitalism'.[156] Meanwhile, the Bank of France broke with its conservative habits and began to support the increasingly important financing of industry by smaller local and regional banks.[157]

Another strategy used by French industrial firms to cope with national, and especially international, competition was to form trade agreements [*ententes*]. Before the last third of the nineteenth century, the French national economic space had been compartmentalised, and this implied a de facto partition of

---

151 Dougui 1981, pp. 281–2.
152 Woronoff 1994, p. 261.
153 Plessis 1996, p. 154.
154 Plessis 1996, p. 152.
155 Plessis 1996, p. 153.
156 Kemp 1971, p. 259.
157 Plessis 1996, p. 154.

markets, ensuring safe profits. With the end of this partition from the 1860s, French industrialists – though never as efficient and institutionalised as their German counterparts – responded to the threat to their profits by forming trade associations, so as to ease competitive imperatives. These associations and agreements emerged from the 1870s, but became widespread only after 1880.[158] The state was in fact often party to these agreements, and tribunals were lenient, especially from the 1890s. Magistrates, however, tolerated agreements only insofar as they did not eliminate, but actually safeguarded, competition. That is to say, firms were allowed to organise only in ways that avoided concentration, which would eliminate competition.[159] While iron producers were somewhat more organised, textile associations were much looser, and neither type of association led to the disappearance of market competition. As Daviet explains, 'agreements achieved their aims only insofar as they went with a market-determined system without commanding markets. There are no examples indicating that a fall of cost prices due to technological progress in the long term had no repercussions on selling prices. The main reason for this was the existence of dissident manufacturers'.[160] Indeed, as mentioned earlier, industrial prices decreased sharply from the 1860s and continued to do so after the formation of trade agreements.

In some cases, as for iron and steel products, initiatives by large private enterprises were instrumental in creating and safeguarding competitive markets. This was the case for railway companies. In 1865, for instance, the *Compagnie du chemin de fer du Nord* distributed steel rails orders to two new firms so as to increase the number of suppliers on which it could rely. Giving up short-term financial gains, the rail company managed its orders with the aim of disrupting a clique of torpid steel producers. In order to rupture a regional monopoly, the rail company's administrators explained that they would favour emerging firms in order 'to create a competitive context from which we will benefit in the future'.[161] This strategy rapidly paid off. Stiffer competition forced all producers to very rapidly adopt two technical innovations that had been developed by new firms, and steel prices fell by 52 percent from 1864 to 1867. Rail companies continued to issue and distribute orders across the 1870s and 1880s, so as to maintain the competitive context that they had helped to put in place.[162]

---

158   Daviet 1988, p. 273.
159   Caron 1988, pp. 128–9; Daviet 1988, p. 275.
160   Daviet 1988, p. 276. On dissident, 'individualist' manufacturers, see also Caron 1995, p. 131 and Charle 1991, p. 238.
161   Caron 1988, p. 132: '[C]réer une concurrence dont nous profiterons plus tard'.
162   Caron 1988, p. 133; Hirsch 2008, p. 73.

The economic impact of competitive markets created by state and economic actors was real and substantial, but it should not be overestimated. In 1870, added value in agriculture still represented around 40 percent of the country's gross domestic product, while artisans supplied at least 70 percent of total manufacturing production.[163] The weight of agriculture declined consistently from the 1880s[164] as industrial capitalism matured, but, at least from our contemporary standpoint, the configuration of France's workforce meant that its economy still looked largely agrarian on the eve of World War I. Even as the opening years of the twentieth century brought an important burst of concentration (the continuation of a process that had been launched in preceding decades), the French industrial structure remained dispersed and characterised by small artisan workshops.[165] The new competitive nature of French markets from the 1860s did kickstart a capitalist transformation of industry, but the limitedness of these markets, and their lack of depth, also slowed down the pace of this process of industrialisation.

From 1851 to 1891, the average annual rate of growth of the French population was 0.1 percent – more then ten times less then English and German growth rates.[166] Urbanisation also proceeded at a much slower pace in France,[167] and this was related to the evolution of the structure of the country's labour force. In 1911, the share of the rural population in the total French population was 55.8 percent. That same year, 41 percent of the French labour force was in agriculture, while British and German shares were respectively 8 and 27 percent.[168] From 1870 to 1914, there was a relatively slow but steady decline of the proportion of the population dependent upon agriculture for its livelihood. But this rural exodus involved almost exclusively waged agricultural labourers, while the proportion of agricultural landholders actually slightly increased. 'There was no agricultural revolution' over this period.[169] International price competition had contributed to a capitalist restructuring of French industry, but not of agriculture, where central economic actors continued to avoid capitalist market-dependence. From the 1860s, France was flooded with international agricultural products. Net imports of wheat, for instance, went from 0.3 percent of total production in 1851–60 to 10 percent in 1871–80, and to 19 percent

---

163   Marchand and Thélot 1991, p. 144; Plessis 1985, p. 92.
164   Barjot 2014b, p. 377.
165   Barjot 2014b, p. 384.
166   Gildea 2003, pp. 144, 278.
167   Gildea 2003, p. 148.
168   Kemp 1971, p. 297; Marchand and Thélot 1991, p. 26; Verley 1996, pp. 102–4.
169   Plessis 1985, p. 96.

in 1888–92.[170] The severe slump in agricultural prices that ensued led swelling numbers of agricultural wage labourers to move to urban centres, while many peasants reacted by requesting permanent rent decreases from their landlords. As rent was declining, the resale value of land fell, by as much as 25 percent in some regions.[171] Many larger landowners responded by selling their estates to redirect their capital into more profitable investments. Small landholders bought substantial shares of the land that was sold, and this had the effect of consolidating an already massive French peasantry, which survived well into the twentieth century and even until the post-war period.[172] While landholding patterns remained largely unaltered, agricultural productivity appears to have declined from 1866 to 1896, and output was slightly negative or stationary over the 1880s and 1890s, after a sharp deceleration during the 1860s and 1870s.[173]

A faster development of French industrial capitalism would have required a large-scale dispossession of the French peasantry; but since this class was perceived as a barrier to social revolution, the French state was not ready to proceed with such a policy.[174] Consequently, France did not experience a capitalist agrarian transition that could have incited, or provided the material preconditions for, a stronger rural exodus, and which would in turn have fuelled the growth of a mass consumer market. Indeed, the French agrarian sector was not capable of supporting the relatively slow process of urbanisation that did take place, and a quarter of France's food had to be imported from foreign countries in order to sustain the industrialisation of the country.[175] As it was, the share of the French population made up of market-dependent individuals in possession of substantial disposable income remained too small to sustain an economy able to catch up with Britain or to keep up with Germany and the United States, the two leading industrialising countries at the time.[176] As was mentioned above, France's internal consumer market remained relatively small, and domestic demand stagnated in the last quarter of the nineteenth century, just as French firms were rapidly losing ground in foreign markets.

---

170 Moulin 1991, p. 92. See also Marchand and Thélot 1991, p. 25.
171 Moulin 1991, pp. 92–3; Zeldin 1993, p. 61.
172 Isett and Miller 2017, pp. 258–67.
173 Marchand and Thélot 1991, pp. 25, 143–4.
174 Kemp 1971, pp. 228–32.
175 Haine 2000, p. 150. That proportion was much smaller (around ten percent) in Germany, as is shown in Ferguson 2000, pp. 100–1.
176 Verley 1996, p. 102. Asselain (1984, p. 165) estimates that 60 to 75 percent of this relative backwardness was due to the persistence of a large peasantry and the related compactness of the French domestic market.

The absence of agrarian capitalism also implied a much slower mechanisation of agricultural production, which in turn limited market outlets for capital goods.[177] The intensification of industrial investments did stimulate demand for steam engines and other equipment from the 1860s, and capital goods production became an increasingly important growth factor in the following decades.[178] But this stimulus was itself ultimately limited by the absence of a mass consumer market for manufactured goods.

Domestic and, especially, international market opportunities began to expand again from the closing years of the century, and did so until 1913, as ongoing urbanisation and proletarianisation began to produce 'vast stockpiles of customers' across North America and Europe, and popular consumption became increasingly massive and diversified.[179] This supported much faster rates of capital accumulation, including in France, where it contributed to a progressive transformation of strategies of surplus appropriation.

5   Changing Modes of Surplus Appropriation and (Partial) State Restructuring

Wood has explained how the capitalist mode of production brings a separation of 'economic' and 'political' spheres that makes possible a new form of exploitation under liberal-democratic regimes.[180] With the rise of capitalism, political powers of command over labour processes and means of production are privatised and serve as a new form of surplus appropriation. Moments of appropriation and of coercion are disjoined, and the ruling class no longer needs direct and exclusive access to the state in order to reproduce itself. Capitalist property replaces politically constituted property and pressure from below can force the democratisation of the state without fundamentally threatening the operation of class exploitation. The state is capitalist since it depends upon, and needs to actively support, the accumulation of capital to function and preserve its legitimacy, yet it appears neutral and autonomous since it is no longer the property and monopoly of a ruling class.

It appears that this capitalist transformation of social power that allows for a partial democratisation and rationalisation of the state, began in France under the Third Republic. Gambetta's classic narrative of rising *nouvelles couches* no

---

177   Verley 1996, p. 123.
178   Verley 1996, pp. 98, 123.
179   Hobsbawm 1994, pp. 49, 53; Verley 1989, p. 56.
180   Wood 1995, pp. 19–48.

doubt needs to be importantly nuanced, yet it seems clear that the world of notables had begun its decline.[181] Politically conservative, notables were divided between Bonapartists and monarchists, backing rival houses. Their electoral defeat led to a consolidation of the Republic by the late 1870s. Though its dominance would be intensely contested by still powerful notables for decades to come, a new 'republican aristocracy' had by then taken control of the state. The presence of notables in parliament and government weakened.[182] Meanwhile, liberal and conservative republicans in government purged notables from a number of administrative bodies,[183] and undertook to democratise and to reform state power. The new capitalist modes of production and of surplus appropriation described in this chapter provided the material foundation of these republican endeavours aimed at restructuring state power.

During the closing decades of the nineteenth century, as the value of land declined, French elites increasingly turned away from landed investments. Likewise, the importance of prestigious and lucrative state functions began to wane. Capitalist investments and business careers were rapidly gaining in popularity. Thus, '[i]n 1848 only about 5 percent of money left at death was in shares while 58 percent was in land or houses. By 1900 31 percent was in shares and only 45 percent in land or houses'. Moreover, 'in the upper echelons more and more graduates of the *grandes écoles* abandoned public service to go into industry and business. Young men of good family became inspectors of finance only as a preparation for careers with large companies'.[184] Under the Second Empire, most great fortunes in France still stemmed from landed property. On the eve World War I, this was no longer the case, and great capitalist businessmen accumulated wealth on a scale that no landowning notables could pretend to reach.[185] Even if they were still considerable, their fortunes had been surpassed within a generation, and this led many notables to adapt to the modern world by joining the boards of directors of industrial firms.[186]

These new sources of wealth freed up the state, which was becoming less and less important as a means of surplus appropriation. The Second Empire incited the transition to industrial capitalism in France, but it was also the regime under which the granting of state offices as a source of ruling class rev-

---

181   Charle 1991, pp. 228, 229, 291.
182   Charle 1991, pp. 257–8.
183   As Magraw (1986, pp. 215, 220) stresses, however, the extent of these purges should not be exaggerated.
184   Zeldin 1993, pp. 59, 124.
185   Charle 1991, pp. 240–1.
186   Charle 1991, pp. 236–7.

enues reached its apex, as we saw in the previous chapter. The growth of the state continued and even accelerated under the Third Republic, but its nature was fundamentally different, and patronage – which had been endemic under former regimes – played at best a marginal role in this process. The massive increase of state employees was now tied to the development of new state functions such as education, postal services, communication and transport, economic development, and others. A comparative analysis of the evolution of state finances from the Second Empire to the Third Republic reveals that budgets for old state functions stagnated, while budgets assigned to the new functions listed above increased very rapidly.[187] The overwhelming majority of new employees received very modest salaries. Meanwhile, highly paid offices tended to stagnate or declined, and were surpassed by the number of lucrative jobs in the private sector: 'At this period [1901] only a thousand civil servants were earning over 15,000 francs a year, and the highest salary was only 35,000. But the department stores of Paris by themselves were paying over 250 of their employees salaries of 20,000 to 25,000, equal to that of most prefects, and in business many could hope to earn 50,000, 100,000, or more'.[188] State parasitism was still very much alive, but its growth had finally been checked.

The Republic brought considerable democratic reforms. Universal male suffrage remained in place, and the democratic electoral process was substantiated with the repeal of mandatory state approval of electoral candidates. The co-optation of senators came to an end, and mayors, who used to be nominated, were now elected.[189] The modernisation of state administration remained limited, but it was not altogether insignificant. Once the republican regime had been stabilised, a substantial renewal of the higher levels of the administration was achieved.[190] While nepotism remained frequent, it was checked and entered into decline, as hiring processes were formalised and *concours* were established. For instance, the number of prefects who were sons of high-ranking officials went from 40.9 percent under the Second Empire, down to 6.6 percent in 1901.[191]

In addition to important popular struggles, this partial democratic and administrative reforming of the state stemmed from a broader, capitalist transformation of social power, which was itself tied to the capitalist restructuring of French industry that has been described here. Considering the emergence of

---

187   Charle 1991, p. 194.
188   Zeldin 1993, pp. 122–3.
189   Charle 1991, pp. 255–6.
190   Charle 1991, p. 261.
191   Charle 1980, p. 28; 1991, pp. 195, 197, 238, 261–2, 263; Zeldin 1993, p. 119.

a new 'economic' mode of surplus appropriation that brought about the emergence of a novel form of state, Zeldin is right to assert that, by the turn of the twentieth century, 'the weight of the exploitation of the rich was felt by the masses in a very different way' than it had been in the middle of the nineteenth century. It was in the face of this unprecedented form of exploitation that the French working class succeeded in remaking itself.

CHAPTER 6

Capitalism and the Re-making of the French Working Class

The rise of capitalism in France led to the re-making of the working class. This re-making was not immediate, and important continuities between the working class that emerged in the 1830s–40s and the one that crystallised at the turn of the twentieth century can be noticed. Fundamental ruptures also took place. From the 1880s and 1890s, French workers began to form much larger labour unions and socialist parties gained significant weight within France's party system, while revisiting their strategic outlook and relationship with republicanism. These ideological and organisational transformations were fuelled by a massive upsurge of strike activity, and Noiriel goes as far as to assert that this represented a climax of combativeness in the history of the working class in France; one that plunged the ruling class into deep disarray.[1]

The present chapter will explore this re-making of the working class by first assessing its progressive structural re-composition under the pressures of industrial capitalism. This will be followed by a discussion of the labour movement under the Second Empire and during the Paris Commune, which will stress continuities with the movement that had emerged from the 1830s. The analysis of the renewal of working-class struggles will then begin with a section on the rapid rise of strike activity from the 1880s, which should be read as a refusal of the de-politicisation of the social relations of production which capitalism entails. The chapter will conclude with a discussion of the renewal of the socialist movement, which became increasingly (though never completely) independent from 'bourgeois' republicanism from the late 1870s until the eve of World War I, as new social property relations brought about a reordering of class relations.

---

1   Noiriel 1986, pp. 83, 99.

1   The Re-composition of the Working Class

The transition to industrial capitalism in France began in the 1860s and accelerated during the following decades, under the Third Republic. Over the closing decade of the century, and until World War I, international competition intensified, as did intra-national competitive pressures, with the development and adoption of new technologies by French companies. The rapid and wideranging fall in prices that ensued progressively 'demolished the big urban and rural craft industries, ruined small, technically unsophisticated producers of textiles and metals, impoverished landowners and bankrupted thousands of shopkeepers'.[2] France was facing rival national economies engaged in faster and deeper processes of industrialisation, and, from the mid-1870s to the mid-1890s, it was hit especially hard by what has been called the 'great depression' of the period[3] – a concept that, it should be noted, is much less fitting as a description of (for instance) the highly dynamic German economy of the period. As we saw in the last chapter, economic growth sharply decelerated, profits collapsed, and firms were compelled to adapt by adopting capitalist strategies in order to stay afloat.

This economic depression, followed by rapid growth resulting from capitalist transformations during the *belle époque*, brought about a 'decisive period' of renewal of the French working class.[4] It was at that time – and especially from the 1880s to 1914 – that a modern industrial proletariat emerged in France.[5] The country now comprised a growing stable industrial workforce that was increasingly dependent on wages.

Until that point, industrialisation had largely been accomplished through the extension and dissemination of industrial work in the countryside, involving vast numbers of isolated domestic workers. The emergence of new competitive imperatives during the last third of the nineteenth century brought a crisis of rural industrial production. While French capitalist industrialisation appeared, as already mentioned, relatively slow on a national scale, it had a deep impact in specific regions and localities. Price competition led to the deindustrialisation of entire regions, sometimes within a few years. From 1860 to 1880, for instance, more than half of Normandy's cotton production was wiped out by English and international competition – the remaining half sur-

---

2   Tombs 1996, p. 289.
3   Noiriel 1986, p. 86.
4   Charle 1991, p. 276; Tombs 1996, p. 289.
5   Noiriel 1986, p. 83.

vived largely thanks to its privileged access to the Algerian colonial market.[6] The industrial map of France was deeply transformed, and industrial production became largely concentrated in the North and North East regions, as well as in large cities such as Paris, Lyon or Lille and smaller towns such as Roubaix and Saint-Étienne.[7]

Seeking to increase labour productivity, industrial firms were now increasingly concentrating production in mechanised factories. The ancestral organisation of industrial production via decentralised regional industrial networks – the *fabriques* – supervised by large merchants and their agents were gradually dying out, and so was the complementarity of agricultural and industrial labour. As cotton hand weaving and other domestic industrial activities moved to factories, peasants, who were often also simultaneously cottage workers, were deprived of crucial ways of supplementing their family income. This situation often became untenable and many were forced to move off the land. The erosion of rural domestic industrial production had a dual impact. Peasants in possession of holdings sufficiently large to sustain their family remained on the land (and even often acquired new holdings) even as cottage industry faded out. Describing this phenomenon, Marchand and Thélot speak of a 'deproletarianisation' of the French peasantry during the period.[8] The reclusive and largely autarkic French peasantry remained massive well into the twentieth century. Meanwhile, the combined effects of disappearing cottage production and of a depression caused by plummeting agricultural prices pushed growing numbers of wage-labourers possessing small holdings away from the countryside and toward towns and cities. The share of the waged workforce in agricultural production decreased steadily, going from 37 percent in 1866 to 26 percent in 1914.[9]

The interpenetration of agriculture and industry that had characterised the French economy for most of the nineteenth century was thus progressively vanishing, as the former sector became increasingly isolated from the rest of the economy. The pluriactivity and incessant mobility from countryside to town and from land to workshop and back of French workers was fading out, as industrial labourers were cut off from their rural environment.[10] Whereas in the past factory owners had had significant difficulties in retaining a stable workforce, they now had access to a growing pool of market-dependent work-

6   Reddy 1984, pp. 298–9.
7   Charle 1991, pp. 277, 280; Noiriel 1986, pp. 85, 93.
8   Marchand and Thélot 1991, p. 90.
9   Marchand and Thélot 1991, p. 93.
10   Noiriel 1986, pp. 83, 91.

ers – a working class that was being uprooted from the land.[11] The seasonal variation of industrial workforces within factories, which had been substantial until then, decreased vastly over the last third of the nineteenth century, and the typical French industrial worker was by then working an average of 295 days per year.[12] Larger firms developed and extended new paternalist schemes to retain workers, controlling housing, consumption and the leisure of their employees.[13]

The rural exodus that stemmed from these transformations was limited, since it involved mainly agricultural wage-labourers and left the peasantry untouched.[14] Until 1914, the number of peasants remained more or less stable. In 1906, industry employed 31.6 percent of the national labour force, but was still 12 percentage points behind agriculture.[15] Still, the growth of the working class represented the defining transformation in the French social structure over the period. The average yearly increase of the number of factory workers from 1866 to 1896 was 1.3 percent – higher than the 1.1 percent yearly increase of the 1920s.[16] Also from 1866 to 1896, the industrialisation of the French economy created an additional two million industrial workers, and also contributed a further two million workers to the service sector.[17] A large majority (62 percent) of industrial workers were still working in small workshops of 10 employees or less, and their numbers continued to grow in absolute terms in parallel to the increase of large scale factory production.[18] Nevertheless, as early as 1896, 21 percent of French industrial labourers were employed in factories counting 200 workers or more.[19]

For the first time, French industrial development implied the growth of a proletarianised workforce of wage-labourers.[20] As a consequence of the expul-

---

11   Noiriel 1986, p. 98.
12   Marchand and Thélot 1991, p. 139; Verley 1996, pp. 106–7.
13   Noiriel 1986, pp. 90–1.
14   Marchand and Thélot 1991, p. 94.
15   Charle 1991, p. 278.
16   Marchand and Thélot 1991, p. 99.
17   Charle 1991, p. 278.
18   Historians do not all agree on this point, however, and these disagreements probably have to do with the unreliability of the nineteenth-century French census. Noiriel (1986, p. 111), for instance, mentions that the number of independent artisans and *boutiquiers* went from two million in 1866 to three million in 1906, whereas Marchand and Thélot (1991, p. 96) assert that their number no longer grew from the first decade of the Third Republic.
19   Charle 1991, p. 279.
20   Hanagan (1989) provides a indepth historical analysis of the emergence of a stable industrial population in the Saint-Étienne region from the 1840s to the 1880s. Contrary to Hanagan, however, I contend that industrial capitalism remained absent in the region

sion of a portion of the agricultural and 'proto-industrial' rural workers from the countryside, larger cities experienced rapid demographic growth. The population growth of Paris – the major industrial centre of the country – already impressive during the first half of the century, was even more spectacular in the second. After the annexation of the inner suburbs in 1860, the capital had a population of just under 1.7 million in 1861; forty year later, it counted over 2.7 million inhabitants. Whereas the first waves of immigration of the early nineteenth century had been propelled by the expansion of traditional Parisian artisanal production, the waves of the last decades of the century tended to proletarianise the capital's population. As Tyler Stocall explains, 'by the turn of the century the metropolitan area was home to a large and prospering heavy industrial sector organised along more modern lines of production ... By 1900 Paris had definitely entered the industrial age'.[21]

In Paris as in other cities and towns, urban craft workers remained a majority, but the ongoing capitalist transformation of French industry did not spare them – and this was especially true across the last two decades of the century. The mechanisation of production directly or indirectly affected artisan producers and threatened the reproduction of traditional skills. Deskilling processes and the imposition of repetitive and alienating tasks was spreading in larger factories, but also in smaller workshops. In many trades, this prompted an identity crisis among skilled urban artisans.[22] The relative slowness of French industrialisation ensured that, for decades to come, the French working class was still divided between an older artisan sector and modern factory production. Gender and ethnic divisions also endured and even grew more entrenched, and this represented 'persistent[s] sources of weakness for the labour movement'.[23] The number of women hired as industrial workers increased during this era. As this unfolded, women were increasingly confined within low-paid and precarious branches of work.[24] Important international immigration also had a substantial influence on the evolution of the working class – not least by contributing to ugly and frequent expressions of xenophobia and racism.[25] Yet, there is also a sense in which the capitalist transformation of French industry began 'the creation of a more permanent, more homogenous industrial labour

---

(and elsewhere) until the Second Empire, as is shown by the ongoing and explicit politicisation of economic life by workers that he very well describes.

21   Stovall 1990, p. 190.
22   Charle 1991, p. 283; Noiriel 1986, pp. 86, 95, 97; Tombs 1996, p. 290.
23   Magraw 1992, p. 60.
24   Charle 1991, p. 278; Noiriel 1986, p. 14.
25   Charle 1991, p. 281.

force'.[26] Growing numbers of French workers were by then coming to share a common experience of capitalist exploitation. These radical transformations, however, unfolded progressively over several decades, and by the end of the Second Empire and at the time of the Paris Commune had really only just begun.

2   The Labour Movement under the Second Empire and the Paris Commune

Capitalism had begun to penetrate France under the Second Empire, but its impact on labour was still very limited in many sectors even during the Empire's closing years. As we saw in the preceding chapter, the process of capitalist restructuring of labour and of the judicial regulation of trades began during the late 1860s and extended over several decades. The Haussmannisation of Paris and other cities, bringing massive urban upheaval, did have a considerable impact on the working class, dismembering many communities and rapidly hiking rents – processes that contributed to republican and socialist mobilisations that will be discussed in a moment.[27] Yet much of traditional urban handicraft production only really began to be affected with the acceleration of the conversion to factory production in French industry, as international competition intensified from the 1880s. The French worker delegates to the 1867 Universal Exhibition mentioned in the previous chapter still depicted the increased exposure of French industry to English capitalist competition as a *threat* to their trades' traditions – though their tone made it clear that this threat was closer from home than it had ever been before. While cotton production was already rapidly being mechanised from the second half of the 1860s, most skilled artisanal trades remained untouched by capitalist restructuring processes. Lyon's silk *fabrique*, for instance, would only begin its mechanisation in the late 1870s, while Paris, the major industrial centre of the country – comprising a fifth of the country's industrial workforce – remained an artisan city where most trades where still traditionally organised. They were still largely untouched by technological or economic innovation on the eve of 1871.[28] In

---

26   Tombs 1996, p. 290.
27   I reject, however, Roger Gould's thesis according to which Haussman's urban restructuring led to a replacement of class by neighbourhood communities as a new basis of popular resistance during the late 1860s and the Paris Commune. For an excellent critique of Gould's work, see Tombs 2014, pp. 59–65.
28   Plessis 1985, p. 97; Tombs 2014, pp. 37–8.

that year, 90 percent of French industrial firms counted ten employees or less.[29] Capitalism had arrived, but its decisive impact on French class politics was still in the making.

After Louis-Bonaparte's coup, the labour and republican movements remained 'silent' for most of the 1850s.[30] When the French labour movement re-emerged from the early 1860s, the continuity with the 1840s was remarkable.[31] Trade socialism and its emphasis on associations still formed the ideological core of the movement – though workers now tended to prefer the term 'cooperative' instead of 'association', the latter remained the envisaged means of organising and regulating labour within trades as well as on a broader social scale.[32] An association movement remained alive in almost every trade, and the number of associations grew throughout the 1860s. There were about a hundred workers' association in Paris at the beginning of 1870, and approximately thirty and twenty in Lyon and Marseille, respectively.[33] These labour organisations were often tied to a similarly expanding number of mutual aid societies. They also often mutated into *chambres syndicales* and contributed to coordinating strikes, especially from the late 1860s. In 1870, 106 labour societies were affiliated to the *Chambre fédérale des Sociétés ouvrières*, while around twenty of them joined the French section of the International Workingmen's Association (IWA), which was established in 1864. Though it was involved in the immediate defence of the workers' interests through strikes, the syndical chambers had broader purposes and was conceived as a sort of 'permanent commission' that directed and enlightened a trade as a whole, taking in hand all issues from wages to unemployment and apprenticeship.

One new element that differentiated the 1840s from the 1860s was a turn away from the state, which was taken by a substantial part of the organised labour movement – and at a time when most of the working class in Paris and in other large cities were still hoping for the coming of a republican regime. As a consequence of the savage repression of the June days of 1848, of further repression over the following years and of a coup that led to an authoritarian regime, many of the labour mouvement's initiatives under the Second Empire organised workers outside of all state institutions and envisaged a decentralised federation of self-managed cooperatives as a mode of emancipation. While Louis Blanc and his statist republican conceptions had been much more influ-

---

29   Tombs 2014, p. 168.
30   Pilbeam 1995, p. 243; Rougerie 2004, p. 270.
31   Stedman Jones 1977, p. 89.
32   Rougerie 2004, pp. 272–4.
33   Rougerie 1988, p. 10.

ential than Proudhon in 1848, the ideas of the latter were dominant in the IWA in France at the time of his death in 1865, and this prefigured not only some of the communards' ideas in 1871, but also the anarcho-syndicalist politics of the Confédération générale du travail (CGT) of the turn of the century.[34] From 1868, however, the leadership of the French section of the IWA broke with Proudhonian 'mutuellism', its focus on autonomous cooperatives and its abhorrence of strikes, and adopted a more revolutionary 'collectivism'. It also supported the federation of local associations, but was much more prompt to form alliances with republicans to target state institutions, as a way of defending the interests of labour. Collectivists also actively supported the strike wave of 1869–70.[35]

The revival of republicanism within the labour movement – amidst the broader recovery and renewal of a disparate republican movement in France – was also expressed and facilitated by the over 900 public meetings that were held in Paris from 1868 to 1870. These meetings raised controversial political issues, and sometimes made open calls for revolution and class struggle. The desire for a democratic and social republic was still in the air, while the ideal of a more direct and participatory form of democratic republic, recalling the initiatives of the sans-culottes of the first republic, had once again matured, having been disseminated among the French labour movement in the two decades that preceded the Paris Commune.[36] The inflammable political ambiance of the period was further evidenced by the Parisian days of riot that followed the elections of 1869 and the plebiscite of 1870 (aimed at validating a liberal reformation of the Empire), which were reminiscent of the revolutionary upheavals that had struck the capital on many occasions since 1789.[37]

Yet, as Tombs convincingly argues, it was not so much these popular assemblies and struggles that led to the Paris Commune of 1871 as the war and France's military defeat at the hands of Prussia.[38] After the French Empire had declared war on Prussia in July 1870, it rapidly became clear that French troops were badly prepared to face Prussians armies.[39] The defeat of Napoleon III in Sedan

---

34   Hayat, 2014, pp. 345–9.
35   Cordillot 2010, pp. 19–55; Léonard 2011; Lévêque 2004; Rougerie 1968.
36   Rougerie 2000.
37   Tombs 2014, pp. 69–74.
38   Tombs 2014, pp. 75–81. See also Pilbeam 1995, p. 256.
39   For a presentation and discussion of the events going from the 1870 Franco-Prussian war to the formation of the Paris Commune, see Rougerie 1988, pp. 22–63; Tombs 2014, pp. 83–133; and Pilbeam 1995, pp. 256–60.

on 2 September of the same year caused the fall of the Empire and the proclamation of a Republic at Paris' city hall two days later. A government of
national defence headed by general Trochu and radical and moderate republican ministers including Léon Gambetta and Jules Ferry, was formed, before
rapidly moving to Tours, and later to Bordeaux. The provisional government
neglected the constitutional consolidation of the republican regimes, and its
authority remained tenuous while it attempted to pursue the war against Prussia. The people of Paris and of other cities and regions rapidly organised in
order to defend the *patrie* against Prussian armies and to preserve the republic
against French monarchists. In Paris, popular vigilance committees were organised and the central committee of the Republican Federation of the National
Guard politically coordinated the republican and patriotic resistance. After the
provisional government's capitulation to the newly formed German Empire on
28 January of 1871, a national assembly was elected on 8 February. The Liberal
Union of Thiers came out victorious, and in the new assembly the monarchists
formed a majority. The preliminary peace project – conceding to the annexation of Alsace and Lorraine by Germany – which would eventually lead to
the Frankfurt treaty, was ratified on 1 March, and sustained republican agitation forced the newly formed government to move to Versailles a few days
later. Then, when Thiers attempted to seize cannons stationed in Parisian popular neighbourhoods, the population spontaneously rose in opposition. Thiers
was forced to order the military evacuation of Paris and the central committee of the Republican federation called for municipal elections that were held
on 26 March. The autonomous Paris Commune was formed, and would survive
until the 'bloody week' of 21 May to 28 May 1871.[40]

Most of the legislative initiatives and executive measures of the Commune
had directly or indirectly to do with the military threats coming from Versailles or the Prussians.[41] Besides military affairs, the Commune's accomplishments during its short existence remained necessarily limited. The ideological
standpoints of politically active communards were diverse: Jacobins sided with
Proudhonians, Blanquists, and moderate republicans.[42] The clear common
denominator was the republican ideal. Some of the measures that were associated with the Commune's republican agenda included the symbolic abolition
of conscription (even as it was unironically proclaimed that all able citizens
would be made to join the national guard), the separation of church and state,

---

40   On communalist movements and municipal governments in other French cities in 1870–1,
      see Aminzade 1993; Leidet and Drogoz 2013.

41   Tombs 2014, p. 177.

42   Lévêque 2004; Tombs 2014, pp. 142, 213.

and the introduction of free, secular, and compulsory education. A thorough democratisation of justice, aimed at making it free, and placing it under the supervision of elected juries, was also envisaged, though never implemented.[43]

While it was the first political regime in France to establish a Labour Commission, the impact of the Commune on labour relations remained limited. The main reforms that were passed were the abolition of night shifts for bakers, the ban of pay deduction and fines, and initiatives to replace hated employment offices with *bourses du travail* that would provide more leeway to workers dealing with unemployment.[44] A decree allowing for the conversion of abandoned workshops into producers' cooperatives was also adopted – it had limited concrete impact, but was seen by some as anticipating a broader plan to build cooperative socialism.[45]

The radical character of the Commune had more to do with its innovative institutional forms of government than with its socio-economic reforms. This is what led Marx to rightly declare that '[t]he great social measure of the Commune was its own existence'.[46] The Paris Commune was an original form of government in which the working people of Paris was a permanent political actor that effectively controlled its representatives.[47] This was a government that was concretely realising aspirations comparable to those that had guided the famous, but never implemented, constitution of June 1793, drafted at a time when the First Republic was governed under the political influence of the sans-culottes.[48] Under the Paris Commune, representatives were constantly made to conform to the wants and needs of their constituents. A municipal assembly directed an executive power, which, through the creation of nine commissions, tightly controlled the administrative structures and employees of the regimes. Information on current political affairs was systematically made public, circulated and debated among citizens. The principle of revocability,

---

43 Rougerie 1988, pp. 66–8; Willard 2000, pp. 17–18.

44 Rougerie 1988, pp. 68–70; Tombs 2014, p. 177; Willard 2000, pp. 18–19.

45 Boisseau 2000, p. 54; Tombs 2014, pp. 170–2. There is no unanimity on the socialist intents of the Commune's political leadership. Tombs insists that leaders were very prudent and went out of their way to assert their respect for private property, while Rougerie shows (as will be discussed below) that the Commune's Labour Commission had plans to pursue a socialist transformation of the economy that was quite similar to earlier attempts during the 1848 revolution. It appears that, while some leaders were strictly Jacobin republicans who had no time for socialist schemes, others were keen to ensure that the republic would indeed be 'social'.

46 Marx 2010, p. 217.

47 For an excellent discussion of the original democratic form of government put in place under the Commune, see Boisseau 2000.

48 Boisseau 2000, p. 52.

though insufficiently clarified and institutionalised, was a practical reality that oriented the decisions and actions of elected officials. As summarised by Boisseau, the Parisian people had gone from being a solicited actor (via elections and plebiscites) to an active institutional actor.[49]

For its contemporary participants, the Paris Commune was not merely a municipal uprising, but rather the beginning of a revolution that would spread across France (and beyond) to inaugurate a new type of republic in which each town and village would gain the right of, and capacity for, democratic self-administration. This was a communalist emancipatory strategy – in which Paris would only act as an ideal to be emulated.[50] Communalism, promoting a radical attenuation of the role of the central state and the democratisation of political power, had matured within the French labour movement since the 1840s, in part under the influence of Proudhon.[51] The Paris Commune's Declaration to the French People of 19 April 1871 clearly expressed this plan for a new republican model in which the political integration of the nation would derive from a voluntary federation of self-managed communes, against the 'oppressive', 'arbitrary' and 'expensive' centralisation imposed by preceding empires and monarchies.

There is a very concrete sense in which this form of government was to serve as a crucial part of an answer to the 'social question'. This was because, inter alia, it was intended as a direct reaction to the state parasitism that had peaked under the Second Empire, in which highly paid and apparently useless offices had multiplied enormously. Establishing a republic was not a mere constitutional formality, but a major step toward achieving social equality and the emancipation of the working class, who called for the abolition of an expensive and oppressive state.[52] The working people of Paris perceived political injustice as the source of economic and social injustice. The ideal of an 'inexpensive' government was a widespread radical popular aspiration, and opposition to 'fonctionnarisme' a recurrent theme. On 1 April, a decree drastically reduced the salaries of public servants and elected officials.[53] Meanwhile, the tight control exercised over the civil service by the executive power and through the constant

---

49   Boisseau 2000, p. 53.
50   Boisseau 2000, pp. 36–7, 45–6.
51   Rougerie 1988, pp. 77–86. Rougerie explains that this communalism also had roots in the great concern for political decentralisation that characterised the outlook of active citizens during the opening year of the First Republic – a concern that has largely been concealed by an overemphasis on the centralising tendencies tied to the politics of the Committee of Public Safety, which seized power in 1793 and implemented the Terror.
52   Tombs 2014, pp. 211–12.
53   Boisseau 2000, p. 53; Tombs 2014, pp. 141, 149.

involvement of active and informed citizens in the political administration of the Commune, amounted to radical ways of abolishing bureaucratic parasitism.

These political concerns were noting new, of course, and had been central programmatic elements in the formation of the French working class during the 1830s and 1840s. Breaking with the Marxist orthodoxy existing at the time, the pioneering work of Rougerie during the 1960s demonstrated that the Paris Commune was the 'dusk, not the dawn' of a revolutionary cycle – the last revolutions in a cycle that had begun in 1789, rather than a rehearsal of the revolution that was to come in 1917.[54] Contemporaries were well aware of the their revolution's connection to those of the past, and consciously revived and celebrated the repertoire and symbols of the great French Revolution, for instance re-establishing the republican calendar that had been created in 1793.[55] For contemporaries, the social composition of the Parisian revolutionary masses was also plain to see: these were common, working people – independent artisans, skilled craft workers, office employees, or small shop owners. This was true in 1871, just as it had been in 1848, 1830, or even during the 1790s.[56] What made the Paris Commune stand out was the fact that a majority of its political leadership was composed of workers.[57]

The enemies of the communards were drawn from the same groups that had composed the reactionary forces – and that had been identified as such by working-class revolutionaries – since 1789: monarchists, the clergy, and idle exploiters and parasites. For communards, the people comprised all workers, including intellectual employees, and even the 'working bourgeoisie', but excluded and was opposed to speculators and overpaid and parasitic state officials who had benefited from the corrupted political system of the Second Empire.[58] Socialist republicans revolving around the Commune's Labour Commission revived the ideal of a democratic and social republic that would complete the transformation that had begun in 1789.[59] The Commission envisaged vast projects aimed at organising labour in ways that continued and expanded the 'trade socialism' put forth by the trades societies and worker associations at the Luxembourg Commission in 1848. Though now closer to Proudhon's than

---

54   Rougerie 1964, pp. 240–1.
55   Tombs 2014, pp. 35, 214.
56   Rougerie 1964, p. 127; Tombs 2014, pp. 38, 202.
57   Tombs 2014, p. 210.
58   Tombs 2014, pp. 214, 218–19.
59   Tombs 2014, p. 211.

to Blanc's idea – and consequently keener to rely on mutualised credit than on financial aid provided by a central state – the aim of this republican socialism was still to favour the generalisation of cooperative enterprises that would sell at cost price, relinquish profits, be more efficient and consequently replace private companies over time.[60]

These planned socialist reforms were never launched. By late April 1871, Thiers's government had assembled sufficient troops to attack the Parisians, and the Commune was barbarically crushed in the closing days of May. This major working-class defeat permitted the continuation of a capitalist transition that had only just begun, but that accelerated over the following decades and brought an important reformation of the French working class. The resistance of French workers to class exploitation was evolving, but it was not disappearing – in some ways, it was only intensifying.

3   The Rise of the Strike: Refusing the Depoliticisation of Production

The capitalist transformation of social power implied a de-politicisation of economic relations and a privatisation of authority over labour processes. French workers ferociously opposed these processes and engaged in a major strike wave. '[T]he 1890s–1900s saw the highest level of strike activity in French history'.[61] Strikes were nothing new, but such sustained intensity certainly was – a new period of working-class resistance had clearly begun. From 1830 to 1880, there was little change in the strike patterns of French workers and no steady upward trend could be identified. Collective work stoppages were de-criminalised in 1864, and impressive strikes were waged at the end of the decade. This new burst of strike activity, however, represented a recovery from a sharp lull over the first decade of the Second Empire; in any case, it remained modest compared to what was to come. It was really only around the turn of the 1880s that a real take-off in strike activity can be observed in France.[62]

The average number of strikes went from barely 100 per year in the late 1870s to well over 1,000 per year during the 1900s.[63] There was a yearly increase of nearly seven percent from 1884 to 1913, and 'the number of strikes per 100,000

---

60   Rougerie 1988, pp. 68–70.
61   Tombs 1996, p. 290.
62   Lequin 1983, p. 440; Rebérioux 1974, p. 147; Shorter and Tilly 1974, p. 48.
63   Magraw 1992, p. 5.

workers increased sixfold in a fairly steady progression' over the same period.[64] Strikes became more frequent, but also longer and more massive.[65] The number of strikers per year reached 39,500 in 1884, more than doubled to 82,960 in 1890, and then skyrocketed to 159,500 in 1900 and 241,767 in 1913.[66]

The strike was becoming a familiar phenomenon and the major form of working-class protest. While their usefulness had been contested by influential Proudhonians during the period of the Second Empire, material conditions were now leading the labour movement to rehabilitate the strike, which was resorted to with much greater frequency. The general strike was in fact about to become the centrepiece of the revolutionary strategy adopted by part of the French labour movement.[67]

Strikes increasingly departed from the old seasonal pattern, still dominant in the 1830s and 1840s,[68] whereby workers would demand wage increases in times of relative prosperity. While this pattern remained in place, a rapidly growing proportion of strikes were now directly waged around the issue of control over production.[69] Workers were resisting the imposition of new forms of payment and the loss of power over labour processes that these entailed. They opposed new factory rules, and expressed their 'abhorrence of fast rhythms, of unjust fines, of implacable schedules and, above all, of meddlesome, unjust, brutal and lewd foremen'.[70] They fought to retain control over hiring processes and against their monopolisation by employers, and to preserve existing tariffs that guaranteed living standards.[71] Workers were striking massively to resist the commodification of their labour power. In 1883, the Parisian stonecutters' union opposed what they called the '"immorality of bourgeois opinion" which assimilates labour to a commodity and treats the wage as a price subjected to the laws of supply and demand'.[72] As capitalist work-discipline was implemented, a concern for dignity became ever more pressing. Labourers were incensed by employers who treated them as 'beasts of burden', as soulless means of pro-

---

64   Friedman 1990, p. 159; Shorter and Tilly 1974, p. 56.
65   Noiriel 1986, pp. 99–100.
66   Friedman 1990, p. 160. Friedman explains that he establishes the 'average number of strikers for five years centered on year given for 1884, 1890, and 1900. The 1913 figure is a three-year average of 1911–13'.
67   Perrot 1974, p. 97.
68   Faure 1974, pp. 55, 57.
69   Charle 1991, pp. 302–3; Lequin 1983, p. 444; Shorter and Tilly 1974, p. 67; Stearns 1971, p. 57; Tombs 1996, p. 294.
70   Perrot 1974, p. 296.
71   Noiriel 1986, p. 102.
72   Perrot 1974, p. 134.

duction, and demanded to be treated respectfully by foremen and for a ban on insults towards workers.[73]

By the turn of the twentieth century, workers had developed a 'flamboyant hatred' for factories, which they assimilated to 'prisons', while depicting themselves as 'convicts' or 'bandits' involved in forced labour.[74] The new capitalist factories evoked feelings of 'terror' and of 'strangeness' among workers – 'for a long time, indeed, life inside the factory was not, in the eyes of the vast majority, life'.[75] Workers fled these new workplaces, and capitalist factories experienced very high turnover rates. Apart from being a way to impose a series of demands, the strike was in itself a direct way of escaping the new capitalist discipline; it 'loosened the vice of rigid schedules, of throbbing rhythms and introduce[d] the liberty of leisure in an exhausting existence without pauses'.[76] Striking workers often took some time to relax, tending to their gardens, hiking in the woods, or playing with their children. Strikes were 'festivals' that often involved banquets and joyful parades around the locality.[77] Disparaging remarks from foremen could spark échapées-belles, during which workers massively exited factories in protest and marched in the streets, chanting slogans and singing songs in which 'workers liked to castigate the oppressing boss, profiteer and pleasure-seeker, who refused to recognise the natural rights of his workers'.[78] Work stoppages also provided time to participate in regular and often enormous meetings that allowed labourers to organise their movement and to control their delegates from below, thus quenching their thirst for direct democracy.[79]

Strikes involved workers from all industrial branches, working in small workshops as well as large factories.[80] This was not simply a rebellion of skilled craftmen and women. Semi-skilled and unskilled workers also joined the struggle.[81] So did white-collar and service workers. Retail as well as restaurant workers formed unions. Postal workers decried speed-ups and the growing volume of

---

73   Magraw 1986, p. 309; Stearns 1971, pp. 58, 59.
74   Charle 1991, p. 311; Perrot 1974, p. 295; Rebérioux 1974, p. 156.
75   Lequin 1983, p. 415.
76   Perrot 1974, p. 548: 'desserrent l'étau des horaires rigides, des cadences lancinantes, et introduisent dans une existence harassante et sans trêve, la liberté du loisir'.
77   Perrot 1974, p. 548.
78   Sirot 2002, p. 146: 'ces chants aiment fustiger le patron oppresseur, profiteur et jouisseur qui se refuse à reconnaître le bon droit de ses ouvriers'.
79   Perrot 1974, pp. 588–96.
80   Lequin 1983, p. 462; Noiriel 1986, pp. 99–100; Perrot 1974, pp. 55, 59.
81   Scott 1974, pp. 92, 113.

mail they were forced to carry, while cab drivers organised against big monopoly firms and café waiters struck for their right to grow moustaches.[82]

Major works dealing with the rise of strike activity in France at this time have focused on sectors such as mining and textiles, where a substantial proportion of all strikes occurred. They have explained this acceleration by relating it to the rapidly changing experience of a workforce that was 'uprooted, disoriented, and uncertain of its social identity, demoralized'.[83] While craft workers could lean on pre-existing solidarity structures, the new industrial workers were depicted as disoriented, and consequently as waging strikes at random. Reddy offers a critique of this perspective, and stresses that most textile workers that left their rural communities actually moved to towns and cities that were only a few miles away. According to him, trade communities in fact remained quite strong in all industrial sectors, and it was the very rootedness of labourers and their community life that fuelled their collective action.[84] While Reddy might be underestimating the dissolving impact of capitalism on trade communities, it is certainly true that these communities, which had been nurtured by *prud'hommes* and other judicial institutions after the Revolution of 1789, lingered on for decades after the first signs of capitalist restructuring in France. It was in fact to defend the moral economy upheld by these institutions and trade communities against its erosion by industrial capitalism that workers struck in rapidly growing numbers at the turn of the twentieth century.

This fact can also partly explain the relatively low membership of French trade unions at the time (which remains a distinguishing characteristic of the French labour movement to this day). In 1913, while there were over four and a half million unionised workers in Germany and over four million in Britain, there were only around one million in France.[85] This amounted to 668 and 901 unionised workers per 10,000 inhabitants in Germany and Britain, respectively, against 259 in France.[86] Many authors have underlined the French paradox of numerically weak trade unions (and socialist parties) that existed side-by-side with the intense class-antagonism nurtured by French workers.[87]

---

82   Magraw 1992, pp. 14, 48; Stearns 1971, p. 59.
83   Reddy 1984, p. 291. These major contributions include Perrot 1974, Shorter and Tilly 1974, Stearns 1971.
84   Reddy 1984, p. 294. For a similar argument, see Calhoun 2012.
85   Carroué, Collet and Ruiz 2005, p. 78.
86   Note that union density in France only slightly inferior to the density found in the United States, Norway, Italy or Belgium, and superior to the density of several other countries such as Switzerland, Sweden and Canada.
87   Berlanstein 1992, p. 661.

The formation of *chambres syndicales* accelerated from the second half of the 1860s, in the wake of the decriminalisation of strikes and the foundation of the IWA in 1864. But it was really only from the 1880s that French unions began to reach substantial portions of the working class, as strike activity also began to rapidly increase.[88] Unions were often formed after the fact, with the purpose of organising a strike, and also often faded away once workers went back to work. Consequently, union density constantly fluctuated in France until World War I, while remaining well below levels reached in Britain or Germany, even as it began to involve growing numbers of workers.[89] Also in contrast with developments in other industrialising countries, the French labour movement failed to federate unions along trade lines before the 1890s.[90] Even after the formation of the CGT in 1895, strikes and unions tended to be organised on a local basis, rather than along trade and sectoral lines, which leads Stearns to speak of the 'pervasive localism' that characterised the French labour movement of the time. As he explains, 'French workers, though ready for an intensive local effort on occasions, resisted industry-wide strikes of the sort that became common in Britain'.[91] First emerging in Paris in 1887, *bourses du travail*, at first envisaged as an alternative to employment offices, rapidly spread across the country – they were present in 144 cities in 1914 – and were often instrumental in organising these local struggles. *Bourses* formed a federation in 1892, which merged into the CGT in 1902.[92] Financially supported by moderate republican politicians, who hoped that they would promote union moderation and smooth collective bargaining, *bourses du travail* rapidly became rallying points for revolutionary syndicalists.[93]

Contrary to their British counterparts, French unions refused to confine their action to an economic sphere – 'the CGT did not see itself as merely a trade union organization – indeed, it explicitly rejected what came to be called in France *trade unionisme* – but as a political movement that provided an alternative to electoral socialism'.[94] French unions 'did not distinguish the political level from the social ... In fact, unions took care of all the tasks of a diverse tradition and did not substitute it with the simple defence of professional interests, the wage above all'.[95] Just as the French labour movement had done throughout

---

88   Lequin 1983, p. 453; Stearns 1971, p. 12.
89   Cottereau 1986, p. 144; Lequin 1983, pp. 449, 459; Zolberg 1986, p. 421.
90   Cottereau 1986, p. 145.
91   Stearns 1971, p. 30.
92   Lequin 1983, p. 456; Shorter and Tilly 1974, pp. 168–9.
93   Cottereau 1986, p. 146; Friedman 1990, p. 157; Stearns 1971, p. 12.
94   Zolberg 1986, p. 419.
95   Lequin 1983, pp. 453–4: 'ne distingue pas le plan politique de celui du social ... Dans les

the century, the unions that were growing at the turn of the century refused
'the compartmentalization between the public sphere (the state, elected representative, public opinion) and the economic or "private" sphere proposed by
parliamentary democracy'.[96]

Union membership in France had a very different meaning than it did in Britain. Union density remained relatively low in France because French workers
'learned from experience that Anglo-Saxon-style unions were unnecessary and
ineffective'; their preference for more spontaneous and informal types of action
'was a rational response to the situation they faced'.[97] French workers evolved
in a (fading) universe of more or less stable, normative regulation of production
and labour relations. Joining a union did not necessarily mean belonging to a
formal organisation as it did in Britain. It simply entailed a solidarity that could
involve participation in actions aimed at enforcing and preserving existing regulations. Once the action was over, there was often no reason or incentive to
retain union membership.[98] Unions were vehicles to maintain or re-establish
proper *usages* and customary practices that were increasingly under threat. The
ad hoc, often informal, and spontaneous character of French syndicalism was
rooted in a culture of 'pragmatic direct action'[99] that stemmed from established
normative regulations – as well as from encroachments on these regulations.

Workers regularly struck to consolidate normative tariffs. Employers were
asked to sign these tariffs and workers made sure that they were printed, publicised, and enforced by public authorities and *prud'hommes*.[100] These were not
understood as mere collective agreements reached by private parties. Perrot
mentions that many strikes turned into 'authentic constitutional conflicts'.[101]
This metaphor hints at the political character of the period's labour conflicts.
Strikes 'were more an instrument to force the intervention of the state in labor
relations than a tool for, say, belaboring employers at the bargaining table'.[102]
Strikes were not confined to workplaces; they were fundamentally public affairs
and unfolded as such. They 'tended to be dramas staged in the forum of the
street or the town square, and all the marching back and forth, the public meetings, the placards and demonstrations were designed to catch the eye of the

---

faits, les syndicats cumulent toutes les tâches d'une tradition diverse et ne lui substituent
pas l'unique défense des intérêts professionels, celle du salaire surtout'.

96   Cottereau 1986, p. 147.
97   Berlanstein 1992, p. 667.
98   Cottereau 1986, pp. 143–4.
99   Ibid.
100   Perrot 1974, pp. 275–6.
101   Perrot 1974, p. 276: 'véritables conflits constitutionnels'.
102   Shorter and Tilly 1974, p. 28.

political powers-that-be'.[103] Bargaining between employers and workers took place in the public sphere and 'in order to communicate with each other the parties resorted to public announcements, notices placarded on the plant gate or the door of the town hall or printed in the local newspaper. Typically, an employer who wanted to end a strike by meeting his workers halfway, or by giving in to their demands, would post the new pay schedule in a public space'.[104]

Workers organised less around plants than on a municipal basis, often using *bourse du travail* as headquarters in larger towns. Spilling across workplaces, strikes took the form of local and community-based struggles during which strikers often paraded with their demands written on placards in order to make their struggle known to the local public.[105] The prime objective of these 'demonstrations-petitions'[106] was to compel public authorities to intervene in labour conflicts. Though Parisian strike leaders sometimes directly appealed to ministers, strikes more often attempted to reach regional and municipal authorities, and prefects and subprefects were the public figures most frequently involved in labour conflicts.[107] Workers addressed letters to prefects which 'evoked the *cahiers de doléances*, they had the sadness and softness deriving from the hope to be read by a benevolent eye. For a long time, workers retained their faith in the mediating powers of the Prefect'.[108]

On most occasions, very little bargaining actually took place directly between workers and employers: 'between 1898 and 1914 ... worker unions formally negotiated with their employers in only 6 percent of all strikes ... We have no reason to think that this minimal share was much different in either the years before or after this time. And in only 1 percent of all strikes in 1905–1914 did employers and workers' unions actually negotiate together to end a dispute'.[109] This certainly had to do with the stubborn refusal of most employers to bargain, but we must also consider that unions 'did not imagine their primary mission to be representing their members in collective bargaining'.[110]

---

103   Shorter and Tilly 1974, p. 343.
104   Shorter and Tilly 1974, p. 35.
105   Perrot 1986, p. 87; Shorter and Tilly 1974, p. 28.
106   Sirot 2002, p. 157.
107   Shorter and Tilly 1974, p. 41; Stearns 1971, p. 67.
108   Perrot, quoted in Shorter and Tilly 1974, p. 378. See also Charle 1991, p. 303.
109   Shorter and Tilly 1974, p. 35. This trend persisted during the interwar period. In 1919, a law formalised collective agreements into civil contracts enforceable in courts. Yet, during the five years that followed, only five percent of all strikes ended with a collective agreement. This figure rose to eight percent for 1925–9 before declining to three percent for 1930–5 – see Shorter and Tilly 1974, p. 29.
110   Shorter and Tilly 1974, p. 28.

272   CHAPTER 6

Workers did not seek collective bargaining *à l'anglaise* with their employers, because they did not consider labour and economic relations as private and depoliticised matters. They remained fundamentally *public* matters. During the 1830s and 1840s, and most dramatically in 1848, the French labour movement attempted to extend normative regulations of the economy by building a social republic that would further democratise social relations of production. By the closing decades of the century, however, they were trapped in a defensive posture, trying to preserve the social embeddedness of economic relations. To the emerging political economy of capital, French workers were opposing their own moral economy. This was illustrated, for instance, by a strike in 1903 led by textile workers in Armentières in Northern France, which has been studied in detail by Reddy.[111] Strikers were demanding the reinstatement of tariffs that had been established in 1889, and wanted to retain their apprenticeship system, as well as their control over hiring. Doing this, 'laborers did not feel that they were engaging in bargaining or in a market maneuver; they expressed their intention of imposing their will on a tyrannous minority [their employers] whose failure to live up even to their own conservative notions of owner-laborer reciprocity had forfeited their last claim to tolerance'.[112]

As the capitalist power of employers continued to increase, some workers also came to accept the new rules of the game. The rhythms of the capitalist restructuring of French industry varied greatly according to trades and regions and, of course, workers had their own agency and historical background that contributed to the development of differentiated organisational strategies and ideological outlooks.[113] Textile workers from the North, for instance, were relatively more receptive to Guedes's translation and importation of Marxist ideas into France, while miners often tended to adopt a reformist outlook and to develop more formalised trade-unions, seeking material gains by bargaining with their employers.[114] As we are about to discuss, the French labour movement of the turn of the twentieth century was ideologically and organisationally diverse. Yet, in the midst of this diversity, the bellicosity of the French working class stands out, and indicates the depth of its refusal of the new capitalist world that was emerging. This spirit of defiance contributed to the rise of a new, autonomous labour movement in France at the turn of twentieth century.

---

111   Reddy 1984, pp. 309–23.
112   Reddy 1984, p. 321.
113   Charle 1991, pp. 276–7.
114   Charle 1991, p. 313; Noiriel 1986, p. 102.

4   The Transformation of Class Relations and the Rise of an
       Autonomous Socialist Working-Class Movement

As we saw in Chapter 4, the fiscal question was a core issue of the class antagonism that had existed under the old regime and for most of the nineteenth-
century. Consequently, republicans had made fiscal reforms a major element
of their programme. Émile-Justin Menier, a pre-eminent republican champion
of fiscal reforms in the 1870s, asserted that

> old politics considered taxation as the main instrument of oppression
> of the weak and of enjoyment for the strong. It was ... under feudalism,
> the exploitation of man by the lord; under the divine right monarchy, the
> exploitation of the people for the benefit of the king and of his courtesans.
> Taxation has retained this form. The state is in an antagonistic relation
> with the taxpayer and tries to extract from him as much as it can by pla-
> cing him in a network of onerous and vexatious taxes. In democratic and
> industrial civilisation, taxation must be completely transformed. Citizens
> of the same country, we must consider ourselves as stockholders of the
> same society.[115]

Menier expressed a sentiment widely shared among republicans. The modest
progressive fiscal reforms of the Second Republic had been rapidly retracted,
and, after its fall, republicans condemned the successive imperial and mon-
archic regimes of the nineteenth century for exacerbating the fiscal inequalities
of the old regime. These regimes had been undemocratic, and this explained
why their fiscal policies had benefited the richest. The fiscal project of republicans was to build an 'inexpensive' state [État à bon marché] so as to supress
'parasitism', and they regularly promoted the idea of a single and progressive
income tax to replace the numerous indirect taxes that were then in place.[116]

---

115   Quoted in Delalande 2011: 'l'ancienne politique considérait l'impôt comme le principal
       instrument d'oppression pour les faibles et de jouissance pour les forts. C'était ... dans
       la féodalité, l'exploitation de l'homme par le seigneur; sous la monarchie de droit divin,
       l'exploitation du peuple au profit du roi et de ses courtisans. L'impôt a encore conservé
       cette forme. L'État se place en antagonisme avec le contribuable et essayé de lui arracher
       le plus possible en l'enserrant dans un réseau de taxes onéreuse et vexatoires. Dans la
       civilisation démocratique et industrielle, l'impôt doit changer complètement de forme.
       Citoyens du même pays, nous devons nous considérer comme actionnaires de la même
       société'.
116   Delalande 2013, pp. 274–5.

Fiscal issues were at the heart of parliamentary and public debates in France from the outset of the Third Republic until World War I. Actual fiscal reforms, however, were slow to materialise and remained modest, and income tax was only introduced in 1914. An income tax proposal was debated in 1871–2, but rapidly sunk by Thiers, who considered it a divisive initiative that could destabilise the new republican regime. Gambetta put forth a new income tax bill in 1876, but this was a half-hearted attempt that was once again easily rejected. 'Opportunist' republicans opted for fiscal realism and folded before the opposition of monarchists who wanted to preserve the privileges of the notability and who were consequently opposed to substantial fiscal reforms.[117] Liberal republicans rationalised this by arguing that an income tax would actually reproduce the fiscal spoliation of the poor by the state – they opposed the redistribution of wealth through progressive taxation and public expenditure that was proposed by radical republicans. Meanwhile the wealthy protected their privileges by evoking the defence of 'middle-class' interests and the republican myth of an egalitarian society of small owners.[118]

One of the most remarkable facts tied to the evolution of class relations, however, is the overall taming of the fiscal debates that occurred in France during the first decades of the Third Republic.[119] This taming was actively pursued by politicians who had in mind the recurrent clashes around these issues that took place under previous regimes. The Republic engaged in sustained and systematic efforts to educate taxpayers in order to legitimate tax payments. Civil and moral instruction manuals insisted on the citizens' duty to pay taxes and stressed that in democratic regime taxes were necessarily serving the general interest.[120] More importantly, republican governments adopted a fiscal policy aimed at building the regime's social basis by satisfying the material interests of specific groups through a series of minor reforms. From the late 1870s and during the 1880s, targeted tax reliefs were established in order to alleviate some of the most blatant injustices of the existing tax system, while some of the most unpopular consumer taxes were eliminated. In addition, administrative and tax collecting procedures were rationalised so as to reduce their costs. The tax collectors' large stipends and arbitrary powers were eliminated, and they were instructed 'to serve the public' and to ease payment terms for the most recalcitrant taxpayers.[121]

---

117   Delalande 2013, p. 276.
118   Delalande 2013, p. 281.
119   Delalande 2011, p. 109.
120   Delalande 2013, p. 279.
121   Delalande 2011, p. 128; 2013, pp. 277, 279.

As tensions around fiscal issues were reduced, the opposition between productive, working people and an idle notability became less salient and was progressively, if partially, replaced by a new class antagonism between workers and capitalists. The emergence of this new class antagonism was reflected in the evolution of French politics and in the development of splits within the socialist and republican movements. From the late 1870s, and partly through the major upsurge of strike activity described above, an important renewal of the French labour movement occurred, which entailed the development of novel socialist and syndicalist organisations. Either revolutionary or reformist in character, these organisations increasingly asserted their independence from a republican movement that was also transforming and slipping toward the right end of the political spectrum while embracing political and economic liberalism. Workers were still eager to defend the Republic whenever it was threatened, but its stabilisation during the late 1870s also marked the beginning of the emergence of autonomous socialist working-class organisations. While still at the margins of French politics at the turn of the 1880s, the socialist workers' movement grew steadily and made significant headway in the decades that followed.

After the fall of the Commune, most of the eminent communards who had not been assassinated during the 'bloody week' were forced into exile. During the first half of the 1870s, monarchists retained a majority in the National Assembly, and the government targeted and repressed socialists. The French socialist movement adapted to this inhospitable context by confining itself to a moderate programmatic outlook, rejecting revolutionary action and promoting the peaceful proliferation of producers' and consumers' cooperatives. For the time being, the labour movement overwhelmingly preferred the Radical republicanism of Gambetta, and the limited social reforms it had to offer, over socialist projects seeking a profound reorganisation of society. From the second half of the 1870s, however, the French socialist movement entered a phase of important, yet contested, self-redefinition that implied a confrontation between mutualists who remained attached to a traditional form of cooperative or trade socialism, on the one hand, and collectivists, who were challenging capitalist property and promoting the collectivisation of means of production through revolutionary action.[122]

A first national workers' congress was organised in Paris in October 1876 and attended by 360 delegates, mainly from syndical chambers of the capital, but also representing a number of provincial organisations. While insisting

---

122   Adler-Gillies 2014, pp. 386, 391.

on the importance of preserving an exclusively working-class character, the congress decided not to participate in electoral politics. Its programme was focused on the development of associations as a means of working-class emancipation, and delegates demanded the dismantlement of legal impediments to the spread of producers' cooperatives. The programme adopted in Paris also explicitly stressed the importance of *prud'hommes* councils as a legal means of solving labour conflicts, another clear sign of continuities with past socialist perspectives. The influence of Proudhon was still tangible, and this first congress replicated the cooperative trade socialism that had been at the core of the French labour and socialist movements ever since the 1830s.[123]

A second congress was held in Lyon in 1878. Since the Paris congress, an important step in the stabilisation of the Republic had been made. After the dissolution by the legitimist president Mac Mahon of a republican-dominated National Assembly that had been elected in 1876, new elections held in 1877 brought about an even stronger republican majority. In this new political context, the Lyon congress stuck to the traditional mutualist programme that had been adopted in Paris, but '[t]he tone of the debate, however, underwent a dramatic shift'. As explained by Adler-Gillies, the debates held at Lyon 'reveal a movement in a moment of negotiation, both with itself, with its own political ideological identity, as well as with its antagonists, the capitalist bourgeoisie'.[124] Delegates agreed on the importance of supporting independent working-class electoral candidates running on a socialist programme. Moreover, the neutrality of the republican state was questioned and appeals to a revolutionary break with the regime were made during debates. Some delegates challenged capitalist property and a collectivist motion was put forth for debate, calling for 'all Workers' Associations in general to study practical means to apply the principle of collective property of land and of means of production'.[125] The motion was rejected by a large majority, and it was clear that '[s]ocial and class reconciliation still underpinned the aspirations of many delegates'[126] – yet signs of change had emerged.

The passage toward collectivism was accomplished at the Marseille congress, held in 1879, and this marked a significant (but not complete) break with the mutualist tradition that had first emerged in the 1830s. The congress adop-

---

123   Adler-Gillies 2014, p. 393; Lejeune 1994, p. 105; Moss 1976, pp. 66–7; Rebérioux 1974, p. 149.

124   Adler-Gillies 2014, p. 393.

125   Rebérioux 1974, p. 149: 'toutes les Association ouvrières en générale à étudier les moyens pratiques pour mettre en application le principe de la propriété collective du sol et des instruments de travail'.

126   Adler-Gillies 2014, p. 395.

ted resolutions in favour of collectivism and declared that the emancipation of the working class could not be achieved merely by developing producers' cooperatives. A revolutionary posture was adopted by a majority of delegates, for whom mere social reforms had become unsatisfactory substitutes for a radical social upheaval that would collectivise the means of production that were monopolised by the capitalist class. Another adopted motion created a workers' party, named the *Fédération du Parti des Travailleurs Socialistes de France*.[127]

The new party, however, was a federation of six significantly autonomous regional organisations and represented a loose coalition of the different socialist and anarchist currents. The limited character of the collectivists' victory was exposed by splits within the movement, taking place at the Havre congress in 1880, and deepening at Reims in 1881. The cooperativist (or mutualist) current still commanded significant influence within the French labour movement, and would continue to do so until World War I. The rupture was completed at Saint-Étienne in 1882, when a Guesdists minority left the Broussiste majority to form the *Parti ouvrier français*.[128] In opposition to Guedes's Marxism, 'possibilists' led by Paul Brousse adopted a more modest and gradualist programme that was to be pursued in large part at the municipal level.

This period marked the emergence of the scission between reformists or '*syndicaux*', on the one hand, and collectivists and anarchists, on the other. Since the 1980s, a new historiography of the French labour and socialist movement of the early Third Republic has challenged the revolutionary/reformist dualism established by an earlier historiography.[129] It appears that 'out of the ideological cleavages and ruptures of the late 1870s–1880s emerged a far more complex movement, one that was neither Marxian nor Proudhonian, one which sought to synthesize its various ideological and philosophical strands'.[130]

The fact remains that, during the opening decades of the Third Republic, the French labour movement was spectacularly fragmented into a myriad of

---

127 Adler-Gillies 2014, p. 396.

128 Adler-Gillies 2014, pp. 400–1; Moss 1976, p. 95; Rebérioux 1974, p. 155. On Jules Guesdes and French Marxism in France under the Third Republic, see Ducange 2017, Stuart 1992 and Willard 1965.

129 Wright 2013; Prochasson, 2012.

130 Adler-Gillies 2014, p. 404; Prochasson 2012, p. 10. Notwithstanding these important points on the porosity between reformist and revolutionary currents at the time, the argument developed in what follows is that the rise of capitalism – to which republicans were in fact contributing – pushed revolutionary issues onto the political agenda. Although always under the influence of the socialism of the past, a new emancipatory politics appeared increasingly necessary, and this was unsettling for reformists – whether moderate socialists, syndicalists, or even left republicans.

political and syndicalist organisation.[131] Only in 1905, answering a call from the International, did socialists form a single party – the *Section française de l'Internationale Ouvrière* (SFIO) – to which the CGT answered in 1906 with the *Charte d'Amiens*, presenting itself as an alternative to electoral socialist politics and promoting the general strike as the key element of its revolutionary strategy.

In spite of this fragmentation, and while they remained very small during the 1880s, socialist parties grew significantly from the 1890s and gained significant weight in municipal and national politics.[132] Party membership remained modest in comparison to other industrialising countries. From 1906 to 1914 the SFIO doubled its membership, which went from 44,000 to 90,000. These figures remained very small in comparison with the million members of the Social Democratic Party of Germany (SPD), but French socialists of this period were still able to experience a real electoral breakthrough. The share of the popular vote secured by socialists in national elections went from under one percent in the late 1880s to nearly 17 percent in 1914. The number of members of the National Assembly belonging to the SFIO went from 52 in 1906, to 76 in 1910, and 103 in 1914, making it the second party in importance behind the Radicals. The share of French cities of 4,000 inhabitants and over with elected socialist officials went from 1.6 percent in 1884 to 31.6 percent in 1913, and, by 1896, socialists had seized power in a dozen large cities while forming majorities within 150 municipal councils. Meanwhile labour unions, which had until then largely been concentrated in urban trades, spread all over the country, as their membership grew by nearly 9.5 percent per year from 1884 to 1913. In absolute terms, union membership went from 72,300 in 1884 to over a million in 1913.[133]

Support for socialism was manifestly growing within the working class. Even after its consolidation in the late 1870s, the Republic was still fragile in a continent where France was the only republican regime besides Switzerland, Andorra, and San Marino – French workers were well aware of this fact and remained loyal to the Republic.[134] The mass of workers rallied in defence of the Republic whenever they sensed that it was threatened, and portions of the socialist left joined the *Bloc des gauches* to back the regime during the Dreyfus affair.[135] Meanwhile, however, many workers also came to support social-

---

131   Tombs 1996, p. 292.

132   Tombs 1996, p. 293.

133   Friedman 1990, pp. 159–60; Magraw 1986, pp. 300, 312; Perrot 1986, p. 108; Rebérioux 1974, pp. 170–1, 213.

134   Friedman 1990, p. 153.

135   Jones 2018, p. 93; Nord 2011, p. 50; Tombs 1996, p. 296.

ist organisations that were getting much more ambivalent about republican institutions than they had been during the middle decades of the nineteenth century,[136] and 'the share of the national vote going to parties of the moderate republican center declined sharply after the early 1880s'.[137]

In the opening years of the twentieth century, the left republican Radical party, founded in 1901, made important gains and came to lead the Assembly and government. But in the meantime, the SFIO was also making significant gains, presenting itself as a 'class struggle and revolutionary' party that rejected alliances with 'bourgeois' republican parties.[138] While only representing a small portion of French workers (who also joined reformist and 'yellow', boss-friendly unions), the CGT formed an active minority of militants that enjoyed a wide appeal among rank-and-file workers, and which promoted a revolutionary programme that was in sharp opposition to mainstream republicanism.[139] The SFIO failed to regroup all socialist organisations outside of the anarcho-syndicalist CGT, but the foundation of the party in 1905 still represented an important organisational break in relation to the republican party family, while contributing to the consolidation of revolutionary tendencies within French socialism.[140] New perspectives on emancipatory working-class politics had emerged from the late 1870s. By the 1900s, the relationship between the state, then under the Radicals' control, and a growing and militant labour movement had become a central issue, if not the central issue, of French politics.[141]

How can we explain the (partial) break with trade socialism and its mutualist programme that took place within the labour movement, and the related increase in the autonomy of this movement from mainstream and even left republican organisations at the turn of the twentieth century? In an influential book, Bernard Moss contends that these transformations were mainly caused by the end of the alliance between the middle- and working-class republicans that followed the consolidation of the Republic. The election of a republican majority in the National Assembly in 1877, and in the Senate in 1879, removed an important restraint on independent working-class politics. In short, independent politics was fuelled by the timidity of the social reforms promoted by republicans. As Moss explains, the evolution of the strategic outlook of the labour movement at the time 'occurred in direct proportion to the disappoint-

---

136   Aminzade 1993, p. 28.
137   Friedman 1990, p. 161.
138   Magraw 1986, p. 312; Rebérioux 1974, pp. 195–6.
139   Magraw 1986, p. 303; Moss 1976, p. 150; Noiriel 1986, p. 106.
140   Prochasson 2012, p. 11.
141   Magraw 1986, p. 251.

ment experienced with the new Republic, its failure to pass a significant pro-
gram of social reforms'.[142] According to him, then, the ideological and organisational transformations of the labour movement were caused much less by
economic than by political factors. France's industrialisation remained relatively slow during the first decades of the Republic, and it was the alignment of
left liberal republicans and their failure to defend the workers' interests that lay
behind the growing independence of labour.[143]

The republicans' moderation on social issues, as well as their active repression of more radical labour militancy, certainly played a crucial role in the shifting of class alliances and, in turn, in the evolution of the labour movement.[144]
Moss's argument, however, remains one-sided. We need to situate the evolution
of class alliances in a historical context characterised not simply by (relatively
slow) industrialisation, but also and crucially by a new mode of exploitive production. Indeed, tensions and splits within the republican movement were
nothing new and had violently surfaced around the social question under the
Second Republic, and especially during the June days of 1848.[145] Similar tensions had emerged under the Paris Commune. The point is that, at the turn of
the century – and on top of these political conflicts among republicans – the
spread of a new form of class exploitation tended to make alliances between
socialists and even left republicans increasingly unstable, just as it called for a
new emancipatory strategy of expropriation of capitalists.

During the 1860s, a new generation of republicans emerged and redefined
French republicanism, blending liberal individualism with representative
democracy and rejecting socialism.[146] After 1871, republican leadership had
passed to this new generation, and the ideas of Proudhon, Blanqui or other
socialist and revolutionary republicans had no influence on the constitutional
consolidation of the new Republic.[147] Left parliamentary republicans under
the Second Republic had stuck to the right-to-work and right-to-life principles
that had been upheld by the socialist workers who died in the streets of Paris
on June 1848.[148] These principles were incompatible with capitalism, and they
were abandoned by republicans under the Third Republic. Radicals, the most
left-leaning republicans, and also, in point of fact, the most moderate socialists,

---

142   Moss 1976, p. 95.
143   Moss 1976, pp. 5, 20, 30.
144   Friedman 1990, pp. 164–5; Nord 2011, p. 48; Tombs 1996, p. 293.
145   Faure and Rancière 1976, pp. 286, 378; Jones 2018, p. 75.
146   Aminzade 1993, p. 52; Pilbeam 1995, p. 249.
147   Pilbeam 1995, pp. 262–3.
148   Jones 2018, p. 76.

promoted social policies that did not threaten capitalism.[149] Moreover, breaking with earlier socialist republicans who had been advocating a participatory form of democracy, radical-republicans adhered to a liberal and representative form of democracy, and made the latter safe for capitalism by separating political from economic power.[150]

The primary reason why growing numbers of workers (though by no means all workers) were led toward collectivist socialism and syndicalism, was not just that radical and more moderate republicans were too slow to implement social reforms to alleviate the effects of capitalist exploitation. It was rather that republicans were directly involved in the implementation of social property relations (described in the previous chapter) from which this new form of class exploitation stemmed in the first place, and that they were mobilising the state's repressive power to do so. Accordingly, republicans attempted to develop a movement that spanned class division and that mobilised the cult of the 'little man', the small independent owner (either rural or urban), as the social basis of the regime.[151] As Aminzade puts it, 'Radicals joined liberals, and parted company with socialists in insisting upon the shared interest of members of all social classes as citizens and calling for class conciliation'.[152] But, while not utterly emptied of its content, the call for unity of all 'productive' citizens against idle aristocrats no longer had the same resonance during this transitory period. Likewise, the myth of a 'middle-class society' of small producers could only be used with diminishing returns in a period in which capitalism was rapidly spreading. This was, indeed, an overblown notion,[153] and France was not a stalemate society – in spite of the resilience of its peasantry, the country had already experienced significant industrialisation by 1914.[154]

The call for cross-class unity against the notability no longer resonated with the workers in the way it had done in the second third of the nineteenth century. It was not just that large-scale factories had emerged in growing numbers. Because of competitive pressures, capitalist restructuring had also spilled over into small urban craft production, sometimes sparking a genuine 'revolt against work' (best expressed by revolutionary syndicalism),[155] and this made forging class alliances with petty employers increasingly senseless for a growing num-

---

149   Delalande 2013, p. 278.
150   Aminzade 1993, pp. 45, 47, 52; Friedman 1990, p. 152.
151   Nord 2011, p. 45; Friedman 1990, p. 153.
152   Aminzade 1993, p. 49.
153   Sick 2013.
154   Nord 2011, pp. 52–3.
155   Berlanstein, quoted in Magraw 1992, p. 47; Noiriel 1986, p. 310.

ber of workers. During this period a *petite-bourgeoisie* parted with the working class and came to share more interests with the incipient capitalist class, as a number of *boutiquier* and small employers formed separate organisations to represent their own interests. An alliance with the 'productive bourgeoisie' was manifestly (and increasingly) less likely to serve the emancipation of the working class, and at this time the very term 'bourgeoisie' tended to be reduced to its narrow economic meaning and to become synonymous with *patronat*.[156] Moreover, as Perrot explains, 'the identification of employers as the principal enemy, to a greater extent than any other factor, contributed to the forging of [working]-class unity'.[157]

The French working class was divided along gendered, and, more than ever before, ethnic and racial lines. It also continued to a significant extent to be divided along trade lines and skills. Women and feminists organised and waged important struggles, but made limited headway within the labour unions and socialist movement.[158] Nevertheless, sustained efforts by labour and socialist activists allowed them to make real progress in uniting into a class workers who were acquiring, in ever growing numbers, a shared experience of capitalist exploitation.[159] By the turn of the century, a distinct, renewed, and often rebellious working-class culture had crystallised.[160] Within large sections of the labour movement, the red flag was preferred to the tricolour flag, the *Carmagnole* and the *Internationale* grew in popularity at the expense of the *Marseillaise*, and May first was adopted as the workers' holyday and as an occasion to wage general strikes. This emerging proletarian culture 'was different from the "*sans culotte*" tradition of the barricades, which involved all "the people"'.[161] As industrial capitalism was taking roots in France, a page had been turned, and the working class had remade itself.

---

156 Charle 1991, p. 239.
157 Perrot 1986, p. 101.
158 Magraw 1986, pp. 288–91, 303; 1992, pp. 60, 68; Rebérioux 1974, pp. 207–8.
159 Noiriel 1986, pp. 104–6; Scott 1974, pp. 110–15.
160 Perrot 1986, p. 105.
161 Tombs 1996, p. 291.

Conclusion

France neither experienced capitalism before, nor as a consequence of the Revolution of 1789. Following the Revolution, the country found itself poised between capitalism and socialism. Things could have gone either way.

The regimes of notables (the First Empire, the Restoration, the July Monarchy, and the Second Empire), reflected a social structure characterised by a mass of conservative peasant proprietors who acted as a buffer against a radicalising urban working class. Yet, while often conservative, the peasantry experienced diverse processes of politicisation during the revolutionary decade that followed 1789 and later, from 1831, through local electoral politics, for instance. By mid-century, large numbers of peasants from different regions had been politicised – many opting for ideas drawn from the radical left. While it is true that the peasantry generally acted as a pillar of conservative regimes, it was not as immovable as has often been suggested.[1]

Following the Revolution, and during the first half of the nineteenth century, capitalism was just outside France; it was knocking at the door, and it was doing so increasingly loudly. Though in a protected, non-capitalist, and therefore deeply different economic context, French merchants and industrialists seized market opportunities and imported technologies used by English capitalists, trying to emulate their industrialisation process. Geopolitical pressures to transform the economic context in which these technological imports were put to work had been felt since the eighteenth century, and attempts to initiate a transition to capitalism were made, though they remained unsuccessful at the time. Many among the French elite had a vested material interest in reproducing old social property relations.

Meanwhile, socialism was growing *within* France. The disappearance of old corporatist structures, of intermediate bodies as basic structures of social and

---

1 Marx, of course, contributed to this perception of French peasants as isolated, hopelessly conservative and politically impotent, famously comparing them to 'potatoes in a sack' – a class incapable of collective, let alone revolutionary, action – in his *Eighteenth Brumaire*. Yet, in this same work (on the very next page), Marx also acknowledged the presence of revolutionary peasants in France. In an influential book, Eugen Weber (1976) asserts that French peasants retained an archaic and parochial political culture until the 1880s. His thesis has, however, been strongly contested by Maurice Agulhon (1978; 1979), who shows how peasants were politicised in several French regions, and sometimes adopted democratic socialist ideas, decades before the coming of the Third Republic. For a review of these debates that also demonstrate the progressive politicisation of French peasants after 1789 and during the first half of the nineteenth century, see Berenson 1987; and Fureix and Jarrige 2015, pp. 233–44.

political integration, and the related elimination of trade guilds, had a destabilising effect on French society – one with which socialist thinkers and activists were trying to cope. Workers had made new gains during the Revolution, they had preserved and developed local customary regulations and institutions, and had formed new, more democratic 'intermediary publics' within their trades. These gains, many of them came to believe, could serve as a base for a new social structure and a way of bringing to fruition socialist utopias. This was the 'trade socialism' which became a central tenet of an emerging republican-socialist labour movement.

Claiming that the Revolution of 1789 paved the way to capitalism is not simply a gross oversimplification – it is actually widely off the mark. But the criticism needs to go further than this. We need to add that, in the decades that followed 1789, the alternative to capitalism was alive and kicking – a real, concrete possibility. In the wake of the 1830s Revolution, a self-conscious working class emerged and became increasingly combative, as the defence of its material interests led it to adopt a republican and socialist political outlook. The Revolution of 1848 then provided an opportunity to bring the democratic and social republic to life by consolidating and 'nationalising' the local 'intermediate publics' of the trades, and through the related establishment of producers' cooperatives. Socialist workers were isolated and violently repressed during the June Days of 1848, but democ-socs were later able to make substantial electoral breakthroughs in different rural regions, where peasants also rose up against Louis Bonaparte's coup in 1851.[2] The Empire prevailed in spite of these insurrections, but when it finally collapsed during its war against Prussia, a fateful, short-lived opportunity to implement a republican-socialist agenda re-emerged during the Paris Commune of 1871. As had been the case two decades earlier, however, the forces of reaction proved too strong.

Socialism had been curbed, and this opened the way to the capitalist alternative. The notability was still torn, and large sectors remained attached to a traditional, agrarian France and to state and social structures that ensured not only its political domination, but also more fundamentally its material reproduction as a ruling class. Yet, as time passed, it became increasingly evident that the reproduction of the ruling class also called for radical social and economic changes. The acceleration of British industrialisation during the second third of the nineteenth century created an international context in which other states – continental European, North American and Japanese – were compelled to rapidly modernise their economies in order to remain contenders, in the

---

2   Berenson 1987, p. 214.

face of stiffer geopolitical competition. France also had to act, and a capitalist restructuring of industry was attempted under the Second Empire and continued under the Third Republic.

The imposition of new, capitalist social property relations implied a concatenation of different transformative processes. By taking pivotal measures to direct financial resources toward the construction of railways, the state acted to create an integrated and competitive national market in which price signals and competition were made operative. In parallel, the French state signed foreign trade treaties that exposed French industrial firms to international capitalist competition from Britain, as well as other increasingly competitive capitalist economies such as those of Germany and the United States. The integration of the French national space, and its insertion within an emerging capitalist world market, rapidly wiped out underperforming French firms, while those that remained afloat were compelled to invest in order to reduce their production costs and to reorganise labour processes, facing deep-seated working-class opposition every step of the way. Lastly, though the process was often internally contested, the French state acted in order to support the subsumption of labour to capital by eradicating the normative regulations of industrial trades, invalidating the jurisprudence that had been kept alive and developed by *prud'hommes* councils and justices of the peace. It was essentially the conjunction of these factors that permitted the making of capitalist social property relations in France.

Exposed to international competition from the 1860s, French peasants had tended to react by retreating to their plots, and by taking advantage of falling land values to buy new ones. To ensure the reproduction of the social class that had formed the basis of successive unstable regimes – regimes that had faced recurrent revolutionary threats since the Restoration, and experienced actual revolutions on several occasions – French political leaders delayed the transition to *agrarian* capitalism – and made sure to re-establish relatively higher tariffs on foreign agricultural products from the 1880s and early 1890s. The preservation of a large peasantry in France limited the growth of domestic consumer markets, and consequently slowed down the capitalist process of industrialisation that had been launched during the 1860s. By the *Belle époque*, however, growing consumer demand brought about by the accelerating uprooting of peasants in different countries led to a new expansion of the world market, which in turn fuelled rapid industrialisation in France.

This process of industrialisation underwent a new and much more important acceleration when the French state finally took measures to induce a capitalist restructuring of French agriculture in the wake of World War II, and then again, and even more decisively, during the first years of the Fifth

Republic.[3] The upshot was the booming French economy of the so-called *Trente Glorieuses*, which, while creating unprecedented economic affluence, also fuelled the intensification of labour exploitation and alienation that was spectacularly opposed in one of the largest general strikes in history, in May and June of 1968. Once more, socialism was curbed, but it remains to this day the only viable alternative to the dehumanising and environmentally destructive system that French workers had struggled to avoid, and later to uproot, across the nineteenth century.

---

3   Isett and Miller 2017, pp. 258–66.

References

Adler-Gillies, Mira 2014, 'Cooperation or collectivism: the contest for meaning in the French socialist movement, 1870–90', *French History*, 28 (3): 385–405.

Agulhon, Maurice 1978, 'Compte-rendu: Eugen Weber, *Peasants into Frenchmen. The modernization of rural France 1870–1914*', *Annales. Économies, Sociétés, Civilisations*, 33 (4): 843–4.

Agulhon, Maurice 1979, *La République au village: Les populations du Var de la Révolution à la Seconde République*, Paris: Éditions du Seuil.

Amann, Peter H. 2015, *Revolution and Mass Democracy. The Paris Club of 1848*, Princeton: Princeton University Press.

Aminzade, Ronald 1986, 'Reinterpreting Capitalist Industrialization: A Study of Nineteenth-Century France', in *Work in France. Representations, Meaning, Organization and Practice*, edited by Steven L. Kaplan and Cynthia J. Koepp, 393–417, Ithaca/London: Cornell University Press.

Aminzade, Ronald 1993, *Ballots and Barricades. Class Formation and Republican Politics in France, 1830–1871*, Princeton: Princeton University Press.

Anceau, Éric 2012, *Napoléon III*, Paris: Tallandier.

Asselain, Jean-Charles 1984, *Histoire économique de la France du XVIIIe siècle à nos jours, tome 1: De l'Ancien Régime à la Première Guerre mondiale*, Paris: Éditions du Seuil.

Asselain, Jean-Charles 1988, 'Histoire économique de la France: regards nouveaux sur le long terme', *Revue économique*, 39 (6): 1223–48.

Asselain, Jean-Charles 1991, *Histoire économique. De la révolution industrielle à la première guerre mondiale*, Paris: Presses de la Fondation des sciences politiques.

Bairoch, Paul 1965, 'Niveaux de développement économique de 1810 à 1910', *Annales. Économies, Sociétés, Civilisations*, 20 (6): 1091–1117.

Bairoch, Paul 1976, 'Europe's Gross National Product: 1800–1975', *Journal of European Economic History*, 5 (2): 273–340.

Baker, Keith Michael 1992, 'Defining the Public Sphere in Eighteenth-Century France: Variations on a Theme by Habermas', in *Habermas and the Public Sphere*, edited by Craig Calhoun, Cambridge: MIT Press.

Ballot, Charles 1978 [1923], *L'introduction du machinisme dans l'industrie française*, Genève: Slatkine Reprints.

Barjot, Dominique 1995, *L'économie française au XIXe siècle*, Paris: Nathan.

Barjot, Dominique 2012, 'Histoire économique et historiographie française: crise ou renouveau?' *Histoire, économie & société*, 31 (2): 5–27.

Barjot, Dominique 2014a, 'L'économie, 1851–1914', in *La France au XIXe siècle, 1814–1914*, edited by Dominique Barjot, Jean-Pierre Chaline, and André Encrevé, 3rd ed., 377–406, Paris: Presses universitaires de France.

Barjot, Dominique 2014b, 'L'économie française, 1815–1851', in *La France au XIXe siècle, 1814–1914*, edited by Dominique Barjot, Jean-Pierre Chaline, and André Encrevé, 3rd ed., 91–134, Paris: Presses universitaires de France.

Beaud, Michel 2010, *Histoire du capitalisme: 1500–2010*, 6th ed., Paris: Éditions du Seuil.

Beecher, Jonathan 2001, *Victor Considerant and the Rise and Fall of French Romantic Socialism*, Berkeley: University of California Press.

Beltran, Alain, and Pascal Griset 1994, *La croissance économique de la France: 1815–1914*, Paris: Armand Colin.

Berenson, Edward 1984, *Populist Religion and Left-Wing Politics in France, 1830–1852*, Princeton: Princeton University Press.

Berenson, Edward 1987, 'Politics and the French Peasantry: The Debate Continues', *Social History*, 12: 213–29.

Bergeron, Louis 1978, *Les capitalistes en France (1780–1914)*, Paris: Gallimard.

Berlanstein, Lenard R. 1992, 'The Distinctiveness of the Nineteenth-Century French Labor Movement', *The Journal of Modern History*, 64 (4): 660–85.

Berlanstein, Lenard R. (ed.) 1993, *Rethinking Labor History: Essays on Discourse and Class Analysis*, Champaign: University of Illinois Press.

Bezucha, Robert J. 1974, *The Lyon Uprising of 1834: Social and Political Conflict in the Early July Monarchy*, Cambridge: Harvard University Press.

Bezucha, Robert J. 1983, 'The French Revolution of 1848 and the Social History of Work', *Theory and Society*, 12 (4): 469–84.

Blanc, Louis 1847, *Organisation du travail*, Paris: Bureau de la Société de l'industie fraternelle.

Blanc, Louis 1849, *La révolution de février au Luxembourg*, Paris: Michel Lévy frères.

Bloch, Marc 1966, *French Rural History: An Essay on its Basic Characteristics*, Berkeley: University of California Press.

Bonney, Richard 1995, 'The Eighteenth Century. II. The Struggle for Great Power Status and the End of the Old Fiscal Regime', in *Economic Systems and State Finance: The Origins of the Modern State in Europe*, edited by Richard Bonney, Oxford: Clarendon Press.

Bonney, Richard 1999, 'France, 1494–1815', in *The Rise of the Fiscal State in Europe c.1200–1815*, edited by Richard Bonney, 123–76, Oxford University Press.

Bouchet, Thomas, Vincent Bourdeau, Edward Castleton, Ludovic Frobert, and François Jarrige (eds.) 2015, *Quand les socialistes inventaient l'avenir, 1825–1860*, Paris: La Découverte.

Bourdieu, Jérôme, and Bénédicte Reynaud 2004, 'Discipline d'atelier et externalités dans la réduction de la durée de travail au XIXe siècle', in *La France et le temps de travail (1814–2004)*, edited by Patrick Fridenson and Bénédicte Reynaud, Paris: Odile Jacob.

Bourguinat, Nicolas 2002, *Les grains du désordre: L'État face aux violences frumentaires dans la première moitié du XIXe siècle*, Paris: Éditions de l'École des hautes études en sciences sociales.

Bourguinat, Nicolas 2005, 'Les "partis" de gauche pendant la monarchie censitaire', in *Histoire des gauches en France*, edited by Jean-Jacques Becker and Gilles Candar, 61–8, Paris: La Découverte.

Braudel, Fernand 1979, *Civilisation matérielle, économie et capitalisme, XVe–XVIIIe siècle. Volume 2, Les jeux de l'échange*, Paris: Armand Colin.

Braudel, Fernand 2008, *La dynamique du capitalisme*, Paris: Flammarion.

Braudel, Fernand, and Ernest Labrousse (eds.) 1993 [1970–82], *Histoire économique et sociale de la France (4 volumes)*, Paris: Presses universitaires de France.

Brenner, Robert 1977, 'The Origins of Capitalist Development: A Critique of Neo-Smithian Marxism', *New Left Review*, I, no. 104: 25–92.

Brenner, Robert 1986, 'The Social Basis of Economic Development', in *Analytical Marxism*, edited by John Roemer, Cambridge: Cambridge University Press.

Brenner, Robert 1987a, 'Agrarian Class Structure and Economic Development in Pre-Industrial Europe', in *The Brenner Debate: Agrarian Class Structure and Economic Development in Pre-Industrial Europe*, edited by T.H. Aston and C.H.E. Philpin, Cambridge: Cambridge University Press.

Brenner, Robert 1987b, 'The Agrarian Roots of European Capitalism', in *The Brenner Debate: Agrarian Class Structure and Economic Development in Pre-Industrial Europe*, edited by T.H. Aston and C.H.E. Philpin, Cambridge: Cambridge University Press.

Brenner, Robert 1989, 'Bourgeois Revolution and Transition to Capitalism', in *The First Modern Society: Essays in English History in Honour of Lawrence Stone*, edited by A.L. Beier, David Cannadine, and James M. Rosenheim, 271–304, Cambridge: Cambridge University Press.

Brenner, Robert 2007, 'Property and Progress: Where Adam Smith Went Wrong', in *Marxist History-writing for the Twenty First Century*, edited by Chris Wickham, Oxford: Oxford University Press.

Brenner, Robert, and Christopher Isett 2002, 'England's Divergence from China's Yangzi Delta: Property Relations, Microeconomics, and Patterns of Development', *The Journal of Asian Studies*, 61 (2): 609–62.

Brewer, John 1989, *The Sinews of Power: War, Money, and the English State, 1688–1783*, Cambridge: Harvard University Press.

Broder, Albert 1993, *L'économie française au XIXe siècle*, Paris: Ophrys.

Bruhat, Jean. 1972, 'Le socialisme français de 1815 à 1848', in *Histoire générale du socialisme, Volume I*, edited by Jacques Droz, Paris: Presses universitaires de France.

Burg, David F. 2004, *A World History of Tax Rebellions*, New York: Routledge.

Cadier, Gabrielle 1988, 'Les conséquences du traité de 1860 sur le commerce franco-britannique', *Histoire, économie et société*, 7 (3): 355–80.

Calhoun, Craig 1983, 'Industrialization and Social Radicalism: British and French Workers' Movements and the Mid-Nineteenth-Century Crises', *Theory and Society*, 12 (4): 485–504.

Calhoun, Craig 2012, *The Roots of Radicalism: Tradition, the Public Sphere, and Early Nineteenth-Century Social Movements*, Chicago: University of Chicago Press.

Calpham, John 1921, *The Economix Development of France and Germany, 1815–1914*, Cambridge: Cambridge University Press.

Caron, François 1988, 'Ententes et stratégies d'achat dans la France du XIXe siècle', *Revue française de gestion*, no. 70: 127–33.

Caron, François 1995, *Histoire économique de la France: XIXe–XXe siècle*, Paris: Armand Colin.

Caron, François 2002, 'L'histoire de l'innovation', *Historiens et Géographes*, no. 380: 157–65.

Carroué, Laurent, Didier Collet, and Claude Ruiz 2005, *La mondialisation. Genèse, acteurs et enjeux*, Rosny-sous-Bois: Bréal.

Chagnollaud, Dominique 1991, *Le premier des ordres. Les hauts fonctionnaires (XVIIIe–XXe siècle)*, Paris: Fayard.

Charle, Christophe 1980, *Les hauts fonctionnaires en France au XIXe siècle*, Paris: Gallimard-Julliard.

Charle, Christophe 1991, *Histoire sociale de la France au XIXe siècle*, Paris: Éditions du Seuil.

Charmettant, Hervé 2006, 'Un modèle conventionaliste de l'autorité dans la relation d'emploi', unpublished doctoral dissertation, Lyon: Université Lumière Lyon 2.

Chassagne, Serge 1989, 'Vers la libre entreprise?' in *La Révolution française et le développement du capitalisme*, edited by Gérard Gayot and Jean-Pierre Hirsch, Villeneuve d'Ascq: Revue du Nord.

Chassagne, Serge 1991, *Le coton et ses patrons. France, 1760–1840*, Civilisations et Sociétés 83, Paris: Éditions de l'École des hautes études en sciences sociales.

Clamageran, Jean-Jules 1867–76, *Histoire de l'impôt en France*, 3 vols., Paris: Guillaumin.

Clough, Shepard B. 1946, 'Retardative Factors in French Economic Development in the Nineteenth and Twentieth Centuries', *The Journal of Economic History*, 6 (S1): 91–102.

Cobban, Alfred 1999, *The Social Interpretation of the French Revolution*, Cambridge: Cambridge University Press.

Cole, W.A., and Phyllis Deane 1965, 'The Growth of National Incomes', in *The Cambridge Economic History of Europe, Volume VI: The Industrial Revolutions and After*, edited by H.J. Habakkuk and M. Postan, 1–55, Cambridge: Cambridge University Press.

Collier, Frances 1964, *The family economy of the working classes in the cotton industry, 1784–1833*, R.S. Fitton, Manchester: Manchester University Press.

Comninel, George C. 1987, *Rethinking the French Revolution: Marxism and the Revisionist Challenge*, London: Verso.

Comninel, George C. 2000, 'English Feudalism and the Origins of Capitalism', *Journal of Peasant Studies*, 27 (4): 1–53.

Considerant, Victor 1847, *Principes du socialisme. Manifeste de la démocratie au XIX siècle*, Paris: Librairie phalanstérienne.

Corcoran, Paul E. (ed.) 1983, *Before Marx: Socialism and Communism in France, 1830–48*, London: Palgrave Macmillan.

Cordillot, Michel 2010, *Aux origines du socialisme moderne. La Première Internationale, la Commune de Paris, l'Exil*, Paris: Les Éditions de l'Atelier.

Cottereau, Alain 1986, 'The Distinctiveness of Working-Class Cultures in France, 1848–1900', in *Working-Class Formation: Nineteenth-Century Patterns in Western Europe and the United States*, edited by Ira Katznelson and Aristide R. Zolberg, 111–54, Princeton, NJ: Princeton University Press.

Cottereau, Alain 1987, 'Justice et injustice ordinaire sur les lieux de travail d'après les audiences prud'homales (1806–1866)', *Le Mouvement social*, no. 144: 25–59.

Cottereau, Alain 1993, 'Review of "Work and Wages: Natural Law, Politics and the Eighteenth-Century French Trades" by Michael Sonenscher', *Le Mouvement social*, 165: 129–34.

Cottereau, Alain 1995, 'Rebelling Against the Work We Love', in *Class*, edited by Patrick Joyce, 271–83, Oxford: Oxford University Press.

Cottereau, Alain 1997, 'The Fate of Collective Manufactures in the Industrial World: The Silk Industries of Lyons and London, 1800–1850', in *World of Possibilities: Flexibility and Mass Production in Western Industrialization*, edited by Charles F. Sabel and Jonathan Zeitlin, 75–152, Cambridge: Cambridge University Press.

Cottereau, Alain 2002, 'Droit et bon droit. Un droit des ouvriers instauré, puis évincé par le droit du travail (France, XIXe siècle)', *Annales. Histoire, Sciences Sociales*, 57 (6): 1521–57.

Cottereau, Alain 2004, 'La désincorporation des métiers et leur transformation en publics intermédiaires: Lyon et Elbeuf, 1790–1815', in *La France, malade du corporatisme? XVIIIe–XXe siècles*, edited by Steven Kaplan and Philippe Minard, Paris: Belin.

Cottereau, Alain 2006, 'Sens du juste et usages du droit du travail: une évolution contrastée entre la France et la Grande-Bretagne au XIXe siècle', *Revue d'histoire du XIXe siècle*, no. 33: 101–20.

Cottereau, Alain 2011, 'L'embauche et la vie normative des métiers durant les deux premiers tiers du XIXe siècle français (Reedited version of the 1995 article)', *Les Cahiers des relations professionnelles*, 10: 47–71.

Crafts, N.F.R. 1984a, 'Economic Growth in France and Britain, 1830–1910: A Review of the Evidence', *The Journal of Economic History*, 44 (1): 49–67.

Crafts, N.F.R. 1984b, 'Patterns of Development in Nineteenth Century Europe', *Oxford Economic Papers*, 36 (3): 438–58.

Crouzet, François 1966, 'Angleterre et France au XVIIIe siècle: essai d'analyse comparée de deux croissances économiques', *Annales. Économies, Sociétés, Civilisations*, 21 (2): 254–91.

Crouzet, François 1985, *De la supériorité de l'Angleterre sur la France: l'économique et l'imaginaire, XVIIe–XXe siècles*, Pour l'histoire. Paris: Librairie académique Perrin.

Crouzet, François 1989, 'Les conséquences économiques de la Révolution française: Réflexions sur un débat', *Revue économique*, 40 (6), 1189–1203.

Crouzet, François 2003, 'The Historiography of French Economic Growth in the Nineteenth Century', *The Economic History Review*, 56 (2): 215–42.

Daumard, Adeline. 1993a [1976], 'Chapitre 1: L'État libéral et le libéralisme économique', in *Histoire économique et sociale de la France. Tome 3*, edited by Fernand Braudel and Ernest Labrousse, Paris: Presses universitaires de France.

Daumard, Adeline. 1993b [1976], 'Chapitre 3: Caractères de la société bourgeoise', in *Histoire économique et sociale de la France. Tome 3*, edited by Fernand Braudel and Ernest Labrousse, Paris: Presses universitaires de France.

Daumard, Adeline. 1993c [1976], 'Chapitre 4: La hiérarchie des biens et des positions', in *Histoire économique et sociale de la France. Tome 3*, edited by Fernand Braudel and Ernest Labrousse, Paris: Presses universitaires de France.

Daumard, Adeline. 1993d [1976], 'Chapitre 5: Progrès et prise de conscience des classes moyennes', in *Histoire économique et sociale de la France. Tome 3*, edited by Fernand Braudel and Ernest Labrousse, Paris: Presses universitaires de France.

Daumard, Adeline. 1993e [1976], 'Chapitre 6: Diversité des milieux supérieurs et dirigeants', in *Histoire économique et sociale de la France. Tome 3*, edited by Fernand Braudel and Ernest Labrousse, Paris: Presses universitaires de France.

Davidson, Neil 2012, *How Revolutionary Were the Bourgeois Revolutions?* Chicago: Haymarket Books.

Daviet, Jean-Pierre 1988, 'Trade Associations or Agreements and Controlled Competition in France, 1830–1939', in *Trade Associations in Business History*, edited by Hiroaki Yamazaki and Matao Miyamoto, Tokyo: University of Tokyo Press.

Delalande, Nicolas 2011, *Les batailles de l'impôt. Consentement et résistances de 1789 à nos jours*, Paris: Éditions du Seuil.

Delalande, Nicolas 2013, 'Le pacte fiscal est-il républicain?' in *Une contre histoire de la IIIe République*, edited by Marion Fontaine, Frédéric Monier, and Christophe Prochasson, Paris: La Découverte.

Delsalle, Paul 1987, 'Tisserands et fabricants chez les prud'hommes dans la région de Lille-Roubaix-Tourcoing (1810–1848)', *Le Mouvement social*, 141: 61–80.

Démier, Francis 2000, *La France du XIXe siècle, 1814–1914*, Paris: Éditions du Seuil.

Deyon, Pierre, and Philippe Guignet 1980, 'The royal manufactures and economic and technological progress in France before the industrial revolution', *Journal of European Economic History*, 9: 611–32.

Didry, Claude 2001, 'La production juridique de la convention collective, The legal production of the convention collective: the March 4, 1919 Act', *Annales. Histoire, Sciences Sociales*, 56 (6): 1253–82.

Dimmock, Spencer 2015, *The Origin of Capitalism in England, 1400–1600*, Chicago: Haymarket Books.

Dormois, Jean-Pierre 1997, *L'économie française face à la concurrence britannique avant 1914*, Paris: L'Harmattan.

Dougui, Nourredine 1981, 'Les origines de la libération des sociétés de capitaux à responsabilité limitée, 1856–1863', *Revue d'histoire moderne et contemporaine*, 28 (2): 268–92.

Dreyfus, Françoise 2000, *L'invention de la bureaucratie. Servir l'État en France, en Grande-Bretagne et aux États-Unis (XVIIIe–XXe siècle)*, Paris: La Découverte.

Ducange, Jean-Numa 2017, *Jules Guesde. L'anti-Jaurès?* Paris: Armand Colin.

Dunham, Arthur Louis 1930, *The Anglo-French Treaty of Commerce of 1860 and the Progress of the Industrial Revolution in France*, Ann Arbor: University of Michigan Press.

DuPlessis, Robert 2016, 'Conclusion: Reorienting Early Modern Economic History: Merchant Economy, Merchant Capitalism and the Age of Commerce', in *Merchants and Profit in the Age of Commerce, 1680–1830*, Perspectives in economic and social history 30, London: Routledge.

Eley, Geoff, and Keith Nield 2007, *The Future of Class in History. What's Left of the Social?* Ann Arbor: University of Michigan Press.

Engrand, Charles 1981, 'Les industries lilloises et la crise économique de 1826 à 1832', *Revue du Nord* 63 (248): 233–51.

Ertman, Thomas 2010, 'The Great Reform Act of 1832 and British Democratization', *Comparative Political Studies*, 43 (8–9): 1000–1022.

Etner, François, and Claire Silvant 2017, *Histoire de la pensée économique en France depuis 1789*, Paris: Economica.

Fairchilds, Cissie 1988, 'Three Views on the Guilds', *French Historical Studies*, 15 (4): 688–92.

Faure, Alain 1974, 'Mouvements populaires et mouvement ouvrier à Paris (1830–1834)', *Le Mouvement social*, 88: 51–92.

Faure, Alain 1986, 'Petit atelier et modernisme économique. La production en miettes au XIXe siècle', *Histoire, économie et société*, 4: 531–57.

Faure, Alain, and Jacques Rancière 1976, *La parole ouvrière, 1830–1851*, Paris: Union Générale d'Éditions.

Ferguson, Niall 2000, 'The European Economy, 1815–1914', in *The Nineteenth Century: Europe 1789–1914*, edited by T.C.W. Blanning, Oxford: Oxford University Press.

Fohlen, Claude 1956, *L'industrie textile au temps du second empire*, Paris: Librairie Plon.

Fohlen, Claude 1973, 'France, 1700–1914', in *Fontana Economic History of Europe: 4, The Emergence of Industrial Societies*, edited by Carlo M. Cipolla. vol. 1, London: Fontana.

Fombonne, Jean 2001, *Personnel et DRH. L'affirmation de la fonction 'Personnel' dans les entreprises (France, 1830–1990)*, Paris: Vuibert.

Fridenson, Patrick 1987, 'Un tournant taylorien de la société française (1904–1918)', *Annales* 42 (5): 1031–60.

Fridenson, Patrick, and André Straus (eds.) 1987, *Le capitalisme français, XIXe–XXe siècle. Blocages et dynamismes d'une croissance*, Paris: Fayard.

Friedman, Gerald 1990, 'Capitalism, Republicanism, Socialism, and the State: France, 1871–1914', *Social Science History*, 14 (2): 151–74.

Frobert, Ludovic 2009, *Les Canuts ou la démocratie turbulente. Lyon, 1831–1834*, Paris: Tallandier.

Fureix, Emmanuel, and François Jarrige 2015, *La modernité désenchantée. Relire l'histoire du XIXe siècle français*, Paris: La Découverte.

Furet, François 1981, *Interpreting the French Revolution*, Cambridge: Cambridge University Press.

Gerstenberger, Heide 2009, *Impersonal Power: History and Theory of the Bourgeois State*, Chicago: Haymarket Books.

Gervais, Pierre, Yannick Lemarchand, and Dominique Margairaz 2016, 'Introduction: The Many Scales of Merchant Profit: Accounting for Norms, Practices and Results in the Age of Commerce', in *Merchants and Profit in the Age of Commerce, 1680–1830*, edited by Pierre Gervais, Yannick Lemarchand, and Dominique Margairaz. Perspectives in economic and social history 30, London: Routledge.

Gildea, Robert 2003, *Barricades and borders: Europe 1800–1914*, 3rd ed., Oxford/New York: Oxford University Press.

Gille, Bertrand 1968 *La sidérurgie française au XIXe siècle*, Genève: Librairie Droz.

Gossez, Rémi 1964, *Les ouvriers de Paris*. Paris: Société d'histoire de la révolution de 1848.

Goubert, Pierre 1970, 'Le paysan et la terre: seignerie, tenure, exploitation', in *Histoire économique et sociale de la France, II, 1660–1789*, edited by Fernand Braudel and Ernest Labrousse. Paris: Presses universitaires de France.

Guicheteau, Samuel 2014, *Les ouvriers en France 1700–1835*, Paris: Armand Colin.

Guionnet, Christine 1997, *L'apprentissage de la politique moderne. Les élections municipales sous la monarchie de Juillet*, Paris: L'Harmattan.

Habermas, Jürgen 1989, *The Structural Transformation of the Public Sphere: An Inquiry Into a Category of Bourgeois Society*, Cambridge: Polity Press.

Haine, W. Scott 2000, *The History of France*, Westport: Greenwood.

Hanagan, Michael P. 1989, *Nascent Proletarians: Class Formation in Post-Revolutionary France*, Oxford: Basil Blackwell.

Harling, Philip 1996, *The Waning of 'Old Corruption': The Politics of Economical Reform in Britain, 1779–1846*, New York: Oxford University Press.

Harling, Philip 2003, 'Parliament, the state, and "Old Corruption": conceptualizing reform, c. 1790–1832', in *Rethinking the Age of Reform*, edited by Arthur Burns and Joanna Innes, 98–113, Cambridge: Cambridge University Press.

Harling, Philip 2004, 'The State', in *A Companion to Nineteenth-Century Britain*, edited by Chris Williams, Malden: Blackwell.

Harris, John R. 1998, *Industrial Espionage and Technology Transfer: Britain and France in the Eighteenth Century*, Aldershot: Ashgate.

Harvey, David 2005, *Paris, Capital of Modernity*, New York: Routledge.

Hau, Michel 1987, *L'industrialisation de l'Alsace (1803–1939)*, Strasbourg: Association des Publications près les Universités de Strasbourg.

Hay, Douglas 2000, 'Master and Servant in England: Using the Law in the Eighteenth and Nineteenth Centuries', in *Private Law and Social Inequality in the Industrial Age: Comparing Legal Cultures in Britain, France, Germany and the United States*, edited by Willibald Steinmetz, 227–64, Oxford: Oxford University Press.

Hay, Douglas 2004, 'England, 1562–1875: The Law and Its Uses', in *Masters, Servants, and Magistrates in Britain and the Empire, 1562–1955*, edited by Douglas Hay and Paul Craven, 59–116, Chapel Hill: The University of North Carolina Press.

Hay, Douglas, Peter Linebaugh, John Rule, E.P. Thompson, and Calvin Winslow (eds.) 2011, *Albion's Fatal Tree: Crime and Society in Eighteenth-Century England*, London: Verso.

Hayat, Samuel. 2014 *Quand la République était révolutionnaire. Citoyenneté et représentation en 1848*, Paris: Éditions du Seuil.

Heywood, Colin 1981, 'The Role of the Peasantry in French Industrialization, 1815–801', *The Economic History Review*, 34 (3): 359–76.

Heywood, Colin 1992, *The Development of the French Economy, 1750–1914*, Cambridge: Cambridge University Press.

Hills, Richard L. 1989, *Power from Steam: A History of the Stationary Steam Engine*, Cambridge: Cambridge University Press.

Hirsch, Jean-Pierre 1979, 'Un fil rompu? A propos du crédit à Lille sous la Révolution et l'Empire', *Revue du Nord*, 61 (240): 181–92.

Hirsch, Jean-Pierre 1985, 'La région lilloise: foyer industriel ou place de négoce?' *Le Mouvement social*, 132: 27–41.

Hirsch, Jean-Pierre 1989, 'Revolutionary France, Cradle of Free Enterprise', *The American Historical Review*, 94 (5): 1281–9.

Hirsch, Jean-Pierre 1991, *Les deux rêves du commerce. Entreprise et institution dans la région lilloise (1780–1860)*, Paris: Éditions de l'École des hautes études en sciences sociales.

Hirsch, Jean-Pierre 2001, 'Retour sur l'ancien esprit du capitalisme', *Revue d'histoire du XIXe siècle*, 23: 87–104.

Hirsch, Jean-Pierre 2008, 'La concurrence: discours et pratiques, hier et aujourd'hui', *L'Économie politique*, 37: 66–76.

Hirsch, Jean-Pierre, and Serge Chassagne 2012, 'Introduction: entrepreneurs et institu-tions', in *La gloire de l'industrie, xviie–xixe siècle*, edited by Corine Maitte, Philippe Minard, and Matthieu de Oliveira, 15–20, Rennes: Presses universitaires de Rennes.

Hobsbawm, Eric 1968, *Industry and Empire*, London: Penguin Books.

Hobsbawm, Eric 1994, *The Age of Empire, 1875–1914*, London: Abacus.

Hobsbawm, Eric 1996, *The Age of Revolution, 1789–1848*, New York: Vintage Books.

Hoffman, Philip T. 1996, *Growth in a Traditional Society: The French Countryside 1450–1815*, Princeton: Princeton University Press.

Hoffmann, Stanley 1963, 'Paradoxes of the French Political Community', in *In Search of France*, edited by Stanley Hoffmann, Charles P. Kindleberger, Laurence Wylie, Jesse R. Pitts, Jean-Baptiste Duroselle, and François Goguel, 1–118, Cambridge: Harvard University Press.

Horn, Jeff 2005, 'Machine-breaking in England and France during the Age of Revolu-tion', *Labour / Le Travail*, 55: 143–66.

Horn, Jeff 2006, *The Path Not Taken: French Industrialization in the Age of Revolution, 1750–1830*, Cambridge: MIT Press.

Horn, Jeff 2010, 'The French Path to Industrialization', in *Reconceptualizing the Indus-trial Revolution*, edited by Jeff Horn, L.N. Rosenband, and M.R. Smith, 87–106, Cam-bridge: MIT Press.

Horn, Jeff 2012, '"A Beautiful Madness": Privilege, the Machine Question and Industrial Development in Normandy in 1789', *Past & Present*, 217 (1): 149–85.

Huard, Raymond 1996, *La naissance du parti politique en France*, Paris: Presses de la Fondation nationale des sciences politiques.

Hunt, Lynn, and George Sheridan 1986, 'Corporatism, Association, and the Language of Labor in France, 1750–1850', *The Journal of Modern History* 58 (4): 813–44.

Isett, Christopher, and Stephen Miller 2017, *The Social History of Agriculture: From the Origins to the Current Crisis*, London/New York: Rowman & Littlefield.

Jakobowicz, Nathalie 2009, *1830, le Peuple de Paris: Révolution et représentations sociales*, Rennes: Presses Universitaires de Rennes.

Jarrige, François 2009, *Au temps des tueuses de bras: les bris de machines à l'aube de l'ère industrielle, 1780–1860*, Rennes: Presses universitaires de Rennes.

Jarrige, François, and Cécile Chalmin 2008, 'L'émergence du contremaître. L'ambi-valence d'une autorité en construction dans l'industrie textile française (1800–1860)', *Le Mouvement social*, 224: 47–60.

Jessenne, Jean-Pierre 2006, *Les campagnes françaises entre mythe et histoire: xviiie–xxie siècle*, Paris: Armand Colin.

Johnson, Christopher H. 1974. *Utopian Communism in France: Cabet and the Icarians, 1839–1851*, Ithaca: Cornell University Press.

Johnson, Christopher H. 1975, 'The Revolution of 1830 in French Economic History', in *1830 in France*, edited by John M. Merriman, 139–89, New York: New Viewpoints.

Jones, P.M. 1995, *Reform and Revolution in France. The Politics of Transition, 1774–1791*, Cambridge: Cambridge University Press.

Jones, Thomas C. 2018, 'French Republicanism after 1848', in *The 1848 Revolutions and European Political Thought*, edited by Douglas Moggach and Gareth Stedman Jones, Cambridge: Cambridge University Press.

Joyce, Patrick 1991, *England and the Question of Class 1848–1914*, New York: Cambridge University Press.

Judt, Tony 2011 [1986], *Marxism and the French Left: Studies in labour and politics in France, 1830–1981*, New York: New York University Press.

Kaplan, Steven 1979, 'Réflexion sur la police du monde du travail', *Revue historique*, 261: 17–77.

Kaplan, Steven 1988, 'Les corporations, les "faux ouvriers" et le faubourg Saint-Antoine au XVIIIe siècle', *Annales. Économies, Sociétés, Civilisations*, 43 (2): 353–78.

Kaplan, Steven, and Cynthia J. Koepp 1986, 'Introduction', in *Work in France: Representations, Meaning, Organization, and Practice*, edited by Steven L. Kaplan and Cynthia J. Koepp, 13–53, Ithaca/London: Cornell University Press.

Kaplan, Steven L. 1976, *Bread, Politics and Political Economy in the Reign of Louis XV*, International Archives of the History of Ideas 86, The Hague: Martinus Nijhoff.

Kaplan, Steven L. 2001, *La fin des corporations*, Paris: Fayard.

Kasdi, Mohamed 2014, *Les entrepreneurs du coton: innovation et développement économique, France du Nord, 1700–1830*, Histoire et civilisations. Villeneuve-d'Ascq: Presses universitaires du Septentrion.

Kemp, Tom 1971, 'Continuity and Change in the French Economy, 1815–1848', in *Economic Forces in French History. An Essay on the Development of the French Economy*, London: Dobson.

Kemp, Tom 2016 [1985], *Industrialization in Nineteenth-Century Europe*, New York: Routledge.

Kieffer, Monique 1987, 'La législation prud'homale de 1806 à 1907', *Le Mouvement social*, 141: 9–23.

King, Peter 2006, 'The production and consumption of bar iron in early modern England and Wales', *The Economic History Review*, 59 (1): 264–64.

Kingston, Ralph 2012, *Bureaucrats and Bourgeois Society: Office Politics and Individual Credit in France, 1789–1848*, Houndmills: Palgrave Macmillan.

Kocka, Jürgen 1978, 'Entrepreneurs and Managers in German Industrialization', in *The Cambridge Economic History of Europe, vol. 7, pt. 1*, edited by Peter Mathias and M.M. Postan, 492–589, Cambridge: Cambridge University Press.

Labrousse, Ernest 1954, *Aspects de l'évolution économique et sociale de la France et du Royaume-Uni de 1805 à 1880*, Paris: Centre de documentation universitaire.

Lacher, Hannes 2006, *Beyond Globalization: Capitalism, Territoriality and the International Relations of Modernity*, New York: Routledge.

Lafrance, Xavier, and Charles Post (eds.) 2018, *Case Studies in the Origins of Capitalism*, New York: Palgrave Macmillan.

Lambert-Dansette, Jean 1991, *Genèse du Patronat, 1780–1880*, Paris: Hachette.

Landes, David S. 1949, 'French Entrepreneurship and Industrial Growth in the Nineteenth Century', *The Journal of Economic History*, 9 (1): 45–61.

Landes, David S. 1969, The Unbound Prometheus: Technological Change and Industrial Development in Western Europe from 1750 to the Present, Cambridge: Cambridge University Press.

Le Bihan, Jean 2008, *Au service de l'Etat. Les fonctionnaires intermédiaires au XIXe siècle*, Rennes: Presses universitaires de Rennes.

Le Roy Ladurie, Emmanuel 1974, 'The Long Agrarian Cycle: Languedoc, 1500–1700', in *Essays in European Economic History, 1500–1800*, edited by Peter Earle, Oxford: Clarendon Press.

Lefebvre, Georges 2005, *The Coming of the French Revolution*, Princeton: Princeton University Press.

Lefebvre, Philippe 2003, *L'invention de la grande entreprise: Travail, hiérarchie, marché (France, fin XVIIIe-Début XXe siècle)*, Paris: Presses universitaires de France.

Lefebvre, Philippe 2009, 'Subordination et 'révolutions' du travail et du droit du travail (1776–2010)', *Entreprises et histoire*, 57: 45–78.

Leidet, Gérard, and Colette Drogoz (eds.) 2013, *Aspects du mouvement communal dans le midi*, Promémo. Paris: Syllepse.

Lejeune, Dominique 1994, *La France des débuts de la IIIe République – 1870–1896*, Paris: Armand Colin.

Lemarchand, Guy 2008, *L'économie en France de 1770 à 1830. De la crise de l'Ancien Régime à la Révolution industrielle*, Paris: Armand Colin.

Lemercier, Claire 2003, 'La chambre de commerce de Paris, acteur indispensable de la construction des normes économiques (première moitié du xixe siècle), Abstract', *Genèses*, 50: 50–70.

Lemercier, Claire 2005, 'La France contemporaine: une impossible société civile?' *Revue d'histoire moderne et contemporaine*, no. 52–3 (3): 166–79.

Lemercier, Claire 2008, 'Discipliner le commerce sans corporations. La loi, le juge, l'arbitre, et le commerçant à Paris au XIXe siècle', *Le Mouvement social*, 224: 61–74.

Lemercier, Claire 2009a, 'Looking for "Industrial Confraternity" Small-Scale Industries and Institutions in Nineteenth-Century Paris', *Enterprise and Society*, 10 (2): 304–34.

Lemercier, Claire 2009b, 'Regulating Apprenticeship in 19th-Century France', Paper presented at *World Economic History Congress*, Utrecht, Netherlands.

Léon, Pierre 1993 [1976], 'La conquête de l'espace national', in *Histoire économique et sociale de la France. Tome 3*, edited by Fernand Braudel and Ernest Labrousse, Paris: Presses universitaires de France.

Léonard, Mathieu 2011, *L'émancipation des travailleurs. Une histoire de la Première Internationale*, Paris: La Fabrique.

Lequin, Yves 1983, *Histoire des Français, xixe–xxe siècles: La Société*. Paris: Armand Colin.

Lévêque, Pierre 2004, 'Les courants politiques de la Commune de Paris', in *La Commune de 1871. L'événement, les hommes et la mémoire*, edited by Claude Latta. Saint-Étienne: Publications de l'Université de Saint-Étienne.

Lévy-Leboyer, Maurice 1964, *Les banques européennes et l'industrialisation internationale dans la première moitié du xixe siècle*, Paris: Presses universitaires de France.

Lévy-Leboyer, Maurice 1968, 'La croissance économique en France au xixe siècle. Résultats préliminaires', *Annales. Économies, Sociétés, Civilisations*, 23 (4): 788–807.

Lévy-Leboyer, Maurice, and François Bourguignon 1985, *L'économie française au xixe siècle. Analyse macro-économique*, Paris: Economica.

Maddison, Angus 2001, *L'économie mondiale: une perspective millénaire*. Paris: Centre de développement de l'OCDE.

Magraw, Roger 1986, *France 1815–1914: The Bourgeois Century*, London: Pearson Education.

Magraw, Roger 1992, *A History of the French Working Class, Volume 2. Workers and the Bourgeois Republic*, Oxford: Blackwell.

Marchand, Olivier, and Claude Thélot 1991, *Deux siècles de travail en France*, Paris: INSEE.

Marcowitz, Reiner 2008, 'Attraction and Repulsion: Franco-German Relations in the "Long Nineteenth Century"', in *A History of Franco-German Relations in Europe. From 'Hereditary Enemies' to Partners*, edited by Carine Germond and Henning Türk, New York: Palgrave Macmillan.

Marczewski, Jean 1961–9, *Introduction à l'histoire quantitative de l'économie française* (11 vols.), Paris: Institut de science économique appliquée.

Margairaz, Dominique 1986, 'La formation du réseau des foires et des marchés: stratégies, pratiques et idéologies', *Annales. Économies, Sociétés, Civilisations*, 41 (6): 1215–42.

Margairaz, Dominique, and Philippe Minard 2006, 'Le marché dans son histoire', *Revue de Synthèse*, 127 (2): 241–52.

Markovitch, Tibor (ed.) 1965, *L'industrie française de 1789 à 1964*, Paris: Institut de science économique appliquée.

Martin Saint-Léon, Étienne 1922, *Histoire des corporations de métiers depuis leurs origines jusqu'à leurs supression en 1791, suivie d'une Étude sur l'évolution de l'idée corporative depuis 1791 jusqu'à nos jours*, Paris: Alcan.

Marx, Karl 1954 [1852], *The Eighteenth Brumaire of Louis Bonaparte*, Moscow: Progress Publishers.

Marx, Karl 1990 [1867], *Capital: Volume I*, London: Penguin Books.

Marx, Karl 1991 [1894], *Capital: Volume III*, London: Penguin Books.

Marx, Karl 2010 [1871], 'The Civil War in France', in *The First International and After Karl Marx*, edited by David Fernbach, London/Brooklyn: Verso.

Marzagalli, Silvia 2012, 'Commerce', in *The Oxford Handbook of the Ancien Régime*, edited by William Doyle, Oxford: Oxford University Press.

McNally, David 1988, *Political Economy and the Rise of Capitalism: A Reinterpretation*, Berkeley: University of California Press.

McPhee, Peter 2013, 'The Economy, Society, and the Environment', in *A Companion to the French Revolution*, edited by Peter McPhee, Chichester: Wiley Blackwell.

Merriman, John M. (ed.) 1979, *Consciousness and Class Experience in Nineteenth-Century Europe*, New York: Holmes and Meier.

Miller, Stephen 2008, *State and Society in Eighteenth-Century France. A Study of Political Power and Social Revolution in Languedoc*, Washington: The Catholic University of America Press.

Miller, Stephen 2009, 'The Economy of France in the Eighteenth and Nineteenth Centuries: Market Opportunity and Labor Productivity in Languedoc', *Rural History*, 20 (1): 1–30.

Miller, Stephen 2012, 'French Absolutism and Agricultural Capitalism: A Comment on Henry Heller's Essays', *Historical Materialism*, 20 (4): 141–61.

Miller, Stephen 2015, 'Ralph Kingston on the Bourgeoisie and Bureaucracy in France, 1789–1848: A Review Essay', *Historical Materialism*, 23 (3): 240–52.

Minard, Philippe 1998, *La fortune du colbertisme: État et industrie dans la France des Lumières*, Paris: Fayard.

Minard, Philippe 2007a, '"France colbertiste" versus "Angleterre libérale"? Un mythe du XVIIIe siècle', in *Les idées passent-elles la Manche? Savoirs, représentations, pratiques, France-Angleterre, xe–xxe siècles*, edited by Jean-Philippe Genet and François-Joseph Ruggiu, Paris: Presses de l'Université Paris-Sorbonne.

Minard, Philippe 2007b, 'L'héritage historiographique', in *Vers un ordre bourgeois? Révolution française et changement social*, edited by Jean-Pierre Jessenne, 21–38, Rennes: Presses universitaires de Rennes.

Minard, Philippe 2008, 'Economie de marché et Etat en France: mythes et légendes du colbertisme', *L'Économie politique*, 1 (37): 77–94.

Mooers, Colin 1991, *The Making of Bourgeois Europe: Absolutism, Revolution and the Rise of Capitalism in England, France and Germany*, London/New York: Verso.

Moriceau, Jean-Marc 1994, *Les fermiers de l'Île-de-France. L'ascension d'un patronat agricole (xve–xviiie siècles)*, Paris: Fayard.

Moriceau, Jean-Marc, and Gilles Postel-Vinay 1992, *Ferme, entreprise, famille. Grande exploitation et changements agricoles: les Chartier (xviie–xixe siècles)*, Paris: Éditions de l'École des hautes études en sciences sociales.

Moss, Bernard H. 1976, *The Origins of the French Labor Movement. The Socialism of Skilled Workers 1830–1914*, Berkeley: University of California Press.

Moulin, Annie 1991, *Peasantry and Society in France Since 1789*, Cambridge: Cambridge University Press.

Nicolas, Jean 2002, *La rébellion française. Mouvements populaires et conscience sociale 1661–1789*, Paris: Seuil.

Noiriel, Gérard 1986, *Les ouvriers dans la société française, XIX–XXe siècle*. Paris: Le Seuil.

Nord, Philip 2011, 'The Third Republic', in *The French Republic: History, Values, Debates*, edited by Edward Berenson, Vincent Duclert, and Christophe Prochasson, Ithaca: Cornell University Press.

O'Brien, Patrick, and Caglar Keyder 1979, 'Les voies de passage vers la société industrielle en Grande-Bretagne et en France (1780–1914)', *Annales. Économies, Sociétés, Civilisations*, 34 (6): 1284–1303.

O'Brien, Patrick, and Caglar Keyder 2011 [1978], *Economic Growth in Britain and France, 1780–1914: Two Paths to the Twentieth Century*, London: Routledge.

Orain, Arnaud 2015, 'On the difficulty of constituting an economic avant-garde in the French Enlightenment', *The European Journal of the History of Economic Thought*, 22 (3): 349–58.

Orgill, Nathan N., Carine Germond, and Henning Türk 2008, 'Between Coercion and Conciliation: Franco-German Relations in the Bismarck Era, 1871–90', in *A History of Franco-German Relation in Europe. From 'Hereditary Enemies' to Partners*, New York: Palgrave Macmillan.

Parker, David 1996, *Class and State in Early Modern France: The Road to Modernity?* New York: Routledge.

Parker, Harold T. 1993, *An Administrative Bureau During the Old Regime. The Bureau of Commerce and Its Relations to French Industry from May 1781 to November 1783*, Cranbury: Associated University Presses.

Perez, Yves André 2012, 'Lendemains de fêtes impériales: retour sur la crise du mode saint-simonien de croissance polarisée en économie ouverte, en France, à la fin du XIXème siècle (1873–1892)', *Humanisme et Entreprise* 5 (310): 1–20.

Pernoud, Régine 1981, *Histoire de la bourgeoisie en France. Volume 2: Les temps modernes*, Paris: Éditions du Seuil.

Perrot, Michelle 1974, *Les ouvriers en grève, France 1871–1890*, Paris: Mouton.

Perrot, Michelle 1983, 'De la manufacture à l'usine en miettes'. *Le Mouvement social*, 125: 3–12.

Perrot, Michelle 1986, 'On the Formation of the French Working Class', in *Working-Class Formation: Nineteenth-Century Patterns in Western Europe and the United States*, edited by Ira Katznelson and Aristide R. Zolberg, 71–110. Princeton, NJ: Princeton University Press.

Phillips, Gordon 1989, 'The British Labour Movement Before 1914', in *Labour and Socialist Movements in Europe Before 1914*, edited by Dick Geary, Oxford: Berg.

Pilbeam, Pamela 1995, *Republicanism in Nineteenth-Century France, 1814–1871*, New York: St. Martin's Press.

Pilbeam, Pamela 2000 *French Socialists Before Marx: Workers, Women and the Social Question in France*, Teddington: Acumen.

Pinaud, Pierre-François 1990, *Les Receveurs généraux des Finances, 1790–1865*, Genève: Droz.

Plessis, Alain 1985, *The Rise and Fall of the Second Empire, 1852–1871*, Cambridge: Cambridge University Press.

Plessis, Alain 1996, 'Le financement des entreprises', in *Histoire de la France industrielle*, edited by Maurice Lévy-Leboyer, Paris: Labrousse.

Plessis, Alain 2001 [1976], *Nouvelle Histoire de la France contemporaine, tome 9: De la fête impériale au mur des fédérés, 1852–1871*, Paris: Éditions du Seuil.

Polanyi, Karl 1957, 'The Economy as Instituted Process: Economies in History and Theory', in *Trade and Market in the Early Empires*, edited by Karl Polanyi, Conrad M. Arensberg, and Harry W. Pearson, 243–70, Glencoe: Free Press.

Pollard, Sidney 1965, *The Genesis of Modern Management. A Study of the Industrial Revolution in Great Britain*, London: Edward Arnold.

Portis, Larry 1988, *Les classses sociales en France: Un débat inachevé (1789–1989)*, Paris: Éditions Ouvrières.

Postel-Vinay, Gilles 1974, *La rente foncière dans le capitalisme agricole. Analyse de la voie "Classique" dans l'agriculture à partir de l'exemple du Soissonnais*, Paris: Maspero.

Price, Roger 1981, *An Economic History of Modern France, 1730–1914*, London: Palgrave Macmillan.

Price, Roger 1987, *A Social History of Nineteenth-Century France*, London: Hutchinson.

Prochasson, Christophe 2012, 'Nouveaux regards sur le réformisme. Introduction', *Mil neuf cent. Revue d'histoire intellectuelle*, 30: 5–20.

Prothero, Iorwerth 1997, *Radical artisans in England and France, 1830–1870*, Cambridge: Cambridge University Press.

Rancière, Jacques 1981, *La nuit des prolétaires. Archives du rêve ouvrier*. Paris: Fayard.

Rebérioux, Madelaine 1974, 'Le socialisme français de 1871 à 1914', in *Histoire générale du socialisme. Tome 2: De 1875 à 1918*, edited by Jacques Droz, 133–236, Paris: Presses universitaires de France.

Reddy, William M. 1979, 'Skeins, Scales, Discounts, Steam, and other Objects of Crowd Justice in Early French Textile Mills', *Comparative Studies in Society and History*, 21 (2): 204–13.

Reddy, William M. 1984, *The Rise of Market Culture: The Textile Trade and French Society, 1750–1900*, Cambridge: Cambridge University Press.

Rioux, Jean-Pierre 1989, *La révolution industrielle, 1780–1880*, Paris: Éditions du Seuil.

Roberts, William Clare 2017, *Marx's Inferno. The Political Theory of Capital*, Princeton: Princeton University Press.

Rosanvallon, Pierre 1990, *L'État en France de 1789 à nos jours*, Paris: Éditions du Seuil.

Rougerie, Jacques 1964, *Procès des communards*, Paris: Julliard.

Rougerie, Jacques 1968, 'Les sections françaises de l'Association internationale des travailleurs', in *La première International, l'institution, l'implantation, le rayonnement*, edited by Ernest Labrousse, Paris: CNRS.

Rougerie, Jacques 1988, *La Commune de 1871*, Paris: Presses universitaires de France.

Rougerie, Jacques 1994, 'Le mouvement associatif populaire comme facteur d'acculturation politique à Paris de la révolution aux années 1840: continuité, discontinuités', *Annales historiques de la Révolution française* 297 (1): 493–516.

Rougerie, Jacques 1997, 'France, Angleterre: Naissance d'une famille démocratique', in *Les familles politiques en Europe occidentale au XIXe siècle, Actes du colloque de Rome (1er–3 déc. 1994)*, Rome: École française de Rome.

Rougerie, Jacques 2000, 'La Commune: Utopie, Modernité?' in *La commune de 1871: utopie ou modernité?*, edited by Gilbert Larguier and Jérôme Quaretti. Perpignan: Presses universitaires de Perpignan.

Rougerie, Jacques 2004, 'Par-delà le coup d'État, la continuité de l'action et de l'organisation ouvrières', in *Comment meurt une République. Autour du 2 décembre 1851*, edited by Sylvie Aprile, Nathalie Bayon, Laurent Clavier, Louis Hinckey, and Jean-Luc Mayaud, Paris: Créaphis.

Rubinstein, W.D. 1983, 'The End of "Old Corruption" in Britain 1780–1860', *Past & Present*, 101: 55–86.

Rule, John 1981, *The Experience of Labour in Eighteenth-Century English Industry*, New York: St. Martin's Press.

Salais, Robert, Nicolas Baverez, and Bénédicte Reynaud 1986, *L'invention du chômage: Histoire et transformation d'une catégorie en France des années 1890 aux années 1980*, Paris: Presses universitaires de France.

Salomon, Jean-Jacques 1991, 'La capacité d'innovation', in *Entre l'État et le marché. L'économie française des années 1880 à nos jours*, edited by Maurice Lévy-Leboyer and Jean-Claude Casanova, Paris: Gallimard.

Sawyer, John E. 1951, 'Strains in the Social Structure of Modern France', in *Modern France, Problems of the Third and Fourth Republics*, edited by Edward Mead Earle, Princeton: Princeton University Press.

Schroeder, Paul W. 2000, 'International politics, peace, and war, 1815–1914', in *The Nineteenth Century: Europe 1789–1914*, edited by T.C.W. Blanning, Oxford: Oxford University Press.

Scott, Joan Wallach 1974, *The Glassworkers of Carmaux: French Craftsmen and Political Action in a Nineteenth-Century City*, Cambridge: Harvard University Press.

Scott, Joan Wallach 1988, *Gender and the Politics of History*, London: Princeton University Press.

Sears, Alan 2014, *The Next New Left: A History of the Future*, Halifax/Winnipeg: Fernwood Publishing.

Sée, Henri 1926, *Les origines du capitalisme modern*, Paris: Armand Colin.

Sewell, William H. 1980, *Work and Revolution in France: The Language of Labor from the Old Regime to 1848*, Cambridge: Cambridge University Press.

Sewell, William H. 1986, 'Artisans, Factory Workers, and the Formation of the French Working Class, 1789–1848', in *Working-Class Formation. Nineteenth-Century Patterns in Western Europe and the United States*, edited by Ira Katznelson and Aristide R. Zolberg, Princeton: Princeton University Press.

Shaikh, Anwar 2016, *Capitalism: Competition, Conflict, Crises*, New York: Oxford University Press.

Shorter, Edward, and Charles Tilly 1974, *Strikes in France: 1830–1968*, Cambridge: Cambridge University Press.

Sick, Klauss-Peter 2013, 'La République, des "nouvelles couches" aux "classes moyennes"', in *Une contre histoire de la IIIe République*, edited by Marion Fontaine, Frédéric Monier, and Christophe Prochasson, Paris: La Découverte.

Sirot, Stéphane 2002, *La grève en France: Une histoire sociale (XIXe–XXe siècle)*, Paris: Odile Jacob.

Skocpol, Theda 1979, *States and Social Revolutions*, Cambridge: Cambridge University Press.

Smith, Michael S. 2004, 'Parliamentary Reform and the Electorate', in *A Companion to Nineteenth-Century Britain*, edited by Chris Williams, Malden: Blackwell.

Soboul, Albert 1974, 'L'historiographie classique de la Révolution française. Sur des controverses récentes', *La Pensée*, 177: 40–58.

Soboul, Albert 1977, *A Short History of the French Revolution*, Berkeley: University of California Press.

Sonenscher, Michael 1989, *Work and Wages: Natural Law, Politics and the Eighteenth-Century French Trades*, Cambridge: Cambridge University Press.

Soulet, Jean-François 2004, *Les Pyrénées au XIXe siècle: l'éveil d'une société civile*, Bordeaux: Sud-Ouest.

Stanziani, Alessandro 2012, *Rules of Exchange: French Capitalism in Comparative Perspective, Eighteenth to Early Twentieth Centuries*, Cambridge: Cambridge University Press.

Stearns, Peter 1965, 'British Industry through the Eyes of French Industrialists (1820–1848)', *The Journal of Modern History*, 37 (1): 50–61.

Stearns, Peter 1971, *Revolutionary Syndicalism and French Labor: A Cause without Rebels*, New Brunswick: Rutgers University Press.

Stedman Jones, Gareth 1977, 'Society and Politics at the Beginning of the World Economy', *Cambridge Journal of Economics*, 1 (1): 77–92.

Stedman Jones, Gareth 1983, *Languages of Class: Studies in English Working Class History, 1832–1982*, Cambridge: Cambridge University Press.

Steinfeld, Robert J. 2001, *Coercion, Contract, and Free Labor in the Nineteenth Century*, Cambridge: Cambridge University Press.

Stokey, Nancy L. 2001, 'A Quantitative Model of the British Industrial Revolution: 1780–1850', *Carnegie-Rochester Series on Public Policy*, 55: 55–109.

Stovall, Tyler 1990, *The Rise of the Paris Red Belt*, Berkeley: University of California Press.

Stuart, Robert 1992, *Marxism at Work: Ideology, Class, and French Socialism During the Third Republic*, Cambridge: Cambridge University Press.

Szostak, Rick 1991, *Role of Transportation in the Industrial Revolution: A Comparison of England and France*, Montreal: McGill-Queen's University Press.

Tarrade, Jean 1972, *Le commerce colonial de la France à la fin de l'Ancien Régime: l'évolution du régime de l'exclusif de 1763 à 1789*, Paris: Presses universitaires de France.

Taylor, A.J. 1949, 'Concentration and Specialization in the Lancashire Cotton Industry, 1825–1850', *The Economic History Review*, 1 (2–3): 114–22.

Taylor, George V. 1967, 'Noncapitalist Wealth and the Origins of the French Revolution', *The American Historical Review*, 72 (2): 469.

Teschke, Benno 2003, *The Myth of 1648. Class, Geopolitics and the Making of Modern International Relations*, New York: Verso.

Teschke, Benno 2005, 'Bourgeois Revolution, State Formation and the Absence of the International', *Historical Materialism*, 13 (2): 3–26.

Teurnier, Jonathan 2015, 'Le programme économique de Napoléon III'. clio-texte. 1 November 2015. https://clio-texte.clionautes.org/le-programme-economique-de-napoleon-iii.html

Thillay, Alain 2002, *Le faubourg Saint-Antoine et ses 'faux ouvriers'. La liberté du travail à Paris aux XVIIe et XVIIIe siècles*, Seyssel: Champ Vallon.

Thompson, E.P. 1968, *The Making of the English Working Class*, 2nd ed., Harmondsworth: Penguin.

Thompson, E.P. 1975, *Whigs and Hunters: The Origins of the Black Act*, New York: Pantheon Books.

Thompson, E.P. 1978, 'Eighteenth-Century English Society: Class Struggle without Class?' *Social History*, 3 (2): 133–65.

Thompson, E.P. 1993, *Customs in Common: Studies in Traditional Popular Culture*, New York: The New Press.

Todd, David 2008, *L'identité économique de la France. Libre-échange et protectionnisme (1814–1851)*, Paris: Grasset & Fasquelle.

Tombs, Robert 1996, *France 1814–1914*, London: Longman.

Tombs, Robert 2014, *Paris, bivouac des révolutions. La Commune de 1871*, Paris: Libertalia.

Toutain, Jean-Claude 1961, *Le produit de l'agriculture française de 1700 à 1958*, Paris: Cahiers de l'institut de science économique appliquée.

Tucker, Kenneth H. 1996, *French Revolutionary Syndicalism and the Public Sphere*, Cambridge: Cambridge University Press.

Vardi, Liana 1988, 'The Abolition of the Guilds during the French Revolution', *French Historical Studies*, 15 (4): 704–17.

Verley, Patrick 1989, *Nouvelle histoire économique de la France contemporaine. 2. L'indu-striaLisation, 1830–1914*, Paris: La Découverte.

Verley, Patrick 1996, 'La dynamique des marchés et croissance industrielle', in *Histoire de la France industrielle*, edited by Maurice Lévy-Leboyer, Paris: Labrous-se.

Verley, Patrick 1997, *L'échelle du monde. Essai sur l'industrialisation de l'Occident*, Paris: Gallimard.

Verley, Patrick, and Jean-Luc Mayaud 2001, 'Introduction. En l'an 2001, le XIXe siècle à redécouvrir pour les historiens économistes?' *Revue d'histoire du XIXe siècle*, 23: 7–21.

Weber, Eugen 1976, *Peasants into Frenchmen. The Modernization of Rural France, 1870–1914*, Stanford: Stanford University Press.

Willard, Claude 1965, *Les guesdistes: le mouvement socialiste en France, 1893–1905*, Paris: Éditions sociales.

Wood, Ellen Meiksins 1991, *The Pristine Culture of Capitalism: A Historical Essay on Old Regimes and Modern States*, London/New York: Verso.

Wood, Ellen Meiksins 1994, 'From Opportunity to Imperative: The History of the Market', *Monthly Review*, 46 (3): 14.

Wood, Ellen Meiksins 1995, *Democracy against Capitalism*, Cambridge: Cambridge University Press.

Wood, Ellen Meiksins 2002a, *The Origin of Capitalism: A Longer View*, New York: Verso.

Wood, Ellen Meiksins 2002b, 'The Question of Market Dependence', *Journal of Agrarian Change*, 2 (1): 50–87.

Wood, Ellen Meiksins 2003, 'Globalization and the State: Where is the Power of Capital?' in *Anti-Capitalism: A Marxist Introduction*, edited by Alfredo Saad-Filho, London: Pluto Press.

Wood, Ellen Meiksins 2012, *Liberty and Property: A Social History of Western Political Thought from Renaissance to Enlightenment*, New York: Verso.

Woronoff, Denis 1994, *Histoire de l'industrie en France: du XVIe siècle à nos jours*, Paris: Éditions du Seuil.

Wright, Julian 2013, 'Socialism and Political Identity: Eugene Fourniere and Intellectual Militancy in the Third Republic', *French Historical Studies*, 36 (3): 449–78.

Wrigley, E.A. 2000, 'The Divergence of England: The Growth of the English Economy in the Seventeenth and Eighteenth Centuries: The Prothero Lecture', *Transactions of the Royal Historical Society*, 10: 117–41.

Zancarini-Fournel, Michelle 2005, *Histoire des femmes en France, XIXe–XXe siècle*, Rennes: Presses universitaires de Rennes.

Zancarini-Fournel, Michelle 2016, *Les luttes et les rêves. Une histoire populaire de la France de 1685 à nos jours*, Paris: La Découverte.

Zeldin, Theodore 1993, *A History of French passions: 1848–1945*, Oxford: Clarendon.

Zmolek, Michael Andrew 2013, *Rethinking the Industrial Revolution: Five Centuries of*

Transition from Agrarian to Industrial Capitalism in England, Chicago: Haymarket Books.

Zolberg, Aristide R. 1986, 'How Many Exceptionalisms?' in *Working-Class Formation: Nineteenth-Century Patterns in Western Europe and the United States*, edited by Ira Katznelson and Aristide R. Zolberg, Princeton: Princeton University Press.

Index